RAVENS & BLACK RAIN is a well researched, serious and fascinating book by a writer who has had a lifelong interest in the subject of second sight. Elizabeth Sutherland, who lives in Ross-shire, has written two novels with Highland second sight as a theme: *The Seer of Kintail* and *The Eye of God,* while *The Prophecies of the Brahan Seer* by Alexander Mackenzie, edited and introduced by her, has been reprinted every year since its publication in a special edition in 1977.

TO IAN

FROM ELLA & FRASER

RAVENS & BLACK RAIN

The story of Highland second sight,
including a new collection of the
prophecies of the Brahan Seer

Elizabeth Sutherland

CORGI BOOKS

RAVENS & BLACK RAIN

A CORGI BOOK 0 552 13181 4

Originally published in Great Britain by
Constable and Company Limited

PRINTING HISTORY
Constable edition published 1985
Corgi edition published 1987

This book is set in 10/11pt Plantin

Corgi Books are published by Transworld Publishers Ltd.,
61-63 Uxbridge Road, Ealing, London W5 5SA, in Australia by
Transworld Publishers (Australia) Pty. Ltd., 15-23 Helles
Avenue, Moorebank, NSW 2170, and in New Zealand by
Transworld Publishers (N.Z.) Ltd., Cnr. Moselle and Waipareira
Avenues, Henderson, Auckland.

Made and printed in Great Britain by
The Guernsey Press Co. Ltd., Guernsey, Channel Islands.

For Graeme Marshall who has a wide enquiring mind

CONTENTS

Contents

Contents

ACKNOWLEDGEMENTS

I would like to thank the following:

Maurice Fleming, editor of *The Scots Magazine,* and those readers and writers who have helped with my research

Jim Henderson, editor of the *Northern Times,* Golspie for his co-operation

Alanna Knight, friend and fellow-writer, for her kindness

Henderson Lynn for his encouragement

Swein Macdonald for his support

Professor A. E. Roy of Glasgow University for his advice

Stewart Sanderson, folklorist, for his assistance

J. Clarence Finlayson, Linnhe Gobby, John Graham, Mrs R. Higginbottom, and all those others whose research and experience have been invaluable

The Scottish Academic Press for permission to quote from Alexander Carmichael's *Ortha nan Gaidheal, Carmina Gadelica,* Volume 5.

The *Scottish Daily Express* for permission to quote from Alex Main's article entitled 'An amazing glimpse into our future'.

I would also like to thank the librarians at Dingwall, Inverness and the Mitchell Library, Glasgow, for their help

My editor, Prudence Fay, for her patience with my text

My husband, family and friends in the Black Isle, and particularly the Torins who housed me, my books and typewriter during the renovation of our home.

E.S.
1985

Part One

Second Sight Through the Centuries

The Waking Dream

The great hall at Durness Castle, lit by a blazing log fire and a galaxy of candles, sparkled with the wit of gentlemen and the jewels of their wives. The long oak table sported venison and game. Goblets glowed with red wine. Above the laughter and conversation of the company, the thin, wild music of the pipes could be heard faintly from the battlements.

This was Lord Reay's autumn house-party, to which he had invited friends and relatives from all over the country in the year 1738. George Reay, fellow of the Royal Society and a distinguished nobleman, was no longer young but was vigorous, a hardy Highland chief and a man of many interests.

Among his guests was a young couple from the Borders: Sir Charles and Lady D. still on their honeymoon, were deeply in love. Also present was Lady Frances Mackenzie of Assynt, grand-daughter of Kenneth, third Earl of Seaforth and Isabella Mackenzie of Kintail.

Although Lady D. attempted to join in the light-hearted spirit of the evening, she was quieter than usual. On the previous day Lord Reay had taken her husband to visit a neighbouring chief and they had not yet returned. She was not particularly anxious for his safety – she knew the distances involved and the rough roads in the remote county of Sutherland – but she missed him. She could not bear the thought of their being parted another night. Every time a servant entered the hall, she turned expectantly, hoping to see her husband.

Lady Mackenzie, too, was quiet that night. Exceptionally tall, white-skinned and black-eyed, she looked as bleak as a cormorant in a pride of peacocks. Withdrawn, disinterested, she seemed almost to be unaware of her surroundings. Those who tried to draw her into conversation soon left her alone to sit as stiff and still as the portraits on the wall. Yet all were uneasily aware of her as they dined and talked.

Then suddenly she cried out.

The effect was frightening. Conversation ceased as every eye turned to look at her. Slowly she rose to her feet. Clinging to the back of her chair, she cried out in horror. Her black eyes started, her arms stretched out, each long finger spread as if to repel some unseen fiend. She was as stiff as a corpse in rigor mortis. Though her lips moved, no words were spoken. After a timeless moment she sank back into her chair, trembling and exhausted.

Everyone spoke at once. What had happened? Was she unwell? What had she seen? Most earnest of her inquirers was the pretty bride.

At first Lady Frances did not seem to understand what was happening. She looked inquiringly at the anxious eyes of the women who had crowded round her. Then, without a word, she spread her hands in a wide gesture that swept them back, until only the bride stood before her. Their eyes met and held. In the silence she spoke to her alone.

'Poor innocent dove, poor child. How cruel for you the news. How sad for me to break it.'

Lady D. could not turn away from those compelling eyes, nor could she stop her ears.

'I saw a boat,' Lady Mackenzie continued. 'In it Lord Reay and your beloved husband were being rowed across a deep and darkening loch. A great wind swept down from the mountains and whipped the waters white. The boat was soon awash. I did not want to see but I could not look away . . . and then one wave, mightier than the rest, upturned the frail craft. Lord Reay and his servants struggled to the shore.'

'And Charles?' whispered the bride. 'Oh, tell me he is safe.'

Lady Frances shook her head. 'His body was washed up on the shore. A moonbeam lay across his face. I saw him drowned.'

Without a word, the young wife fainted into the arms of her friends, but before any could speak to comfort or protest, Lady Mackenzie was again seized by the same convulsion and rising, cried out in a high-pitched eerie voice. 'They are bringing him home. Oh, how pale and cold he looks, how his long hair drips, how white those lips that once were warm with love!' She fell back in her chair and her voice sank. 'He is gone for ever. Never again will he see his own fair home and fertile fields . . . yet all is not lost for his son shall live after him and bring back again the image of his father.'

Though the women, gathered round the weeping bride, protested that Lady Mackenzie had suffered a brainstorm, each in her own mind was deeply uneasy, aware of impending disaster. Confusion outside the castle drew the men down to the courtyard while the women crowded to the windows. Torches flared below and the piper struck up a lament. In the jostle of servants could clearly be seen a stretcher, and on it a body. One of the bearers was an ashen-faced Lord Reay. Later he gathered his guests together to tell them what had happened; needlessly, for Lady Mackenzie's account had been true in every detail.

Although Lady D.'s pregnancy had not been suspected even by herself, she bore a son in due course who was to carry on the family name.

The story appeared in *Blackwood's Magazine*, September 1818. It had been sent to the editor by an unnamed friend with a covering letter:

> Were I permitted to bring the story forward supported by all the evidence of those who could speak to its truth, it could be established as the best authenticated of any of those instances which have been given of the seer's prophetic insight. Delicacy forbids me to corroborate its truth by names, many connections of the personages to whom the story relates being yet alive.

Here are some of the ingredients of what has come to be recognized as traditional Highland second sight: spontaneous unsought vision; the precognition of impending disaster; the physical changes that affect the seer; the prophecy that looks to the far future. It is unusual only in the sex of the seer: most visionaries were men.

Highlanders believe that there is something special about Celtic precognition, that it is involuntary, spectre-haunted, not to be confused with fairground fortune-telling, requiring no gimmicks such as crystal balls, cards or stars. Never should it be used for gain or amusement, nor should it be affected, vaunted or assumed. Although not in the same class as Biblical prophecy, it has on occasions come close to it. Although its existence is taken for granted, it is generally considered to be better suppressed, left alone, not talked about, and not cultivated.

That is not how it started, nor how it evolved and (to judge by those who remain loyal to the legend of the Brahan Seer and those who flock to consult his contemporary counterpart, Swein Macdonald) not how it is today.

Perhaps the greatest myth of all, and one that has been perpetuated by Highlanders themselves throughout the centuries, is that second sight is not now so prevalent as it once was. But out of the hundreds of people I have spoken to over the past two years, most have either experienced at least one paranormal incident or have had a friend or relative with psychic power. A woman from Harris who began by telling me that there were no seers left on the island soon remembered a husband and wife, both gifted, who lived down the road. She considered it particularly unusual for a married couple to share the faculty.

Another myth is that second sight is solely the ability to see into the future. The host of tales recounted by psychic investigators and folklorists through the ages show that it includes a wide range of paranormal phenomena each having its own ancient Gaelic terminology, which still accurately describes the varying experiences known today. Only the images have changed. Seers no longer have visions of shrouded corpses, phantom funerals drawn by horses over the moors, bloody battles and arrow-pierced thighs. Instead they see car crashes, rail and plane disasters, and other incidents relevant to the twentieth century.

Attitudes and images may change with the changing centuries, but the experiences – natural or supernatural, latent talent or specific gift, God-given or Devil-spawned – remain remarkably the same.

Second sight is not, of course, peculiar to the Highlands and Western Isles of Scotland: psychic talent exists in every country and every race. Yet it is often regarded as a prerogative of the northern Celt. Why this should be so requires a glimpse back into the remote past.

1   Origins

Modern anthropologists maintain that there is no such thing as primitive man, only primitive conditions. Before sheets of paper there were cave walls for artists, before the written alphabet there were words for story-tellers, and there were always dreams, visions, and the interpretation of signs for communicators and forecasters, just as there are today.

The psychic who had a vision of his neighbour dripping with water or gleaming with scales needed no further proof that he was drowned. If he 'saw' a whale stranded on distant rocks, he knew there was meat for winter. If he dreamed of strange coracles approaching the beach, he prepared his tribe for a confrontation. Whether he saw symbols which needed interpretation, or visions of the future, or whether he witnessed apparitions of the dead or living, he must have been as necessary to his tribes as the hunter or the chief. Such a talent would have been cultivated with care and nurtured in the young, those that showed promise being set apart for further initiation.

In the Highlands, second sight all began with the fairies. Only one fact is certain when researching the world of the 'little people': there can be no proof of how they originated or even of their existence. We can only speculate. One theory is as follows: The Neolithic farmers who settled in the north were obviously a religious people. Remains of their burial cairns – so huge that it is reckoned each one contained as many stones as would build five parish churches today – abound, and all we know of these people is contained in the artefacts found in those tombs, which point to a strong conception of after-life. Possibly they believed in the power of the dead to influence and protect, to punish or destroy their descendants, and some sort of priestly ritual may have included the ability to appease with offerings, interpret signs and, above all, communicate with ghosts. These spirits of the dead – the *sluagh sith* or people of peace – may in time have been turned into the *sithean* or fairies, a host of demi-gods that predated and later became fused into the Celtic pantheon.

'*Sith*' is a confusing Gaelic word. It can mean 'peace', it can mean 'mound', and it can also mean 'fairy'. Thus the *ban-sithean* and the *fear-sithean* were not only the women and men of the mounds and of peace, but also the fairies, a term that includes the elves, brownies and goblins that still abound in Highland folklore. The 'mounds' may have been, in the first instance, the burial cairns; certainly there are cairns today which are known as fairy hills.

But some glens, caves, and knolls also known as fairy sites would appear to have nothing to do with burial mounds. This fact might point to a distant fusion of the Neolithic ghosts of the dead with the capricious Celtic godlings that lurked behind every oddity in nature from bubbling springs to inaccessible glens. The clootie wells, many festooned with placatory offerings to this day, are only one example of the thousands of fairy sites that once existed and still linger on in tradition and place names. The ghosts of the mounds, then, over centuries became the fairies that haunted the countryside and the *ceilidh* hearth of the Highlander. Again, we can only speculate as to how this might have happened.

As the centuries of prehistory merged into history, wave upon wave of immigrants, mostly Celts, invaded the northern shores and brought with them new gods and a new priesthood in the Druids. Probably some of the Neolithic people married the incomers and taught their children their own beliefs and traditions. Others possibly, served the new masters in menial positions. But many may have retreated into the more inaccessible glens and forests, perhaps into the burial mounds themselves. In time, through the skill of story-tellers and the power of myth, the *sluagh sith* the ancestral ghosts, may have become confused with the remnant of their descendants, living in seclusion. Thus a shy old woman emerging from her hide-out at dawn or dusk to fetch water from the burn may have been regarded as a 'fairy washer-woman'. Others, welcomed at the hearth in exchange for doing menial chores, might be remembered as *bòcan* or brownies. Family groups surviving in the deep glens may have come to be regarded as the *sithean* themselves, part supernatural, capricious by nature, to be appeased by offerings of milk and meal and appealed to for charms and spells.

What eventually became of these Neolithic remnants? Perhaps a few lingered on as nomads, by-passed by Christianity, travellers who linked up with the Celtic cairds and tinklers who themselves were to join with the gypsies of a later generation.

Fairies are not ghosts, as is evidenced in one of the many sightings of fairies at the Eathie Glen in the Black Isle recorded by Hugh Miller of Cromarty. On one occasion the miller at Eathie – a wild and inaccessible place to this day – while working late at night heard 'the neighing and champing of horses and the rattling of carts; and on going to the door he saw a long train of basket-woven vehicles laden with sacks and drawn by shaggy little ponies of every diversity and colour. The attendants were slim, unearthly-looking creatures, about three feet in height, attired in grey, with red caps; and the whole seemed to have come out of a square opening in the opposite precipice. Strange to relate, the nearer figures seemed to be as much frightened at seeing the miller as the miller was at seeing them; but, on one of them uttering a shrill scream, the carts moved backwards into the opening, which shut over them like the curtain of a theatre as the last disappeared.'

The difference between fairy and ghost, it would seem, can be defined thus: the fairy is a creature in its own right, whereas the ghost represents a person who has lived on earth, or who is still alive.

Second sight was possibly cultivated as part of the religious practice of Neolithic man, not just for the purpose of ascertaining the wishes of the dead, but also of receiving from them predictions of future success in battle, hunting or crop-raising.

It was also believed (as we shall see in the writings of the Revd Robert Kirk in 1690 or 1691) that second sight was within the bounty of the *sithean*, so that not only could they take on the shape of the living or the dead, but they could also confer upon mortals the ability to see them in this guise. Second sight, therefore, was thought to be a gift from the *sithean* to enable human beings both to witness and communicate with them. The *sithean* were involved in both versions of how the Brahan Seer received his prophetic stone. The east Ross-shire version has him finding it on a fairy mound, while the Lewis story has his mother receiving it from the hands of an apparition, one of the *sluagh sith* themselves.

Second sight, then, might perhaps have originated in a lively talent, common to man from the earliest times, which the Neolithic tomb-builders interpreted as the ability to see and communicate with their ancestral gods. This ability may have been regarded as a gift within the gods' bounty, in order to allow an early priesthood to ascertain their wishes.

While modern man still struggles to account for – and to believe in – psychic phenomena, our remote progenitors had no difficulty in accounting for the same sorts of experience that mediums and seers encounter today. The coming of Druidism to the Highlands and Islands, with its emphasis on the practice of divination, would have enhanced a talent that had probably been encouraged and cultivated from earliest time. That Druidism lasted in the north until the seventh century at least, long after it had died out in other parts of the United Kingdom, may well be one of the reasons why the cult of second sight was to become such a characteristic of the Highlands.

THE DRUID DIVINERS

From about the seventh century BC the first Celts arrived in Britain heralding the Iron Age with new tools, weapons and ornaments, burial customs and language. Gradually, and in successive waves, they penetrated the Highlands and Islands where they eventually dominated the indigenous people by force of arms and superiority of culture.

Though the Romans, somewhat contemptuously, dubbed those north of the Forth and Clyde, Picts – painted people – for their custom of streaming into battle naked and possibly tattooed, they were never able to subdue them. Consequently the north of Scotland remained 'uncivilized' by Rome, not at all a matter for regret, but another reason perhaps why the cult of second sight survived there. Their customs certainly were different. In a story told of a meeting between a Roman matron and a Pictish princess, the former queried the Pictish custom of what might be termed 'sleeping around', but the princess pointed out that it was surely more civilized to give oneself to a brave and chosen warrior than to be raped by an unattractive enemy. This particular custom may have led to the practice of matrilinear descent; many of the dramatic Pictish symbol stones include, among crescents, discs and rods, the mirror and the comb representing the female line.

There is no period in Scottish history that arouses greater argument among scholars than that of the Picts. The facts to emerge from the earliest Gaelic manuscripts demonstrate that the inhabitants of north Scotland collectively called Picts were a splendid race with a rich mythology, a high code of chivalry, and a disciplined fighting force able to resist the might of Rome. Cattlemen and warriors by profession, they were ruled by chiefs said to be divinely descended from their hero-gods. Their women were treated with chivalry and were important in society. Children were fostered out of the immediate family, which led to close bonds of loyalty and friendship within the clan. They lived in beehive huts roofed with bracken and heather, and in times of danger retreated to duns and forts which usually were sited on hilltops.

Pictish clothing, according to the illustrations on their symbol stones, varied from long priest-like tunics with richly embroidered hems to short pleated garments and cloaks fastened with brooches. Dioderus, the Greek historian alive during Caesar's time, records that the material was criss-crossed with little squares and lines, no doubt the forerunner of tartan, which made, according to the prolific Roman writer Varro, 'a gaudy show'. Their jewellery was rich, made of gold, amber, jet and glass. Their weapons were iron and bronze and they carried shields similar to those used at the Battle of Culloden in 1746. In war, they stiffened and dyed their long hair and brushed it forwards. They were superb horsemen and charioteers.

The clan system that was to linger on in the Highlands until Culloden was, when working well, one of the finest forms of government devised for the times. The chief was not only semi-divine, but also father of the family. The clan, or children, were therefore related to him both naturally and supernaturally. Though in theory the territory belonged to the chief, it was cultivated in common and awarded in part to the greatest battle-heroes.

Unfortunately, as the clans increased in number, so too did the disputes. The *righ* or king of a family group which had been defeated in battle had to submit to a higher king, who in turn was subject to the high king or *ard righ*. Kings were not necessarily the direct heirs. Heroic virtues of courage, truthfulness, and physical perfection decided who was best suited to reign. At the time of the Romans there were seven Pictish provinces each with its own ruler, from among whom the *ard righ* was elected. (One of the reasons for the appalling dynastic troubles that were to beset Scotland after the union of the Picts and the latest immigrant wave of Celts known as the Scots, was the change-over from choosing a king from among the strongest chiefs to kingship by linear descent. This produced a series of wasteful dynastic battles and also a succession of minority reigns.)

Second only in importance to the chiefs, and on a par with the warrior aristocracy, were the Druids – a name derived, Pliny suggests, from the Greek word *drus* meaning an oak tree. Not simply priests, the Druids were also physicians, astronomers, historians, poets, law-givers and diviners. Their decisions were final, their perks immense, and their hierarchy included men of the noblest rank. They were also – and most importantly as regards this book – itinerant and inter-tribal. Professor David Greene has said that the literary class 'could pass freely through the iron curtain which separated the tribes from each other'.

Stuart Piggott in his book entitled *The Druids* tells us that there are two kinds, the 'Druids-as-known' through archaeology and contemporary documentation, such as it is, and the 'Druids-as-wished-for', those created by romantic writers of a later age. We see them polished with the wax of romance, as white-haired sages guiding the noble savage through the golden age or as sadistic priests presiding over obscene and bloody rites. That we know so little about their doctrines is owing to the fact that these were not recorded in writing. The factual Druid, from the evidence of archaeology, had an awesome pedigree: he would have inherited the Indo-European traditions of his race, would have absorbed the long-forgotten religion of the Neolithic tomb-builders, and possibly also the unknown rites and taboos of even earlier Stone Age nomads. Stuart Piggott reckons his pedigree could stretch back a good 20,000 years. Julius Caesar tells us that Druids believed in the transmigration and reincarnation of souls, which encouraged bravery in war, and also that they taught the young the science of the stars, the world, the earth, and the power of the gods.

Human sacrifice was certainly part of their ritual, particularly at the great feast of Samhain when the sun god waned and the powers of darkness awoke. Samhain was also the time for divination. In the second century before Christ, the Greek geographer Strabo wrote that the Druids read the omens in many ways – studying the flow of blood after a stab in the back was one of the cruder methods. Other methods such as shoulder-blade divination survived, as we shall see, into comparatively recent times. It was this savage side to the cult of Druidism that was to lead to its abolition throughout Roman Europe. Those who survived in Britain took refuge behind the Antonine Wall, or in Ireland, where the priesthood remained untouched until the coming of Christianity.

St Patrick was the first to challenge the power of the Druids in Ireland, but it was not until the sixth century that Columba confronted them in the Highlands. At the court of King Brude in Inverness the royal Druids raised storms and spells to thwart the coming of Christ, but the fact remains that within a century or two the Picts had abandoned the old religion for the new. Superficially, at least.

There were, according to Strabo, three classes of Druids. First were the bards, story-tellers, lawyers, philosophers and teachers. The young Columba was taught by monks who were also bards, and is generally thought to have been a bard himself. From these imaginative, cultured men the Gael has inherited the powerful art of story-telling, the faithful recitation of hundreds of poetic tales which were passed on in the oral tradition at the *ceilidh* hearth for the best part of 2,000 years. It was not until the middle of the last century that folk-lorists began to write down collections of these tales, fearing that in a world dominated by science they might well be forgotten.

After seven years of training the bard was initiated into the Druid priesthood, instructed in the secret Ogham alphabet, the art of poetry, and in the knowledge of herbalism and of ritual in the sacred groves. From these vates, the Gael has inherited a talent for poetry, a knowledge of natural lore, and an affinity with and respect for the physical world. This strong, abiding love for a countryside peopled with rock, wells, and mountains all with personalities of their own was one of the reasons why the Gael suffered so deeply during the eighteenth- and nineteenth-century evictions.

A further seven years later, the vates began their initiation into the mysteries of magic, divination and prophecy. Through strictly observed rituals they were taught to tap their latent psychic powers, so that they might enter a collective dream state where natural and supernatural realms merged in a timeless dimension. Celtic mysteries occurred in twi-states between night and day, in dew that was neither rain nor river, in mistletoe that was not a plant or a tree, in the trance state that was neither sleep nor waking. The Christian sense of duality – good and bad, right and wrong, black and white, body and soul – was unknown to the Druid. The key to Celtic philosophy is the merging of dark and light, natural and supernatural, conscious and unconscious. The *sithean* themselves existed in this twi-state, beings who dwelled between one world and another, creatures who were neither men nor gods. Their habitation was in ancient tombs, themselves halfway houses between this world and the next.

These beliefs led to the creation of a caste of seers which was to linger on in the remoter Highlands at least until the seventeenth century; to a natural acceptance of the existence of second sight among the Gaels; and to an inherited tendency to greater psychical awareness than other races.

Another side to the cult of the future, which has nothing to do with the waking dream, was yet to become a high skill in the repertoire of the seer-Druid. According to Justin, the third century Roman historian, forecasting future by signs and omens, augury and divination, was a speciality of the Celts. A flight of birds guided the Gauls to Illyrium, and an eagle's appearance turned a Celtic king back from war. The idea of good and bad omens lingers on as a superstition to this day, and though we no longer study the blood-flow of a dying man, we still consult the tarot cards, the teacup and the stars.

Those who experienced the waking dream, then, were also skilled interpreters of signs and deliberate diviners of omens. The duality of Christianity was to separate the two, excusing second sight as involuntary and possibly containing revelation of God's purpose, and condemning deliberate divination as an invasion into God's territory.

In the earliest days, the nomadic Celts wandering through Europe had few named gods but rather worshipped the sun, the moon, and the elements. Wherever they settled, however, they adopted and adapted local deities. Thus Caesar was able to write, 'The Gauls declare that they are all descended from Father Dis, who was Pluto in Roman mythology. It was natural, therefore, that on their arrival in the Highlands, the Celts came to regard the burial cairns and earthworks of an older creed as sacred, and included in their own heroic tales the ancestral spirits of the Neolithic men, taking over and adapting the ancient long-forgotten mysteries to their own needs and rituals.

So it must have been with Christianity. Not imposed from without, nor stamped upon the surface of an ancient cult, but drawn in, intermingled with the best that already existed in poetry, tradition and religious observance. Celtic heroes and goddesses merged into Christian saints. St Brigit or Bride, revered as a saint and said to have been born on 1 February, the Celtic festival of Imbolc, was believed to have been the daughter of a Druid and fused in legend with the Celtic triple-goddess, the giver and taker of life. Christ himself was identified with the warrior-hero Cú Chulainn.

Isle Maree, a jewel in the heart of the loch, is a beautiful example of this fusion between the old and new beliefs. Maree is thought by some to have been St Maelrubha, the red-headed Abbot of Applecross, by others to have been the pagan 'ane god Mourie'. On this small wooded sanctuary, the oak trees of the Druids intertwine with the holly of the Christians. Fragments of St Maelrubha's cell and a Christian burial ground stand close to a dead tree studded with copper coins and nails, offerings to the god of the spring who was supposed to cure insanity. Here too are the graves of a Viking and his Norse lover. In the seventeenth century, Presbytery records give an account of the sacrifice of a bull to Mourie for the cure of a woman, by her four sons.

If Isle Maree is the geographical example of the fusion between two creeds, Columba must surely be its finest personal embodiment. Through the early Celtic saints, and in particular Columba, Christianity was to make its own strong contribution to the evolution of second sight. Prince and bard, priest and prophet, Columba is often thought of as the father of second sight.

THE CHRISTIAN INFLUENCE

The last of the Celts to invade the north were the Scots from Ireland who founded the Kingdom of Dalriada in Argyll in AD 503. Already racially related to the Picts, they were to bicker and battle with them mainly over territory until, through intermarriage, they finally amalgamated under the Scottish King Kenneth Macalpin, in AD 843. Already evangelized by St Patrick, the Scots established Christianity in the north under the leadership and zeal of the remarkable Columba whose story is told on page 152.

Although Columba was the outstanding hero of the early Celtic Church, 'not to be compared with philosophers or learned men but with the Patriarchs, Prophets and Apostles', as Fintan recorded, yet he was steeped in the beliefs and traditions of the Druids. Iona where he built his monastery has also been called the Isle of Dreams or the Isle of the Druids. On the one occasion in thirty years when he returned to his beloved Ireland, it was to attend the Synod of Drumceatt in AD 574 where he spoke on behalf of 1,200 bards who were about to be expelled as trouble-makers. His enlightened argument was that their expulsion would deprive the country of a wealth of knowledge and tradition that could never be replaced.

The simple Christian ethic of prayer, work and Bible-reading appealed to the Picts whose Druids had become decadent, just as the simplicity of the Reformed Church centuries later was to supersede Roman Catholicism for much the same reason. Second sight was not an alien concept to the Columban Church. The Old Testament is brightened by visions predicting the coming of Messiah. The Gospels record the precognitive dreams of the Magi and of Joseph the carpenter. Christ foresaw the destruction of Jerusalem. St Paul called prophecy one of the gifts of the Spirit, and St Columba gloried in that gift. Nor did the concept of Christian vision differ so greatly from the waking dream of the Celts. Just as the ancient Neolithic priesthood sought by dreams and visions to contact the *sithean*, so the prophet-seer existed to interpret the will of God. The ancient cult of the dead is not, after all, so very different from the communion of saints, nor Tir nan Og so far removed from the idea of Paradise.

As time passed, the duality of Christianity began to confuse the issue. Either second sight came from God, as was manifested in the prophets and saints, or it came from the Devil. As men were naturally sinful creatures, second sight was probably evil, certainly best left alone, and on no account to be cultivated. That attitude is little changed today.

Under Christian influence, therefore, the telepathic and precognitive talent of Stone Age man, fostered and cultivated by the Celts to such a degree that it was considered a natural part of ritual and of life, changed. The emphasis shifted from the deliberate cult of the waking dream to its involuntary nature; away from the superstitious consultation of omens or divination by artificial means, to trust in the providence of God. To those of deep spirituality, second sight could be

28

accounted a gift from the Almighty, but to those who were ignorant or who did not profess the Christian faith, it was a key to self-destruction.

Because ordinary people who were neither saints nor sinners did not stop seeing apparitions and dreaming the future, the gift that Columba had cherished came in time to be regarded as an affliction, dreaded and suppressed. At the same time, second sight, however unacceptable, never ceased to be regarded as a gift, now no longer in the bounty of the *sithean*, but (depending upon the personality and motivation of the seer) direct from Satan or the Christian God.

It is interesting to note that the earliest researchers into the history and manifestation of second sight were mainly ministers of the Reformed Church. Their attitude was not, on the whole, condemnatory but curious. Nor was second sight generally associated with witchcraft and seers punished accordingly.

Largely because of the Columban influence, second sight – provided it came involuntarily and unsought – was generally tolerated by the church in the Highlands and Islands, and not regarded, as were divination and fortune-telling, as necessarily evil.

THE VIKING SIGNIFICANCE

Although the Scots were the last Celts to dominate the Highlands and Western Isles, they were not the final colonizers in the north. A century before the Scots and Picts united under Scottish King Kenneth in AD 843, the Vikings had started their piratical raids on the northern coast. The reasons for their instant success were mainly the invention of the keel, the development of sail, and the destruction by Charlemagne of the Frisian fleet which left the seas wide open. At the same time, Scandinavia's supply of iron ore, allied to the skill of her smiths in constructing the two-edged slashing sword, contributed to the Vikings' success on land. As a result, they dominated the Western Isles for 400 years, the Highlands until the eleventh century, and the Northern Isles until the fifteenth century.

A need for territory and a love of liberty brought the first Viking colonizers to the Islands – exiles from the despotism of Harald Harfanger who were to spread from the Shetlands south to the Isle of Man. Although Europe was outraged by the murder and pillage of defenceless Christian settlements such as Iona, gradually the Lochlanners imposed their own set of values, laws and beliefs on the Celts and in turn absorbed, through hostages and intermarriage, many of the customs and characteristics of the Celts, including a gradual conversion to Christianity. Profession of the faith was pursued with vigour in times of victory but abandoned for Thor and his promise of Valhalla when defeat loomed. To the Vikings, natural death was a disaster: entry to heaven was only possible for those who had died gloriously in battle.

Norsemen throughout history have been pictured as savage, lacking in sensitivity, and ruthless. Certainly they were rough, strong men, quick to resent an insult and terrifying in battle as the *berserkir* – bear-shirted initiates of Odin – worked themselves into a frenzy and howled into the fray. Their coming brought chaos and disruption to the Gaels, and probably a return to paganism for as long as the Scandinavians themselves remained unconverted, but there was still much to admire in these sturdy sons of the sea. Implacable enemies could also be loyal friends. Forthrightness, honesty, and generosity characterized these robust and expert sailors whose love of justice was so ingrained in their nature that any form of despotism or oppression was anathema. Certainly their ferocity cannot be condoned but their virtues of practicality, hardiness, and durability deserve to be commended.

Their women, too, were tough and able to cope with responsibility, often left to manage the farm and household while their men were raiding or trading. The sagas are full of tales of their courage and qualities of leadership. Interestingly, one of the most famous, the mother of Earl Sigurd who is celebrated for remarking to her son, 'I would have reared you in a wool basket if I had known you expected to live forever. It is fate that controls man, not his comings and goings, and it is better to die with honour than live in shame,' was born a *Celtic* princess.

Many of the clans as we know them today owe their origin to the intermarriage of the Celts and the Vikings. Not only was Sigurd's mother a Celt, his wife was the daughter of Malcolm II of Scotland and their son, Thorfinn, spent time in the Scottish court with his grandfather and cousin Macbeth. (Current thinking suggests that Thorfinn and Macbeth may be one and the same person.)

Sir George Mackenzie of Tarbet, later to be the first Earl of

Cromarty, called himself 'a little chief of the only Norwegian family remaining in Scotland, viz., the race of Olaus, one of the last Royalists of Man and of his son Leodu who was heritor of Lewis.'

Western Islanders inherited their strong physique and skilled seamanship from their Norse ancestors, and also many of the controlled characteristics which, blended with those of the emotional, artistic Celt, have produced both a cultured and a hardy race. Norse genes may also have contributed towards a particular outlook on life sometimes called Celtic gloom. Moodiness and fatalism are not part of the Irish temperament. Doctor Beddoe has stated that, 'It is curious that wherever in the North of Scotland Scandinavian blood abounds, hypochondriasis, hysteria, and other nervous diseases are remarkably frequent.' Harsh conditions, continual poverty, a rocky coast imprisoned by restless seas, are influences which, acting upon a nature inclined to moodiness, have produced not just an admirable strength of character in the Highlander, but also a tendency to depression.

An analogy – fanciful perhaps – may be seen between Norseman and Celt in the doctrine and expression of worship in the Islands. The sober, strongly disciplined service of the Free Kirk in Lewis offers an intriguing contrast to the colourful imagery of Catholic ritual in Barra. That the two creeds survive together without the animosity that exists in Northern Ireland forms part of the analogy, and is owing perhaps to the dour, commonsensical attitude of Viking intermingled with the creative nature of the Gael.

The Norsemen also left an enormous legacy of superstition. No expedition was undertaken without consulting the runes. Belief in witchcraft, spells, and the power of omens and dreams became – like the mingling of blood – inextricably mixed with Celtic belief and custom. Thus, according to the *Bannatyne Manuscript History of the Macleods*, the mother of the seer Coinneach Odhar received his divining stone from the ghost of a Viking princess.

According to another legend, entirely Norse, Coinneach Odhar found it in a raven's nest. The gift of prophecy, according to Norse tradition, was to be found in the Victory Stone. To obtain this, the seeker has to remove, boil, and replace a raven's eggs. When she finds she cannot hatch them she flies off to find the Victory Stone, which she places in her nest to encourage the eggs to hatch. When next she leaves her nest, the stone is there for the taking. It will not only endow the finder with the gift of prophecy but also assure him of victory in battle.

Norse and Celtic superstitions regarding the raven, which features in so many of Coinneach Odhar's prophecies, differ in that the 'bird of Odin' was regarded with respect by the Norseman while to the Gael he was the harbinger of death.

Highland second sight, then, stems from the imposition of the Celt's cultivated vision upon the unknown ancestral rituals practised by the Neolithic tomb-builders, of Christian dualism on Celtic mysteries, of Norse fatalism upon Celtic imagination. All have played a part in shaping, encouraging and preserving the latent talent that lies within us all. That it is such an interweaving of many traditional beliefs and superstitions is evident from the number of Gaelic terms that exist to describe it, detailed in the next chapter.

2   The Many-Faceted Gift

Out of sight. Through space. Beyond time.

These facets of vision, of the psychic crystal – clairvoyance, telepathy, pre- and retrocognition – combine to form the greater part of what is understood today as Highland second sight. Just as the lights in the crystal turn from deep loch-blue to heather-pink, so there are many variations in the nature of the vision. Separate Gaelic terms exist for all of them.

John Gregorson Campbell, minister of Tiree, folklorist and Gaelic scholar, in his *Superstitions of the Highlands and Islands of Scotland* published in 1902, was the first to collect and define the extensive lexicon that would seem to cover all aspects of the faculty.

Dà-Shealladh

Literally two-sights, *dà-shealladh* (pronounced daa-halugh), implies the ability to see normally and to witness the world of apparitions, both of the dead and the living. The spectre seen was thought to be entirely independent of the person it represented. That person knew nothing of its appearance, and, more important, the spectre was not considered to be his spirit or some eerie manifestation of his soul. This belief originated in the early Celtic, or possibly pre-Celtic, conception of the ancestral god, the *sith* or fairy who was able to take on the appearance of dead or living persons in order to convey some message to the seer.

No one thought that the apparitions emanated from the seer's mind or from any wish or fantasy on his part. He was not considered to be insane, abnormal, or possessed by evil spirits. The important fact underlying the term was that second sight enabled seers to have visions of persons known or unknown, dead or alive, which came from the *sithean* for some good purpose of their own.

Taibhsear, Taibhsearachd and Taibhs

In Gaelic, many of the words used to describe psychic phenomena start with the syllable 'ta'. *Taibhsear* – pronounced ty-sher – means literally 'he who is spectre-haunted'. The spectres seen are the manifestations described above, beings that exist in the twilit world between heaven and earth, doubles of the persons they represent.

It was thought that the *taibhs* enacted all that would one day happen – or had already happened – to the person it represented. Thus, the *taibhs* who was seen in a shroud heralded the death of its human double. Seers differed in their interpretation of the position of the grave clothes: some thought that if the face was covered, death was imminent, but others placed more importance on the feet.

The *taibhs* of a fisherman gleaming with phosphorous or dripping water was usually the sign of drowning, but not always. Campbell tells of a certain man from Tiree who was sent to fetch wood from Loch Creran and forgot his parcel of dry clothes. As expected, he got wet through to the skin and had to sit all evening in damp clothing. When he returned, the woman with the gift of second sight asked him if he had got wet at all when he was away, for she had 'seen' him soaked to the skin and was sure he must have drowned. The fisherman, who repeated the story at the turn of the century, said there was no way by which she could have heard of his condition.

Thus it took skill to interpret the messages conveyed by the spectres. Care, too, was needed in dealing with them for they could be spiteful and capricious. It was dangerous for a *taibhsear* to walk in the middle of the road at night for fear of being run down by a phantom funeral. A certain young seer, while travelling along the south side of Loch Rannoch, was joined by a funeral procession. One of the poles of the bier was thrust into his unwary hands and he was forced to carry it for about a mile. As he was on the loch side of the coffin, he had great difficulty in keeping to the path, for the phantom bearers continually tried to push him into the water. About a mile later they vanished as mysteriously as they had appeared.

Silence in the presence of a *taibhs* was essential, for if the seer were to speak first, the apparition would have the power to force him to keep it company by night. The *taibhsear* would then become *taibhsearan*, haunted by this particular *taibhs*. As it was usually hard to distinguish between the spectral double and its human original, seers tended to be silent men, recognizable by their brooding, melancholy look. A young seer in Tiree about the year 1900 was on his way home after drying corn in a kiln at the mill. As his head was bowed against a gale, he collided with a figure whom he took to be a friend. Without thinking he spoke, but as soon as the answer came in broken, unintelligible words he knew it was a *taibhs*. Every night for six months thereafter he was forced to box with the apparition after dark, or so he told his companions. One of these, doubting his story, followed him outside one night and watched him spar with some unseen assailant until he fell to the ground.

A *taibhs* could also be treacherous. A young labourer from Mull was given a pair of knitted gloves by a fellow servant which he wore for the first time when crossing a mountain pass on his way home to his family. At the most dangerous point he was joined by the *taibhs* of the maid who had knitted the gloves. As she was on the safe side of the path, he was terrified that she would push him over the precipice. Praying hard, he continued in safety until he reached level ground. Then he took off the gloves, flung them at her and said, 'That is all the business you have with me.' On his way back to work, he noticed the gloves on the path, but he did not touch them. The vision never returned. How he accounted for the loss of the gloves to his fellow servant is not recorded!

If the *taibhs* became too troublesome and if the seer were brave enough, he could tell its living double to stop annoying him. The latter, who knew nothing of the haunting, might well be very angry, and the *taibhs*, too, would be furious, often giving the seer a 'thundering lashing' – but it usually then disappeared.

Part of the *taibhsear's* code was never to wish too strongly for anything, for this could cause a *taibhs* to appear and do harm to its double. John Gregorson Campbell tells of a young girl from Morven who, while sitting sewing her trousseau with her friends, sighed and wished aloud that she could see her lover. At that precise moment he happened to be crossing a mountain pass, when she appeared to him. Recognizing her *taibhs*, he struck at it with his dirk. At home, the bride took ill and died soon after. Strong wishing by a woman in Perthshire who was being battered by her husband brought the *taibhs* of her dead brother to her side. It asked her unpleasantly what she wanted and when she explained, it went out to the field where her husband was ploughing. She watched her man drop dead.

Fiosachd and Fiosaiche

Derived from *fios* (pronounced 'feess') the word for knowledge, *fiosachd* (pronounced feessak) is associated with augury, divination and fortune-telling, while *fiosaiche* (pronounced feessa-cher) – literally 'one who knows' – has come to mean a seer in the occult sense: sorcerer, soothsayer, fortune teller.

Not usually connected with second sight, *fiosaiche* is still the word used in the oral tradition to describe Coinneach Odhar, generally regarded as the greatest of Highland seers. It is also mentioned by John Aubrey as an alternative style for seer.

Tannasg

Tannasg (pronounced tannask) narrows the *taibhs* to the apparition of someone already dead.

A particularly good example of a *tannasg* was seen by Sir George Mackenzie of Rosehaugh during the time he was Lord Advocate for Scotland in the reign of Charles II. Sir George, cousin of Kenneth, third Earl of Seaforth who was to feature in one of Coinneach Odhar's most intriguing prophecies (page 202), was a seer himself. While in Edinburgh it was his custom to take an evening stroll down Leith Walk. On one occasion he was stopped without introduction or apology by a distinguished, if somewhat eccentric-looking, old gentleman, 'There is a very important case coming up in London a fortnight from now,' he said earnestly. 'It concerns a large city estate where a false claimant is doing his utmost to disinherit the rightful heir on the grounds that he had no title deeds. If you will be so good as to visit the mansion house on the estate, you will find in the attic an old oak chest with two compartments. Between the layers you will find hidden the titles required. I desire you to attend the case.'

The old man gave details of the address and walked away. Sir George was surprised, thought the old man mad, and forgot the matter. Next evening, however, he met him again in the same place, and again he was urged to hurry south to attend the case, assuring him he would be well paid for his trouble. Sir George listened patiently but promised nothing. On the third day, the old man pleaded with him not to waste another hour, or the case would be lost.

His insistence, obvious anxiety, and advanced age finally persuaded Sir George to ride south, and he arrived in London on the day before the case was due to be tried. Within an hour he reached the address and met two men, one of whom was the rightful heir, the other his London barrister. The latter, understandably put out by Sir George's interference, was extremely rude about Scotland and Scottish law. Sir George replied that, lame and ignorant as his learned friend took the Scots to be, yet in law as well as in other respects they would effect what would defy the London clique.

The heir, much intrigued, invited Sir George into his house and offered him refreshment. The drawing-room was hung over with grand portraits, one of which immediately attracted Sir George's attention. He knew that face.

'There's the man who spoke to me three times, three days running in Leith Walk, and who persuaded me to come here. Who is he?'

His host eyed him strangely. 'My great-grandfather,' he replied, 'dead for the past fifty years.'

Both hurried upstairs to the attic and eventually found the old trunk lying dusty and unused in a corner – empty, or so it seemed. At a kick it disintegrated and there, just as described, between the two layers lay the original title deeds.

After winning the case, and incidently proving the superiority of Scottish law to his English counterpart, Sir George returned to Edinburgh. He never saw the strange old gentleman again.

Tamhasg

Tamhasg (pronounced tavask) distinguishes the *taibhs* as a spectre specifically of the living. One of the commonest instances of second sight today is the *tamhasg* of a close friend or relative on the point of death.

Only recently a young woman told me that she had woken up one night to see her mother standing at the foot of her bed, smiling. So vivid was the vision that she cried out, 'Mother, what are you doing here?' As soon as she turned to waken her husband, the *tamhasg* departed. Within minutes the telephone rang to tell her that her mother had just died. She found the vision deeply comforting, for her mother had looked well, not crippled with arthritis and old age as she had been in life.

A *tamhasg* was not always the herald of gloomy events. A common

37

sighting was that of a future bride or groom. Campbell tells of a man from Coll who, while serving with his regiment in Africa, caught glimpses over a period of five years of the *tamhasg* of the woman he eventually married. Sometimes she even touched him. On his way home he called in at a house in Dervaig, Mull, where he saw a woman sitting at a loom, weaving. She was identical to the *tamhasg* who had haunted him over the years. They fell in love and married.

Tàsg

Another word for apparition, *tàsg* (pronounced task) is generally associated with an unearthly wail heard before a death. The cry comes not from the dead person but rather from his closest mourner.

In the case of a man drowned in Tiree, a cry consisting of three loud drawn-out wails was heard on the site where his closest friend later received the news of his death. At the old quay in Port Appin, Argyllshire, the wailing of a woman was heard in the night: some days later the mother of a lad killed in Glasgow was heard to utter the same lamentation. In July 1870, a ship struck a sunken rock near Skerry-vore Lighthouse and sank. Though the crew was rescued, the skipper was swept away by the current and drowned. Crying heard in the district four years before was reckoned to have heralded the event.

Taslach

The *taslach* is an unseen *taibhs*, recognizable only by the noise it makes: a cry, a knock, or footsteps perhaps. It is usually a ghost of the living and might even be of someone completely unknown to those who hear it.

During the '30s, Dr David Johnston of Strathallan, Fortrose, was wakened by the persistent ringing of his doorbell. He rose and went downstairs, but could find no one there. Later he learned that a patient who had been much on his mind had died at the exact moment he heard the bell. The *taslach* of the patient was responsible for the sound. Dr Johnston was to be wakened on another occasion in the same way – this time the *taslach* was a tramp who had died close by and who was entirely unknown to the doctor.

Animals were credited with being able to witness *taslach*. A man from Skye, when asked why the dogs were barking near a churchyard one night, replied that it was because they could see the *taslachan* of the living. He called it a premonition of a funeral.

38

Taradh

Noises made by a *taslach* were called *taradh* (pronounced tarugh). Often they were connected with a change of tenancy. My grandparents, home from India on leave at the turn of the century, took a large house in Fife for six months. On their first night the household was wakened by shouts, screams, weeping, doors banging and the continual tread of footsteps on the ground floor. Watched by a huddle of frightened servants, my soldier-grandfather took his sword and descended to investigate. He found nothing, and the noises were never heard again.

My own experience of *taradh* was equally alarming. Towards the end of November 1965 we had just moved into an old house in the Black Isle, Ross-shire. Between four and five in the evening I was writing letters in the old kitchen, waiting for my family to come home for tea. The Aga stove gave out a gentle heat, and a newly baked cake cooled fragrantly on a wire tray. I felt relaxed and at home for the first time in the new rectory. Then, through the length of the house, I heard the front door slam. Heavy footsteps climbed the stairs and strode down the corridor towards the bathroom directly above where I was sitting. I thought it was my husband come home from his round of visiting and gone upstairs to wash, so I moved the kettle on to the hot plate and waited. Meanwhile the footsteps continued backwards and forwards along that upstairs passage, an angry heavy tread that shook the ceiling above me. What was he doing, I wondered? Why should he be so upset? I hurried along the corridor that led to the dining-room, and out into the hall. At the foot of the stairs I called out, and the sound ceased suddenly. The silence was profound.

I turned to look at the front door. It was locked. The key was there and the bolt drawn. No one could possibly have come in. My husband returned about half an hour later.

That old house had also been haunted by a *tannasg* for many years. An old woman, thought to have been housekeeper to the daughters of Sir Alexander Mackenzie, the explorer, was said to have watched her son drown in Fortrose Bay. She was frequently seen by truthful men and women of my acquaintance, standing by an upstairs window. Officially laid in the '30s by bishop, bell, and book, she was never seen thereafter. I had no reason to suppose that hers were the angry footsteps.

Tachar
Tachar is a rarely used word for spectre, whose derivatives are better understood as 'haunted' in place names. Sron an Tachair, the ghostly nook, is a rock between Kinlochrannoch and Druim-a-Chastail in Perthshire, which was supposed to be haunted. A long tree-lined avenue near Tore in the Black Isle could be said to be haunted by a *tachar*. Local inhabitants avoid it at night.

Taran
Taran, meaning the ghost of an unbaptized child, is also very uncommon these days. A legend connected with the ruined Redcastle on the Beauly Firth dates from the old custom of burying a child beneath the cornerstone of an important building to ward off evil spirits. Redcastle was first built by the brother of William the Lyon in 1179, and the child allegedly buried in the foundations is said to haunt the castle to such an extent that it has been left to ruin. That ghost may have been a *taran*.

Tathasg
Another word for apparition, *tathasg* (pronounced taask) is particularly connected with the spirit of a mother seen and heard by her orphaned children. Some of the loveliest Gaelic lullabies were said to have been composed by these apparitions while watching over the cradles of their infants. It was surely a *tathasg* who, in 1982, stood at the shoulder of her young Glasgow daughter and touched her reassuringly as she bent over the crib of her newly born baby.

Dreug
Dreug (pronounced drayk), which means meteor, falling star, or fireball, is also used in connection with ghostly lights in the night sky which portend death. A woman from South Uist told me that only recently she saw these death-lights like the tail of a comet come to rest over the house on the night her brother died. In Tiree they are also called *teine-sithe* – fairy fire – and, as we shall see in Chapter 5, these were witnessed by Father Allan McDonald in Eriskay.

Sometimes these lights were said to be caused by other spirits awaiting the soul of a dying person. They had a greenish appearance and could be seen moving about the room where a body awaited burial. The Gaels also believed that the soul after death had the appearance of a flame. On the night three men were drowned near Kyle, the lights were seen by the Rev. D. MacEchern who officiated at the funeral in 1919. Mr MacEchern was also told by a certain Mr Young that his mother, who lived in Latheron, had been sitting by the bed where her children slept when she saw a light brighter than a candle rise from one of her bairns. Within a couple of days, the child was dead.

One woman in the Black Isle told me that the whole bedroom lit up at the moment her mother died. She and the district nurse were dazzled by its brightness. Both found the experience comforting and unforgettable.

Naisg
A verb and noun connected with binding, sealing, or making fast, *naisg* (pronounced nashk) was also used in the sense of 'binding away' second sight. With so much to see and so much to dread in the world of apparitions, it is little wonder that the gift was generally unwanted. It takes a person of immense courage and personality to be able to cope with so much knowledge, and most of it painful.

John Gregorson Campbell tells a sad story of a seer who had two sons, both in the army and both fighting overseas. In his visions he continually saw what was happening to them. To get rid of these disturbing sights he gave half-a-crown to an old woman and prayed for the removal of his second sight. His wish was granted, and for a while he knew nothing of the fate of his sons. He found this as upsetting as knowing too much, so he sent for a seer in Tiree, and set him beside the hearth so that he might look through the flames, for it was an old belief that the best visions were seen through fire.

Soon the seer began to sweat and the father, who knew this heralded some unhappy vision, begged him to say what he could see. The *taibhsear* told him that both his sons were dead, one killed by a bullet through the heart, the other shot through the head. A letter corroborating these tragic events arrived soon afterwards.

But apparitions were not all tragic or malevolent. Some, like Sir George Mackenzie's old man, returned to give good advice. Others, too fond of their earthly possessions, returned to watch over them. One appeared to complain to his widow that she had not shaved him before burial! Whatever their intentions, the reappeared dead were not particularly welcome, and to prevent their return the plant called

41

trailing perlwort (*Sagina procumbens*) or the bog violet, in Gaelic *Mothan* (*Pinguicula vulgaris*), was hung over the lintel in houses where a corpse awaited burial. A tradition which must date back to our prehistoric ancestors dictated that a cup of water be placed by the corpse in case it should return and be thirsty. It was also a belief that if the strings of the winding sheet were not tied, the spirit could not rest.

To make a pact with a friend that whoever died first would return to inform the survivor was considered unholy and unwise. In Kintail two herdsmen entered into just such a bond. One died, and a new-comer was employed in his stead. The survivor clung to the company of the stranger but one night, in spite of every precaution, he found himself alone. He sang and mended his shoes to keep his courage up but he could not keep his thoughts from his dead friend and the compact they had made. Sure enough, at midnight he heard a scratching on the roof. The noise grew louder and the terrified man called out in the hope that it was his living companion, 'I know you're just trying to scare me.' As soon as he spoke, his dead friend entered wrapped in his shroud. Fortunately the outcome was happy, for the apparition assured him that he had gone to a pleasant place and went away again.

The ancient cult of the dead, strengthened by a natural pride of ancestry, usually gives the Celt a respect for human remains. A tailor who was irreverent enough to kick a skull was haunted thereafter by the *taibhs* of its owner. The Highlander also has a sense of humour where ghosts are concerned – as is shown in the story of the man who disturbed a grave one night by lifting a skull.

'That's mine!' said the angry *taibhs*.

When he dropped it and picked up another, a similar voice cried out, 'That's mine!'

'What,' said the man, much surprised, 'had you two skulls then?'

DREAMS

Visionary dreams, though not the spectre-haunted sightings traditionally meant by second sight, were certainly part of the seers' repertoire. It is, after all, only a short step from the dissociated waking state of the seer to the subconscious disposition of the dreamer.

Bruadar, Bruadarach and Bruadaraiche

Bruadar (pronounced broo-e-tar) means 'dream' but it may also mean 'vision' with the adjective 'visionary', while *bruadaraiche* (broo-e-taracher) means 'dreamer' in the visionary sense of precognitive or retrocognitive dreaming.

Campbell tells the story of a widower who dreamed that his dead wife appeared and said, 'Man, who hast shut the door upon me and left me lying here, before the Christmas is come a greater loss will befall you. Man, who hast the children, rearing them unpeaceably, if oft your hand be raised I will not long be at peace with you.'

An Inverness policeman in 1892 dreamed that while he was at the Northern Meeting Games, a message came that the Duke of Sutherland had died at 10.30 the previous night. He awoke, trembling, and while he was trying to calm down, the telephone rang. The Chief Constable was on the line to tell him that the Duke had died at 10.30 p.m. and would not be at the Games.

Precognitive dreams are as frequent today as ever they were. In Balmacara recently I met a psychotherapist who told me she had trained herself to dream when in search of a solution to some problem. She had been planning a holiday with friends but, feeling deeply uneasy for no apparent reason, she decided to 'sleep on it'. In her dream she had a strong image of fire and read it as a warning. On the night she should have been away, the house where she would have stayed was destroyed by fire with a heavy loss of life.

A woman from Nairn, writing in 1982, states that she dreams 'a lot that comes true, especially to myself, for example the initials of my husband. I saw the wedding cake and the room we had our honeymoon in. I can walk into a room or building and say I've been here before, even to the exact words the people say to me. I've never met anyone who can say the same and I know a lot who don't believe me, but it comes to pass as in my dream, even if it's months or years later. I described my mother-in-law to my husband before I met her, that she walked with a limp and had a walking stick and her name was Helen.

'I've even dreamed of a little girl murdered in London, about twenty years ago. I saw her down a coal-cellar in a pink party dress, and an axe beside her. I told my husband this the next morning and on switching on the wireless, I heard the girl missing in London had been found dead in a coal-cellar, and that she was wearing a pink party dress.

'I never "see" things, only dream about them.'

That writer was born at midnight on midsummer day, the seventh child in her family.

Mrs Johnston, wife of the Fortrose doctor, had a vivid dream that her husband would have an accident with a chauffeur-driven car containing a nanny dressed in a blue uniform and two children. She warned him to be careful. Next day, as he drove towards the junction with the main road near his home, he drew out, taking extra care. Suddenly a large car driving too fast flashed past, just catching the end of his bonnet. It was driven by a chauffeur and contained a nanny and two children, exactly as his wife had described.

Long before Freud and Jung, the Gaels had their own interpretations of dreams, and saw them as indications of the future. To dream of raw eggs, for example, meant trouble; eggs in general indicated gossip or scandal. Herrings presaged snow, a grey horse stood for the sea, while a white horse indicated a letter. To dream of women was unlucky, and of the dead meant that they were not at peace. Those who could not interpret their dreams went to a recognized seer for elucidation, just as they consulted him as to the best days for travel or doing business. This fact links the traditional seer closely to the deliberate cult of the future, which has been part of his repertoire since the days of the Druids.

OMEN, AUGURY AND DIVINATION

Second sight in its finest form is a natural talent in which some people are more proficient than others. It is also spasmodic, involuntary, and elusive. Not surprisingly then, some who had the talent naturally also sought to boost it artificially. The girl who tapped on the seer's door to ask 'Whom will I marry?' expected an answer. The seer, unable to depend upon his fluctuating talent and wanting to answer her, often turned to artificial methods of augury and divination.

Frith and Frithir

Though *frith* (pronounced free) is a word connected with rage and angry glances, it also means augury, divination and incantation used to discover the fate of absent friends or sick relations. It was the *frithir* (pronounced free-ir), the augurer's or seer's, task to cast the *frith*.

44

There were certain rituals to be observed. The *frithir* had to fast, and on the first Monday of every quarter, before sunrise, had to go bare-headed, barefooted and blindfolded to the doorstep. There he would place a hand on each jamb and invoke God or the Trinity to reveal the mystery. He would then predict from the first thing he saw on opening his eyes.

The influence of Christianity on old Celtic custom is shown in the lovely old Gaelic legend which describes how Mary cast a *frith* to find the boy Jesus when he was lost in Jerusalem.

> God over me,
> God before me, God behind me,
> I on the path, O God,
> Thou, O God, in my steps.
>
> The augury made of Mary to her Son,
> The offering made of Bride through her palm,
> Sawest Thou it, King of life?
> Said the King of life that he saw.
>
> The augury made by Mary for her own offspring,
> When he was for a space missing.
> Knowledge of truth, not knowledge of falsehood,
> That I shall truly see all my quest.
>
> Son of beauteous Mary, King of life,
> Give thou me eyes to see all my quest,
> With grace that shall never fail, before me,
> That shall never quench nor dim.

This beautiful poem, recorded by A. Carmichael in his fifth volume of *Carmina Gadelica*, is a perfect example of how the old Celtic religion and the Christian faith existed side by side in the Celtic church.

Taghairm

There were, however, far more sinister ways of divination dating directly from Druidic rites, which survived in the Highlands from East Ross-shire to Skye until comparatively recent times. In the ancient mode of divination known as *taghairm* (pronounced ta-herm), the performance consisted of roasting cats one after another for several days, without eating. This was said to summon a legion of evil spirits in the form of black cats all screeching in a terrifying manner. In another form, the diviner was wrapped in the hot skin of a newly slaughtered ox and laid at full length in the recess behind a waterfall or on the edge of the incoming tide. Clad in the 'cloak of knowledge', his mind in a ferment, his ears deafened by the roar of water, his garbled answer to the question put to him was considered to come from the spirit who haunted the falls or the shoreline.

Slinneanachd

Derived from *slinnean* for shoulder (pronounced sleenyan), *slinneanachd* (sleenyanachk) is a term used for shoulder-blade divination which was still practised in 1746. Thomas Pennant, in his *Tour of Scotland* in 1796, records Lord Loudon's story of the common soldier who, while the Battle of Culloden was raging, predicted victory for the Hanoverians by 'pretending to have discovered the event' through studying the speal bone. The best beast for the purpose was a black sheep, or possibly a pig. The animal was slaughtered and boiled till the flesh fell from the bones. The diviner then studied the shoulder blade, careful to see that it had not been scraped or marked by knife, tooth or nail. The largest mark indicated the inquirer's grave, and from its position, his prognosis was determined. Other spots represented gatherings of people either at funerals, weddings or battles.

Deuchainn

Literally meaning trial, experiment or proof, *deuchainn* (pronounced jaiheen) can also mean trial by omen 'for him and for his luck' in order to discover the outcome of some important undertaking. The best time to perform these complicated rites was Hallowe'en or Hogmanay. If, for example, you wanted to know something about the person you would eventually marry, you climbed to the cairn on a hill 'which no four-footed beast could reach'. The first creature seen on the way home indicated the nature and person of your future mate. A sleek brown cow pointed to prosperity and happiness; a fox, on the other hand, was a decidedly bad omen.

Those who wanted to know their luck in the new year would close their eyes, walk to the end of the house and look round. The sight of an old woman was unlucky, but a young horseman was particularly fortunate. A man digging indicated death, as did a duck or hen with its head under its wing. The story is told of a seer who once made a trial for a sick person at the request of a friend. After performing the rite he opened his eyes and saw six ducks, all with their heads under their wings. The patient was dead within two days.

If a girl wanted to know whether her betrothed loved her, she would look at him secretly between her fingers and whisper a charm:

> I have a trial upon you,
> I have a looking at you,
> Between the five ribs of Christ's body;
> If it be fated or permitted you
> To make use of me,
> Lift your right hand,
> And let it not quickly down.

If her lover's first gesture was then to lift his left arm, she would know that he did not care for her.

We still use our 'he-loves-me-loves-me-not' daisies.

Manadh

Translated as luck, chance, prediction and omen, *manadh* (pronounced manugh) dates back to the Druid art of augury and survives today merely as superstition.

Birds were particularly significant. A cuckoo calling from the roof predicted the death of an inhabitant, as did the call of a golden plover at night. A pied wagtail seen between the tenant and his croft meant eviction. Cock-crowing at midnight presaged news in the morning. The cry of a curlew or the sight of a heron forecast disaster to the traveller.

To this day the sight of a minister or certain women turns fishermen back from their boats, and a story is told in Skye of one of them who, rather than encounter *droch comhalaichean* – bad people to meet – sent his son out ahead of him!

Tealeughadh chupaichean (pronounced tea-l-yaevugh hoopa-han)

Teacup reading was a later, but recognized form of prediction which reached its height in popularity when tea was still a luxury, expensive and hard to get. The spae wife who read the tea-leaves was in great demand in every township as far south as Glasgow, and some raised it to an art. Although the practice has almost died out these days, it was not long ago that spae wives chapped at the door with their little cases containing a decorative cup and packet of tea, offering to give a professional reading.

I well remember a family cook who, as a special favour, would read my cup when I was a child. Part of the ritual was to drink it down to the dregs – penance enough, for I disliked the drink – turn the cup *deiseal* (to the south) so that the last drops spread the leaves. A large amount of dregs promised worldly wealth, a small isolated speck predicted a letter. Other single leaves stood for my enemies. Annie-the-cook could weave such a fantasy round the bottom of a teacup that it seemed as if my whole life was spread out in the lie of the leaves.

ANIMALS AND SECOND SIGHT

The Gaels believed that animals were able to see apparitions more clearly than the greatest seers. Rising hackles, whitened eyes, barking or whinnying at night for no good cause, were all evidence of their possession of second sight, and their power to witness *taibhsean*. Their visions were usually considered to be omens of death. Horses were thought to be better seers than dogs, and when they shied or refused to move on the road it was because they could see an accident or funeral soon to take place.

John Gregorson Campbell tells of a grey tail-less bitch in Lorn who howled for a fortnight at the side of a burn. On the fourteenth day, a young woman and her child were swept off a bridge upstream by a sudden spate, and their drowned bodies were washed up on the spot where the dog had kept vigil.

Not all sightings presaged disaster, however. In Professor Archie Roy's account of a haunting in a farmhouse, the dogs were observed to crowd round an empty chair wagging their tails and begging for attention as if aware of a friendly presence.

In most sightings, if there are animals present they are usually the first to show psychic awareness. This should not be surprising. If second sight is natural to man, it would be strange if it were not also present in animals. That fact makes a mockery of any occult or supernatural explanation, and underlines the normality of the possession of a sixth sense, however latent and misunderstood, in man.

Second sight may be a natural, latent talent, but as seers themselves will tell you it is as easily abused as any other. Any talent should be used to promote truth, and the seer who employs his gift to exploit others or to gain wealth is as despicable as the writer or artist who turns to pornography for the same reasons.

There were plenty of imposters in the past, just as there are today. A Highlander of note who believed in the faculty itself once remarked, 'I never knew a truthful, trustworthy man who was a *taibhsear*.' Thomas Pennant while in Caithness recorded the story of the laird who pretended to have second sight in order to enhance his reputation in the clan. In time he developed the faculty and wished that he hadn't. A boat owned by him was caught in a storm one night. Obsessed with anxiety, he started to his feet and declared that all would be drowned for he had seen a vision of them passing before him in wet garments and with dripping locks. Later he learned that all on board had perished.

The dangers of exploitation of second sight are great. Doctor H. H. Bros, writing in the American magazine *Fate*, suggests that only those free from mental and emotional problems can safely experiment, and few could claim to be that. Bros also places a strong emphasis on the motives lying behind psychic exploration. Henderson Lynn, a follower of the old Celtic religion, believes that the misuse of his talent when he was a young man led to a spell of temporary blindness.

Though attitudes have changed over the years, the supply of psychic experience has remained as constant as a railway line running through the countryside of time. To follow that line, and the views and opinions of psychic investigators over the last three centuries, makes an intriguing journey.

3   The Age of Inquiry

George Sinclair, Professor of Mathematics at Glasgow University, published in 1685 a best-seller entitled *Satan's Invisible World Discovered*, which was written mainly as an argument against the current attacks of 'atheists and Sadducees' upon Christianity. Of second sight, he states that he is credibly 'informed that men and women in the Highlands can discern fatality approaching others by seeing them in waters or with winding sheets about them'. He heard also that 'others can lecture in a sheep's shoulder-bone a death within the parish seven or eight days before it come'. All preternatural knowledge, he says, came to people 'first by a compact with the Devil, and is derived downwards by succession to their posterity'. On the other hand, he admits that 'many are innocent and have the second sight against their will and inclination'.

This highly readable account of spooks, devils, 'thundering noises', invisible hands, and the thud of ghostly hoofs contains one story which might have involved a seer, or, as we are led to believe, the ghost of a seer.

While the king stayed at Lithgow, attending the gathering of his armie, which was defeated at Flowdon, being full of cares and perplexity, he went into the Church of Saint Michael, to hear Evening-song, as then it was called.

While he was at his devotion, an ancient man came in, his amber-coloured hair hanging down upon his shoulders, his forehead high, and inclining to baldness, his garments of azure colour, somewhat long, girded about with a towel or table napkin, of a comely and very reverend aspect.

50

Having inquired for the king he intruded himself into the prease, passing through, till he came to him, with a clounish simplicity, leaning over the canons-seat, where the king sat.

'Sir,' said he, 'I am sent hither to entreat you, to delay your expedition for this time, and to proceed no further in your intended journey: for if you do, you shall not prosper in your enterprise, nor any of your followers. I am further charged to warn you, not to use the acquaintance, company or counsel of women, as you tender your honour, life and estate.'

After this warning he withdrew himself back again into the prease. When service was ended, the king inquired earnestly for him, but he could be nowhere found, neither could any of the bystanders (of whom diverse did narrowly observe him, resolving afterwards to have discoursed with him) feel or perceive how, when or where he passed from them, having in a manner vanished in their hands.

The king was James IV who was killed in the Battle of Flodden at the age of forty in September 1513.

Sinclair was one of the very few investigators to ascribe second sight to witchcraft and the Devil. Although, as we shall see, the historical Coinneach Odhar was indicted for witchcraft there is no record that he was, in fact, a seer in the traditional sense. Certainly there were, and are, fortune-tellers and crystal-gazers involved with witchcraft, but true second sight in the Highland sense has seldom been ascribed to any compact with the Devil.

THE WELSH SCHOLAR

The second sight descends from father to son for some generations. Those who have it can prevent the evil which doth threaten others, but cannot save themselves. It's so very troublesome to many that they'd gladly be free from it. These persons observe that spirits are great lovers of flesh and they see them sometimes taking flesh out of pots, putting in its place that which is worse of which they'll not taste.

These who have this foresight by compact give responses being asked.

Sometimes they bring back to life those who are giving up the ghost; but another dies in his place, and it always proves fatal.

They come, as some say, by the second sight thus: they look through the knot in a piece of tree and the boals of sheers at a south door upon a burial as it passeth by.

This early reference to second sight comes in a manuscript discovered and copied by Edward Lhuyd, a Welsh Celtic scholar who was made keeper of the Ashmolean Museum, Oxford in 1691. Thought to have been written by the Revd James Kirkwood of Dunbar, *A Collection of Highland Rites and Customes* was collated at the request of the famous Robert Boyle, the scientist who laid the foundations of modern chemistry and physics and whose chief work, *The Skeptical Chymest* was published in 1661.

Boyle, himself the seventh son of an Irishman, was also passionately interested in the promotion of a Gaelic Bible for Protestants, not just in Ireland but also in the Highlands. He became a close friend of his two assistants, the Revd James Kirkwood and the Revd Robert Kirk of Aberfoyle, himself an addicted investigator as we shall see.

The manuscript now in the Bodleian Library has recently been edited by J. L. Campbell of Canna and the above extract is important on two counts. It clearly reveals the paradox that has affected the approach to second sight through the ages: the gift that is an affliction, the natural talent that is at the same time supernatural, the moral dilemma that makes it good if unsought and sinful if cultivated.

More important, the manuscript was the spring of that first stream of interest that was to draw into its current the research and curiosity of men like Samuel Pepys and Dr Johnson, right down to the folklorists, parapsychologists and scientists of today.

ROBERT KIRK AND THE FAIRIES

'Then a spirit passed befor my face, the hair of my flesh stood up. It stood stil, but I could not discern the forme thereof: an Image was befor my Eyes.' This is as good a description of a *taibhs* as ever was found in the Highlands. In fact, it comes from the Bible (Job 4:15–16) and is quoted in the frontispiece to the Revd Robert Kirk's treatise, *The Secret Common-Wealth*, probably written in 1691 or 1690.

Robert Kirk is thought to have been born in 1644 to the minister of Aberfoyle. He was a seventh son, which was believed in itself to convey the gift of second sight, and this may account for his fascination with the subject. In due course he was to become a minister himself, serving for twenty years in the parish of Balquhidder before moving to his father's church at Aberfoyle where he remained until his death in 1692.

Living right on the doorstep of the 'barbarous Highland rebels', he devoted himself to their evangelization by translating the psalms, the Bible, and the catechism into Gaelic. At the same time he was a meticulous notebook-keeper, and he is chiefly remembered today for his collection of information about fairies and second sight which he called *The Secret Common-Wealth*.

This marvellously entertaining essay, recently edited and produced in its fullest form by the folklorist Stewart Sanderson, is about 'the Nature and actions of the Subterranean (and for the most part) Invisible people heirtofor going under the name of Elves, Faunes, and Fairies, or the like . . . as they are described by those who have the Second Sight.'

Belief in fairies or the *sithean* is a cult which is still – if rarely – subscribed to in the twentieth century. Childhood bedtimes are still enchanted by tales of fairies' deeds. Whether they were, as some believe, the remnants of an earlier Neolithic race driven back to their cairns and tombs to find refuge from the hordes of incoming Celts, and emerging by night to steal milk and butter unless it was freely given; or whether they were the relic of a far-away religion that predated the Celtic pantheon, it is impossible to know. Certainly Robert Kirk believed in their existence, and held that second sight was not only within their power to bestow but also necessary to those who wished to make contact with them.

For the would-be seer, there were certain rituals to be observed. 'There be odd solemnities at investing a man with the priviledges of the whol Misterie of this Second Sight.' This included finding a tether of hair which had bound a corpse to its bier and binding it round his waist. He must then lower his head, look back through his legs till he saw a funeral, or look back in the same way through a hole which had once contained a knot of wood in a branch of fir. If the wind should change while the tether still bound him, he was in mortal danger.

'The usuall method for a curious person to get a transient sight of this otherwise invisible crew of Subterraneans (if impotently and over-rashly sought) is to put his foot on the Seers foot, and the Seers hand is put on the Inquirers head, who is to look over the Wizards right shoulder (which has an ill appearance, as if by this ceremonie, an implicite surrender were made of all betwixt the Wizards foot and his hand ere the person can be admitted a privado to the art.) Then will he see a multitude of Wights, like furious hardie men flocking to him hastily from all quarters, as thick as atomes in the air, (qch are no nonentities or phantasms. . . . but Realities, appearing to a stable man in his awaking sense and enduring a rational tryal of their being.)' The initiator 'defending the Lawfulness of his skill, forbids such horrour and comforts his Novice by telling of Zacharias being struck speechless at seeing of apparitiones Luc.1.20. . . . Elisha also in his Chamber saw Gehazi, his servant, at a great distance taking a reward from Naaman 2.King.5:26. Hence were the prophets frequently called Seers or men of a second or more exalted sight than others.'

Such a ritual as Kirk describes would seem to point both to a caste of seers and also to the remnant of genuine Druidic rites.

In the true psychic tradition, 'men of that second sight' did not discover strange events on being asked, but 'at fits and Raptures, as if inspyred with som Genius at that Instant, which befor did lurk in or about them.' Apparitions were not always friendly. A certain seer told Kirk that he was forced to cut the body of his vision in two with 'his iron weapon' in order to escape attack. At other times the same seer was forced to wrestle with his apparition. Second sight could also be bestowed by evil spirits. Kirk's example is that of the Devil who showed Jesus 'a sight of all nationes, and the finest things in the world at one glance, tho in their natural situations and stations at a vast distance from other'.

Of symbolic second sight, Kirk writes: 'As Birds and Beasts whose bodies are much used to the change of the free and open air, forsee stormes', as 'the Deer scents out a Man (and powder (tho a late invention)) at a great distance; a hungry hunter, Bread; and the Raven, a Carrion; their brains being long clarified by the high and subtil air, will observe a verie small change in a trice. Thus a Man of the second sight perceiving the operations of these forecasting invisible people among us . . . told he saw a winding-shroud creep up on a walking healthfull persons legs, till it came to the knee, and afterwards it came up to the midle, then to the shoulders, and at last over the head, which was visible to no other person. And by observing the spaces of time betwixt the several stages, he easily guess'd how long the man was to live who wore the shroud, for when it approached his head, he told that such a person was ripe for the Grave.'

That second sight could be inherited was also part of his theory. 'Men of the Second Sight (being design'd to give warning against secret engynes) surpass the ordinary vision of other men; which is a native habit in some, descended from their ancestors, and acquired as an artificiall improvement of their naturall sight in others; . . . For some have this second sight transmitted from Father to Son, thorow the whole family, without their own consent, or others teaching, pro-ceiding only from a Bounty of providence, it seemes; or by compact, or a complexionall quality of the first acquirer.'

An allusion to the special gifts of seventh sons, which included psychic healing and second sight, explains that these might be due to some secret virtue in the mother's womb which increased until it reached its zenith at the conception of a seventh son. As we have seen, Robert Kirk himself was said to have been a seventh son.

Women were not normally seers, according to Kirk, except for one who lived on the Island of Colasnach (Colonsay) in the time of Montrose. When consulted by the islanders, she saw by 'earnestlie looking', strangers close to the shore though she could not distin-guish them as friend or foe. It seemed to her that they were leaving the island rather than approaching it. This put the inhabitants off their guard, but it turned out that the boat had been stolen by the enemy and that they were rowing with their backs towards the island. 'Thus', wrote Kirk, 'this old Scout and Delphian Oracle was at last deceiv'd and did deceive.'

Referring to magic, it was necessary for novices to believe in their initiator's skills. A person called Stewart who scorned second sight was so tormented by a seer that he lost his powers of speech and movement. Seers were, in fact, often dreaded, as is indicated in the following story. At Killin in Perthshire, a yeoman happened to enter an inn where a seer was seated. At the sight of him, the seer arose to leave, his excuse being that the newcomer would be dead in two days. Angry and frightened, the yeoman stabbed the seer and was, as a result, executed two days later.

A vision of the departed at the hour of death was experienced by a minister, 'verie intelligent, but misbeleiving all such sights as were not ordinarie,' who happened to be in a narrow lane at the same time as a seer. When a labourer approached them 'furiously', the seer warned the minister to move out of his way, but the latter stayed his ground and both he and the seer were 'violently cast aside, to a good distance' and lamed by the fall. Soon after the minister had returned home, he heard the bell toll for the death of that labourer whose *taibhs* he had seen not half an hour since.

Kirk also tells the story of a seer in Kintyre who suddenly ducked his head aside at the table where he was having a meal. When asked why, he told the company that a friend of his, known to be in Ireland at the time, was threatening to throw a dish full of butter in his face. Those present wrote down the day and the time, and sent word to the gentleman in Ireland who confessed that he had made the threat at that precise moment, knowing his friend 'would make sport with it'.

Many points of interest emerge from Kirk's theories and research. Firstly, at that period second sight was considered to be closely bound up with the cult of ancestral worship in the persons of the *sithean*. Also there would seem to have been a caste of seers still influential in small isolated communities, who were feared for their powers, and disliked. Second sight was not only inherited, or natural in some, but also something that could be acquired at the instigation of experienced seers. That it was still then closely linked to magic and ancient religious rites is evident from the text. But however acquired, however interpreted, the experiences of seers in Kirk's time do not really differ from accounts of psychic happenings today. The visions he recorded were, as they still are, both trivial and portentous, symbolic and deceptive, fraudulent and genuine.

A strange tradition surrounds the death of Robert Kirk, perhaps born out of his particular beliefs and writings. It seems that he collapsed and died while out for a stroll in his nightshirt on the fairy knoll near the manse of Aberfoyle. Later he appeared to one of his relatives, telling him that he was not dead but a prisoner in Fairyland and that he would appear at the baptism of his child yet to be born. The relative should throw a knife over his ghost, which would break the spell. The spirit duly appeared as predicted but the relative was so astonished that he forgot to throw the knife. For many years Kirk was thought to be trapped among the fairies, and the legend still persists in the area – a strange memorial to a man whom Stewart Sanderson describes as 'in the truest sense a scholar, a gentleman, and a Christian, who strove in all humility to discharge his duties and exercise his talents in the cause of his faith'.

JOHN AUBREY'S QUESTIONNAIRE

Though not a Highlander nor even a traveller to the north, John Aubrey Esquire, Fellow of the Royal Society at Gresham College, added to his many interests and enthusiasms a strong curiosity regarding second sight. His information about it was obtained from 'two letters from a learned friend of mine in Scotland' which he was later to include in a chapter called 'An Account of Second Sighted Men in Scotland' which was part of his *Miscellanies*, published in 1696.

Of the letters he writes: 'This is the surest and clearest account of second sighted men that I can now find, and I have set it down fully as if I were transiently telling in your own presence, being curious for nothing but verity so far as I could.'

In the first letter, Aubrey's learned friend tells him that he drew up a questionnaire about seers, sent it all over the Highlands, and received many answers which he arranged and collated before sending them to Aubrey. The second letter, dated some months later in the year 1694, contains fuller answers to certain of these original questions. The queries are succinct, very much to the point and the sort of questions still asked today. They follow in their original form, but I have shortened and edited the answers.

Query One: If some few credible well-attested instances of such knowledge as is commonly called the second sight can be given?

The answer to this is that there are many. One of the examples offered describes a young woman who refused to take meat from the servant who offered it to her because she saw him 'full of blood' and was afraid to touch him. Next day the servant was involved in an alehouse brawl. While trying to separate the antagonists he was cut on the forehead by a sword and returned home drenched in blood.

57

Query Two: If it consists in the discovery of present or of past events only? Or if it extend to such as are to come?

Second sight relates only to things which will shortly come to pass. In his second letter, Aubrey's correspondent quotes an example which must even then have been of great antiquity and already have entered the realms of myth. Certainly it occurs from time to time in slightly altered versions throughout the early history of second sight. The story describes how a seer told his master that he had seen an arrow pass through the thigh of an acquaintance, without drawing blood. His reputation, he believed, was at stake over this vision, for such a thing was not possible and he was afraid that he would be thought an imposter if the story was widely known. Some years later, the acquaintance died of natural causes. On the way to his burial a quarrel broke out as to where he should be laid. The argument swelled into a fight, and bows were drawn. One of the arrows passed throught the thigh of the corpse on the bier, and naturally drew no blood.

Query Three: If the objects of this knowledge be sad and dismal events only – such as deaths and murders? Or, joyful and prosperous also?

'Sad and dismal events are the objects of this knowledge, as sudden deaths, dismal accidents; that they are prosperous or joyful, I cannot learn.'

One instance which 'might be judged as prosperous to one, but dismal to another' is of interest in that it involved an aunt of the notorious Countess Isabella Mackenzie of Seaforth who allegedly was responsible for the burning of the Brahan Seer. John Macleod of Dunvegan married the beautiful Sybella Mackenzie, sister of the second Earl of Seaforth, in 1628. One evening they returned from a stroll round the castle to find the wet-nurse in tears. Anxiously they asked whether the baby was ill, or the nurse's milk dried up? Still weeping, she shook her head.

'What, then?' Sybella pressed her.

At last she told them that she had experienced a vision. She had seen a man wearing a scarlet cloak and a white hat who had come between Macleod and his lady, and was kissing her over her shoulder. The nurse interpreted the vision as a prediction of Macleod's death and Sybella's remarriage, which is exactly what happened.

After Macleod's death, Sybella married the Master of Lovat who arrived dressed for his wedding in the bright clothes foreseen by the nurse. (Though Aubrey does not mention it, Sybella was to be married a third time in 1672, to the Tutor of Grant. The Revd James Fraser, author of the *Wardlaw Manuscript*, was even more critical of her than he was of her niece, Isabella, for he described her as 'a woman of great parts but bad practices and far worse principles'.)

In the second letter, the learned gentleman adds in answer to the third query that those with second sight see murders, drownings, burials, combats, and manslaughters, but also weddings and sometimes more prosperous events. The Bishop of Caithness – father of five daughters – had a servant who was also a seer. When one of the girls complained that she had all the work to do, the seer comforted her by saying that soon she would be free, for he saw a tall gentleman in black walking on the Bishop's right-hand side, whom she would marry. He described the table covered with good food and the clothes of those asked to the wedding breakfast. Within three months the prediction was literally fulfilled.

Query Four: If these events which second sighted men discover or foretell, be visibly represented to them, and acted as it were, before their eyes?

The answer was in the affirmative, sometimes within and sometimes without doors, 'as in a glass'. If a man's death were by drowning, they would see him in water up to his throat, or if by decapitation, they would see the body without its head. Unexpected death was represented by a winding sheet bound round the head.

Query Five: If second sight be a thing that is troublesome and uneasy to those that have it and such as they would gladly be rid of?

Again the answer was yes. Some visions could be very frightening, causing the seer to 'sweat and tremble and shriek' at the apparition. One seer prayed to be rid of it, and at last lost the faculty.

Query Six: If any persons truly godly, who may justly presumed to be such, have ever been known to have this gift or faculty?

The answer given in the first letter was an uncompromising 'no'. The second letter contradicts this statement and adds 'persons that have a sense of God and religion and are presumed to be godly are known to have the faculty'. This was evidenced by those who, possessing it, judged it a sin, believed it to come from the Devil, and earnestly desired to be rid of it. Some had gone so far as to beg the Presbytery to appoint public prayers and sermons, before confessing in the sight of the congregation 'with deep sense on their knees'. After which they were no longer troubled.

Query Seven: If it descends by succession from parents to children? Or, if not, whether those that have it can tell how they came by it?

By succession. 'I cannot learn how they came by it, as hard to know, neither will they tell; which if they did, they are sure of their stroaks from an invisible hand.'

Query Eight: How came they by it?

'Some say by compact with the Devil. Some say by converse with fairies. I have heard that those that have this faculty have offered to teach it to such as were curious to know it, upon such and such a condition they would teach them, but their proffers were rejected.'

Second sight could, however, be shared if the seer put his foot over that of his companion during a vision.

Aubrey's *Miscellanies* also included a letter written to himself on the subject of second sight by 'a gentleman's son in Strathspey, being a student in divinity'. The instances given were attested by 'several of good credit yet alive'.

The student's first story featured Andrew Macpherson of Cluny. While courting Mackenzie of Gairloch's daughter, Cluny was seen by Lady Mackenzie and her attendants while out walking.

'There he goes,' said she, 'off to visit his young lady.'

One of her attendants who had second sight replied, 'If you be he, unless he marry within six months, he'll never be wed.'

'How do you know?' asked Lady Mackenzie.

For a while the man would not tell her; then, reluctantly, he described how he had seen Cluny enclosed in his winding-sheet, except his nostrils and his mouth which would also be closed within six months. It happened as foreseen. Cluny was dead six months later, and his brother Duncan succeeded him.

It was customary in those days, just as it is today, for folk who were anxious about lost relatives to consult a seer. A certain gentleman, wrote the student, whose son had gone abroad was told that on that very day the lad had married a French woman who had brought him a dowry of many thousands of crowns. He would come home in two years to visit his father, but without his wife and son. And so it happened.

'All that have the gift are not equally proficient,' continued the theological student, going on to give an amusing account of two seers at work, one a gentleman and the other 'a common fellow', who were both visiting the manse of an Inverness minister. All at once the common fellow began to weep and cry out that a certain sick woman about five miles away was either dead or dying. The gentleman seer – naturally the expert – replied, 'No, she's not dead, nor will she die of this disease.'

'Oh?' said the fellow. 'Can't you see her covered in her winding sheet?'

'Aye,' replied the gentleman, 'I see her as well as you do, but do you not also see that her linen is wet with sweat? She will soon be cooling of her fever.' And so it turned out. The Revd Hector Mackenzie vouched for the story's truth.

The most remarkable episode recorded by the student concerned a seer called Archibald MacDonald who lived near Glencoe, for the young man was actually present when his prediction was made. In 1683 Archibald happened to be visiting the student's home when he declared that within two years Archibald, ninth Earl of Argyll, would come to the West Highlands and raise a rebellion, which would be divided and dispersed. Argyll would be taken prisoner and decapitated in Edinburgh, where his head would adorn the Tolbooth like his father's before him. In 1685, Charles II was succeeded by James VII and II, and Argyll was arrested after a reign of terror inaugurated by the south-west Covenanters. He was condemned and executed as a traitor, just as predicted.

Strangely enough, although the student does not record it, Argyll's father, the eighth Earl, had featured in a prophecy made during Cromwell's occupation. He was playing bowls with friends at Inveraray when suddenly one of his companions turned white and

61

fainted. When he recovered he cried out, 'Bless me, what do I see? My lord with his head off and his shoulders all bloody.'

The student writing to Aubrey was certainly no expert in Gaelic for he stated that 'second sight is generally called "taishitaranghk" (a somewhat confused rendering of *taibhsearachd*) and seers "phissichin", (*fiosaichan*) which is properly foresight or foreknowledge'.

Aubrey may perhaps be criticized for being too credulous in his account of, and acceptance of, second sight, but he is typical of his age: curious, eager to learn, open-minded. His correspondent makes several interesting observances. We learn that gentlemen besides 'common fellows' laid claim to the faculty, and – true to the times – were naturally better at it. The church's ambivalence is made very clear. The first uncompromising negative answer to Query Six is subtly moderated by the divinity student's tale of rival seers at work in the manse. The Protestant ethic which runs like a thread through the narrative would seem to point to Aubrey's correspondent's being a minister himself. But it was not only the Reformed Church that was unsure of its ground, for we find in Bellesheim's *History of the Catholic Church*, in Volume IV, a report by Bishop Nicolson of a Visitation in 1700.

> In this island of Barra many people are under the power of a kind of vision called by the native, second sight, in virtue of which they foresee and predict unexpected and wondrous events. This power is quite beyond their own control and the effects actually correspond to the predictions. The Bishop proposes certain spiritual remedies with a view to delivering these poor people, but desires to refer the matter to the impartial judgement of your eminences.

Two hundred years later, the Society for Psychical Research used the same method of distributing a questionnaire in their researches led by the third Marquess of Bute, into the faculty of second sight.

THE LETTERS OF SAMUEL PEPYS

Considering the interest in second sight shown by Aubrey, Lhuyd and Boyle, it is not surprising that others in the social, academic and scientific worlds, such as Lords Reay, Tarbat and Clarendon, should share that fascination: still less surprising that Samuel Pepys, whose interests ranged so widely, should be intrigued by what was probably a fashionable topic for coffee-house and drawing-room conversation.

Pepys was Secretary to the Admiralty after the Civil War and came into contact with Highlanders not only in the course of his duty but also socially. His famous diary, which he began on 1 January 1661, was kept regularly for nine years and reflects every aspect of life during the Restoration. Less well known, perhaps, is his correspondence, which contains six important letters on the subject of second sight.

The first is from George, third Lord Reay of Durness in Sutherland, who was a Fellow of the Royal Society and, according to Wood's *Peerage*, 'a nobleman of parts and learning'. With it Lord Reay includes an earlier letter from Lord Tarbat to the Honourable Robert Boyle which must have been written before 1691, the year of Boyle's death.

Lord Tarbat, later to become the first Earl of Cromartie, whose seat was Castle Leod in Strathpeffer, was also brother to Isabella Mackenzie of Seaforth who allegedly burned the Brahan Seer for his predictions. He was a man of great learning and organizing abilities, who played a prominent part in the Restoration and who was also Senator of the College of Justice, Clerk Register, a Privy Councillor and Justice-General.

The Lord Reay to Mr Pepys   Durness, the 24th October 1699
Honoured Sir,

Conforming to my promise, I send you all the information I have met with in the inquiry you recommended to me touching the Double-Sight, and have just now received my Lord Tarbat's answer to me relating thereto, as follows:-

'I remember that several years ago in answer to a letter of Mr Boyle I wrote to him about the Second-Sight: a copy whereof received enclosed. Since that time I was not much in the north, nor did I either make any inquiries on that purpose, what I occasionally heard then differ considerably from what I had heard formerly. One particular of which was of a footman of your great-grandfather's, who was mightily concerned upon seeing a dagger in the Lord Reay's breast. He informed his master of the sight,

63

who laughed at it. Some months after he gave the doublet which he did wear when the Seer did see the dagger in his breast, to his servant, who did wear or kept it about a year, and then gave it to this footman, who was the Seer, and who was stabbed in the breast by another when this doublet was upon him. My lord, you may inquire further into the truth of this.'

This, sir, is the answer I have had from my Lord Tarbat, and I enclose you a copy of his letter therein. I have since informed myself of the truth of the story about my grandfather's footman, and find it literally true; as also another, much of the same nature, which I shall give you an account of, because I have it from a sure author, a friend of my own, of unexceptionable honesty, to whose father the thing happened, and he himself was witness to it all.

John Mackay of Didril, having put on a new suit of clothes, was told by a Seer that he did see the gallows upon his coat, which he never noticed; but some time after gave his coat to his servant, William Forbes, to whose honesty there could be nothing said at the time, but he was shortly after hanged for theft, with the same coat about him, my informer being an eye-witness of his execution and one who had heard what the Seer said before.

I have heard several other stories, but shall trouble you with no more than what happened since I last came into the country.

There was a servant woman in Mindo Aubry's house, in Langdale on Strathnaver, in the shire of Sutherland, who told her mistress that she saw the gallows about her brother's neck, who had then the repute of an honest man; at which her mistress, being offended, put her out of the house. Her brother, nevertheless, having stolen some goods, was sentenced to be hanged the 22 August, 1698; yet by the intercession of several gentlemen, who became bail for his future behaviour, was free (though not customary by our law) which occasioned one of the gentlemen, Lieutenant Alex. Mackay, to tell the woman servant that she was once deceived. The man being set at liberty, she replied, he is not dead yet, but shall certainly be hanged, and accordingly he, betaking himself to stealing anew and being catched, was hanged the 14 February, 1699.

I was this year hunting in my forest, having several Highlanders with me; and speaking of the Second-Sight, one told me there was a boy in the company who had it, and had told many things that had fallen out to be true, who being called and confessing it I asked him what he saw last; he told me that he had seen the night before such a man by name, who lived thirty miles from that place, break my forester's servant's head, which the servant overhearing laughed at him for saying that that could not be, they being very good friends, so as I did not believe it, but it certainly happened since.

These stories, with what is considered in my Lord Tarbat's letter, are the most satisfactory for proving Second-Sight I have heard, and the people are so persuaded of the truth of it in the Highlands and Isles, that one would be more laughed at for not believing it there than for affirming it elsewhere.

For my own part I do not question it; though that be of small weight towards the persuading others to the belief of it. But I dare affirm had you the same reasons I have, you would be of my opinion. I mean had you heard all the stories I have, attested by men of honour not to be doubted, and been eye-witness in some of them yourself; as the breaking of a man's head, foretelling of another's death, and another story which the same boy told me long ere they happened.

There was a blind woman in this country in my time who saw them perfectly well, and foretold several things that happened, as hundreds of men will attest. She was not born blind, but became so by accident, to that degree that she did not see so much as a glimmering; yet saw the Second-Sight as perfectly as before. I have got a manuscript since I came last to Scotland, whose author, though a parson, does (after giving a very full account of the Second-Sight) defend there being no sin in it for reasons too long to be here inserted, but with the first opportunity I shall send you a copy of his books, and I have this day received a letter from a friend I had employed for that purpose, promising me the acquaintance of this man, of which I am very covetous, being persuaded it will give me much light in this matter.

There is a people in these countries surnamed 'Mansone', who see this sight naturally, both men and women, though they commonly deny it, but are so affirmed to do by all their neighbours. A Seer with whom I was reasoning on the subject, finding me very incredulous in what he asserted, offered to let me see as well as himself. I asked whether he could free me from seeing them thereafter, whereto he answering me he could not, put a stop to my curiosity. The manner of showing them to another is thus: the Seer puts both his hands and feet above yours, and mutters some words to himself, which done, you both see alike.

This, sir, is all the information I can send you on this head till I have the opportunity of sending you the fore-mentioned Treatise,

Remaining, honoured sir, your most obedient servant,

Reay.

Thus we learn that Lord Reay who was later to become part of Lady Assynt's terrifying vision of death and drowning (see page 16), had no doubts on the subject of second sight, though he recognized – as do all those who have experienced the inexplicable – the difficulty in convincing others.

Who the Mansones were is not known today, but their existence hints strongly at the survival of a caste of seers descended from pre-Christian culture who lingered on until the seventeenth century at least. The fact that one of the seers offered to initiate Lord Reay strengthens the argument. Henderson Lynn, the Celtic Clairvoyant of today, would go so far as to suggest that the caste is in existence now, surviving in the cairds and tinkers, nomadic Celts who continue to practise the old beliefs and rituals.

Lord Reay's enclosure of Lord Tarbat's letter to Robert Boyle now follows:

Sir,

I had heard very much, but believed very little, of the Second-Sight; yet its being affirmed by several of great veracity, I was induced to make some inquiry after it in the year 1652, being then confined to abide in the North of Scotland by the English usurpers [Cromwell and his forces].

The general accounts of it were that many Highlanders, yet far more Islanders, were qualified with this sight; that men, women, and children, indistinctively, were subjected to it, and children whose parents were not; sometimes people came to age who had it not when young, nor could any tell by what means produced.

It is a trouble to most of those who are subject to it and they would be rid of it at any rate, if they could.

The sight is of no long duration, only continuing so long as they keep their eyes steadily without twinkling. The hardy therefore fix

66

their look that they may see the longer, but the timorous see only glances, their eyes always twinkling at the first sight of the object.

That which generally is seen by them are the species of living creatures, and of animate things which are in motion, such as ships, and habits upon persons. They never see the species of any person who is already dead.

What they foresee fails not to exist in the mode and place where it appears to them. They cannot tell what space of time shall intervene betwixt the apparition and real existence. But some of the hardiest and longest experience have some rules for conjectures, as if they see a man with a shrouding-sheet in the apparition, they would conjecture at the nearness and remoteness of his death by the more or less of his body that is covered by it.

They will ordinarily see their absent friends, though at a great distance, sometimes no less than from America to Scotland, sitting, standing or walking in some certain place, and then they conclude with assurance that they will see them so and there.

If a man be in love with a woman, they will ordinarily see the species of that man standing by her, and so likewise if a woman be in love, and they conjecture at their enjoyments (of each other) by the species, touching the person or appearing at a distance from her (if they enjoy not one another).

If they see the species of any person who is sick to death, they see them covered over with a shrouding-sheet.

These generally I had verified to me by such of them as did see, and were esteemed honest and sober by all the neighbourhood, for I inquired after such for my information; and because there were more of these seers in the Isles of Lewis, Harris and Uist than in any other place, I did entreat Sir James MacDonald (who is now dead), Sir Normand Macleod and Mr Daniel Morison, a very honest person (who are still alive), to make inquiry into this uncouth sight and to acquaint me therewith, which they did, and all found an agreement in these generals, and informed me of many instances, confirming what they said, but though men of discretion and honour, being but at second hand, I will choose rather to put myself than my friends on the hazard of being laughed at for incredible relations.

I was once travelling in the Highlands, and a good number of servants with me, as is usual there, and one of them going a little before me to enter a house where I was to stay all night, and going hastily to the door, he suddenly started back with a screech, and fell by a stone which hit his foot. I asked him what the matter was, for he seemed to be very much frightened. He told me very seriously that I should not lodge in that house, because shortly a dead coffin would be carried out of it, for many were carrying it when he was heard cry.

I neglecting his words and staying there, he said to other of the servants he was very sorry for it, and that what he saw surely would come shortly to pass; though no sick person was then there, yet the landlord, a healthy Highlander, died of an apoplectic fit before I left the house.

In the year 1653, Alexander Munro (afterwards Lieutenant-Colonel to the Earl of Dunbarton's regiment) and I was walking in a place called Ullapool in Lochbroom on a little plain at the foot of a rugged hill. There was a servant working with a spade in the walk before us, and his face was to the hill. Before we came near to him he let the spade fall, and looked toward the hill. He took notice of us as we passed near by him, which made me look at him, and perceiving him to stare a little strangely, I conjectured him to be a seer, wherefore I called to him, at which he started and smiled.

'What are you doing?' said I. He answered, 'I have seen a very strange thing, an army of Englishmen, leading horses, coming down that hill, and a number of them are come down to the plain, and eating the barley which is growing in the field near to the hill.' This was the fourth of May (for I noted the day) and it was four or five days before the barley was sown in the field he spoke of.

Alexander Munro asked him how he knew they were Englishmen; he answered, 'Because they were leading horses, and had hats and boots, which he knew no Scotchman would have on there.'

We took little notice of the whole story as other than foolish vision, but wished that an English party were there, we being at war with them, and the place almost inaccessible for horsemen. But in the beginning of August thereafter, the Earl of Middleton, then Lieutenant for the King in the Highlands, having occasion to march a party of his towards the South Highlands, sent his foot through a place called Inverlawell, and the forepart which was the first down the hill, did fall to eating the barley which was on the little plain under it, and Munro, calling to mind what the Seer told

68

us in May preceeding, wrote of it, and sent an express to me to Lochslin in Ross (where I then was) with it.

I had occasion once to be in company where a young lady was (excuse my not naming of persons) and I was told there was a notable Seer in the company, and I called to him to speak with me as I did ordinarily when I found any of them, and after he had answered several questions, I asked him if he saw any person to be in love with that lady. He said he did, but knew not the person, for during the two days he had been in her company, he perceived one standing near her with his head leaning on her shoulder, which he said did foretell that the man should marry her, and die before her, according to his observation. This was in the year 1655.

I desired him to describe the person, which he did so I could conjecture by the description that it was such a one who was of that lady's acquaintance, though there was no thought of their inter-marriage till two years later, and having occasion in the year 1657 to find this Seer, who was an Islander, in company with the other person whom I conjectured to have been described by him, I called him aside, and asked him if that was the person he saw beside the lady near two years then past.

He said it was he indeed, for he had seen that lady just then standing by him hand-in-hand. This was some months before their marriage, and the man is since dead, and the lady is still alive.

I shall trouble you with but one more, which I thought the most remarkable of all that occurred to me. In January 1652, the above-named Lieutenant-Colonel Al. Munro and I happened to be in the house of William Macleod of Fierinhed, in the County of Ross; he, the landlord and I sitting on three chairs near the fire, and in the corner of the great chimney there were two Islanders, who were that very night come to the house, and were related to the land-lord. While one of them was talking with Munro, I perceived the other to look oddly towards me, and from his looks, and his being an Islander, I conjectured him a Seer, and asked him why he stared. He answered by desiring me to rise from the chair for it was an unlucky one.

I asked why?

He answered, 'Because there was a dead man in the chair next to it.'

'Well,' said I, 'if it be but in the next, I may safely sit here; but what is the likeness of the man?'

He said he was a tall man with a long grey coat, booted, and one of his legs hanging over the chair, and his head hanging down to the other side, and his arm backward as if it were broken.

There were some English troops then quartered near the place, and there being at that time a great frost after a thaw, the country was wholly covered with ice. Four or five Englishmen riding by this house, not two hours after the vision, while we were sitting by the fire, we heard a great noise, which proved to be these troopers, with the help of other servants, carrying in one of their number who got a very mischievous fall, and his arm broken; and falling frequently into swooning fits, they brought him into the hall, and set him in the very chair and in the very posture which the Seer had proposed; but the man did not die, though he revived with great difficulty.

Among the accounts given me by Sir Normand Macleod, there was one worthy of special notice, which was this. There was a gentleman in the Island of Harris who was always seen by the Seers with an arrow in his thigh; such in the isle who thought these prognostications infallible did not doubt but he would be shot in the thigh before he died. Sir Normand told me that he heard it in the subject of discourse for many years, when the gentleman was present; at last he died without any such accident. Sir Normand was at his burial in St Clement's Church, in the Isle of Harris. At the same time the corpse of another gentleman was brought to be buried in the very same church. The friends on either side came to debate who should first enter the church, and in a trice from words they came to blows. One of the number (who was armed with a bow and arrows) let fly among them. (Now, every family in that isle have their burying place in that church in stone chests, and the bodies are carried on open biers to the place of burial.) Sir Normand having appeased the tumult, one of the arrows was found shot in the dead man's thigh; to this Sir Normand himself was a witness.

In the account Mr Daniel Morison, parson in the Lewes, gave me, there was one, which, though it be heterogeneous from this subject, yet it may be worth your notice. It was of a young woman in this parish who was mightily frightened by seeing her own image still before her, always when she came into the open air, and the back of the image always to her, so that it was not a reflection as in a mirror, but the species of such a body as her own, and in very like habit, which appeared to herself continually before her.

The parson kept her a long time with him, but had no remedy for her evil, which troubled her exceedingly. I was told afterwards, that when she was four or five years older, she saw it not.

These are matters of fact, which I assure you are truly related; but these and all others that occurred to me by information or otherwise, could never lead me into so much as a remote conjecture of the cause of so extraordinary a phenomenon; whether it be a quality in the eyes of some persons, in those parts, concurring with a quality in the air also. Whether such species be everywhere, though not seen for want of eyes so qualified, or from whatever cause, I must leave to the inquiry of clearer judgments than my own.

But a hint may be taken from this image which appeared still to this young woman aforementioned, and from another mentioned by Aristotle, in the fourth of his Metaphysics, if I remember right, for it is so long since I read it; as also from the common opinion that young infants (unsoiled with many objects) do see apparitions which are not seen by those of older years; likewise from this, that several who did see the Second-Sight when in the Highlands or Isles, yet when transported to live in other countries, especially in America, quite lose this quality; as it was told me by a gentleman who knew some of them in Barbadoes, that did not see any visions there, although he knew them to be Seers when they lived in the Isles of Scotland.

In this lucid account, Lord Tarbat not only proves himself to be an excellent investigator, keeping notes of years, dates and events with scientific precision, but he also raises some important points. Seers abounded at that period and were instantly recognizable by their staring looks. Their visions were of the future only and not of any past event. Their visions were very often symbolic and needed interpretation by the seers themselves. Possibly most interesting of all, children were natural visionaries. This is a theory very much in vogue today.

Open-minded, curious and knowledgeable, Lord Tarbat, a

Highlander by birth and upbringing, had no doubt at all of the existence of second sight, though not much to offer by way of explanation

His letter must have been well circulated, for Robert Kirk was to add a copy to his *Secret Common-Wealth*, his reason being that he 'might not be thought singular in this disquisition, that the mater of fact might be undenyably made out, and that I might with all submission given some annotations with animadversions on his supposed causes of that phaenomenon, with my reasons or dissent from his judgment'.

Some of the points Kirk makes about Lord Tarbat's letter are as follows: few women have second sight and those that do are less accurate. Second sight cannot be criminal, because of its involuntary nature. A strong desire to attain the art is helpful. The vision then seen is 'no fantastic shadow of a sick apprehensione' but a recreation of that person by the *sith*. The girl who witnessed her own image was in fact seeing her double or co-walker, recreated by a *sith*. Kirk argues that second sight cannot depend upon a 'qualitie of the air, nor of the eyes' for a number of reasons, including the fact that 'a Seer can give another person this sight transiently by putting his hand and foot in the posture he requires of him'. If this were the case, all that the girl who was haunted by her 'reflex-selfe' had to do to be cured was move away to another district. Kirk's description of the physical and mental changes experienced during a vision matches those of mediums today. 'Our Seer is put in a rapture, transport, and sort of death, as divested of his body, and all its senses.' Only 'clownish and illiterat men' are frightened and disturbed by what they see. Seers, he concludes, are 'for the most part candid, honest and sociable People'. Kirk had no doubt at all that second sight existed, that the visions seen were 'real intelligent creatures' and that the sight of the seers was clear, lawful, and void of deception. Tarbat too was convinced.

Pepys' reaction was very different. His reply to Lord Reay is that of a courteous yet sceptical old man. Regarding second sight, he writes; 'I little expected to have been ever brought so near to a conviction of the reality of it, as by your Lordship's and Lord Tarbat's authorities I must already own myself to be.' He does not think much of Lord Tarbat's theory regarding 'a quality in the eyes of some persons, in those parts' and insists that visions of 'daggers, shrouds, arrows, gibbets, and God knows what . . . must be the creatures of the mind only (however directed to them) and not of the eye'. He points to inconsistencies such as the fact that 'your seers are both desirous to be themselves rid of it, and ready to communicate it to any other that will venture on it.' Yet he also recognizes the 'unquestionable faith, authority, and capacity to judge' of the eye-witnesses which 'will not permit me to distrust the truth of it'.

He asks Lord Reay for further information, and also for his permission to discuss his letter with 'some of my learned friends'. He also asks about the manuscript mentioned by Lord Reay and hopes to obtain a copy.

In Lord Reay's answer, dated Inverness, 9 January 1700, he gives that permission and includes another instance out of the many more stories of second sight that he has heard. Unfortunately the manuscript so coveted by Pepys was not included.

A gentleman who was married to a cousin of Drynie's lying at this house, called him to the door (the very ordinary compliments being passed) to speak to him about some business. But when he went out he was so frightened that he fainted, and being recovered would not stay in the house that night, but went to a farmer's near by; where she asking him why he left the house, he told her he went to the door, he saw his winding sheet about him.

And accordingly, the gentleman did die that night, though he went to bed in perfect health, and had no sickness for some time before.

I had this story from Drynie's own son, the farmer, his servant, and the man himself saw it.

For my part I am fully convinced of this sight; but what to attribute it to I know not, nor can I be convinced, any more than you, that it depends on any quality, either of the air or eyes, but would gladly know your opinion of it.

Samuel Pepys took advantage of Lord Reay's permission to circulate his letter, and the following written to Pepys by the Revd Dr George Hickes, one-time chaplain to the Duke of Lauderdale, is obviously a result of these discussions:

Dr Hickes to Mr Pepys   London, June, 19, 1700

Honoured Sir,

I have been ill of a cold since I had the honour to wait upon you and Mr Hewer, and that hath been the cause why I have been so long in performing the promise I made, of sending you in writing some things you gave me occasion to say, by imparting to me my Lord Reay's letter to you, and the letter my Lord Tarbat wrote to him concerning the Second-Sight.

This is a very proper term for that sight which those Scottish Seers or visionists have of things by representation; for, as the sight of a thing itself is, in order of nature, the first or primary sight of it; so the sight of it, by any representation, whether really made without, as all apparitions are, or within upon the stage of imagination, as all sorts of visions are made, is in order of nature the second or secondary sight of that thing; and therefore, the sight of any thing by representation, though first in order of time, may properly be called the Second-Sight thereof. . . .

But the Scotch have restrained the use of the term only to that sight of the things by appearance, or representation, which those Seers or Visionists among them used to have; but whether in outward apparitions always, or inward visions, or sometimes one way, and some the other, I have not yet learned, but it would be an inquiry proper for the subject, and fit for that ingenious Lord to make.

I told you, when I was in Scotland, I never met with any learned man, either among their divines or lawyers, who doubted the thing.

I had the honour to hear Lord Tarbat tell the story of the Second-Sight of my Lord Middleton's march with his army down a hill, which you read in the letter written by his Lordship to Mr Boyle. It was before the Duke of Lauderdale he told it, when his Grace was High Commissioner of Scotland, about twenty-two years ago.

About the same time, as I remember, he entertained the Duke with a story of elf arrows, which was very surprising to me; they were of triangular form, somewhat like the beard or pile of our old English arrows of war, almost as thin as one of our old groats, made of flints or pebbles, or such like stones, and these the country people of Scotland believe that evil spirits (which they call elves, from the old Danish word Alfar, which signifies Daemon, Genius, or such) do shoot them into the hearts of the cattle; and, as I remember, my Lord Tarbat, or some other Lord, did produce one of these elf arrows, which one of his tenants or neighbours took out of the heart of one of his cattle that died of an unusual death.

I have another strange story, but very well attested, of an elf arrow that was shot at a venerable Irish Bishop, by an evil spirit, in a terrible noise louder than thunder, which shaked the house where the Bishop was; but this I reserve for his son to tell you, who is one of the deprived Irish clergymen, and very well known, as by other excellent pieces, so by this late book, entitled *The Snake in the Grass*.

I mention this to encourage you to desire my Lord to send you a more perfect account of these elf arrows; the subject being of so near alliance to that of the Second-Sight, and to witch-craft, which is akin to both . . .

Sir, I beg your pardon for this digression from Second-Sight to witches; and perhaps the divine whom my Lord Reay tells you hath written a book in defence of the innocency of seeing things by the help of it, would be offended with me for joining them together. In truth, sir, I long to see that book, being myself uncertain in my opinion whether that way of seeing things be from a good or evil cause, or some times from one, and some times from the other. One would hope that in good men, who contribute nothing towards the having of it, it should be from good spirits, which the old Danes and Norwegians, from whom the Scotch have a great part of their language, called Lias Alfar, i.e., Spirits of Light; but in those who come to have it by certain forms of words, which we call charms, or doing and performing such ceremonies as are mentioned in my Lord's letter, one would think it proceeded from evil spirits, which the old Danes and Norwegians called Suart Alfar, i.e., Black Spirits.

It may also be presumed to proceed from the same cause, in men of otherwise unblamed lives, who are addicted to study magic, or judicial astrology, or who are known to converse with demons, as many amongst the learned, both ancient and modern, both foreigners and our own countrymen, are said to have done.

A good number of well-attested stories out of good historians and records, as well as living witnesses, would help to resolve these doubts. Among the former are to be consulted the histories of old Northern nations, written in old Danish or Swedish, which commonly have the title of Saga, which signifies a narration or history, and have been printed of late in Denmark and Sweden. But it may be these theories, and many more, are sufficiently resolved and accounted for in the book above mentioned, which my Lord hath promised to send you; but as by phenomena, they may be resolved.

It was commonly reported, when I was in Scotland, that Lord Seaforth, then living had the Second-Sight, and thereby foretold a dreadful storm to some of his friends, in which they had like to have been castaway. Once I heard the Duke of Lauderdale rally him about it, but he neither owned it nor disowned it; according to that maxim of the civil law, 'Qui tacet aut non negat, sic utique non fatetur.'

At the same time there were a girl in custody in Edinburgh, whose name was Janet Douglas, about twelve or thirteen years of age, famous for the Second-Sight, and discovery of witches and their malfices and enchantments therby. This girl first signalized herself in the Western Islands, where she discovered how one Sir G. Maxwell was tormented in effigy by witches. She was not known there where she made this, which was her first discovery, but from thence she came to Glasgow, whither her fame having got before her, the people in great numbers ran out to meet her. As she was surrounded by crowds, she called out to one man, a goldsmith, as I remember, and told him that of so long a time he had not thriven in his trade, though he was very diligent in it, because an image was made against him, which he might find in such a corner of his shop; and when the man went home, there he found it where she said it was, and the image was such both as to matter and form as she had described it, viz., a little rude image made of clay.

She told another that he and his wife, who had been a very loving couple, of late had lived in great discord, to the grief and astonishment of them both; and when the man asked the reason, she answered as she did before, that there was an image against them. I have forgot whether she named the witches who made these images, as she did those who made that in which they tortured Sir G. Maxwell. But by these and other discoveries, she made such tumults and commotions among the people of Glasgow, that the Magistrates thought fit to confine her, and send an

76

account of her to the Privy Council at Edinburgh, who sent for her up in custody; but when she came near the city the people went out in vast crowds to meet her, and as she was surrounded by them, she accused several people of witchcraft, which obliged them to put her in close confinement, to keep the people and their minds quiet from the commotions she had raised in them.

This happened a little before the Duke of Lauderdale went the last time as High Commissioner into Scotland in May 1678, when I had the honour to attend him as his domestic chaplain.

One thing I must not fail to tell you – that in all her marches from Sir George Maxwell's to Edinburgh nobody knew her nor would she discover to any one who she was . . .

After I returned from Glasgow I renewed my petition to my Lord Duke for leave to see Janet Douglas, which he granted me. My desire of seeing her arose from a great curiosity I had to ask her some questions about the Second-Sight, by which she pretended to make all her discoveries. I took a reverend and learned divine with me, one Mr Scott, minister of the Church of the Abbey of Holyrood, now the Palace of the Scottish Kings.

When we were first brought to her, I found her as I had heard her described, a girl of very great assurance, undaunted, though surprised at our coming, and suspicious that I was sent to betray her; this made her very shy of conversing with us, but after many and serious protestations on my own part, that I came for no other end but to ask her some questions about the Second-Sight to which she pretended, she at last promised she would freely answer me, provided I would use my interest with my Lord High Commissioner to obtain her liberty upon condition she went into England, never again to appear in Scotland, which I promised to do.

Upon this I began to premise something of the baseness of lying and deceiving, and especially of pretending to false revelations and the dangerous consequences of such practices, which made all such lying pretenders odious to God and man, and thus requiring her in the presence of God to tell me nothing but truth, she promised me with a serious air to tell me nothing but the very truth.

I then asked her if indeed she had the Second-Sight, and if by that she knew those things she discovered, to which she replied in the affirmative. I then asked her if she thought it proceeded from a

77

good or evil cause, upon which she turned the question upon me and asked me what I thought of it.

I told her plainly that I feared it was from an evil cause, but she replied quickly, she hoped it was from good. I then asked her if it came upon her by any act of her own, as by saying any words or performing any actions or ceremonies, to which she replied No. I asked her upon this, if she remembered her baptismal vow, but she did not understand my question till I began to explain it, and with great quickness replied she remembered it and called to mind that she had renounced the Devil and all his works; and then I told her that by the devil was meant Satan, the Prince of Devils and all spirits under him, and asked her if she renounced them all; which she said she did.

Then I asked her if she would renounce them all in form of words that I had provided; which promising to do, I bid her say after me, which she did in the most serious and emphatic expressions that I was able to devise. Then I asked her if she could say the Lord's Prayer, she said yes; I bid her say it upon her knees, which she did. Then I asked her if she had ever prayed to God to deliver her from the power of the Devil and all evil spirits; but she not answering readily and clearly to that question. I then asked her if she would make such a prayer to God on her knees as I would compose for her, which she did without any difficulty.

Then I proceeded to ask her at what distance she saw persons and things by the Second-Sight, she replied, at the same distance as they were really from her, whether more or less.

Then I asked her if the Second-Sight came upon her sleeping or waking; she answered, never sleeping, but always when she was awake. I asked this question to know whether the Second-Sight was by outward representation, which I call apparition, or by inward representation on the theatre of imagination caused by some spirit; or, that I may use my own terms for distinction, whether these Second-Sight folks were Seers or Visionists, or sometimes one and sometimes the other.

Then I asked her if she was wont to have any trouble, disorder, or consternation of mind, before or after the Second-Sight came upon her, to which she answered never, but was in the same temper at those as at all other times.

Then I asked her if the Second-Sight never left any weariness or faintness upon her, or listlessness to speak, walk, or do any other business, to which she answered no, adding that she was always then as before.

These two answers of hers do not agree with some of my Lord's Letters, wherein, as I remember, he speaks of one who said he had always perturbation of mind attending the Second-Sight; but as to this there may be a difference, from the different temper of the patients, and the different stock and temper of the animal spirits in them.

This girl, as I have observed before, was of a bold, undaunted spirit, and might bear those sights, from what cause soever, without any fear or perturbation, which others of more passive tempers, and a less stock of animal spirits could not so well endure.

There seems to have been this difference among prophets themselves, whereof some, as we read, received the prophetical influx with great terrors, labour and consternation, of which they complained when their visions of apparitions were over, and desired God to be excused from the prophetical influx and burthen of it; but of others, we do not read they had any such complaints.

One of the last questions I asked this girl was: if she desired the Second-Sight to be taken from her; to which she replied, what God pleased.

After I had discoursed with her in this manner, as long as I thought convenient, I returned home, and gave the Duke an account of my conversation, with which he was pleased; and I told him of my promise to intercede with his Grace for her liberty, upon condition she might go into England, but he said that that would not be convenient for certain reasons. After receiving which answer, I sent her word that I could not obtain her liberty, and so she was shut up all the while we were there, but soon after we came away she was set at liberty.

When I heard of it I made all inquiry I could what had become of her, and how she came to obtain her liberty; but I could not get any further account of her, which made me suspect that she was the child of some person of honour or quality, for which sake all things were hushed. When I was with her I asked her of her parentage, but she would tell me nothing of it. I also told her how I observed that all her words and expressions were of the better sort,

79

and asked her how, she, being a Highlander and in appearance a poor girl, came to speak so well.

To this she artfully replied why I should suppose it so difficult for her to learn to express herself well. Indeed her wit and cunning were both answerable to her assurance. The famous Lord Advocate, Sir George Mackenzie, of immortal memory, designed to write her history; but why he did not, I can give no account, etc.

Geo. Hickes

The above is possibly the most interesting of the six letters, not just for the portrait the minister gives of the child seer, Janet Douglas, but also for the tolerant, inquiring approach of the man himself. He is more or less convinced of the fact of second sight but unable to make up his mind as to its source. He wants to believe that it is not just a by-product of witchcraft, which makes him as anxious as Pepys himself to get hold of the elusive manuscript promised by Lord Reay.

His curiosity would seem to stem not just from a naturally inquiring mind but also from his interview with Janet Douglas. The young girl certainly knew how to handle the inquisitive cleric, at once submissive to his religious requirement and at the same time bold and precocious. She must have had all the charisma of a twentieth-century star to have drawn such crowds and intrigued the interest of the Lord Advocate, Sir George Mackenzie, himself a seer as we have seen. It is highly probable that she had some sort of psychic talent which reached a peak at puberty and which, allied to a strong personality, she knew how to use to full advantage. It would be interesting to know what happened to her; it is thought that she was sent to the West Indies where she subsequently married.

As for her visions, they would seem to reflect the cults and obsessions of the age. Swein Macdonald, the Highland Seer of today, is able not only to sense good and evil motives in his clients but also to find or describe lost or hidden articles. The contexts may be different, but the faculty remains the same.

The final letter in Pepys' collection was written to him by Henry, second Earl of Clarendon and is a typical instance of second sight, experienced in much the same sort of way from the beginning of recorded time.

London, May 27, 1701

Sir,

I cannot give you a greater instance of my willingness to gratify your curiosity in anything within my certain knowledge than the sending you this foolish letter. The story I told you the other day relating to what they call in Scotland the Second-Sight, is of so old a date and so many of the circumstances out of my memory that I must begin as old women do their tales to children, 'Once upon a time'.

The matter was thus: one day, I know by some remarkable circumstances it was towards the middle of February, 1661–2, the old Earl of Newborough came to dine with my father at Worcester House, and another Scotch gentleman with him, whose name I cannot call to mind.

After dinner, as we were standing and talking together in the room, says my Lord Newborough to the other Scotch gentleman (who was looking very steadfastly upon my wife), 'What is the matter, that thou hast had thine eyes fixed upon my Lady Cornbury ever since she came into the room? Is she not a fine woman? Why doest though not speak?'

'She's a handsome lady indeed,' says the gentleman, 'but I see her in blood.'

Whereupon my Lord Newborough laughed at him, and all the company going out of the room, we parted, and I believe none of us thought more of the matter. I am sure I did not. My wife was at that time perfectly well in health and looked as well as ever she did in her life.

In the beginning of the next month she fell ill of the small-pox. She was always very apprehensive of that disease, and used to say if she ever had it she should dye of it. Upon the ninth day after the small-pox appeared the blood burst out again with great violence at her nose and mouth, and about eleven of the clock she dyed, almost weltering in blood . . .

Clarendon

THE DEAN'S INGENIOUS THEORY

It would be tempting to think that the 'manuscript by a parson who gave a very full account of second sight and saw no sin in it' referred

81

to by Lord Reay and awaited so eagerly by Pepys, Hickes and their friends, was the booklet compiled by the Very Revd John Frazer, Minister of Tiree and Coll and Dean of the Isles, but modern scholarship has decreed this to be unlikely.

Born in Mull in 1647, the son of the Revd Farquhar Frazer, John Frazer was educated at Glasgow and inherited his father's charge in 1680. As an Episcopalian and a Jacobite he earned no stipend, but he was not suspended and continued in his parish until his death in 1702. His book was published posthumously in 1707 by a relative of his wife, Andrew Symson of Edinburgh, who also contributed a preface. Dedicated to the same Lord Tarbat whose letter to Robert Boyle on the subject of second sight also impressd Pepys and Reay, it carried the imposing Greek title of *Deuteroscopia, or a Brief Discourse Concerning Second Sight Commonly So Called*.

Frazer, whose experiences were first hand, had no trouble in believing in second sight and certainly 'saw no sin in it'. 'That such representations are made to the eyes of men and women is to me out of all doubt, and that effects follow answerable thereunto, as little questionable.' However, he admits: 'I have found so many doubt the matter of fact, which I take to be the reason that so little has been written of it, that I think it necessary to saӯ something briefly that may put the existence of it beyond all scruple, if I should insert all the clear instances that I had of this matter.'

The examples he gives are typical instances of death warnings and predictions of momentous events.

On one occasion, his servant came to him in great distress after having spent the night in the barn lying beside a phantom corpse in a winding sheet. No amount of persuasion would induce him to sleep there again. Six months later, a young man was brought to the manse in extremis. When he died he was laid out in the barn, and the servant was quick to remind his master of his frightening vision.

On a visit to Sir William Sacheverill in Mull, who had a commission from the Admiralty to explore the wreck of a Spanish ship in Tobermory Bay, the Dean took with him his personal servant, a young, handsome lad of whom he was fond. Before they set off by boat, a woman who had the gift begged one of the sailors to warn Frazer not to take the boy, but the seaman refused, believing the woman's interference to be 'an unwarrantable trifle'. Frazer spent an agreeable time with Sir William, himself keenly interested in second sight, and after a few days left for home. While at sea, the boy took ill of a 'vehement bloody flux' and the winds turned so unfavourable that the crew 'could neither sail nor row'. On the eleventh day at sea the poor boy died, and immediately the seaman told the minister of the old woman's warning. The Dean himself carried the lad ashore, and after the burial paid the woman a visit. She told him she had 'seen' the boy walking with the minister through a field, and he had been sewn up in his shroud.

Another example concerned a certain Duncan Campbell, 'a gentleman of singular piety and considerable knowledge, especially in divinity', who was working at that time in Kintyre. One morning he saw twelve men carrying a bier and recognized all except one. When he looked up again, they had vanished. Next day he saw the company again. This time they were no vision but in the flesh, and with only eleven bearers – so he stepped forward and himself made up the dozen.

Another tale was told to the Dean by a seer called John Macdonald who was servant to Captain Lachlan Maclean, the laird of Coll. One day he saw his master crossing a field and though the weather was bright, the captain's periwig was wet and his clothes glistened like fish scales. Macdonald told a friend that he feared it presaged the laird's death. A year later the Captain was drowned in Lochaber.

In 1685, a seer who was a tenant of Clanranald and living on the Island of Eigg told his priest, Father O'Rain, and the whole congregation one Sunday after Mass, that they would all be driven from the island by the sword, by 'deflowering of women' and by fire. Those who valued their lives should leave immediately. At first no one believed the warning, but the seer was so persistent that several families flitted on the strength of it to Canna and other islands. Four years later the seer became ill. Father O'Rain and some close friends gathered round his death bed to persuade him to confess that the vision was a lie, but he refused, maintaining that very soon his prediction would come true. After a fortnight, in June 1689, Redcoats, Whitecoats and Grenadier Capes armed with musket, pike and sword under the command of Major Ferguson and Captain Pottinger, descended on the island as foretold. Frazer himself was taken prisoner.

The Dean ends his book with an ingenious theory as to the nature of second sight. Species and images, he states, pass into the brain through the ear and eye and are there stored up in several compartments. Visions witnessed by seers are formed by good or bad angels by way of the nerves. Their foreknowledge may account for visionary appearances of future events. This theory is similar to the old belief that all visions are within the bounty of spirits, be they fairies or angels. Where the Dean finds the way too difficult to explain, he ascribes the matter to the direct will of God and is sure that such visions are sent for our edification.

MARTIN MARTIN, GENT.

One of the fullest and most entertaining accounts of second sight is to be found in *A Description of the Western Isles of Scotland* by Martin Martin, factor to the laird of Macleod, who died in 1719. First published in 1703, this edition was revised and re-issued in 1716, 'very much corrected'. Both editions contained a dedication to *His Royal Highness, Prince George of Denmark, Lord High Admiral of England and of Ireland and of all her Majesty's Plantations, and Generalissimo of all her Majesty's Forces* . . . The reason for this dedication was the earlier Norse occupation of the north: the islands 'can now, without suspicion of infidelity to the Queen of England, pay their duty to a Danish prince, to whose predecessors all of them formerly belonged. They can boast that they are honoured with the sepulchres of eight kings of Norway, who at this day, with forty-eight kings of Scotland and four of Ireland lie entombed on the Island of Iona.'

Martin was very much impressed by the history and genealogy of the Islanders and his book contains a full account of their lives and also a lengthy chapter on second sight, 'in Irish called Taish'.

'The Second-Sight,' he writes, 'is a singular faculty of seeing an otherwise invisible object, without any previous means used by the person that sees it for that end; the vision makes such a lively impression upon the seers, that they neither see nor think of anything else except the vision as long as it continues; and then they appear pensive or jovial according to the object which was represented to them.' Vividly he portrays the seer in the act, with 'eyelids erect over unblinking eyes', as was obvious to observers including Martin himself who had often witnessed the spectacle. The eyes of a certain Skye seer turned so far up during a vision that he had to draw them down with his fingers, or get someone else to do so.

Contrary to other observers, Martin maintains that second sight was not inherited, as he knew several gifted parents whose children were not endowed and vice versa. Nor was it acquired 'by compact' (presumably with the Devil) nor was it communicable unless witnessed by two seers who touched each other.

The sight of a shroud was always a sign of death, and depending on how much of the body was covered, the date of demise could be roughly calculated. The time of day when the *taibhs* appeared was also relevant to the time of death. A morning vision forecast death within the hour; if seen at noon, death would probably occur that day; but if seen after 'candles be lighted' the person whose image was seen might live for weeks, even years.

Clearly Martin believed that seers could be made as well as born. Novices, he tells us, were apt to 'swoon' at a vision seen out of doors or through fire. A novice once predicted the demise of one of Martin's friends, which he did not believe until the event took place. Within time, that novice who came from St Mary's parish in north Skye, graduated to become a 'skilled' seer.

Marriages were frequently predicted. Martin records the story of a seer's vision of two young men, both known to him, both well-born, seen standing to the left of a young gentlewoman. No one except the seer doubted that she would marry one of them. Later the seer saw a third man, unknown to him, yet whom he was able to describe in fine detail, standing close to the girl. Later that man turned up in the district and the two were eventually married.

Martin himself was the object of several visions. Often when he was hundreds of miles away, seers had predicted his appearance even before he had made up his mind to visit that particular island. Panoramic visions of the future were another part of the seer's repertoire. Mogflot in Skye was the scene of a repeated vision of houses, orchards and cultivated land at the time when the place contained 'but a few sorry cow-houses thatched with straw'. Later the vision was realized.

That seers also used omens to predict is illustrated in the following story. Daniel Dubh (Black), a well-known seer, observed a spark from the fire fall on his master's left arm and predicted the imminent death of his young son, which occurred. Thereafter sparks from the fire that fell on the arm or breast were considered omens of death. Ghostly sounds of music, singing, cock-crowing or the grinding of corn also usually presaged death, and Martin added the sense of smell to the seer's stock. The odour of cooking fish or meat in a house that contained none promised a good meal.

Martin also mentions the fact that children experience visions. He was visiting friends one day when a child suddenly cried out at the sight of 'a great white thing lying on the board which was in the corner'. He was not believed until a seer who was also present told the company that the child was right: he too had seen a shrouded corpse on a board which would be used to make a coffin. So it turned out.

Cows, like horses were also thought to have the sight, for often during milking they would run away in fright for no apparent reason. (Perhaps the dairymaid's hands were cold!)

Knowing how sceptical non-believers in the supernatural could be, Martin continues his discourse with a section which sets out to refute all possible argument.

Objection One: These seers are visionary and melancholy people, and fancy they see things that do not appear to them, or anybody else.
Answer: The people of these isles, and particularly the seers, are very temperate and their diet is simple and moderate in quantity and quality. Martin also tells us that they are not prone to hysterics, fits, or convulsions and that there are no lunatics nor any instances of suicide among seers.

Objection Two: There is none among the learned able to oblige the world with a satisfying account of those visions, therefore it is not to be believed.
Answer: If everything for which the learned are not able to give a satisfying account he condemned as impossible, we may find other things generally believed that must be rejected as false by this rule. The examples Martin gives are 'yawning' and 'magnetism'.

Objection Three: Seers are imposters, and the people who believe them are credulous and easily imposed upon.
Answer: Seers are generally illiterate and well-meaning people, and altogether void of design, nor could I ever learn that any of them made the least gain by it, neither is it reputable among them to have that faculty.

Islanders, Martin argues, are not credulous and do not believe blindly in a prediction until it has come to pass. If seers were liars, is it reasonable, he asks, to believe that Islanders would go on believing a lie from age to age? Many believers were persons of birth and education with nothing to gain from concurring with any imposture of simple, illiterate men.

Continuing his passionate advocacy of second sight, Martin points out that those who deny it are happy to believe in strange events in history on the word of long-gone historians, yet they would deny their contemporaries – men of probity and reputation – the freedom to believe in what is much more certain than ancient history.

True visions, he states, always come to pass exactly as seen, though there are novices and 'heedless' people who do not always know how to interpret the visions. Sometimes visions are seen yet not accomplished for many years; sometimes they are seen but not understood until they have been fulfilled. For example, a boy known to Martin was often surprised by the glimpse of a coffin close to his shoulder which made him think it must be an omen of his own death. An experienced seer told him he was wrong, next time he went to a funeral he should act as bearer. He did this some days later, and thus saw in reality that which he had previously seen in vision. He was never again troubled by that particular sight but grew to be one of the 'exactest' seers in Skye.

Martin's final point in his defence of the faculty is that second sight was no new discovery experienced by 'one or two in a corner', but was undergone by many of both sexes who had no contact with each other. Nor was it confined to the Western Isles. A woman in Holland saw a 'smoke about one's face' which presaged death. 'Death men's lights' in Wales were well-known forecasters of death. The Isle of Man also had its seers. How ridiculous, says Martin, to suppose that there could be a pact of deceit between the seers of Scotland, Holland, Wales and the Isle of Man, people of different languages separated by sea, government and interests.

He ends his chapter with a number of case histories, some of which are expanded versions of stories already told by Frazer, Aubrey and Lord Tarbat. For example he knew more than Frazer about the seer on Eigg who foresaw the violation of that island, for he had heard the prediction in Edinburgh from the mouth of Norman Macleod of Grabin who had just come south from Skye in September 1688. Macleod's version was that the seer had been troubled with frequent visions of a man in a red coat with a blue lining and wearing a blue cocked hat who was kissing one of the prettiest girls on the island. His interpretation was that the girl would either marry or be debauched by the stranger. The story was well known all over Skye, and was scorned for it was unusual for strangers to visit Eigg and the girl had no intention of leaving.

A year later, however, in 1689, Major Ferguson was sent with 600 men and some frigates to quell the islanders who had supported James VII and II. Probably Eigg would have not been invaded, in spite of the fact that some of its inhabitants had fought at the Battle of Killiecrankie, had it not been for an unfortunate accident. The crew of a boat from Eigg, while in Skye, were involved in the murder of one of the Major's men. In reprisal, the major invaded the island and due revenge was taken. The girl mentioned in the prediction was seized, taken on board one of the frigates, raped and 'brutishly robbed' of her beautiful hair. The story ended happily for her, in that her reputation was pronounced undamaged and she married in due course.

Sir Norman Macleod of Bernera, who featured in Tarbat's letter, supplied Martin with further interesting instances. One of his stories concerned his butler who was watching his master play a complicated game with dice – possibly backgammon. When the other player paused to deliberate over a move, the butler whispered in his ear, and as a result he won the game. Sir Norman was surprised for he did not think the butler knew the rules, but the latter told him he had seen a spirit called 'Browny' reach his arm over the player's head and touch the counter with his finger. Browny featured in another of Sir Norman's tales. While he was away on business, his servants gathered in the great hall when one of them, probably the same butler, told the rest to clear out for he had 'seen' a great crowd in the hall that night. The others demurred, pointing out that it was dark outside and the rocky coast made the approach by boat too dangerous, but within the hour Sir Norman and his clansmen returned. Questioning his servant, Sir Norman was told that Browny had reappeared, and had made a great parade of removing an old woman sitting by the fire by clasping her by her neck and heels. The vision, so amusing that the seer had laughed aloud, had been interpreted by him as a warning that the hall would soon be needed by his master.

In Gaelic, *gruagach* or brownie was one of the *sithean* who watched over herds or performed menial household tasks. Martin's tale is particularly interesting with reference to the old belief in the ancestral spirit, which was seen only by those with second sight.

Martin also recounts some remarkable instances connected with a seer called Archibald Macdonald from Trotternish in Skye. On one occasion he predicted that a certain invalid called Lachlan would never die in his own room. 'If that sick man dies in the room where he now lies, I shall from henceforth renounce my part of heaven. I tell you that he will be carried alive out of his room and never return alive.' Lachlan lived longer than expected but proved such an impossible patient that his family decided they would have to take him into the adjoining room. Not surprisingly, Lachlan refused to be moved. However his friends were so exhausted by his ravings that they lifted him against his will. He died as he crossed the threshold.

This would seem to be a strong case of auto-suggestion, and would explain why Macdonald was a dreaded neighbour. Afterwards he told the minister, Daniel Nicholson that he had 'seen' the patient in the doorway to the other room, clad in his shroud. Mr Nicholson suggested that Macdonald attempt to give up his unhappy power, as 'it is not true character of a good man', but the seer was not pleased and answered that he hoped he was no more unhappy than any of his neighbours just because he could perceive what they could not.

He then went on to predict: 'I had as serious thoughts as my neighbours during your sermon today, for I saw a corpse laid on the ground close to the pulpit, and I assure you it will be accomplished soon, for it was in daylight I saw it.' The minister attempted to silence him, for there were no sick in the neighbourhood and never more than one burial a year in that particular kirkyard, but the seer claimed loudly that this prediction, like all the rest, would come true. A week or two later when Mr Nicholson returned to preach in that parish, he found a burial party awaiting him and the corpse lying on the very spot where it was seen by Macdonald.

At this time the minister was a widower aged forty-four, and Macdonald had a vision of a young gentlewoman, well-dressed, standing at his right hand. He described her minutely, with reference to her complexion, height and clothing, and predicted she would marry the minister. Mr Nicholson told his parishioners to pay no heed to such 'a foolish dreamer', for 'it's twenty to one if ever I marry again'. But Macdonald persisted and so it occurred, for some years later the minister attended the Synod where he met a widow, a Mrs Morison, with whom he fell in love and whom he married. As soon as the congregation saw her, they recognized her from Macdonald's description.

One night before supper Macdonald told his host – a certain Daniel

Martin, who vouched for the truth of the tale – that he had just had a vision of the strangest thing in his life: 'a man with a long cap with bells attached which he was always shaking and playing a small harp with four strings and two deer horns fixed to the front of it'. The host and his family had a good laugh, but Macdonald declared huffily, 'You must excuse me if I laugh at you when my vision is accomplished.' Some days later the 'vision' turned up dressed as described – no doubt a professional one-man-band.

These stories about Archibald Macdonald give an interesting clue to the character of a seer, the nature of his visions, and the way he was regarded in the community. He must have been a respected neighbour; a man of power, not to be crossed, and exuding all the arrogance that such a reputation breeds; able to get the better of the minister, his chief rival for esteem within the community. Though he was not approved by the church, neither was he utterly condemned. His relationship with Mr Nicholson would seem to have been one of friendly rivalry rather than downright enmity.

Not all enjoyed their psychic ability, however, and Martin records several who wanted to be rid of their gift. He was particularly critical of the first, a maidservant whose mistress threw over her holy water snatched from the font during a baptism. The minister, John Morison, was somewhat surprised at this homespun attempt at exorcism, but recollected himself so far as to say a prayer, after which the girl was cured. 'I think it to have been one of Satan's devices to make credulous people have an esteem for holy water,' Martin remarks sententiously.

Two stories, both from the parish of St Mary in Skye, relate to the darker side of second sight. A servant was suddenly taken ill for no apparent reason, and one of his masters, who was a seer, told him his illness was due to a strange cause. An ill-natured woman from the next village was angry with him for not offering to marry her. The seer had witnessed her berating and reproaching him in a vision, and finally threatening him with 'her head and her hands' at the very moment he was taken ill.

The other story concerned a kiln belonging to the Revd Dougal Macpherson which caught fire and was quickly extinguished. When one of his servants predicted that it would catch fire again, the minister was angry and threatened to beat him if he continued to prophesy such mischief 'by the lying way of the second sight'. The seer told him he could not help his gift. 'Just now,' he added, 'I have seen that boy sitting by the fire with his face red with blood from his forehead. I could not help seeing this and certainly it will happen within a few days, for I have seen the vision in the daytime.'

The minister ordered the seer to hold tongue or find a new master. 'You are an unhappy creature,' he added, 'who likes to frighten the people with false predictions.'

Next day the boy came in with blood on his face, having fallen over a stone and cut his forehead. Somewhat less aggressively, the minister then asked his servant to predict when his kiln would catch fire and was told 'before Hallowtide'. Determined to run no risks, Mr Macpherson removed the key and told his servant he would take care of it until after that date. 'By this means,' said the minister, 'I shall make the Devil, if he is the authority of such lies, and you, both liars.'

Hallowmas duly passed with no fire, and the seer was scorned as a fool and a cheat. Then the servants gathered into the kiln to dry the corn with special instructions to watch out for fire. Needless to say, the place was burned – the seer's revenge, perhaps.

Taghairm was also practised in Martin's day. The minister of North Uist told him that a certain John Erach of Lewis had, out of curiosity, joined a group who 'consulted the oracle'. As the newcomer he was elected to pass the night in a bull hide, 'during which time he felt and heard such terrible things that he could not express them'. The experience was so dreadful that 'he would not for a thousand worlds' repeat the performance.

A hint that seers at that time might belong to the remnant of a particular caste is contained in the statement that when one seer was in doubt as to the outcome or interpretation of a vision 'he did not fail to consult his fellow-seers in the neighbourhood in which he lived'.

'These accounts', says Martin concluding his discourse, 'I had from persons of as great integrity as any are in the world.'

Martin's book is not only invaluable as a comment on the life and superstitions of the Islanders, but also as a comprehensive account of all aspects of second sight, which includes instances of what would today be regarded as coincidence, downright deceit, and mental illness. But among the dross of myth, exaggeration and superstition there are nuggets of genuine vision. He puts up a passionate case, and if not all his examples can be classed as genuine, there are certainly enough cases to prove his point.

Just as significant as the examples given is the one omitted. Martin was researching in the Islands shortly after the period ascribed by oral tradition to the legendary Coinneach Odhar. Reputedly born in Lewis in the first half of the seventeenth century, his fame would surely have been at its peak some twenty or thirty years after his alleged burning. Yet there is no mention of him or of his prophecies, a point to bear in mind when we come to look at the life of the Brahan Seer.

THE MIRAGE AND THE ONION

In 1763 Messrs Ruddiman, Auld and Co of Edinburgh published a curious little volume called '*A Treatise on the Second Sight, Dreams and Apparitions* with several instances sufficiently attested; and an appendix of others equally authentic. The whole illustrated with letters to and from the author on the subject of his treatise; and a short *Dissertation on the Mischievous Effects of Loose Principles*.'

The author called himself Theophilus Insulanus and to this day it is not absolutely certain who he was. James Boswell in his *Journal of a Tour to the Hebrides* refers to him as being William Hamar in Skye whose daughter, Molly, he met at Dunvegan, 'past sixty but affected youthfulness'. Dr William Mackay, the distinguished Gaelic scholar, agreed with this supposition, his proof being a reference in the *Letter-Book of Baillie John Stuart of Inverness* – Scottish History Society.

But Norman Macrae, editor of *Highland Second Sight* published in Dingwall in 1908, believed him to have been the Revd John Macpherson, a minister in Skye who travelled extensively through the Highlands and Islands during the first half of the eighteenth century, and today this is who he is generally thought to have been.

Still more muddling is the fact that Theophilus's book was republished and edited in 1818 by a certain 'W' who added to it a theory of his own which has continually been confused with the views of Theophilus himself. 'W' attempts to explain second sight by comparing it with the appearance of the Fata Morgana, a vision seen in the Straits of Messina and attributed to the enchantress Morgana or the Spectre of the Brocken, a giant shadow cast on cloud or mist below by someone standing on a hill above. (Brocken is the highest peak in the Hartz Mountains in Saxony and is famous for witch revels and as the setting for Goethe's *Faust*.) He also likens the faculty to a mirage. Even in modern terms this is not an unreasonable theory. A mirage is an optical phenomenon which may occur in an atmosphere heated or cooled in horizontal layers, when the light is refracted while passing from one layer to another. Under certain conditions the light is at such a large angle that it can act as a mirror. We all know how light shimmers in a heat haze. When this shimmering occurs at a higher level it can reflect distant objects well beyond the horizon. To 'W' the mirage must have seemed as supernatural as second sight is thought to be today.

One of the examples recorded by Theophilus certainly reads like the sighting of a mirage. A certain tacksman in Harris, Angus Campbell, saw a fleet of nine ships drop anchor at Corminish opposite his home. He called his family and servants and all took particular note of a large sloop among the other ships. As the mooring chosen by the fleet was unsafe, he decided to send some of his servants out by boat to pilot the ships into a safer anchorage. While they were discussing what to do for the best, the scene gradually faded and disappeared. Two years later the very same ships, including the sloop, dropped anchor at Corminish just as witnessed in the 'mirage'. The story was vouched for by many witnesses, including the minister of Harris.

Theophilus's book is crammed with instances which he insists all came from 'persons of undoubted veracity who had no interest or design to falsify or disguise the truth of their narrations'. The story of Lieutenant Armstrong's sighting of one of his own sergeants in Skye could easily belong to the twentieth or any other century. As the officer was crossing the mountain called Hornivall on his way to visit Macleod of Dunvegan, he saw his sergeant dressed in uniform down in the valley below. Although his servant could not see him, Armstrong insisted they both go down to look; but once there could see no sign of him, or of anyone else. Next day he heard that his sergeant had died at the moment he had been seen 'by a waking dream, which', adds Theophilus, 'I take to be the best definition of the Second Sight.'

Again in Skye, Theophilus tells of a young tenant farmer from Waternish who, while harvesting late one night, saw a crowd of neighbours carrying a corpse through his cornfield. Not pleased, he went home and told his wife who suspected that it might have been a vision and advised him not to complain. Next day to his relief he found his corn undamaged, and a year later the vision was realized when a funeral party passed right through the same field on its way to the churchyard at Trumpan.

In Lewis, a gentleman called Donald Macleod told him of a certain young woman who was betrothed to a highly suitable partner. A local seer told her, however, that she would never marry this particular man. Even on her wedding day, the seer persisted in his prediction. At the last moment another suitor appeared at the head of a party of twelve, kidnapped the girl, and bore her off to another island where he married her. This story reads like a blueprint for the ballad 'Lochinvar' and probably belongs to the realms of myth.

Women featured as seers in Theophilus' account. He writes of a certain Marion Macaskill who once saw a corpse carried by six men through a narrow pass of rock. Twelve years later a woman in search of herbs fell down that same pass and it took six men to retrieve her body. Of this particular vision, Theophilus himself is critical, pointing out that it had not been written down before the event. Another of Theophilus' informants, called Christine Macaskill, told him that her experiences of second sight were always unpleasant. On one occasion as she sat by her fire she 'saw' a neighbour steal one of her sheep and cut its throat. Hurrying to the man's croft, she forced open the door and caught him in the act of skinning the beast, which she identified by 'Challenging her mark on it'. The thief bribed her with four ells of new linen to hold her tongue.

The Lady of Coll, 'one who had a pious education, and one who lived in the practice of untainted virtue', told Theophilus of an elderly gentleman, Maclean of Knock, living on the Coll estate, who had a strange experience. He was walking in the fields at dusk when he was joined by a neighbour who had been ill for some time. 'How far do you intend to go?' he asked his friend, who told him he was on his way to a certain village and that he was in a hurry. Next day he heard that his sick friend had died the previous day at the hour when he was seen by Maclean.

One of the many visions that foresaw the Jacobite risings is recorded by Theophilus. In Benbecula a servant, Lachlan Maculloch, was coming out of his master's house one night in 1744 when he saw close to him 'a promiscuous heap of Redcoats on the path to his cottage'. In his attempt to escape he cut his shin on a rock. In 1746, the captain in command of the warship *Furnace* arrived and his men disembarked just as had been seen.

Seers, Theophilus found, were men with 'minds of a melancholy cast' who 'in some instances are weak-sighted' – an interesting theory shared today by Henderson Lynn, the Celtic clairvoyant, who believes that seers very often have something wrong with their normal sight.

Theophilus's own view on the existence of second sight is unquestioning. He attributed it to divine revelation and his object in writing his book was to shed light on the immortality of the soul and the existence of a Providence to guide and assist. To add weight to his conviction, he draws upon an argument of Lucretius who, he writes, 'though by the course of his philosophy, he was obliged to maintain that the soul did not exist separate from the body, makes no doubt of the reality of apparitions, and that men have often appeared after their death. This I think very remarkable; he was so pressed with the matter of fact, which he could not have the confidence to deny, that he was forced to account for it by one of the most absurd unphilosophical notions that ever was stated. He tells us that the surfaces of all bodies are perpetually flying off from their respective bodies, one after another; and that these surfaces of thin cases that included each other, whilst they were joined in the body, like the coats of an onion, are sometimes seen entire, when they are separated from it; by which means we often behold the shapes or shadows of persons who are either dead or absent.'

Far-fetched though this may sound, the theory of Lucretius so scorned by Theophilus has something in common with the modern conception of radio-activity today.

Theophilus was the last of the serious researchers to accept second sight as a fact. Although he and the earlier seventeenth-century investigators could no more account for it than later researchers, they seldom doubted its existence. By the mid-eighteenth century, however, the age of reason was well under way and thinkers were no longer able to accept readily what they could not account for by logic. Acceptance gave way to doubt, scepticism, and in many cases contempt, which matched the general opinion of the rest of Britain regarding the Gaels after their defeat at Culloden. For a time, Highlanders were forbidden to wear their national dress and discouraged from speaking their own language. Their chiefs, impoverished and humiliated, lost not only their self-respect, but also regard and responsibility for their clans. Gradually eviction and grinding poverty oppressed the Gaels as they entered the darkest era of their history. During this colder shift in the climate of opinion, second sight did not cease, but it stayed within the cottage and the croft. The Gael is proud and sensitive; from this time on he became less willing to expose himself, his customs and beliefs, to the speculation of outsiders. He learned to hold his tongue. He has, to a certain extent, held it ever since.

4   The Age of Reason

THOMAS PENNANT, TOURIST

Shortly after the Battle of Prestonpans in 1745 – a win for the
Jacobites – the Lord President, Duncan Forbes of Culloden, was
talking to a friend about the consequences of the battle. During the
conversation he moved to the window in Culloden House and gazed
out over the moor. 'All these thing may happen,' he said, 'but depend
upon it, all the disturbances will be terminated on this spot.' This
famous prediction was fulfilled when the last battle to be fought
on British soil took place at Culloden in 1746, and the prophecy
was recorded by Thomas Pennant who received it first-hand from
Duncan Forbes's friend.

Pennant, born in 1726 in Flintshire, educated at Wrexham and
Queen's College, Oxford, was eventually to become one of the most
eminent naturalists of the eighteenth century. Although *The British
Zoology* published in four volumes was his most important work, it
was his Highland exploration, first written about in *A Tour in
Scotland*, published in 1769, that was to make him famous. The book
was an immediate success and as a result 'the remotest part of North
Britain' was thereafter to become 'inondee with southern visitors'. As
a travel-writer, he had, as Dr Johnson said, 'a greater variety of
inquiry then almost any man, and has told us more than perhaps one
in ten thousand could have done in the time that he took'.

In fact, only Dr Johnson himself was to write so well of the Highlands.

Pennant has several observations to make on the subject of second
sight and superstition which place him firmly in the 'age of reason'.
The following paragraph on Perthshire demonstrates his attitude.

The country is perfectly highland; and in spite of the intercourse this and the neighbouring part have of late years had with the rest of the world, it still retains some of its ancient customs and superstitions; they decline daily, but lest their memory be lost, I shall mention several that are still practised, or but very lately disused in the tract I had passed over. Such a record will have this advantage when the follies are quite extinct, in teaching the unshackled and unenlightened mind the difference between the pure ceremonies of religion, and the wild and anile flights of superstition.

Such 'wild and anile flights of superstition' that still persisted included belief in ghosts, though the 'notion of witchcraft is quite lost' owing to the repeal of the Witch Act in 1736, 'a proof what a dangerous instrument it was in the hands of the vindictive or of the credulous'. But Pennant observed that there was still a belief in auspicious days. No Highlander, he tells us, would ever begin anything of consequence on 3 May, known in Gaelic as the 'dismal day'.

That *slinneanachd* or shoulder-blade divination, was still practised is instanced in two examples. Lord Loudon's soldier predicted a Hanoverian victory at Culloden, and a certain Molly Maclean pronounced by the examination of 'a well-scraped shoulder-blade' that five graves would soon be opened, one for an adult and four for children, one of whom would be her own.

Pennant records a case of *taghairm* in Trotternish in Skye and describes how the diviner was clad in an oxhide and placed under a waterfall. 'These pretenders to second sight,' he writes, 'like the Pythian priestess, during their inspiration fall into trances, foam at the mouth, grow pale, and feign to abstain from food for a month, so over-powered are they by their visions.'

Although he mentions a belief in Iona that St Columba was thought to be the first possessor of second sight, in that he predicted the victory of Aidan, King of the Scots, over the Picts 'on the instance it happened', he is generally sceptical of the faculty and contemptuous of seers. 'I must not omit,' he adds, 'a most convenient form of second sight, possessed by a gentleman of a neighbouring isle, who foresees all visitors, so has time to prepare accordingly: but enough of these tales, founded on impudence and nurtured by folly.'

Of Skye he writes: 'Very few superstitions exist here at present: pretenders to second sight are quite out of repute except among the most ignorant and at present are very shy of making boast of their faculties.'

No wonder! Pennant's impatience must have been obvious.

For the purposes of this book, however, Pennant's most important observation relates to Coinneach Odhar. Writing of Sutherland and reflecting on the poverty, bad management and early evictions that so damaged that county, he states: 'Every country has had its prophets . . . and the Highlands their Kenneth Oaur. Kenneth long since predicted these migrations in these terms; whenever a Maclean with long hands, a Frazier with a black spot on his face, a Macgregor with the same on his knee, and a club-footed Macleod of Rasa should have existed; whenever there should have been successively three Macdonalds of the name of John, and three Mackinnons of the same Christian name, oppressors would appear in the country, and the people change their own land for a strange one. These predictions, say the good wives, have been fulfilled, and not a single breach in the oracular effusions of Coinneach Oaur.'

Considering that the legendary Coinneach Odhar, who was allegedly born in Lewis, prophesied throughout Ross-shire and was burned during the second half of the seventeenth century, it might seem strange that the first literary allusion to him should come from an English traveller in Sutherland. Significant too that, as we have seen, there is no mention of him in the works of Martin, Frazer and Theophilus Insulanus, who were writing of Ross-shire and the Western Isles. But not so strange, perhaps, when we look at the life of the historical Coinneach who was living in 1577 and involved with the Rosses of Balnagown. The estates of the latter marched with the County of Sutherland. David Ross, the eleventh Laird of Balnagown, married the Earl of Sutherland's daughter and no doubt there was much contact between the two families during which the seer's name and deeds would often have been discussed. Possible, too, that the historical Coinneach knew and travelled in Sutherland himself.

Apart from his reference to Coinneach Odhar, Pennant's observations are of interest because he was the first to take a cool, critical look at the faculty of second sight. Though his instances and conclusions are not sufficient to constitute a reasonable argument either for or against its existence, they counterbalance the credulity of earlier observers.

For true reasonableness, we need to look at his contemporaries, those delightful followers in his trail, James Boswell and Samuel Johnson.

'A FAVOURABLE PRESUMPTION'

It was probably Pennant's *A Tour of Scotland* that stimulated Dr Samuel Johnson to realize his long-projected jaunt to the Highlands and Islands with his friend and biographer James Boswell in 1773.

In his *Journal of a Tour to the Hebrides* Boswell records that 'after supper at Dunvegan in Skye the conversation turned to Pennant and some objected he was superficial but Mr Johnson defended him warmly'. Both men were also stirred by Martin's account which, as Boswell says, 'impressed us with a notion that we might there contemplate a system of life totally different from what we had been accustomed to see; and to find simplicity and wildness, and all the circumstances of remote time and place, so near to our native great island, was an object within the reach of reasonable curiosity.'

Boswell admitted that Johnson was prejudiced against Scotland. 'The truth is, like the ancient Greeks and Romans, he allowed himself to look upon all nations but his own as barbarians.' It would therefore not be unreasonable to find him contemptuous of second sight, but this was not the case. General Macleod, one of Johnson's hosts, remarked in his memoirs that the Doctor 'listened to all the fables of that nature which abound in the Highlands; and though no one fact was so well vouched for as to command his particular belief, he held that the thing was not impossible; and that the number of facts alleged formed a favourable presumption.'

In Boswell's *Journal* there are several references. After dinner on a wet and stormy day while the two men were staying in Skye, the conversation concerned the subject of second sight. Dr Johnson turned to the Revd Martin Macpherson, minister of Sleat, 'a very poor companion', and asked him if he knew of any instances. Macpherson answered pompously that he was resolved not to believe it because it was founded on no principle. 'Then,' said Dr Johnson, 'there are many things which we are sure are true that you will not believe. What principle is there why the loadstone attracts iron? Why an egg produces a chicken by heat? Why does a tree grow upwards, when the tendency of all things is downwards? Sir, it depends upon the degree of evidence you have.'

The son of their hostess, 'young Mr Mackinnon told us of one Mackenzie who is alive whom he had often seen faint, and when he recovered he told he had seen things. He told Mr Mackinnon that on such a place he would meet a funeral, and that such and such people would be the bearers, naming four; and three weeks after he saw just what Mackenzie had told him. The naming the very spot in a country where a funeral comes a long way, and the very people as bearers when there are so many out of whom a choice may be made, seems curious. We would have sent for Mackenzie had we not been informed that he could speak no English. Besides, the young man seemed confused in his narration.'

Mrs Mackinnon, their hostess, 'who was a daughter of old Kingsburgh, told us that her father was one day riding in Skye, and some women who were at work in a field on the side of the road told him they heard two taisks, that is two voices of persons about to die; "and what", said they, "is extraordinary one of them is an English taisk, which we never heard before." When he returned, he at that very place met two funerals, and one of them was of a woman who had come from the mainland and could speak only English. This, she told us, made a great impression upon her father.'

On 16 October, after a hard day of riding in Mull, Boswell and Johnson were ferried across to the island of Ulva to stay with Lachlan Macquarry. Though his house was 'mean', the two travellers were impressed by the man who was intelligent, polite, very much a man of the world whose family had owned Ulva for 900 years.

'Macquarry told us a strong instance of second sight. He had gone to Edinburgh and taken a man-servant with him. While he was away, an old woman who worked in the house remarked one day, "Macquarry will be at home tomorrow and will bring two gentlemen with him," and she said she saw his servant return in red and green. He did come home next day. He had two gentlemen with him; and his servant had a new red and green livery, which Macquarry had bought for him at Edinburgh upon a sudden thought, not having the least intention when he left home to put his servant in livery; so that the old woman could not have heard any previous mention of it. This, he assured us, was a true story.'

Boswell was somewhat surprised to find that all who lived in Scotland did not believe in second sight. One of the greatest put-downs of his life must have occurred when he and Johnson were staying with the Duke of Argyle at Inveraray. 'I made some remark,' he writes, 'that seemed to imply a belief in second sight. The Duchess said, "I fancy you will be a Methodist." This was the only sentence Her Grace deigned to utter to me; and I take it for granted, she thought it a good hit at my credulity . . .'

Boswell's personal views on second sight were written in November when he and his friend were back in Edinburgh.

I beg leave to say something upon second sight, of which I have related two instances, as they impressed my mind at the time.

I own I returned from the Hebrides with a considerable degree of faith in the many stories of that kind which I heard with a too easy acquiescence, without any close examination of the evidence; but since that time my belief in those stories has been much weakened by reflecting on the careless inaccuracy of narrative in common matters, from which we may certainly conclude that there may be the same in what is more extraordinary. It is but just, however, to add that the belief in second sight is not peculiar to the Highlands and Isles . . .

However difficult it may be for men who believe in preternatural communication, in modern times, to satisfy those who are of a different opinion, they may easily refute the doctrine of their opponents who impute a belief in second sight to superstition. To entertain a visionary notion that one sees a distant or future event, may be called superstition; but the correspondence of the fact or event with such an impression on the fancy, though certainly very wonderful, if proved, has no more connection with superstition than magnetism or electricity.

In Dr Johnson's account of his and Boswell's tour, A Journey to the Western Islands of Scotland, he writes with great seriousness on the subject of second sight. His summary is still the most-quoted literary description and deserves to be given in full.

We should have had little claim to the praise of curiosity, if we had not endeavoured with particular attention to examine the question of the second sight. Of an opinion received for centuries by a whole nation, and supposed to be confirmed through its whole descent, by a series of successive facts, it is desirable that the truth should be established, or the fallacy detected.

The second sight is an impression made either by the mind upon the eye, or by the eye upon the mind, by which things distant or future are perceived, and seen as if they were present.

A man on a journey far from home falls from his horse, another, who is perhaps at work about the house, sees him bleeding on the ground, commonly with a landscape of the place where the accident befalls him. Another seer, driving home his cattle, or wandering in idleness, or musing in the sunshine, is suddenly surprised by the appearance of a bridal ceremony, or funeral procession, and counts the mourners or attendants, of whom, if he knows them, he relates the names, if he knows them not, he can describe the dresses. Things distant are seen at the instant when they happen. Of things future I know not that there is any rule for determining the time between the sight and the event.

This receptive faculty, for power it cannot be called, is neither voluntary nor constant. The appearances have no dependence upon choice: they cannot be summoned, detained, or recalled. The impression is sudden, and the effect often painful.

By the term second sight, seems to be meant a mode of seeing, superadded to that which nature generally bestows. In the Erse it is called Taisch; which signifies likewise a spectre, or a vision. I know not, nor is it likely that the Highlanders ever examined, whether by Taisch, used for second sight, they mean the power of seeing, or the thing seen.

I do not find it to be true, as it is reported, that to the second sight nothing is presented but phantoms of evil. Good seems to have the same proportion in those visionary scenes, as it obtains in real life; almost all remarkable events have evil for their basis; and are either miseries incurred, or miseries escaped. Our sense is so much stronger of what we suffer, than of what we enjoy, that the ideas of pain predominate in almost every mind. What is recollection but a revival of vexations, or history but a record of wars, treasons, and calamities? Death, which is considered as the greatest evil, happens to all. The greatest good, be it what it will, is the lot of but a part.

That they should often see death is to be expected; because death is an event frequent and important. But they see likewise more pleasing incidents. A gentleman told me, when he had once gone far from his own Island, one of his labouring servants predicted his return, and described the livery of his attendant, which he had never worn at home and which had been, without any previous design, occasionally given him.

Our desire of information was keen, and our inquiry frequent. Mr Boswell's frankness and gaiety made every body communicative; and we heard many tales of these airy shows, with more or less evidence and distinctness.

It is the common talk of the Lowland Scots, that the notion of the second sight is wearing away with other superstitions; and that its reality is no longer supposed, but by the grossest people. How far its prevalence ever extended, or what ground it has lost, I know not. The Islanders of all degrees, whether of rank or understanding, universally admit it, except the ministers, who universally deny it, and are suspected to deny it, in consequence of a system, against conviction. One of them honestly told me, that he came to Skye with a resolution not to believe it.

Strong reasons for incredulity will readily occur. This faculty of seeing things out of sight is local, and commonly useless. It is a breach of the common order of things, without any visible reason or perceptible benefit. It is ascribed only to a people very little enlightened; and among them, for the most part, to the mean and the ignorant.

To the confidence of these objections it may be replied, that by presuming to determine what is fit, and what is beneficial, they presuppose more knowledge of the universal system than man has attained; and therefore depend upon principles too complicated and extensive for our comprehension; and that there can be no security in the consequence, when the premises are not understood; that the second sight is only wonderful because it is rare, for, considered in itself, it involves no more difficulty than dreams, or perhaps than the regular exercise of the cogitative faculty; that a general opinion of communicative impulses, or visionary representations, has prevailed in all ages and all nations; that particular instances have been given, with such evidence, as neither Bacon nor Boyle has been able to resist; that sudden impressions, which the event has verified, have been felt by more than own or publish them; that the second sight of the Hebrides implies only the local frequency of a power, which is nowhere totally unknown; and that where we are unable to decide by antecedent reason, we must be content to yield to the force of testimony.

By pretension to second sight, no profit was ever sought or gained. It is an involuntary affection, in which neither hope nor fear are known to have any part. Those who profess to feel it, do not boast of it as a privilege nor are considered by others as advantageously distinguished. They have no temptation to feign; and their hearers have no motive to encourage the imposture.

To talk with any of these seers is not easy. There is one living in Skye, with whom we would have gladly conversed; but he was very gross and ignorant and knew no English. The proportion in these countries of the poor to the rich is such, that if we suppose the quality to be accidental, it can very rarely happen to a man of education; and yet on such men it has sometimes fallen. There is now a second sighted gentleman in the Highlands, who complains of the terrors to which he is exposed.

The foresight of the seers is not always prescience: they are impressed with images, of which the event only shews them the meaning. They tell what they have seen to others, who are at that time not more knowing than themselves, but may become at last very adequate witnesses, by comparing the narrative with its verification.

To collect sufficient testimonies for the satisfaction of the public, or of ourselves, would have required more time than we could bestow. There is, against it, the seeming analogy of things confusedly seen, and little understood; and for it, the indistinct cry of national persuasion, which may be perhaps resolved at last into prejudice and tradition. I could never advance my curiosity to conviction; but came away at last only willing to believe.

This is a masterly description which covers every feature of second sight. Delicately Johnson examines each argument for and against its existence and neatly balances the theories with their counterparts. After discussing each aspect he comes to the conclusion that he cannot make up his own mind, not because he is prejudiced one way or the other, but for lack of sufficient research.

'Not a man in a million . . . believes in ghosts.' Thus wrote the critic of *The Monthly Review* in his discussion of Sir Walter Scott's *Demonologie* in 1830.

Did Scott believe in second sight? Byron certainly thought so. 'Who can help being superstitious?' he wrote. 'Scott believes in second sight.'

Mrs Anne MacVicar Grant of Laggan, author of *Essays on the Superstitions of the Highlanders of Scotland* and herself a seer, wrote to a friend: 'I was amused at Sir Walter's caution in keeping so entirely clear of the second sight: like myself, I am pretty confident he has a glimmering belief of, though not the same courage to own it.'

To define second sight, Scott turned to Johnson's superb definition and added, 'Spectral appearances thus presented, usually presage misfortune; . . . the faculty is painful to those who suppose they possess it . . . and . . . they usually acquire it while themselves under the pressure of melancholy.'

He experienced one vision himself. At dusk he saw a cart and horse led by a man which 'at once, tumbled down the bank and vanished'. Two hours later a servant on his way home from Melrose, leading a laden cart, skidded down the same brae, fortunately without too much damage. Hardly an example to convince the seer, let alone his friends, yet typical of innumerable random sightings that would seem to have no significance.

A lawyer born in Edinburgh in 1771 and called to the bar in 1792, Scott entered an age when it was fashionable to doubt everything and believe nothing. His head was turned towards scepticism, but, as a poet and novelist of superb imagination, his heart leaned towards credulity. In his note on second sight in *The Lady of the Lake* he wrote: 'If force of evidence could authorize us to believe facts inconsistent with the general laws of nature, enough might be produced in favour of the existence of second sight.' For Scott the lawyer, however, its true existence was probably only to be found in the realms of poetry. Whatever his private belief, he was always intensely interested in the marvellous and this included every aspect of prophecy, divination and second sight. He was to use them frequently in his writing, his correspondence and his conversation.

One of his favourite stories, recorded by John Lockhart in his

Memoirs of Sir Walter Scott, concerned the Laidlaw family in the sixteenth century. When Laidlaw chided his wife for practising the black arts, she cursed his name and lineage. Although their only son begged her to revoke the curse, she forced him to kill a heifer which she sacrificed to the Devil in his presence. Then she took the ashes to a stream and flung them into the water. 'Follow them,' she ordered, 'from stream to pool, as long as they float visible; and as many streams as you shall then have passed, for so many generations shall your descendants prosper. After that they shall like the rest of the name be poor, and take their part in my curse.' There were nine streams.

After telling the tale, Scott pointed out that the Laidlaws were landless men except Laird Nippy of Peel who went bankrupt, thus fulfilling the prophecy, which Scott always repeated 'with an air that seemed to me [Lockhart] in spite of his endeavours to the contrary . . . grave.'

The Mackenzie prophecy (see page 25), in the same vein, also caught his imagination to such an extent that he wrote the following *Lament for The Last of the Seaforths*

In vain the bright course of thy talents go wrong
Fate deaden'd thine ear and imprison'd thy tongue,
For brighter o'er all her obstructions arose
The glow of the genius they could not oppose;
And who, in the land of the Saxon or Gael,
Might match with Mackenzie, High Chief of Kintail?

Thy sons rose around thee in light and in love,
All a father could hope, all a friend could approve;
What 'vails it the tale of thy sorrows to tell?
In the springtime of youth and of promise they fell!
Of the line of MacKenneth remains not a male,
To bear the proud name of the Chief of Kintail.

And thou, Gentle Dame, who must bear, to thy grief,
For thy clan and thy country the cares of a Chief,
Whom bright rolling moons in six changes have left,
Of thy husband and father and brethren bereft:
To thine ear of affection, how sad is the hail
That salutes thee – the heir of the line of Kintail.

The prediction, which is given in full in Chapter 7, prophesied that the last Lord Seaforth would be deaf and dumb and outlive his four sons, that his estates would be inherited by a widow and his lands pass to strangers. On 11 January 1815 Francis Humberston Mackenzie, Chief of Kintail, died stone-deaf and virtually dumb, having outlived his sons. His heiress Mary was the widow of Admiral Sir Samuel Hood.

Scott was deeply moved. A week later he wrote to J. B. S. Morritt: 'You will have heard of poor Cabarféidh's death – what a pity it is he should have outlived his promising young representative . . . I do fear the accomplishment of the prophecy that when there should be a dumb Caberféidh the house was to fall.' On 21 January, he again wrote to Morritt after watching Lord Seaforth's funeral procession in Edinburgh: 'There is something very melancholy in seeing the body pass, poorly attended, and in the midst of a snow storm whitening all the sable ornaments of the undertaker, and all corresponding with the decadence and misfortune of the family.'

In his letter to the Marchioness of Stafford written on the same day, Scott said: 'All the Highlands ring with a prophecy that when there should be a deaf Caberféidh the clan and chief shall all go to wreck, but these predictions are very apt to be framed after the event.' However, he goes on to say that Morritt had 'heard the prophecy quoted in the Highlands at a time when Lord Seaforth had two sons both alive and in good health – so that certainly was not made après coup.' As we shall see later, this small piece of evidence is of great importance in establishing the existence of the Mackenzie prediction before the actual event.

Like most of us, Scott was inconsistent in his attitude to superstition. On one occasion when troubled by financial problems he resorted to trial by augury and planted some acorns in order to 'judge by their success in growing whether I will succeed in clearing my way or not'. Later, when reminded that Friday was considered an unlucky day for a journey, he answered, laughing, 'Superstition is very picturesque, and I make it at times stand me in great stead; but I never allow it to interfere with interest or convenience.'

Being a writer contemporary with Scott must have been hard. John Galt certainly found it so. Often he had an idea for a novel, only to find that Scott had just published one on the same theme. 'What a cursed fellow that Walter Scott has been to drive me out of my original line,' he was to cry in exasperation; but•Scott's favourable review of one of his books eventually cooled his anger.

Galt was born in Ayrshire in 1779 and moved to Greenock ten years later, where he was educated and where he worked in the Custom House until he left for London in 1804 to make his way as a writer. It was not until 1820 that his first novel was published, and three years later he became secretary to the Canada Company which went bankrupt. He was arrested for debt and, like Scott, worked hard to pay his way by editing and writing biographies and novels. In 1834 he returned to Greenock, where he died five years later.

Unlike Scott, Galt was a Calvinist who believed in predestination and 'the unchangeable nature and purposes of the Deity' in which 'temporary meddling and uncertainty in the universe play no part'. To Galt there was no such thing as free will. In *The Bachelor's Wife* he wrote: 'Men and gods vainly struggle to free themselves from the adamantine bonds of destiny. The oracle, or the omen which declares the impending evil, affords no method of averting it. All insight into futurity proves a curse to those on whom the power descends. We hear the warning which we cannot obey.'

As a young man, Galt was obsessed with alchemy, precognition, astrology, omens and ghosts, and during his travels in the Levant he made a study of the paranormal including the sense of 'second hearing'. Man, he believed, was endowed 'with more senses that he is aware of'. Highland second sight was 'one of the seven senses of the human species which every one possesses to a certain degree'.

Second sight played a particularly important role in his novel *The Spaewife*, the plot of which was based on a vision of the death of James I. Signs and portents abound in *The Omen*, while 'strange intimations by auguries and signs' make up the plot of *Southennan*. With Galt, however, visions and omens never encourage the characters to break away from their destination. Rather, they paralyse the will and emphasize the stupidity of fighting against what has been ordained.

Although in general Galt believed that occult experience probably came from within man rather than from any outward supernatural force, he is at his best as a writer when he uses the occult as an external force in which he only partly believes.

A DARKER SUPERSTITION

'An intus-suception of transient events at a distance from the seer, not unlike reverie occupying the mind in a moment of abstraction, is denominated the second sight.' Thus wrote Sir John Graham Dalyell, lawyer, naturalist, antiquarian and prolific author, in his *Darker Superstitions of Scotland Illustrated from History and Practice* which was published in Glasgow in 1835.

His theories on second sight are a hodge-podge of the works of previous researchers, his examples being taken mainly from Robert Woodrow's *Analecta* – a delightful account of life in Scotland in 1679 – and accounts of witchcraft trials in Orkney. Considering that the Northern Isles have never claimed second sight as one of their commoner beliefs, this seems a strange choice, though it makes interesting reading.

Sir John emphasized that, strictly speaking, second sight is limited to visions of incidents and objects seen at the moment of their happening, however distant in space, and that it only borders on prognostication. Although other countries claim it, the Highlands and particularly the Islands enjoy it 'in the highest perfection'. 'Not only they, but their cattle also,' he adds contemptuously.

'The faculty must be ascribed to past rather than present times because although not entirely extinct, the same credulity which fostered its subsistence has long been on the wane.' (For all his research into documents, Sir John cannot have spent much time in the field, or if he did his unsympathetic approach must have shut every seer's mouth for miles.) 'Nor can it be claimed as an antiquity, for all that is known of it was written in the two last centuries.' It was not until the reign of Charles II that it became the object of research and discussion, he argues. Such a superstition could not have sprung up over night: 'Probably the lower the state of rude society, the slower the dissemination of novelties.'

Second sight was 'enjoyed' by either sex, young and old, inherited or acquired, taught or untaught, imparted as in cases of augury and witchcraft. It might also be bestowed by supernatural beings, as happened to Isobel Sinclair, the Orcadian witch, who 'sex times at the reathes of the year, she hath bein controlled with the Phairie; and that be thame, she hath the secund sight; whereby she will kno giff thair be any fey bodie in the house.'

Just as the faculty may be acquired, says Sir John, so too may it be lost, depending upon the circumstances of the seer. Those who emigrated to the West Indies, for example, 'did sie no visions there'; but a trip south was not enough to banish the sight, as was evidenced by the Provost of Glasgow who was talking in the street to a High-lander when a mutual acquaintance passed by. The Highlander informed him that their friend would 'very soon be a dead corpse'. Sure enough, minutes later he was run over by a carriage and his body was removed in the Provost's presence. On the other hand, a seer could not get rid of the faculty by wishing, try though he might. Public prayer and confession was the only hope.

However acquired, second sight was always accompanied by 'a troublesome and painful sensation'. Seers shrieked, trembled and sweated in the power of their vision. Although second sight some-times witnessed joyful occasions, the visions were usually dis-mal – as in the case of the Revd John Cameron, minister of Lochend in Kintyre who on the morning of the Battle of Bothwell Bridge in 1679 became very melancholy. His elder, watching him 'throu his chamber dore, saw him weeping and wringing his hands, and con-tinued knocking till at length he opened to him, and he asked what was the matter; if his wife and bairns were weel? "Little matter of them," says he, "our friends at Bothwell are gone." '

When the elder suggested Cameron might be mistaken he cried, 'No, no. I see them fleeing as clearly as I see the wall.' As near as could be calculated by later accounts, the vision occurred at the crisis of battle.

The object seen by the seer, continues Sir John, was generally represented in some dismal aspect, shrouded or manacled. For example the trial of Elsbeth Reoch in Orkney, 1616, records that she 'by the secund sicht saw Robert Stewart, son naturall to the late Patrick, sumtyme Earle of Orknay, with Patrick Traill, to whom she was with bairne, and certane utheris with ropes about their necks, in Edmond Calendares house, at the eftirnoones drink, before the Earle of Cathnes' cuming to the cuntry.'

Although second sight was 'of something contemporary, it might border on futurity', says Sir John, and quotes another example from the Northern Isles. The husband of Jonkie Dyneis was fishing six miles from home and in danger, when she was 'fund and seen standin at her owin house wall, in ane trans, that same hour he was in danger; and being trappit, she could not give answer, but stude as bereft of her senses: and when she was asked as why she was so movit, she answerit, gif our boat be not tynt, she is in great hazard – and wes proved so to be.' Poor Jonkie was also tried for witchcraft.

Sir John then discusses the organic functioning of a seer. The vision, he believed, existed for only as long as the seer could keep his eyes open. Those with trembling or tired eyes, such as Albinos, could never be good seers.

Should a seer lose his faculty by travelling abroad, he might still retain the ability to experience predictive dreams. In the year 1628, to amuse his colonel at the storming of Stalsund while on an expedition with Mackay's Regiment, a young officer called Monro told him 'of a vision that was seen of the Colonel's Company that morning before the enemy did storme, being a predictive dreame, and a true.' The seer was a soldier called Murdo Macleod, described as tall and courageous, who woke two of his companions who were sleeping while on watch. When they complained, he told them, 'Before long you shall be otherwise stirred.'

In reply to their questions he answered, 'You shall never see your country again.'

One of the two answered bravely that the loss would be small if the rest did well.

'No,' said Murdo, 'for there was great hurt and dearth of many being neare.'

When asked who else would die, he gave the names of all who would be killed.

'And yourself?'

'I will be killed with the others,' said Murdo Macleod.

A young lad nearby asked, 'What of the major?' meaning Monro himself.

Murdo answered that he would be shot but not killed, and that the lad would be at his side when he was wounded, which, added Munro, he was.

No wonder the army still dislikes seers and fortune-tellers in the ranks. Such a dream must surely have been a true recipe for defeat!

111

'In general,' writes Sir John, 'Second sight has been ascribed to the Highlands as a peculiar faculty but examples of something analogous seem to be known elsewhere, though not recognized under the specific name.' He ascribes this fact to the 'nurseries of superstition which encourage delusions which seem to correspond to each other'. Or possibly the physical conditions of the country may cause 'generale peculiarities': Holland, France, Padua, and Rome provide him with examples.

Illusions, too, depend upon the mental and personal characteristics of the seer, but he grudgingly admits that 'there are intelligent persons in Skye' who were convinced of its existence, and that in Shetland there lived a family who claimed the faculty through inheritance, though it existed in the head of that family alone.

He firmly distinguishes between second sight and prediction, prognostication and divination, but is no more disposed to accept the existence of prophetic powers than of second sight. Nevertheless, he quotes one story of prophecy which seemed to him to be well authenticated, although it dated from 1436. While James I was travelling from Edinburgh to Perth, he was stopped at Leith by a 'woman from Ireland', who stepped out into the middle of the road and cried out, 'My Lord King, and ye pass this water, ye shall never come back alive.' The King was astonished at her words, as he had already heard of an old prophecy that declared that a Scottish king would be slain that year, so he sent one of his knights to go and speak to the woman. She insisted that her words were true, for a certain 'Huthart' had told her them.

The knight was sceptical. He advised the King to pay no attention to the ranting of a drunken fool, so they set off for Perth – St John's Town, as it was called in those days – where the King held a great feast. During the merrymaking, the Irish woman again appeared and tried unsuccessfully to get near enough to the King to warn him. Meanwhile conspirators plotted the assassination, and the King was murdered. Sir John tells us that the 'woman from Ireland' was probably a Gaelic-speaking Highlander.

The Orcadian, Bessie Skebister, was also credited with the power of prophecy. During her trial it was alleged that 'all the honest men of the Yle declarit that it was ane usuall thing when they thoucht boatis war in danger, to come or send how they war, and if they would come home weill? Whereupon an common proverb is usit: giff Bessie say it is weill, all is weill.' Bessie too was strangled and burned for her advice.

'New generations of prophets are constantly rising,' says Sir John and one can sense his sigh. 'The world is never altogether free of them.'

Sir John has no theories as to the nature and origin of second sight, simply because he has no belief in it. As a result he has no original examples to quote. His contribution has been largely ignored by Highlanders and investigators who could not fail to sense his contempt and impatience with the 'superstition'. Perhaps his lameness, after a fall as a child, prevented him from travelling north to undertake some original research. A pity, this, for in spite of being so widely read and such an inveterate researcher into ancient manuscripts – he claimed to have examined 700 of them for his book on sixteenth-century poetry – Sir John does not give a balanced view. He was, of course, a man of his times with all the prejudices of his day, and he was not young when he wrote *Darker Superstitions*. Certainly he was entitled to his opinion, but for a man of his knowledge and interests, that opinion might have been reached in a fairer way.

Sir John Dalyell's attitude heralded yet another approach to paranormal experience in the Highlands. An explosion of inventions, discoveries, and doctrines such as Darwinism brought in a new age of science where nothing that was not visible, demonstrable and comprehensible was to be believed. Because second sight together with other paranormal phenomena violated this new attitude to the nature of the world, they were considered to be unscientific and therefore not credible.

At the same time the attitude to the Highlands also underwent a subtle change. Thanks to the patronage of Queen Victoria, mountains and glens, tartan and reels had become fashionable. Highlanders were considered on the one hand quaint and endearing; on the other uneconomic and therefore less important as tenants than sheep, grouse, and deer.

Highlanders who did not emigrate or find comfort in the newly formed Free Kirk with its strict doctrines and high ideals tended to value themselves as they were valued and saw their beliefs and abilities as worthless. But interest in the paranormal, far from ceasing, flourished and became a fascination for table-tapping, trances, and the ectoplasmic apparitions of mediums, for ghost stories and a morbid attraction for the trappings of death.

This was also the age of the folklorist who – afraid that the scientific attitude might put an end to the oral tradition and other customs of the Gael – collected and recorded all he could glean for the sake of posterity. Thus second sight was linked with witchcraft, social customs, clan lore and the tales and legends of the race. On the whole folklorists did not claim to believe or disbelieve in the faculty of second sight. They observed, questioned, and recorded, and their contribution to our understanding of the whole subject is invaluable.

5   The Age of Science

HUGH MILLER, GEOLOGIST AND GENIUS

Born in 1802 in the cottage at Cromarty which is now a National Trust museum, Hugh Miller reflected the contrasting characteristics of his parents which were to make him both scientist and poet, stone-mason and seer, churchman and suicide.

His father was a level-headed forty-four-year-old skipper when Hugh was born, descended from a long line of seamen and counting a pirate among his ancestors. Hugh's mother Harriet – a fey eighteen-year-old girl with a talent for story-telling – was the grand-daughter of Donald Roy Ross, a Gaelic-speaking Highlander with second sight and a fanatical religious convert. That Hugh inherited a measure of old Donald's talent for second sight as well as his religion is demonstrated in the following account taken from his autobiography, *My Schools and Schoolmasters*, published in 1854 two years before his untimely death.

My mother was sitting beside the household fire plying the cheerful needle when the house-door, which had been left unfastened, fell open, and I was despatched from her side to shut it. What followed must be regarded as simply the recollection, though a very vivid one, of a boy who had completed his fifth year only a month before.

Day had not wholly disappeared, but it was fast passing on to night, and a grey haze spread a neutral tint of dimness over every more distant object, but left the nearer ones comparatively distinct, when I saw at the open door, within less than a yard from my breast, as plainly as ever I saw anything, a dissevered hand and arm stretched towards me. Hand and arm were apparently those of

115

a female; they bore a livid and sodden appearance; and, directly fronting me, where the body ought to have been, there was only transparant space, through which I could see the forms of the dim objects beyond. I was fearfully startled, and ran shrieking to my mother, telling her what I had seen; and the house-girl, whom she next sent to shut the door, also returned frightened, and said that she too had seen the woman's hand, which, however, did not seem to be the case. And, finally, my mother going to the door saw nothing, though she appeared much impresed by the extremeness of my terror and the minuteness of my description.

Miller suggests that the coincidence of this sighting with the probable time of his father's death by drowning seemed 'at least curious', for his father's ship had left Peterhead that day in a storm and was never heard of again.

As a boy he was playing at the foot of the staircase in his cottage when he was aware of a presence on the landing above him, and when he looked up he saw the figure of a large, tall, very old man dressed in a pale blue greatcoat who was watching him intently. The young Hugh was naturally frightened for he took the ghost to be that of his buccaneering great-grandfather who had been dead for sixty years.

Among Hugh Miller's comprehensive collection of old tales connected with Ross-shire and contained in *Scenes and Legends in the North of Scotland*, he mentions Coinneach Odhar. This important East Ross reference – one of the earliest – places the Brahan Seer firmly in the east and makes no mention of any Lewis connection. The character described by Miller seems to have little in common with Alexander Mackenzie's ill-used, anti-Establishment figure, and this has accounted for the belief that there were at least two Brahan Seers, a point which will be discussed in Chapter 7.

Meanwhile the reference is important enough to quote in full:

Kenneth Ore, a Highlander of Ross-shire, who lived some time in the seventeenth century, when serving as a field labourer with a wealthy clansman who resided somewhere near Brahan Castle, he made himself so formidable to the clansman's wife by his shrewd, sarcastic humour, that she resolved on destroying him by poison.

With this design, she mixed a preparation of noxious herbs with his food when he was one day employed in digging turf in a solitary morass, and brought it to him in a pitcher; she found him

116

lying asleep on one of the those conical fairy hillocks which abound in some parts of the Highlands, and, her courage failing her, instead of awaking him, she set down the pitcher by his side and returned home.

He awoke shortly after, and seeing the food, would have begun his repast, but feeling something press heavily against his heart, he opened his waistcoat and found a beautiful smooth stone, resembling a pearl, but much larger, which had apparently been dropped into his breast while he slept. He gazed at it in admiration, and became conscious as he gazed, that a strange faculty of seeing the future as distinctly as the present, and men's real designs and motives as clearly as their actions, was miraculously imported to him: and it is well for him that he should become so knowing at such a crisis, for the first secret he became acquainted with was that of the treachery practised against him by his mistress.

But he derived little advantage from the faculty ever after, for he led, it is said till extreme old age, an unsettled, unhappy kind of life – wandering from place to place, a prophet only of evil, or of little trifling events, fitted to attract notice when they occurred, merely from the circumstances of their having been foretold.

Hugh Miller goes on to describe some of his prophecies (see the Appendix) and ends by saying: 'The prophet, shortly before his death, is said to have flung the white stone into a lake near Brahan, uttering as his last prediction, that it would be found many years after, when all his prophecies would be fulfilled, by a lame, humpbacked mendicant.'

This whole story, factually untrue no doubt, shines with that other truth that may only be found in myth. Within these few short lines is contained the whole of Highland prophetic history.

First there is the fairy hillock, the burial mound that was the dwelling place of the ancestor gods, the *sithean* or the fairies; then the bestowal of the gift of second sight by the *sithean* on their territory. Interestingly, the gift is given in the form of a stone, the symbol of prophecy in Norse mythology. The gift confers the semi-divine powers not only of seeing the future but also of knowing the heart and minds of men, so that Coinneach seems to become both high-priest and ancestor god, a man greatly to be feared, indeed hated, but indestructible.

117

The Christian influence permits miracle and prophecy, provided the gift is used responsibly. Coinneach is saved by a miracle, but for what? He is no Saint Columba. The sterner doctrines of the post-Columban churches, Catholic and Protestant, cannot let him enjoy his gift: like Lucifer he has climbed too high and in some versions of the story he is actually burned for his pride. Hugh Miller has him leading an 'unsettled, unhappy kind of life till extreme old age', which is far more subtle and, in view of the slender evidence for the story, more likely.

THE 'CLACH'

Alexander Mackenzie was the son of a crofter, born in Gairloch and bred on the old myths and legends that were so much part of Highland life in 1838. He must have been a bright child for in spite of limited schooling and a youth spent as a labourer he was taken on by the Scotch Drapery Trade in England and managed to make his way in the business world. At the age of thirty he returned to Inverness where he opened a drapery shop called Clachnacuddin House, which earned him the nickname of 'Clach'.

This left him time to pursue his passion – research into clan history and Highland lore. Before long he had founded and was contributing extensively to the *Celtic Magazine* and later the *Scottish Highlander*, monthly papers full of items of particular interest of Gaels which ran from 1875 to shortly before his death in 1899. He also published several clan histories including that of the Mackenzies (not always accurate), an account of the Highland Clearances which has recently been re-issued with a foreword by John Prebble, and several collections of old tales including *The Prophecies of the Brahan Seer*, a top seller from its first edition in 1877.

The *Prophecies* began as a series of articles in the *Celtic Magazine* and proved so popular that Mackenzie was persuaded to publish them in book form. He dedicated it to his close friend, the Revd Alexander Macgregor, minister of the West Church in Inverness. Within eight months the first edition was sold out, and a larger volume followed it, containing a lengthy appendix by the Revd A. Macgregor based on his own contributions to the *Celtic Magazine*. In 1899 the two collections were separated, and Aeneas Mackay of

118

Stirling printed two editions, one of Mackenzie's *Prophecies*, with an introduction by Andrew Lang, and the other entitled *Superstitions of the Highlanders* by the Revd Alexander Macgregor. Though both sold well at the time, it was Mackenzie's book that survived. Until the publication of an edition brought out by the Sutherland Press in 1970, there were never less than fifty people on the waiting list at Inverness Library, and the illustrated Constable edition of 1977 has already been reprinted five times.

Why it has proved to be so popular is no mystery. Coinneach Odhar Fiosaiche – Sallow Kenneth the One-who-knows, also known as Kenneth Mackenzie – had featured for many years in the oral tradition of the Gael. Reared on the tales himself, Mackenzie was afraid that they might be forgotten as times and customs changed, so he set about making as comprehensive a collection as possible both of the predictions and of the legends surrounding the seer's life. Assisted by Donald Macintyre, the schoolmaster at Arpafeelie on the Black Isle, and by A. B. Maclennan, author of *The Petty Seer*, he soon had collected sufficient material to fill a volume, and the interest aroused must have been gratifying. It is possible that some of the book's success was due to the title *The Brahan Seer*. This was Mackenzie's own invention and had no Gaelic precedent, nor was there any proof that Coinneach was a Mackenzie. He may have been – Mackenzies dominated Ross-shire in the seventeenth century – but there was no foundation for the assertion.

In fact, many Gaelic scholars and Highland historians of today have been quick to point out that Mackenzie's imagination was altogether too active to produce a balanced account; that in addition to repeating the old stories and prophecies, he actually invented some and certainly ornamented others; that his Gaelic translation was as suspect as his research; and that his whole approach to the subject of second sight was naïve.

Mackenzie, however, was not so credulous as his critics alleged. In his foreword to the *Prophecies* he writes: 'Second sight or *taibhsearchd* claimed for and believed by many to have been possessed by Coinneach Odhar, the Brahan Seer, is one, the belief in which scientific men and others of the present day accept as unmistakeable signs of looming, if not of actual, insanity.'

In his address to the Inverness Gaelic Society of which he was a founder member, in 1875, he was even more explicit: 'I must therefore be careful, in reading a paper on such a dangerous subject, to guard against any suspicions on your part that I believe in what I am about to relate, however unsatisfactory the question may appear to my own mind, or however difficult it may be to explain away what follows.'

On the other hand, he states that many of the prophecies were known in the Highlands for generations before they were fulfilled and that some had only recently come to pass. 'We are all grown so scientific, that the mere idea of anything being possible which is incomprehensible to our cultured scientific intellects cannot be entertained, even although it be admitted that in many cases the greatest men of science, and the mightiest intellects, find it impossible to understand or explain many things as to the existence of which they have no possible doubt.'

In his book he divides Coinneach's prophecies into four categories: those which might be attributed to natural shrewdness, such as that which foretold there would be a road among the hills of Ross-shire from sea to sea, with a bridge over every stream; those not yet fulfilled, which included the prediction that when nine bridges spanned the River Ness 'the Highlands, would be full of ministers without grace, and women without shame'; those that had already come to pass, such as the prophecy that a cow would calve in Fairburn Tower, which was well known to Mackenzie's parents 'and to many others I could mention, years before it actually came to pass'; and finally those whose fulfilment was in doubt. For example, 'the Canonry of Ross would fall when full of dead Mackenzies' might refer to the original ruin of Fortrose Cathedral after the Reformation, or to a future fall of the remaining south aisle which is certainly full of buried Mackenzies to this day.

The most outstanding prophecy, in the author's estimation, refers to the downfall of the Seaforth Mackenzies and much of the book is taken up with a description of the clan and the facts leading up to the end of the Kintail male line. (This is set out in full in Chapter 7.)

Perhaps it is Alexander Mackenzie's shining enthusiasm for his subject that gives his book charm and credibility. There are many in the Highlands today who look on the legends as gospel and believe them to be fact. For all the author's protestations, there can be no doubt that, in spite of lack of historical evidence, he was hooked on his prophet, and his faith is infectious. He confesses to having had 'experiences of our own, which we would hesitate to dignify by the name of second sight', but unfortunately does not disclose them. These experiences no doubt predisposed him to belief in his hero and it was certainly his estimation that Coinneach Odhar was 'beyond comparison the most distinguished of all our Highland seers, and his prophecies known throughout the country for more than two centuries'.

Nowadays Mackenzie would have been supported by the 'scientific' acceptance of psychic phenomena such as second sight, but in his day it was not so easy. In vindication, he falls back on the 'sacred writers – who are now believed by many of the would-be-considered-wise to have been behind the age, and not near as wise and far-seeing as we are' – as being examples of those who believed in the faculty. 'But then,' he adds on a note of irony, 'we shall be told by our scientifc friends that the Bible itself is becoming obsolete, and that it has already served its turn; being only suited for an unenlightened age in which men like Shakespeare, Milton, Newton, Bacon and such unscientific men could be considered distinguished.'

He finds the clergy 'slightly inconsistent' in their beliefs, in that they 'solemnly desire to impress us with the fact that ministering spirits hover about the couches of the dying, but refuse to all the possibility of any mere human being, in any conceivable manner' having the ability to witness them, or 'discovering any sign or premonitions of the early departure of a relative or of an intimate friend'.

That it was Mackenzie's misfortune to be born in such a 'scientific' age is not relevant to his collection of tales, nor is the fact that they were not based on documentary evidence. They shine with that deeper truth illuminated over centuries by the morals and emotions of a courageous breed, moulded by the imagination and words of a poetic people, set against a background of personal and collective hardship. Within the legends of the oral tradition may be clearly seen the true spirit of Highland men, the heartline of Highland history.

And Mackenzie, the crofter's son, knew it.

THE INVERNESS MINISTER

Genial, beloved, and scholarly, the Revd Alexander Macgregor, friend of the 'Clach', succeeded to his father's parish at Kilmuir in Skye before his induction to the West Church, Inverness, in 1852.

There, with a congregation of a thousand, he was only able to continue his writing (which included the translation of the Apocrypha into Gaelic) by rising at 5 a.m. and working till breakfast at his desk. Flora Macdonald, who had been buried at Kilmuir, the Jacobites, and Highland folklore were his particular interests, and he was a regular contributor to Alexander Mackenzie's *Celtic Magazine*. Eventually his collection of folk tales was published as a book under the title of *Highland Superstitions* in 1891, eight years after his death.

His instances of second sight come mainly from Skye. One dating from 1830 records how a septuagenarian minister paid a visit to his ailing brother, Captain Macleod, who lived in Portree with his large family. On the way home a sudden storm forced the old man to spend the night with a Mrs Nicolson at Scorribreck. She was delighted to welcome him to her thatched farmhouse and entertained him well. During the evening she had occasion to go up the attic where the parish mort-cloth was kept, spread out on a table. While she was up there, her family heard her scream and the sound of a fall. Running up the trapstair they found her insensible. When she recovered, she told them she had seen the mort-cloth lit up, and in the centre of it the image of the minister's niece, the daughter of Captain Macleod. Shortly afterwards the girl took ill and died, and her coffin was the first to be covered by the mort-cloth since Mrs Nicolson's vision.

Years later in the district of Kilmuir an old woman seer had a vision of a boat sunk in a storm and many people drowned. Few heeded her moanings until, on the day of the Portree fair, a boat bound for Kilmuir full of people in a hurry to return home was sunk in a sudden squall, and all passengers were lost.

In 1850, in the village of Earlish in the parish of Snizort, a cottar's wife had a baby. As was the custom, mother and child were visited by all the neighbours bringing gifts. One woman whispered that she feared the child would not long be spared and that one day it would be the cause of great grief to its mother: she had seen a vision of the baby torn and mangled in its cradle. A few months later, while the child was asleep, the mother left the croft for a few moments to fetch water from the well. When she returned she found the child exactly as predicted. A large pig had forced its way into the cottage and had partly devoured the infant.

In one of the laird's houses, the young people decided to celebrate the New Year with a dance while their parents were away from home.

During a quadrille, a lady glided along the side of the ballroom wall and was seen by all those near by.

'My mother! It's my mother!' cried one of the girls and fainted with distress. At the exact moment she had been seen, the mother died in a city in the south.

Macgregor records that a local minister in Skye, while on a visit to the miller's wife, found her in her kitchen surrounded by pieces of driftwood picked up on the shore and brought in to dry out. She was in a great state of excitement. The local seer, Christy Macleod, had been sitting on one of the planks warming herself by the fire when suddenly she had fainted and fallen to the floor. At that very moment she was recovering on one of the beds. 'Please go and see her,' begged the miller's wife, 'and get her to tell you what she saw, for I am afraid she had an unlucky sight of one of my children.'

The minister reluctantly agreed. He found Christy recovered but unwilling to speak. Eventually, however, she told him she had seen the broken, bleeding body of a lad called Macdonald who at that moment was alive and well. Six weeks later there was a wedding to which this lad was invited. On his way home, probably hung-over, he fell down a precipice and his body wedged tightly in a crevice. The neighbours wondered how best to bring up his body and one had the idea of bringing a plank from the miller's kitchen. The one chosen was the piece of wood on which Christy had seen the corpse.

Alexander Macgregor also recounts a story of General Stewart of Garth, which he records in his *Sketches of the Highlanders.* On an autumn evening in 1773 when the General was a young man, a neighbour's son called in to see him. Usually a talkative, amusing fellow, he was on this occasion remarkably quiet. After a while he asked if he could see the youngest member of the family, a boy aged three who was upstairs in the nursery. There he found the nurse trying to fit a pair of shoes on the toddler's feet, and complaining they were the wrong size. 'They will fit him before he will have use for them,' said the young man sadly.

The nurse chided him for predicting evil for a healthy child, and the others were none too pleased. At last he told them that he had seen a funeral party with a crowd of people accompanying a small coffin on their way over a bridge to the graveyard. The twenty gentlemen there were all known to him, and the principal mourners were his own father and the father of the three year old child. The following night the boy died suddenly and the funeral took place exactly as seen. 'The gentleman was not a professed seer,' wrote the General. 'This was his first and last vision, and it was sufficient.'

SUPERSTITION – THE LESSER OF TWO EVILS

It is better to believe too much than too little, says the Revd Alexander Stewart FSA(Scot), minister of Ballachulish and Ardgour, in his humorous, kindly volume entitled *Nether Lochaber, the Natural History, Legend and Folklore of the West Highlands* published in 1883.

> We live in an age of intense literary and intellectual activity; the tendency of the highest culture of our time, however, it is complained, being towards materialism and scepticism, the latter either in the form of indifferentism or absolute negation. The great mass of our people, however, stand at the other extreme, for whilst it is complained that those of the highest culture believe too little, or don't believe at all, the common people, it is averred, believe too much . . .
>
> A man with any form of creed, even if it be false, may be led in time to believe aright, whereas the case of the utterly creedless man is well-nigh hopeless.

The Highlander, he believes, would not be 'so religious and devout if it were not for the substratum of superstition that underlies their better-founded beliefs and religious aspirations', in spite of a 'multiplication of ministers, churches, schoolmasters and school boards . . . Those who believe in it implicitly are by no means the worst people.'

The example he quotes, though not second sight in the narrow sense, had by then come to be classed in the same category. He recounts it in the form of a conversation overheard at a local gathering.

> Mrs B: I suppose you have all heard of the death of X.L., poor fellow. It was reported that he was better yesterday, but I knew last night that I should hear of death some time today, and knowing of no one else at present unwell, I decided that it must be X.L.'s death that was foretold me.

Mrs C: Foretold you! How?

Mrs B: Why, thus: long after dark last night, as I was busy getting the children's supper, the cock, that had gone to roost as usual, suddenly stood up on his perch, and crowed a long and loud crow that startled us all; and I made Katie say the Lord's Prayer, for I knew that a cock crowing at an hour so untimeous meant a death in our neighbourhood and nothing else. On inquiry, I find that X.L. died just about that time.

Mrs D: I knew it too, that there was to be such a death in our neighbourhood. My nose itched so much all last evening and the itching was on the left nostril side, and I was certain that it was to be the death of a male that I should hear of. I had not, however, heard that X.L. was poorly.

Mrs F: While at breakfast this morning, I could hardly eat anything, so loud and persistent was the ringing in my ears. It was just like the tolling of the church bell.

Far from laughing at the women, who were all highly respected members of the parish with some education, and while admitting that it 'was rank superstition and sheer nonsense', the minister reckoned that the beliefs had value in that the conversation led to 'much moralizing' and that it was 'perhaps more effectual than would be the most carefully composed sermon'.

'To sneer at such beliefs and pooh-pooh them superciliously,' says the minister, 'is too easy. A true philosopher will admit like Hamlet that "there are more things in heaven and earth than are dreamed of in our philosophy".'

THE FAIRY-TALE COLLECTOR

Andrew Lang, energetic collector of folklore and legend from all over the world, has delighted a host of children from the days of Victoria right up to the new Elizabethan age with his twelve volumes of coloured books of fairy-tales which started with the blue in 1889, and ended with the violet in 1910. He was also a Greek scholar famed for his translation of Homer, and a pioneer of research into world-wide myths and religion.

He believed that 'second sight is only a Scotch name which covers many cases called telepathy and clairvoyance by psychical students, and casual or morbid hallucinations by other people' and that 'either it is very common, or people who choose to claim the possession of it are very common'.

In his foreword to the 1899 edition of Alexander Mackenzie's *Prophecies of the Brahan Seer* he goes so far as to admit that 'unlike Mr Mackenzie, I can unblushingly confess the belief that there probably are occasional instances of second sight, that is, of premonitions', and he backs his belief by quoting Hegel 'who was not ashamed to include second sight in his vast philosophic system' (*Philosophie der Geistes*, 1845).

Although Lang believed, tentatively at least, in the existence of second sight, he had no theories as to how it occurred, but, he argues, 'if there is a psychical element in man, if there is something more than a mechanical result of physical processes in nerve, brain and blood, then we cannot set any limit of the range of knowledge supernormally acquired.' Rather than listen to 'rumours of the Brahan Seer' he preferred examples of modern instances which could be corroborated at first hand, and he quotes a couple of what he believed to be authentic cases.

One of these was told him by a Royal Academician and a close friend. He and a lady also known to Lang were being shown over a beautiful new house by its owner when the Academician, while in the owner's bedroom, turned pale and silent. When they were alone, his lady friend asked him what was wrong. 'I saw X, the owner of the house, lying dead in his bed,' he replied unhappily. The owner died within the month.

Lang's other case concerned a lady, also well known to him, who while calling on a friend had seen a vision of a man – previously unknown to her – who thrust a knife into her friend's left side. Lang offered to bet £100 against the fulfilment of the vision, but some months later the lady, again visiting her friend, saw the man of her vision on the doorstep. Inside, she found her friend close to death after an operation on her left side performed by the man of the vision, who was a surgeon.

Both these stories, says Lang, were in the Celtic tradition, though only one of the seers was a Highlander.

Lang likens Coinneach Odhar to a crystal-gazer rather than a traditional seer because of his use of a 'gibber' – the Australian word for a divining stone. The use of stones 'usually crystals, or black stones, I have found among Australians, Tonkaways, Aztecs, Incas, Samoyeds, Polynesians, Maoris, Greeks, Egyptians, in Fez,' and he refers readers to his own book on the subject, *Making of Religion*, which expands this theory. Highland visions, he writes, were usually spontaneous and uninvoked, except where the seer used the blade bone of a sheep. If there were more examples of divination by the use of a stone in the Highlands, then they should be recorded.

He wished that predictions of 'second-sighted men' who were to his personal knowledge very prevalent in Sutherland, Lochaber and Glencoe, should be taken down before their fulfilment. 'Unless this is done, the predictions, as matter of evidence, go for nothing.' It was also essential to discover the percentage of failures before pronouncing on the successes, which might be due to chance, coincidence, mis-statement or downright lying.

'In fact,' he ends his foreword, 'like Dr Johnson, I want more evidence. He was ready to believe, but unconvinced. I am rather more credulous, but it would be very easy to upset my faith, and certainly it cannot be buttressed by vague reports on the authority of tradition. It may be urged that to inquire seriously into such things is to encourage superstition. But if inquiry merely unearthed failure and imposture, even superstition would be discouraged.'

Highlanders like the Revd Dugald MacEchern of Caithness found Lang's approach too flippant to be taken seriously. His book on the subject, *Cock-Lane and Common Sense*, while valuable as a collection of interesting facts, offended those who regarded second sight more respectfully. His theory that our ancestors were subject to 'mental confusion' and could not distinguish between waking and dreaming certainly seems thin; his thesis that hard conditions of life favoured hallucination and that primitive people practised some sort of hypnotism might be tenable if it were not for the prophetic element in second sight. To account for the fulfilment of a prediction, Lang fell back on that overworked and too convenient theory, coincidence.

Lang also offended by giving the impression that he thought that since second sight was practised in other countries, it was therefore of less value and interest than if it were peculiar to the Highlands alone. 'Because crystal-gazing has been practised in all ages and in every part of the world, and because other practices and beliefs are co-extensive with the human race, therefore Lang concludes that there is nothing in them,' writes MacEchern. 'Is it not more likely that experiences that are common to all nations, ages and climes, have something in them? Spiritual instincts deep-seated in the human race, and supported by occurrences that are reported, not only by the Bible writers, but by the records of all nations, are not to be lightly scoffed at or dismissed as delusions.'

FATHER McDONALD AND THE CHARMING MISS X

For most of the year the dunes and peat hags of South Uist are moody with rain and sour under lashing winds; then, by a blink of the sun, they are changed into paradise. This was Father Allan McDonald's first parish, where he arrived in 1884, a dedicated young priest, cultured and full of zeal for his 2,000 parishioners who mostly spoke only Gaelic.

Brought up in Fort William, educated at Blairs and at the Scots College in Spain, he studied and improved his knowledge of his parishioners' language to such an extent that he was able to write fine Gaelic poetry, make a collection of Gaelic hymns, and compile a dictionary of local Gaelic words. His most valuable contribution to literature was undoubtedly his comprehensive collection of folklore, local history and tales in the oral tradition, including many instances of second sight. His ministry lasted nineteen years until his untimely death at the age of forty-six, and he is still remembered with affection and admiration in the islands of South Uist and Eriskay.

His examples of second sight cover every aspect of the faculty, from symbolic vision, divination, omens and death-lights to spectres, voices, and phantom funerals. A typical example from his first notebook describes how Margaret Macdonald of Dalibrog in South Uist, a servant at the inn, while carrying an armful of peats from the stack met a man at the door whom she had never seen before.

'Are they in?' he asked.

She told him to come inside, but he did not appear there. The household laughed at her at the time, but later she met and recognized a stranger who had just come off the ship on a visit from America. She knew him by his clothes and, in particular, a gold watch guard.

An instance of the double or *alter ego* is vividly described in the

128

story of the man who woke up in bright moonlight to see outside his window the apparition of a woman he knew. Alarmed, he consulted a local wise man who warned him to speak severely to the woman herself, or he would be in trouble. When he did so, she admitted that she had been thinking of him at the time.

Father McDonald also collected the prophecies of a seer called Angus MacInnes who prophesied: 'The beginning of the troubles was to see a white raven. The next sign was to see a white crow.' Aonghus Og of Arivullain saw the raven and killed it. He was drowned in Loch Eynort not long after, and his family line came to an end. Angus MacInnes himself saw the white crow at a place called Kilbride, which soon after was lost to the family who had it.

Two prophecies were related to the Highland Clearances. 'The living will envy the dead': this foresaw the day when those evicted from their homes would sooner be in their graves than alive in another country. 'The son of the slender black wife will place a foot on each side of the Rogha Glas': when the small tenant crofters were evicted, the land at Rogha Glas was made into one farm.

The old MacNeils of Barra had a *fiosaiche* called Mac a'Chreachainn who prophesied: 'Barra will yet be under rats and grey geese'. The prediction came true when the township of Eoligarry was cleared for sheep, and became well known for its rats. Later, after the First World War, it became a village again.

It is thought that Father McDonald himself was a seer, in that he experienced several visions one of which he confided to Amy Murray a month before his death. In her book, *Father Allan's Island* published in New York in 1920, she writes: 'Father Allan had *seen* but once, he said, and that nothing more than the corpse-candle (a sight nowise out-of-the-way) and in another island. Looking down from a hillside at night, he saw it move across the plain, then down a glen, to a house where he knew a man was dying: walking homewards, he met a messenger to say the man was dead.'

Amy Murray also recalls how one night at Dalibrog, while sharing his room with a fellow-priest named Canon Chisholm of Barra, himself also a seer, Father Allan woke to hear the low murmur of voices outside the house. Father Chisholm also heard it and suggested it might be the wind. 'You know it is not the wind,' said Father Allan, but outside there was nothing to be seen. Next day, Father Allan was in the same room when he heard the same murmuring voices outside.

A drowned man from his congregation was being carried into the chapel.

In his diary, Father Allan recorded several strange incidents. Once, while reading his office at night, he heard what sounded like a woman's voice calling outside. When he looked, there was no one to be seen in the moonlight. A servant who had also heard the voice thought it had said, 'Come here.' She was convinced it had been a *manadh*, or ghostly warning.

On a fine calm evening in August 1897 he heard what sounded like a crowd of schoolchildren cheering across the Sound of Eriskay. After listening to about six calls, he fetched his housekeeper and they both heard it four or five times more. Each 'hurray' was punctuated by a pause as if someone were calling for the cheer. He was sure it was the children of Garrynamonie school enjoying a Jubilee picnic. Very shortly afterwards came the news of the death of a fellow-priest and close personal friend. Though he could find no logical reason to connect the two events, yet he felt sure they were linked, especially when the headmistress later assured him that there had been no picnic that day.

In March 1898, again in Eriskay, he looked out of his window at midnight and saw a little red candle-sized flame about as high as a window by the near end of the church. It stayed for some three minutes, then went out, and reappeared elsewhere. It was not dark enough for a torch, nor could he believe that anyone would be about at that hour, so he called his housekeeper to have a look. 'It's only a *manadh*,' she said. 'It's a long time since people first saw that light at the church.'

These stories, together with a comprehensive collection of Father Allan's folklore, may be read in *Strange Things* by John L. Campbell and Trevor H. Hall, which also includes the sad account of Father Allan's association with the Society for Psychical Research and their investigator, the charming Miss X. In August 1894, the *Oban Times* reported that several members of the SPR were in the Highlands and Islands collecting information on second sight and other similar subjects. The columnist wrote: 'It is reported that the tour has been inaugurated at the instance of the Marquess of Bute, who is one of the vice-presidents of the Society.' Among the party was the 'lady editor of Borderland'. This lady editor was Ada Goodrich Freer, alias Miss X.

The SPR had been founded in 1882 'for the purpose of making an organized and systematic attempt to investigate various sorts of debatable phenomena which are *prima facie* inexplicable on any generally recognized hypothesis.' In 1889, John, third Marquess of Bute, a wealthy Catholic convert with wide interests, became a member of the Society, and the following year was made a vice-president. When it was proposed that an inquiry be made into Highland second sight, Lord Bute responded with a donation of £150 and a promise of help.

A circular letter and schedule of questions was printed, and 2,000 copies went out to the clergy, doctors, schoolmasters and other professional people including the landed gentry of the Highlands. The results were disappointing. Only fifty-four forms were returned, and twenty-eight of these were negative, so the following year the questionnaire went out again, this time accompanied by a personal letter from Lord Bute. Out of the 157 answers, only 42 were positive. Obviously the approach was wrong. Someone was needed to investigate in the field and to interview those who had replied to the schedule. Ada Goodrich Freer was chosen.

Described as a bright, sprightly, energetic lady of thirty-seven, she was able to charm Lord Bute and convince him of her suitability. Not only Lord Bute: many others were captivated by her charm. F. W. H. Myers, a leading member of the SPR wrote: 'I saw Miss X the other day; extremely interested in the Hebrides investigation, which she hoped to make more and more thorough. I think you have got the right woman and in the right place!'

It was not Miss Freer, however, who first discovered Father Allan's collection of folklore, but the Revd Peter Dewer, a Gaelic-speaking minister of North Bute who was secretary of the SPR's inquiry. In a letter to Lord Bute, he praised the help given by the young priest and as a result was able to come to several conclusions about the attitude of seers to their faculty. He established that seers believed it was dangerous for them to communicate with their visions. Rather than do so they would walk accompanied by some apparition for many miles in complete silence. He also established that they looked on crystal-balls and hypnotism as 'black arts'; that they had never heard of spiritualism or automatic writing; that they invoked the three persons of the Trinity to test their visions.

Meanwhile, Miss Freer and a friend, with an Ordnance Survey map, set out to tackle the seers. In order to gain their confidence she claimed to be clairvoyant herself, which she believed 'had a good effect on the evidence'. Certainly her reports impressed the SPR. She reached South Uist in the autumn of 1895 and immediately suggested to Lord Bute that he acquire Father Allan McDonald's collection outright, but the priest had plans of his own and proposed writing a book himself. Lord Bute was not pleased, and sent an ultimatum to Father Allan by way of his bishop: either to sell his material outright for about £100, or collaborate with Miss Freer in editing such of his material as was suitable, for a sum of £50.

By now Ada Goodrich Freer realized that it would not be to her advantage to buy the manuscripts outright, preferring that Father Allan should continue to collect material that might be of use to her. The offer of collaboration was made, but Miss Freer took it upon herself to cut Lord Bute's suggested offer of £50 as a fee to £10. Father Allan, charmed by her personality, sent her all his manuscripts and promised to continue his research. He started on these immediately, under the title of *Strange Things*. Fortunately the SPR inquiry petered out before he had finished.

Meanwhile his main collection of folklore passed into her hands, two notebooks of which were never to be seen again. A cheque for £10 was duly forwarded to the priest. In her letter of thanks of Lord Bute's secretary, Miss Freer wrote condescendingly, 'I have allowed Mr Macdonald to continue his researches.' It was this arrogance, this patronizing attitude, that was to make her so thoroughly disliked and disapproved of in the Islands. Yet Father Allan admired her almost to the end. 'My acquaintance with her has been an education of mind and soul, and has thrown sunshine over the last two years of my life.' It was not until he saw her work in print that he realized that she was an extensive copyist and a flagrant plagiarist of his works. Amy Murray records: 'He had been little pleased with the working up one pair of hands, at least, had given them.'

Certainly in her subsequent lectures, papers and books on folklore, there are occasionally acknowledgements of his help, but only as befited someone who had introduced her to her sources or who had accompanied her on her interviews. Such ill-usage of a gentle priest's beloved life-work is not easily forgiven in the Highlands.

The failure of the SPR's inquiry into second sight was mainly owing to their choice of investigator. Ada Freer made no effort to study the work of previous folklorists or the literature that already existed on the subject of second sight. She had no knowledge of Gaelic or of the Highlander's way of life. She made no attempt to analyse her findings. Her subsequent ghost-hunt at Ballechin House brought her into disrepute with the SPR.

Perhaps she is best described by the name given her in Eriskay and South Uist, '*Cailleach Bheag nam Bocan*'. John L. Campbell translates this as 'the little middle-aged lady who is preoccupied with ghosts'. Somehow that description puts her neatly in her place.

A GUIDE-BOOK TO THE GIFT

One of the first books to deal exclusively with the subject, *Highland Second-Sight*, was compiled by Norman Macrae, editor of the *Northern Weekly*, and was published by George Soutar of Dingwall in 1908. Macrae's contribution consists of an uncritical, straightforward account of the work of previous investigators and a short collection of contemporary instances. For comment and explanation he calls upon the scholarship of the Revd William Morrison MA FSA(Scot), one of the Morrisons of Cross in Lewis, who was minister of the United Free Church of Duthil.

Macrae reckoned that second sight had changed over the years. Now it had 'no other future event than death to disclose'. Crystal-gazing, tea-cup reading, tingling ears and itchy palms may prognosticate other events, but 'these things are not to be confounded with the second sight . . . it is always some phantom that the second-sighters see, and the phantoms betoken but the one sad event'.

As examples he cites two cases from the parish of Avoch in the Black Isle, contributed by A. B. Maclennan who learned them more or less first-hand. One refers to a farmer known to Maclennan who could tell in advance the death of an acquaintance. 'He knew this by the fact that he saw the phantom funeral processions pass along the road at the east side of his farm to the graveyard so distinctly that he could easily recognize, and often told the names of, the persons forming them.' The other instance refers to an uncle of Maclennan called Kenneth Bain, a saintly elder in the Independent Chapel at Avoch who saw his son approaching his door on horseback. As soon as he greeted him, both horse and rider vanished. 'Och, och, wae's me!' mourned the old man, 'it is my son's spectre that I have seen.'

Exactly a week later his son arrived in the flesh, wearing the same clothes and riding the same horse. He was unwell at the time and died soon afterwards.

An old lady 'living in Dingwall till recently', says Macrae, frequently saw the ghosts of those about to die. Once she saw a particular person known at the time to be in America. Some weeks later, news was received of his death which had occurred at the same time as the vision. The poor woman had few friends bold enough to call on her, for invariably she would have some sad message to give.

Another seer in Newtonmore disliked his ability to see phantom funerals so much that he preferred to keep quiet about the visions. On one occasion he met a spectral burial party near a bridge. The ghostly horse shied and lashed out at him with his hoof. The poor man was in agony for the rest of the day and the night. Next morning he had recovered and happened to be crossing the same bridge when the actual funeral passed by. The same horse reared and kicked him in the same place. It was no more painful than the phantom bruise but this time there was a mark to show for it.

'Occasionally,' says Macrae, 'the second sight takes the form of direct divination, not exactly the foretelling of future events as in the case of the prophecies of the Brahan Seer but in the discovery of things secret or obscure such as revealing the exact spot where anything that is lost may be found . . . the incredulous may smile, and they may be pardoned for doing so in the absence of any satisfactory explanation of the "gift", but that the "gift" exists is proved again and again by well accredited instances.'

His two examples first appeared in *The Rowan Tree Annual* for 1907/8 which was published in Perth. They concerned a Mrs Rachel Cameron, born a MacGregor of Ardlaroch in 1815, a crofter's wife from Rannoch, whose second sight had descended from one generation to another by way of red-haired daughters. Mrs Cameron's daughter, also a red-headed Rachel, inherited the gift from her mother and had the same ability to find those who were lost. The ninth Duke of Argyll recorded in 1896 that old Mrs Cameron had told a grieving mother exactly where and how she would find the body of her drowned son. Her daughter's powers were equally convincing. When on a wet and stormy day in Aberfeldy a farmer disappeared on his way home from market, his family wrote to her. She had never been to Aberfeldy, and knew nothing of the district or the people who had come to her for help.

134

After prayer, she had a waking dream. 'A sort of mist rose up,' she explained, 'then cleared, and like a picture I saw a dead man lying in a reclining position, kept down by some tree roots at the bottom of a pool at the side of a river, below a queer bridge. I did not know the place.' However, she sent for one of the farmer's relatives who drew a sketch of the famous Wade Bridge at Aberfeldy.

'That's the place,' she said, 'and the hole below it is at the side.'

The relative protested that they had dragged the river and searched the same spot again and again. 'Nevertheless,' said Rachel, 'the body is there.' And so it proved to be.

On another occasion, in 1900, Mrs Cameron was asked to help find a groom who originally came from Rannoch but who had disappeared in England while in service to his master. She 'saw' that the young man had been murdered and his body buried under stones in a quarry near the stables. She also 'saw' that his murderers had removed the body from the quarry and thrown it into a lake. The police not only found the place where the body had lain in the quarry, but on dragging the lake they also recovered the corpse.

Local opinion regarding the powers of the Camerons was that faith had much to do with second sight. Here were good Christian women, healthy in mind and body, asking God, who had bestowed the gift upon them for his own wise reasons, to sanctify it and make it a blessing and comfort to others, and their prayers were answered.

Macrae intended his book to 'prove as helpful to the serious student as, it is believed, it will be welcome to the general reader – not in the light of the superstitious or merely curious, but as a subject of particular interest in view of present-day research into matters psychological'. To deal with the deeper aspects of the faculty, he called upon the Revd William Morrison. Morrison a minister of the Free Kirk was very decided in his opinions. He ascribes the origins of second sight – as did past researchers – to belief in the *sithean* 'generally called *Fiosaichin*, those that know'. Strictly speaking, he says, second sight is not the ability to see ghosts of the dead, though many who have the faculty claim that ability also. Second sight may also exist independent of any vision at all: the seer may foretell 'spontaneously and as if from certain knowledge' an event about to happen. Though second sight may surprise the educated and stretch their credulity to the limit, there is no doubt in the minds of most Highlanders that it exists, and in almost every rural community in the

135

north there are one or more persons who claim to be seers with the power to predict what may be about to happen, either in their own neighbourhood or elsewhere.

Morrison maintained that second sight was not so prevalent as once it was, the reason being that people were no longer obliged to live solitary lives dominated by loneliness, distance and wilderness. The scenery may have been one reason for its prevalence; racial composition was certainly another. The Norse influence, says the minister, which is absent in the Irish and the French temperaments, accounts for coolness in crisis and also 'feelings of intense enjoyment, yea, to peals of almost super human laughter, in the acme of their conflict with men and waves'.

When it comes to the psychology of second sight, Morrison is not flattering to his fellow Highlanders. 'It is a matter of ordinary observation that there is an analogy between the different states of mental growth in the individual and in those of a community of even age . . . It is the simple truth to say that in the Highlands of Scotland today many are in a state of pupilarity as regards their mental attitude to this question of the second sight.' We should not be surprised, then, that 'men of the standing of George Sinclair, Professor of Mathematics in Glasgow from 1654 to 1696 – in spite of his knowledge of exact sciences – should be unable to rise above the gross delusions of his age.'

Though superstition may be denounced superficially, Morrison says, deep down the old beliefs still linger. He tells an ironic story of a fellow minister who continually denounced from the pulpit the superstitious notions of his flock. As a result he was attacked by some who caused a tree to fall across the road, narrowly missing himself and his servant. Next Sunday the congregation was startled not just to learn about the attack, but to hear the minister declare that 'he had it given to him' to predict that the three men responsible would none of them leave this world until all had been punished. One would die suddenly, another would die 'where he'd have the burial of an ass', and the third was to become a pauper before he died. 'Rumour had it, to my knowledge, that the prediction was literally fulfilled,' wrote Mr Morrison.

On the whole he believed that second sight was a matter of self-deceit. Simple people were 'tricked by their own excited feelings into giving reality to delusions of their senses of sight and sound'. Many predictions were 'discovered' after the event. Knowledge of the past was the only platform from which we could conjecture the future: no wonder, then, that there had been no visions of 'railways, steamships, electric telegraphs, and the thousand and one feats of science'.

Waking dreams and reveries, he tells us, are common enough. When these are combined with a high degree of probability of an event, either feared or desired, and where the event justifies the expectation, then there is a tendency to account for the vision as a supernatural event rather than due to natural causes. It is, he claims, the same in the moral world – the 'still small voice' within us, those moral judgements 'flashed upon the inner eye' we call conscience. When rapid judgements as to probable events are thrown up on the 'screen of the external world', we call it second sight. Perhaps this vision – if it is later realized – should be termed 'first' rather than 'second' sight of the event.

To back his argument, Morrison examines Bacon's essay on *Prophecies*. Excluding divine prophecy, and looking only at those 'that have been of certain memory and hidden causes', his conclusion was that 'they ought all to be despised and ought to serve but for winter talk by the fireside'. As guides to future behaviour they are worse than useless, for if the 'gift of foreseeing future events in our lives were universal, there would be no place for freedom of the will to adapt means to ends'. God alone can avert the inevitable.

Bacon isolates three factors that have given prophecies 'grace and some credit'. Firstly, men notice only what they hit and never mark what they miss. Secondly, conjectures and obscure traditions sometimes turn themselves into prophecies, and thirdly, 'almost all seers, being infinite in number, have been imposters, and by idle and crafty brains merely contrived and feigned after the event passed.' Morrison refutes this third factor, though he accepts that hallucination, hypnotism and auto-suggestion may play a large part in some instances. He prefers the second factor, that 'probable conjectures, aided by the subtle and rapid action of one's judgement, raised by the imagination to the height of certainty, turn into firm conjectures that such and such an event will take place.'

Morrison goes on to point out that there is no limit to the imagination of emotional men where vision is concerned. Most know the story of the orator who so impressed a group of fishermen with his description of a storm that he was interrupted by a cry from the audience, 'Man the life-boat!' So vivid was his word-portrayal that one of his listeners actually saw the sinking ship.

From Bacon, Morrison moves on to Kant who examined the question of vision in his *Dreams of a Visionary Explained by Dreams of Metaphysics*. In answer to the question, 'What is spirit, how is its presence detected, how is it related to matter, and why does spirit and body constitute a unity?' he came to the conclusion that such questions are beyond our intelligence. The soul has relations with two worlds, the inner one of the mind and the outer of matter. But 'departed souls and pure spirits, though they can never produce an impression upon our outward senses, or stand in any community with matter, can still act upon the soul of man, which, like them, belongs to a great spirit commonwealth.' Kant comes to no conclusion about the alleged intercourse between spirits and men. 'I reserve my scepticism about each story separately while allowing them some credibility as a whole.'

Kant and Bacon, according to Morrison, were of a like mind in that they believed that prophecies of second sight were not altogether illusions, though their accompanying of vision were. Predictions were conjectures which if they came true were remembered, and if not, were forgotten. 'This analysis of second sight is suggested by all the observed facts of this peculiar mental phenomenon,' Morrison concludes.

To other Highlanders, Morrison's views were not only controversial, they were insulting. He seemed to believe that seers were subject to gross delusions, that their predictions came from memory and 'the experiences of the past rapidly balancing probabilities'. Although he stated that his analysis was based on observed fact, this was not borne out by example. The 'balancing of probabilities' says Morrison 'may lead a seer to predict a funeral of an old and ailing person, but not to the foresight of a highly improbable accident. Take the well-known story of the seer who saw a corpse with an arrow in its thigh. The probability is that the dead man was shot. Yet he died of other causes and the arrow pierced him on the bier. How could *probability* account for the dream of a minister that his upper lip was swollen to an enormous extent, and the fact that he was stung next day and his lip affected in the manner of his dream?'

He says that visions of 'the thousand and one feats of science' are never witnessed, but this is not true. Coinneach Odhar and others witnessed the railway and described trains as 'chariots without horses' for lack of the correct terminology. Coinneach also predicted that 'fire and water' would run side by side through the streets of Inverness, long before the coming of piped water and electricity.

Although Morrison's theories do not always match up to the experience or evidence for second sight, he was one of the first to attempt a serious psychological analysis. His essay heralds the slow dawn of a new attitude towards the paranormal.

TELEPATHY AND SECOND SIGHT

On 6 February 1919, the Revd Dugald MacEchern, Minister of Bower in Caithness, and Bard to the Gaelic Society of Inverness, presented a marvellous open-minded paper to that society in which he suggested that second sight was particularly relevant to the immediate post-war era. 'War and death have broken and crushed the flower of Europe. Men, therefore, with renewed interest ask, "Does the spirit survive? Is the spirit different from the body and independent of it, even as music is something distinct from the violin, the instrument of its manifestation?" The subject of second sight here obviously has a value. It contributes to an answer to the supreme questions which religion and philosophy try to answer.'

Forty years ago, says MacEchern, such a statement would have been unthinkable. 'Nothing was to be believed that could not be accounted for by a material philosophy.' The age of reason was itself a reaction against the excessive superstition of earlier centuries. Once again, opinion had changed. Today physicists and scientists held more open views and were more prepared to 'explore life's magic and mystery'.

Nowhere was magic and mystery more prevalent than in the Celtic race. 'To the Celt, the ideal is the only reality and outward things are but the vesture and shadow of unseen realities that surround us . . . the Celt has never allowed the claim of the so-called logical faculty to be the sole avenue of knowledge.' Nor were Highland Celts the only believers in second sight. A certain Eugenie Le Port who lived near the standing stones of Carnac in Brittany was acclaimed as a seer of ghosts, fairies and spirits. The natives of that region were convinced that the spirits of the dead lived among the stones, and most of their other beliefs were paralleled by those held in the Highlands.

MacEchern was adamant that we should not consider second sight to be a violation of natural laws. If it existed it must be part of life, of which things material may only be a small particle of the greater whole. Miracles happen not according to a known law but as part of the general order of the universe. Although that law is as yet unknown, it is part of a higher force and subject to a higher code. Thus the appearance of a spirit would be 'the result of some beautiful law and force in a higher order – perhaps not a physical order, but of a sphere which yet impinges on and affects the physical sphere'. Physicists such as Alfred Russell Wallace and Sir William Crookes both took the view that spirit phenomena were part of the general order of the Universe of Being. Such laws and forces were capable of neutralizing those of the physical world. Anyone, the minister continues, who admitted that the world was created by God must believe in miracles, for creation is itself the neutralizing of a lower law by the superimposition of a higher.

In discussing the five senses, Mr MacEchern reminds us how limited they are. We can only hear sounds within the range of eleven octaves. Our perception of light is similarly limited. Five senses confine us to recognition of five sets of phenomena: there may be 5,000 others which we cannot perceive. The physical world may only be one of many.

The universe, says MacEchern, has a permanent character independent of the human mind, since it was conceived by an eternal mind. This eternal mind imposes ideas upon the individual human mind, for the eternal mind is God who spoke and the world stood fast. The world is the word of God; in other words, the expression of God's thought. Thus the world is the eternal idea expressed. What it is in itself we cannot say, for it may not correspond to our idea of it. All we know of the physical world is what we think of it in our minds, but we can never get outside it, so to speak, to see it whole. We know it only by ideas.

With regard to the unseen, MacEchern insists that materialists may scoff and attempt to identify the brain as its instrument, but materialism may be contradicted on three counts. Firstly, by identity: though we are not the same bodies as we were ten years ago, yet we are the same persons. Secondly, by the fact that we are moral creatures with free will to shape our destinies, which could not happen if our thoughts and wills were determined by the effect of matter on our minds. Thirdly, because matter could not produce sensation and sensation could not produce thought unless there was first a person who could feel.

To the question. 'Why should some people have second sight, and not all?' the minister replies that perhaps all men do have it, but in varying degrees. Or perhaps all may once have had it, but some have lost it through contact with modern life which is overly concerned with material needs and pleasures. On the other hand, perhaps we are only just beginning to develop the faculty and some have forged ahead where conditions are favourable. We may all yet develop it.

'Is telepathy or thought-transference from one human mind to another at a distance, an adequate explanation of second sight?' Mr MacEchern asks, and suggests that there are many cases of second sight which could be thus explained (where the seer has a vision of an event distant in space but which is happening simultaneously) and many that could not.

With regard to the former, he tells the tale of two Highland clerics called Cunnison, father and son, who were ministers of Kintyre and Mull. One night the son in Mull was visited by a neighbour who was being followed by a large and rabid greyhound. After the household had retired to bed, the dog killed the family cat and attacked one of the servants. The minister hurried to her rescue and was also bitten, as was his wife and her young sister. The dog then savaged several people in a nearby cottage, and all who were bitten died eventually in appalling agony, except for Mr Cunnison junior who, knowing what lay ahead for him, caused himself to bleed to death. Meanwhile his father, the minister in Kintyre, had a vision of the terrible scene while it was happening, and told his wife and family what he had witnessed.

There was nothing prophetic about that vision, says Mr Mac-Echern. The sighting and the tragedy were contemporaneous and might well have been telepathic. His own mother – a descendant of the famous Rannoch seer, Rachel Cameron, whom we read about in *Highland Second-Sight* by Norman Macrae – once dreamed that her son was in great danger and awoke in time to save his life. While in Perthshire, she dreamed that her eldest son who was in America had written home to tell her he was earning twelve shillings a week. A fortnight later she received a letter from him which told her he was earning twelve dollars. So struck was she by the coincidence that she wrote back to ask him when he had written to her. The time was identical to the time of her dream.

'Human Radiation', says MacEchern, 'is one theory of telepathy when the brain constantly radiates by means of vibrations – like those of light and electricity. Thought thus radiates in all directions.' Those minds capable of receiving such radiations would be in tune with the sender, just as the minister's harp, piano and cello were all tuned to each other. In moments of great stress, such as the sinking of the *Titanic*, the mind would be capable of greatly increased radiation, so that friends at a great distance could be affected. Distance would be no object to radiation: all that mattered would be that transmitter and receiver should be in tune.

'Can mind move articles at a distance? asks Mr MacEchern. If so, perhaps Human Radiation might account for that also. Mind or thought can certainly move muscles for the distance of a few feet, so why not objects further apart? In his family, events like births or deaths were often heralded by the mysterious ringing of bells, and in Coll, where he was once parish minister, he saw in the schoolhouse the portrait of Sir Hector Macdonald – 'Fighting Mac' – fall from the wall on the day he died in Paris.

But Human Radiation could not account for precognition and prophecy; nor could telepathy, unless it came from some higher spirit. With regard to prophecy there were two views, that of the Pantheist and that of the Theist. The former saw the human soul as part of the universal soul which is a mirror in which past and present events are seen at the same time. Theists, like the minister himself, believed that the Divine Spirit or other holy spirits were able to reveal the future, and that all second sight that predicted the future could be thus explained. 'To the Hebrew seer, cradled on the Nile, it was given to behold the burning bush. To the Celt cradled beside the Atlantic wave and nursed on breasts of the mountains, it is given to apprehend that ever-living world that penetrates the world of matter.'

Of the many examples MacEchern quotes in his paper, one tells how Mrs Faed, wife of the artist, recalled that she and her husband, enveloped in mist while climbing in the Highlands, suddenly saw a figure dressed like a Highland chief standing before them on the path and warning them not to advance another step. The vision then vanished. When the mist cleared they found themselves on the edge of a precipice. Mrs Faed was convinced that the spectre had saved their lives, and told her London acquaintance that it had been the most striking experience of her life.

Although in his parish of Bower in Caithness there were few examples of second sight, he records one incident of a seer called Ewan Mcleod, a farm labourer who was always seeing strange sights. He could predict a funeral a week before hand, see a coffin delivered to a house where no one was ill, look into the fire and see weird apparitions. One was of a boat labouring in a heavy sea, whose crew were all known to him save one who had his back turned. He described in detail the loss of the boat and the struggle of the drowning men. Strangely enough, Ewan was later lost at sea in the same manner: the person whose back was turned and whom he could never recognize had evidently been himself.

While minister of Coll, MacEchern had a strange experience of his own. At a children's party in the castle he was leaning against the piano when a candle set fire to the sleeve of his jacket. Next day he stopped at Glasgow, en route for Kent, and he bought a ready-made jacket for the journey as the other had been ruined. He could get nothing to fit him except an indigo-blue suit. While in the train he wore his royal-blue university cricket cap. On arrival in Rochester his host's daughter immediately exclaimed, 'Oh! Last night I dreamed that you came dressed in blue.'

'Now,' records Mr MacEchern, 'I had never worn a blue suit in my life since a child in a sailor's suit, grey being my favourite colour and black the colour of ministerial dress. It was the accident of the burning – an accident improbable and wholly unforeseen – that led me to buy a suit otherwise not required and of a colour not desired. In ten thousand days I had only worn a blue suit once, and it was the only day on which anybody dreamed of me in that colour.' (The minister likens the story on page 103 which was told to Boswell and Johnson by Macquarry of Ulva, whose servant was seen by an old woman dressed in a coloured livery.)

With regard to Coinneach Odhar, 'that most famous of Highland seers', MacEchern has some points to make about his divining stone. Not necesarily a badge of his profession nor a means of concentrating the attention, it may well, he thinks, have had chemical or radio-active powers conducive to the trance state with the ability also to affect the seer's nervous system. The old story mentions that in the acquisition of second sight he lost the natural sight of one eye, which suggests that the stone must have had some strange properties. 'Reichenbach and others have experimented to show, and claim to have proved, that quartz, limestone, metals and other materials affect the body, and therefore the nervous system, which again is the organ of the mind.' Charcot demonstrated that a rapport exists between the sensitive subject and foreign bodies in proximity. Quartz, crystal, or rock crystal have been found throughout the ages to facilitate the faculty of vision. Thus the visions of Coinneach Odhar were not to be found in the stone, but the stone was conducive to producing an ecstatic state.

Contrary to the views of many researchers, Dugald MacEchern held that the faculty of second sight was still very prevalent in the Highlands. The reason for so many statements to the contrary by other folklorists was probably due to the sensitivity of the Highlander, who would not speak of his beliefs to a sceptical stranger nor yet to the unsympathetic.

He concludes by saying that however second sight may be accounted for, it assuredly exists, a fact which scientists must admit whatever their explanations.

Dugald MacEchern's paper on second sight raises several points. Firstly, he was the son of a woman famed for her inheritance of the faculty whose talent was known throughout the Highlands. He grew up in a family that never questioned the existence of second sight and regarded it very much as a gift from God. Such close proximity to a seer could have had a variety of effects on a clever, inquiring young man, ranging from passionate advocacy to disapproval and disavowal. For a man of his integrity, the slightest suspicion of fraud on his mother's behalf, whether deliberate or made through ignorance, would have manifested itself later in silence on the subject, or in denunciation. In fact he saw the way it worked at first hand, and had no doubts.

Having accepted that second sight existed, it became his concern to describe how it worked, but using all the latest theories of scientists and psychologists of the day. His paper effectively spans the gap between the closed minds of the nineteenth-century materialists and the great boom of experimentation that was to become the hallmark of a new age of psychic exploration.

144

In 1951 a busy journalist, Lewis Spence, added to his daunting lists of books published on all aspects of mythology, occultism and fairy lore a volume entitled *Second Sight, its History and Origins*. Perhaps he wrote too quickly and too much, for his research is generally considered to be unreliable by modern scholarship. For all that, he had some intriguing theories.

He believed that second sight was 'a species of supernormal vision latent in man', cultivated in Stone Age times by a priestly sodality associated with ancestor worship. Over the years its character changed from official use by a high caste to predict for the tribe, to personal fortune-telling by a remnant of displaced augurs. Spence makes no attempt to explain the mental and psychic aspect of the talent, but maintains that 'by assembling and linking it to the motifs of folklore' he has prepared the way for the psychologists.

One interesting belief he holds – which cannot in any way be proved, but which is worth consideration – is that second sight had a distinct purpose in the lives of Stone Age men, its object being the survival of the tribe through the guidance of ancestral spirits. One of the reasons why it has survived only on the fringe of society, disbelieved and discounted by so many, must surely be that it is now purposeless and therefore irrelevant to modern society. Even the predictions of Coinneach Odhar, so respected throughout the Highlands, seem to have little point. The fact that a future event such as the coming of the railway was seen before it happened is intriguing, certainly, but not of momentous importance to the survival of the nation. Since the days of Stone Age priests, second sight would seem, therefore, to have lost its purpose.

Until today, when the wheel has come full circle. Just as the ancient priest-seers – if indeed they existed at all – would prophesy to benefit the tribe, so the 'distant viewers' of today are thought by some, as we shall see, to be of equal value to the governments and businesses in contemporary life.

Part Two

Seers Once and Now

Portrait of a Taibhsear

Tall, severely handsome, he stands at the door of his cottage and solemnly watches the strange woman's approach already heralded by all the animals on the croft. After the courtesies, she questions him about his gift.

'And if I have the second sight, it is not a thing to be talking about,' he answers icily.

She pleads with him to reply to her questions.

'I would rather not, no, I will not,' he replies. 'The thing we are talking about is a fact and by no means a joke. I know that I "see before me" and if you want corroboration of such experiences, read your Bible.'

Florence protests that she is a firm believer that second sight is a gift from God. The *taibhsear* wheels round on her.

'And are you calling it a gift from God? Well, at least, I will be telling you how I dealt with one fool.' His story concerns a young man in the south who laughed at him, so he challenged him to go out with him that night and he would show him a vision. They met at midnight in a quiet, misty street and soon saw a youth walking towards them. 'Who is it?' asked the *taibhsear*. 'God,' cried the young man, 'I think it's myself.' The *taibhsear* agreed. 'Make what you will of it,' he told the youth, 'but I am tired of meeting your spectre whenever I go out at night.' The young man was dead within three months.

'And that will teach you not to mock at things too big for you and for me and for all the scientists and philosophers that ever were,' he adds to Florence.

'Can you then make other people see?' she asks in awe.

'You see that road where it winds out of sight?' The *taibhsear* points to the hill across the loch. 'Once I saw a funeral there with

149

the mourners walking two by two and the corpse carried behind. I called to my wife. At first she did not see it, but then when I touched her she did see it. Neither of us knew who had died. I went to fetch my field-glasses but I could see no sign of the procession through the lens, only with my eyes. A week later, did I not stand here and watch the real funeral go past the way I had seen it in my vision? A young girl, it was.'

'Do you believe that animals have the second sight?' Florence asks, as one of the dogs begins to bark.

'Most certainly. Many humans think they have it, but beasts don't think, they know. The hen that crows is the best seer of all. You may kill her, the others may peck her to death, but whenever a hen crows, look you for a death in that household.'

After a pause the *taibhsear* turns to Florence. 'Do you not think that these things are best forgotten?'

'No, a hundred times no,' she cries. 'People are too materialistic these days. They need to feel and touch and see before they will believe.'

At this, the *taibhsear*'s reserve is broken and he tells her how he inherited the gift as a boy from his forebears. He pours out his many experiences of pre-vision. 'And now,' he concludes, 'you will be thinking mine a life of fear, a haunted life. Well, I have to be telling you that never in my life was I afraid of what I saw. And it is this that lets me know that they are good, the things I see. With regard to this gift, I can only say it is a fact, perfectly normal, and one that carries no fear with it whatsoever.'

This romanticized portrayal of a traditional seer comes from Florence Cameron, daughter of E. C. C. Stanford who was managing director of the British Chemical Industry, manufacturing kelp, at the turn of the century. in her little book, *Told in the Furthest Hebrides*, published by Eneas Mackay of Stirling in 1936, she confesses to 'something approaching reverence for the gift of second sight, or what they call "seeing before them".' As a result of her interview and research, she came to the conclusion that the realm of the spirit lies as closely round us as the sea round the earth and that second sight is another manifestation of what Wordsworth called 'intimations' that we belong not to time nor place nor even to the physical plane, but to eternity.

Here then is the identikit portrait of a Celtic seer, the man of visions, intolerant of fools, unafraid of his powers which he believes to be inherited and good, a dangerous enemy, a man apart. In him are incorporated the high-priest of the burial mounds, the Druid diviner, and the Christian saint. He is an amalgam of every seer described in the oral tradition, a figure deeply rooted in the racial memory of the Gael.

In the following chapters we shall be looking in depth at five seers who between them span a period of 1,500 years. Unwrapping the tissued layers of time, tradition, myth, and fantasy we shall find that they shared and still share the same talent, as inexplicable today as it ever was.

6   *The Columban Tradition*

THE FATHER OF SECOND SIGHT

Rain in Mull. A gull dirges over the sour sea. Mist shrouds lowering mountain tops. Wind like a stepmother's breath nags as the ferry casts off from the pier. A glimmer lightens the western sky. The colours shift and merge like water-paints on paper, grey into lilac, olive to jade. Suddenly the white sands glitter. Sapphire, emeralds and diamonds. The sun is shining on Iona.

Perhaps it was the simple beauty of this bird-loud, light-filled island that induced Columba to build his monastery here, or perhaps it is Columba himself – the light of the Celtic Church – that gives the place an aura. Whatever the reason, Iona is still an island of mystery and magic. Even in rain and storm, the sun still seems to shine.

Columba was magnificent, a genius who could have excelled in any profession from high king to poet. His choice of the priest-hood and sanctity was no easier for him than it was for any other man, for he had all the vices of temper, guile, partisanship, and pride as well as the virtues of compassion, courtesy, and kindness. But it is not Columba the statesman, poet, or saint who concerns us here, but Columba the seer, who has been called the father of second sight.

Most of what we know about him is contained in a gem of biography written in Latin by the Gaelic-speaking St Adamnan, himself Abbot of Iona, in AD 676 within 100 years of Columba's death. Adamnan was very aware that stories about his celebrated predecessor might well be considered exaggerated so he makes this statement:

> Let no one think of me as either stating what is not true regarding so great a man, or recording anything doubtful or uncertain. Let

him know that I will tell the truth with all candour, and without any ambiguity what I have learned from the consistent narrative of my predecessors – trustworthy and discerning men – and that my narrative is founded either on written authorities anterior to my own times, or on what I have myself heard from some learned and faithful ancients, unhesitatingly attesting facts, the truth of which they had themselves diligently inquired into.

Certainly Adamnan and his sources were men of their times, eager to promote all aspects of the Gospel including the prophetic and the miraculous, but they were not just propagandists or hagiographers. They were honourable men who would not stoop to cheap lies for quick conversions. They were also men of culture, breeding, and learning who not only founded monasteries all over the known world but who also taught in all the ancient seats of learning. Moreover, they were Celts reared in the bardic tradition of careful and accurate narration. Bards were not merely poets but historians and chroniclers who knew the importance of honest reporting. Thus there is no reason to suppose that Columba's biography is untruthful. Adamnan and his sources were what we today would call 'reliable witnesses'.

Before examining some of the fifty or so examples of second sight recorded, it is necessary to look briefly at the life and background of this extraordinarily powerful man.

Gartan in Ulster is a wild and lonely place on a hillside, over-looking three lochs, overhung by wild mountains, and over-run in those days by wolves. Here Columba was born on 7 December 521, descended on his father's side from the kings of Donegal, and on his mother's from the kings of Leinster. He was also related through his paternal grandmother to the kings of Argyll in Scotland.

He inherited his gift of second sight from his mother, Ethne, who just before he was born had a vision of an angel bringing her a beautiful flowered mantle which pleased her greatly. Presently the spirit returned and removed the robe which he cast into the sky. Gradually it unfurled to cover the whole of the north from Innes Mod in the west of Ireland to Carn nam Broch – Burghead – on the Moray Firth. To console her, he declared, 'Woman, do not grieve, for thou shalt bring forth a son so beautiful in nature that he shall be reckoned among his own people as one of the prophets of God . . .'

153

At Columba's baptism he was given two names which as he grew up seemed to typify the two aspects of his character – Crimthann, a wolf or fox, and Colum, the dove. According to Celtic tradition, he was fostered by a priest who one day saw his face shining so brightly that it illuminated the whole house. (Time and again Adamnan's narrative describes the brilliance of Columba's aura.) It was during this period that he was given the nickname of Columkill. Even as a child he spent so long in his cell or prayer oratory that local children would demand to know, 'Has our little Colum come out of his cell yet?'

As he grew older he was sent to the great monastery at Moville where one of his teachers was Master Gemman, the aged Bard of Leinster, from whom he learned poetry and music, heraldry, the laws of precedence, and good manners. Columba and Gemman were reading together in the open air when a young girl ran up to the old bard and claimed sanctuary from her angry father. Though both struggled to protect the poor girl, her father speared her to death and started to run away.

'How long, O Colum, will God the Just Judge allow this crime and our dishonour to be unavenged?'

Outrage released the full force of Columba's powers. 'He will avenge it even now,' he cried. 'The murdered one's soul soars to heaven, but the murderer sinks to hell.' At that moment the wretched father tripped over a stone and fell down dead.

While at the monastic school at Clonard founded in 520 by St Finnian, Columba was told by the abbot to build his hut at the door of the church. He disobeyed, however, and built it further away. When the abbot remonstrated, he answered, 'The door will hereafter be here' – which in time it was, as the monastery was enlarged.

When he was priested, Columba entered the monastery of Glasnevin near Dublin where he stayed until the Yellow Plague disbanded the community and he returned to Ulster to begin his public life. Given by his family the stone hillfort at the Oak Wood of Calgaich, he built his famous monastery of Derry, known for centuries as Daire Columkille, and later called Londonderry.

For nineteen years his chief task was organizing the monastic work of copying manuscripts and illuminating their pages. It was his intense love of books that was eventually to cause his exile to Iona. Having borrowed a psalter from St Finnian he was determined to copy it, which he did secretly at night. Someone reported him and

St Finnian demanded the copy as his by right. Columba, who had worked long and hard, refused and the matter was brought to the high king for judgement. Diarmait decided, in the first copyright case to be tried, that 'to every cow belongeth its calf' but still Columba refused to give up the copy. The result was war, which in turn led to Columba's exile in 563.

With twelve chosen followers, he set out in coracles to visit his kin in Argyll, but he was beguiled by Iona. From the practical point of view it afforded good pastureland, and discipline was always easier to maintain on an island. On the emotional side, this was the first place he had visited from which Erin was no longer visible.

Picture, then, the early settlement surrounded by a drystone dyke: the little huts with earthen floors for the monks, two barns, a stable and a byre, a mill, bakery and kiln, the refectory and guest-house, the heather-thatched church with a sacristy to house the bell and, set apart on rising ground, the abbot's house. Most of the monks were laymen and all took a share of manual labour. The seniors or older men, taught the juniors or novices and were considered especially holy. The working brethren took the bulk of the responsibility. All wore shirts of undyed wool that reached to the heels, upper garments with hood and sleeves, and hide sandals. There were white surplices for festivals. They slept on boards covered with straw.

Though Columba spent most of his later life on Iona he travelled widely in the north of Scotland and on one occasion at least returned to Ireland where he attended the Synod at Drumceatt to plead, among other things, for lenient dealings with the 1,200 itinerant bards who perambulated the country praising the great or satirizing the unpopular, and sometimes making a nuisance of themselves to the rulers. That he was acknowledged as one of themselves is evident from the great welcome the Synod gave him and the song of praise composed in his honour.

And so to Columba the seer.

The account which Adamnan gives of the faculty of second sight is much the same as we give today: that it is the power of perception of facts or scenes often still in the future, by some extension of our ordinary faculties for which at present we are unable to account.

Among the miracles which this same man of God . . . performed by the gift of God, was his foretelling the future . . . and making known to those who were present what was happening in other places, for though absent in body he was present in spirit and would look on things that were widely apart. . . . There are some, though very few, who are enabled by divine grace to see most clearly and distinctly the whole compass of the world, and to embrace within their own wondrously enlarged mental capacity the utmost limits of the heavens and the earth at the same moment, as if all were illuminated by a single ray of the sun.

Columba's visions – and we can only look at a few of them here – fall into three of the categories covered by ESP today: telepathy or thought-transferance, clairvoyance or remote viewing, and precognition or premonition of future events. The following instances would seem to fall into the first group:

The vision of an unexpected guest

One stormy day Columba told the brethren to prepare the guest chamber quickly and draw water to wash a stranger's feet. When they told him that it was too dangerous to cross the Sound in such weather, he told them, 'The Almighty has given a calm even in this tempest to a certain holy and excellent man who will arrive before evening.'

The monks gathered to look out for the boat and sure enough it arrived just as Columba had predicted, with St Cainnach on board. The sailors later reported that God had given both tempest and calm in the same sea and at the same time. They could see the storm but they could not feel it.

The vision of Laisran

One freezing winter day, Columba was found weeping by his servant, Diormit, who asked him why he was so unhappy. The saint replied that Laisran, who was eventually to become his second successor at Iona, was working his monks too hard. At that very moment Laisran felt impelled to allow the labourers to rest. It was as if he were consumed with an inner fire not only to have compassion on the workers but also to give orders that they were never to work in severe weather. The saint 'hearing in spirit' Laisran's new command, ceased weeping 'and told all these circumstances to the brethren'.

The following fall into the category of clairvoyance, or remote viewing as it is called today:

Erc the Robber

Columba called two of the monks and told them to sail to Mull and 'on the open ground, near the seashore, look for Erc, a robber, who came alone last night in secret from the Island of Colonsay.' Columba could see him hiding by day among the sandhills under his boat which he had covered with hay, planning to come out at night and sail over to the little island where the monks kept a seal farm. There he would kill as many as his boat would carry and return into hiding. The two monks set off at once and found the thief crouching under his boat just as the saint had seen.

Two battles

On the very day and at the same hour when the Battle of Ondemone was being fought in Ireland, Columba, who was in Britain staying with King Connall, told him everything not only about the battle but also about the kings who were victorious. He also prophesied that the king of the Picts would escape in his chariot.

On another occasion while in Iona, he told his servant to ring the bell. The monks hurried to the church and found Columba on his knees. 'Pray,' he urged them, 'for King Aidan and our people, at this very moment engaged in battle.' After a while he went outside and looking up to the sky declared, 'The barbarians are put to flight and Aidan is victorious.' He was also able to tell them that 303 of Aidan's men had been killed.

Cronan the Bard

Columba was sitting with his brother monks near Lough Key in Roscommon when a bard called Cronan joined them for a while. When he had gone the others asked why Columba had not asked him to sing for them. The saint replied, 'How could I ask for a song of joy from that unfortunate man who, even now, killed by his enemies, has come so soon to the end of his life?'

At that moment a man shouted to them that the bard had just been murdered.

The destruction of a Roman city

Lugbe, one of Columba's monks, saw his face shining with such brilliancy that he dared to ask, 'Has any vision been shown to you just now?' Columba answered that 'a sulphurous fire' had that moment fallen on a city in Italy destroying 3,000 men, women and children. Some months later Lugbe met the captain and crew of a ship who told them that the city known as Citta Nuova in Istria had been destroyed at the time of Columba's vision.

The letter 'I'

Baithene, one of the monks, came to Columba and asked if one of the brethren would look over the text of the psalter he had just finished copying and check it for mistakes. 'Why trouble us without a reason?' said the saint. 'Your psalter is correct except for the omission of a single "I".' Later this was found to be true.

Death of two kings

While travelling near Ardnamurchan in the Highlands Columba listened for a while to his companions discussing two kings, then he turned to them. 'O my dear children, why do you talk so foolishly of these two men? Both are newly slain and have had their heads cut off by their enemies. This very day some sailors will arrive from Ireland and give you the news.'

The sailors duly arrived as predicted and told how the kings had been killed.

The gift of precognition, so much a part of Highland second sight, is demonstrated in a variety of instances, some important, others trivial – which is typical of the way the faculty works.

Foreknowledge of fire

One night while travelling in the Grampian area with his friends, Columba woke suddenly and aroused them to fetch the boat from its anchorage by the village and bring it nearer to where they were sheltering. A little later, when this was done, he woke his friends again. 'Go out and see what has happened to the village where we left the boat.' It was in flames.

The damaged book

While Lugbe was reading by the fire, Columba warned him to take care, 'for I think the book you are reading is about to fall into a vessel of water'. Later the young man rose in a hurry and the book fell into a water pot. A tragedy indeed in an age when every book was copied by hand.

The spilled inkhorn

When a shout arose on the other side of the Sound, Columba was heard to say, 'The man who is calling is not very bright for when he arrives he will upset my inkhorn and spill the ink.' Diormit decided to stand in front of the door and wait for such a troublesome guest in order to prevent the damage. However, for some reason he was called away and at that moment the unwanted visitor arrived. In his eagerness to kiss Columba, he upset the ink with the hem of his robe.

Prophecy of the Battle of Cethirn

While Columba was sitting by a well outside the fort of Cethirn talking to Abbot Comgell, water was raised for them to wash their hands. Filled with knowledge, he declared to his friend, 'The day will come when the water from this well will no longer be fit to drink.' In reply to the abbot's question he continued, 'It shall be filled with human blood when your people and mine, the Picts and the Scots, have a battle at this place. A kinsman of mine shall be slain and his blood, mingling with that of many others, shall fill up the well.'

An old man present at the battle many years later referred to the prophecy and pointed out its literal fulfilment: of the dead bodies cast into the well, one was a relative of the saint.

One of the commonest predictions in the Highlands throughout history has been that of imminent death. Columba, too, prophesied in the same manner as his descendants through the centuries to come.

Prophecies of death

A father brought his two sons to Columba and asked him about their future. One would be dead within the week, the saint replied, but the other would live to old age and die on Iona.

To Colca, Columba gave the following warning: 'One day you will be head of a church and you will hold this position for many years, but if at any time you happen to see your cellarer enjoying a party with his friends and whirling the jug by its neck, know that you will soon be dead.' This, too, was exactly fulfilled.

While travelling in Skye, Columba struck the ground with his staff and declared, 'Strange to say, my children, this day an aged heathen, whose natural goodness has preserved him all his life, will receive baptism, die and be buried on this very spot.' And hour later, a boat carrying an aged man landed on the shore and the saint was able to fulfil his prophecy, by teaching, baptizing and burying the old man whose name, Artbranan, was given to the spot.

A similar story is told of an old Pict on the shores of Loch Ness. As they were travelling, Columba told his companions, 'Angels wait for us by the bedside of an old Pict who has lived well by the light of nature; we must hasten and baptize him before he dies.' They found the old man in a hut in Glen Urquhart, and so the saint was able to convert him before his death.

On another occasion when the monks heard the voice of a man calling across the Sound, Columba predicted that he was coming for a cure of his body, but had better seek penance for his sins, for he would be dead at the end of the week. The man took no heed of the warning, but it was literally fulfilled.

Two brothers came to take the vows, and Columba foretold their end when he predicted, 'These two strangers who are presenting themselves a living sacrifice to God shall pass away in peace this very month.' He admitted both to the Order that very night. One died in seven days, the other a week later.

He also warned a peasant of his death, which would be caused 'by a travelling companion of whom he had no suspicion'. He refused to say more, 'lest the frequent thought of the fact should make thee too unhappy.' The man died from a wound inflicted by his own knife.

But Columba did not only predict death. On many occasions he foresaw future life, as may be seen in the following examples:

Prophecies of life

While he was at Cloyne, a kinsman, ugly and ill-dressed and generally despised, came up behind him as he processed to church, and touched his robe. Though the others urged Columba to take no notice of the troublesome lad, the saint drew him forward and said, 'Son, open your mouth and show me your tongue.' The boy obeyed and the saint blessed him and predicted, 'Though this lad seems so unimportant now, let none of you despise him, for he will please you well. Upright and strong of soul shall he be; wisdom and foresight shall be his portion, and he will be great in this house. His tongue shall receive from God the gifts of both wholesome doctrine and eloquence.' The boy grew up to be the celebrated St Ernan.

When King Aidan consulted Columba about the succession, he was told that none of the three sons of whom he spoke would survive battle, but it would be one of his younger sons – 'the one whom the Lord shall choose should rush into my lap'. Eochoid Buide, a child at the time, ran into the saint's arms and afterwards inherited the throne.

For Scanlan, a prisoner at the time, Columba predicted freedom and a return to his own kingdom for thirty years, then exile, and a second return, before his death after 'three short terms'. All this was fulfilled, but the 'three short terms' turned out to be months rather than years as Scanlan had expected.

One of the monks called Berach, wanting to sail to Tiree, was warned by Columba of danger from 'a huge monster'. It would be wiser for him to sail round by some of the smaller islands to escape. However Berach ignored the warning and on his journey encountered a huge whale leaping out of the water. He barely escaped with his life. On the same day, Baithene, who was afterwards to become Columba's successor, received the same warning. 'That beast and I are both under God's power,' Baithene replied. The saint then blessed him and promised him a safe journey. When the boat encountered the whale, Baithene blessed it and passed on in safety.

One of the most pleasing features in Columba's character was his love of, and care for, birds and animals. The following story is a typical example.

One day he called one of the brothers and told him that on the morning of the third day he must cross to the west of the island, sit down on the shore and watch for a crane, 'a stranger from the northern region of Ireland', who would lie down on the beach, exhausted by wind and weather. 'Treat it tenderly, take it to some neighbouring house where it may be kindly received and carefully nursed and fed by thee for three days and three nights. When it is refreshed and unwilling to stay any longer, let it fly back to the pleasant place it came from.'

The monk obeyed, found the crane as the saint had predicted, cared for it, and after three days set it free. When he returned to the monastery, Columba, without any inquiry, thanked him for what he had done.

It was not until Columba was an old man and longing for the

adventure of death that he received information concerning himself. 'One day,' Adamnan tells us, 'his holy face lighted up with a certain wondrous and joyous cheerfulness, and lifting up his eyes to heaven, filled with incomparable joy, he was intensely gladdened. Then, after a moderate interval of some little moment or so, that savoury and delightful gladness turned into a mournful sadness.' When Columba's friends asked the reason he answered:

Because I love you I will not give way to sadness. You must promise me first that never in my lifetime will you betray to any man the holy secret about which you are asking . . . Up to this present day thirty years of my sojourning in Britain are accomplished. Meanwhile for many days past, I have devoutly besought my Lord, that at the end of this present thirtieth year He would release me from my dwelling here and call me thither to the celestial country. And this was the cause of my gladness . . . for I saw holy angels sent from the throne on high to meet me and to lead out my soul from the flesh . . . but they are not allowed to come near because that which the Lord granted me, He, giving more heed to the prayers of many churches for me, hath changed quicker than can be said. To which churches, indeed, so praying for me, it has been granted by the Lord that, although against my own will, four years from this day are to be added for my remaining in the flesh . . . And when you see these four years yet to come in this life, please God, are ended, I shall pass away rejoicing to the Lord, by a sudden departure, without any previous bodily pain, with the holy angels coming to meet me at the time.

Accordingly four years later, after several more signs, Columba told his servant Diormit on Saturday 8 June, 597 that the end was near. At midnight, when the bell tolled for service, he entered the church and Diromit who followed him saw the whole building light up with his aura. He found his master on the altar step and hastily summoned the brethren. There, after blessing them, Columba died, 'with a countenance full of joy and gladness, as seeing the angels coming to meet him'. So strong were his telepathic links with his friends and followers that many had visions coincident with his death.

Of all his prophecies the most significant, perhaps, written down by Adamnan long before its realization, concerned Iona itself.

Small and mean though this place is, yet it shall be held in great and unusual honour not only by Scotic kings and people but also by foreign and barbarous nations and by their subjects; the Scots also of other churches shall regard it with no uncommon reverence.

In time it was to become the burial place of some forty-eight Scottish sovereigns, four Irish and eight Norwegian kings, and today it is regarded by all the churches as the birthplace of Christianity in the north.

How are we to regard Columba today in his role of seer or psychic? His attitude was certainly the ideal for Christian seers throughout the centuries, in that he regarded his talent as a privilege and a responsibility, as a gift unsought by himself but to be used for the benefit and edification of others. Unlike many of his successors born into scientific or reasonable ages, he never for one moment doubted his ability or its source. He never regarded it as an affliction to be hidden or feared.

Columba's attitude reflected his age, his race, and his bardic education. Second sight was part of the Celtic way of life, its traditions and its culture. As a Christian he no longer regarded it as within the bounty of the *sithean* but as a direct gift from God. He saw no harm in predicting death and using his power to pronounce on the accession of kings. On one occasion he even used a stone to demonstrate God's power to the Druids: by blessing it, he caused it to float in a vessel of water.

His precognitive and clairvoyant visions are typical of those experienced today. The battles and devastations that he witnessed correspond to sightings of the great disasters of today, such as the sinking of the *Titanic*, the collapse of the Tay Bridge, and the tragedy of Aberfan. Equally, and in keeping with modern experience, many of his visions were of trivial, unimportant events.

Although Columba believed, as many today still do, that his visions came from an outward source rather than from a natural latent talent within the human mind, and though, obviously, many of the instances recorded by Adamnan have been twisted to prove a moral, yet the types of experience match up remarkably closely to the visions, incidents, and coincidences of psychics today.

The Revd John Morrison's style came not as a comment on his abilities as preacher or prophet, but from the name of his parish. The Lordship of Petty, thought to be a Pictish name meaning 'the place of farms', is situated on the south shore of the Moray Firth and stretches, eight miles long by two or three broad, between Inverness and Nairn. The undulating country is a green and golden patchwork of fertile fields pocketed with bright farm-houses, each snug in its circle of garden and trees. Sheltered to the south by the rise of Culloden Moor and the Monaliadh Mountains, it is still the pleasant green oasis it must have presented to the prehistoric settlers who first came there to build their burial mounds – the Clava Chambered Cairns lie just beyond the parish boundary – and leave as litter their axes and arrowheads.

Columba, it is thought, saw it as his 'desired haven' when, in the sixth century, he visited King Brude of the Picts at his fortress near Inverness. The story, chronicled by Adamnan, tells how Columba rebuked Briochan, Brude's chief Druid, for keeping an Irish girl as slave. When he demanded her freedom, Briochan threatened to raise a storm to prevent the saint from sailing. Columba accepted the challenge and the Picts crowded to the shore to witness the event. True to his threat Briochan summoned the elements, but Columba ran up his close-reefed sail and set off in the teeth of the wind. Legend relates that he landed in Petty Bay where he established a church which is still dedicated to him. The first building there would probably have been no more than a small oratory of uncemented stone shaped like a beehive and having two rooms. With one or two of Columba's followers to serve in it and to cultivate the surrounding land, it would soon have become a centre for evangelism, culture, and education, and probably remained unchanged for the next 500 years.

After the Celtic Church was reformed and superseded by the Catholics, St Columba's became the centre of the new Parish of Petty in the Diocese of Moray, looking to Elgin where the cathedral marked the centre of the See. The newly erected church, built on the foundations of the old, would have been commodious, Gothic in design, and funded by the Moravia family. One of the early rectors of Petty must have stood out against the trend of the times which was to abolish anything to do with the old Columban Church, for he retained the name of its founder, an indication of local loyalty to the saint.

After the Reformation in 1560, a certain Andrew Macphail, schoolmaster in Inverness, was inducted as the Gaelic Minister of Inverness and Petty, but in due course Petty was to have its own minister, who was also a Gaelic speaker. (Gaelic was the language of the people right up to the early nineteenth century.) During Covenanting times, the locals remained Royalist and Episcopalian, though there were some who were summoned to the High Court at Elgin for non-conformity. The Bishop of Moray visited Petty Church at that time and found it 'very bare'. The minister confessed that everything except one table was borrowed, so two handsome silver Communion cups were presented by Lady Doune, which are still used in the parish.

The arrival of Cromwell's troops, who camped throughout Petty, terrified the inhabitants at first, and the church was closed, but not for long. The English soon became popular, especially with the lassies. Farmers and merchants appreciated the trade they brought, and the minister was delighted for the church was so full that services had to be held outside.

In those days the pillar and jougs were familiar objects by the church door when it was the custom for sinners to stand in sackcloth before the congregation. The Kirk Session for February 1657 recounts how Donald Roy was 'appointed to stand barefoot in saco at the kirk door between the second and third bells, and to stand at the pillar after the same manner in time of sermon.'

A very strange funeral custom known as the 'Petty step' decreed that mourners should run, not walk. The origin lay in an old superstition that the spirit of the last person buried had to keep watch over the kirkyard till the next funeral. When two took place on the same day it was a race to be first at the graveside. The custom appears to have been abandoned after some bearers tripped while carrying the coffin of a witch. They were afraid her curse might blight them!

Tombstones are always an intriguing record of parish life and there is one that reads:

Sixty winters upon the street,
No shoes or stockings on his feet,
Amusement both for small and great
Was poor Johnnie Laddie.

165

This, then, was the parish inherited by the Revd John Morrison in 1749. What of his congregation?

The most notable figures connected with Petty in the thirteenth and fourteenth centuries were the descendants of Freskyn de Moravia, a Flemish supporter of David I, and most important of them were the two Andrew Morays who owned Hallhill Castle in Petty and Ormonde Castle in Avoch across the water in the Black Isle. The first Andrew was a military genius who raised an army for William Wallace but who was killed at the Battle of Stirling Bridge in 1297. The son followed his father's example and was Robert the Bruce's chief lieutenant in the north. He was twice Regent of Scotland and died at Avoch in 1338, sadly mourned.

The Earldom of Moray which gave its name to the county was to become closely associated with the House of Stuart. The old family home – Castle Stuart – still stands on the road to Dalcross Airport, well-maintained, and the family were and still are the principal land-owners in the area. Other top people were the Mackintoshes who in early times were the *toshears* or chamberlains of Petty. They were the principal tenants or tacksmen of the Earls of Moray, who sub-let to small farmers who in their turn rented out patches of land to the cottars.

Mostly the Morays and the Mackintoshes agreed, but occasionally there were rows and evictions which involved the local people in great hardship and unhappiness. The Morays feuded with the Huntlys, and the Mackintoshes with the Camerons, which also affected the cottars. The sixteenth century was a particularly unsettling time as no less than four Mackintosh chiefs met violent deaths and the clan was continually in the hands of minors.

Local people were described as strong, muscular, capable of great endurance. The historian, Hector Boece, in 1521 described the corpse of an inmate of Petty kirkyard – a certain 'little' John – as measuring fourteen feet, 'his member well-proportioned according to his stature'. This was proof, Boece thought, 'that mighty people grew up in the region before they were overcome with gluttony and excess'.

The parish was also a popular place with the gentry. In 1717, Lord Moray's factor complained, 'I must say I am sick of too many gentle-men tenants in Petty.' There were ninety farms by the end of the eighteenth century, all of a good size and in the hands of the better-born.

The houses of the sub-tenants were not so prosperous. Clay and turf huts, heather-thatched, with a central hearth, were the norm. John Morrison's successor, William Smith, was to point out that the mean accommodation in no way matched the character of the inhabitants. 'They are in general sober, peaceable and industrious. Crimes of an atrocious character are extremely rare or rather unknown. They are far from being unsocial but have pretty frequent convivial meetings as at weddings and the like . . . Drinking to excess and quarrels are accounted reproachful.' May Day was a popular festival, and the Shian or Fairy Hills were bright with young people rolling the Beltane Bannock or painted eggs. Fairy cult was strong, and the clootie well, where people hung up rags or similar offerings to the spirit of the water in exchange for good luck, was frequently visited. In the early eighteenth century, itinerant beggars regarded the parish as a place of plenty, while the native poor with their metal discs were well provided for from the church box and by kindly neighbours.

But life in Petty was to change drastically with the Jacobite Risings of 1715 and 1745. The people were Royalists at heart and when Lachlan Mackintosh declared for King James, recruitment in the parish was brisk. Many able young men went off to fight for the cause, but few returned. The crops failed and for three years there was famine in the parish. 'All your tenants are bankrupt,' wrote the factor to Lord Moray. 'You must cancel one year's rent out of the three bad years.'

By far the most memorable event in the history of the Highlands – the Battle of Culloden – occurred in the Lordship of Petty. Local men were solidly for Prince Charles and rallied to his standard. Clan Mackintosh went into battle 700 strong and 400 were killed: the longest trench-grave at the battlefield belongs to that clan. Supporters who survived to be caught were shot, hanged, or deported.

After the disaster the pattern of life changed in Petty, as it did all over the Highlands. The peat trade dried up as Invernessians turned to coal. Carting of sand for flooring ceased as carpets came into fashion. Herring shoals dwindled in the Moray Firth. Improvement of agricultural land was adopted on some of the larger farms but not on the smaller ones. So slow were they to learn new methods that the saying arose, 'Out of the world and into Petty.' For labourers, conditions were pitiful. A farm servant earned 13s 4d for six months' work with a few perks. Poverty and hardship were the norm.

But Petty's greatest loss was her people. There had been deaths in

167

battle and by reprisals; now many left of their own accord to better themselves, some to the army, some to Canada, some to work on the new roads. Those with trades found employment in the towns. Even the beggars deserted for wealthier parishes elsewhere. When John Morrison was inducted at the age of forty-eight there were barely 2,500 souls in the whole parish.

His grandfather John was a Morrison of Lewis described as possessing 'ladies' modesty, bishops' gravity, lawyers' eloquence and captains' conduct'. He was well known as a poet and a wit. His father, also John, was minister at Muir of Ord in the parish of Urray. He inherited his father's gifts, and is generally supposed to have been the author of *A Description of the Lewis* 'by John Morrison, a dweller therein'. Our John was born in 1701 in the parish of Dull in Perthshire. Nothing is known of his schooling or university days except that it was said that 'his scholarship was of a superior cast'. He had probably been ordained for eighteen years before his translation to Petty from the post of missionary in Amulree.

The *New Statistical Account of Inverness-shire* records how he came to be offered the living. A member of Clan Fraser living in the Aird was deeply in debt to an Inverness merchant. As no local lawyer dared handle the case for fear of Fraser reprisals, the merchant employed an Edinburgh Writer to the Signet – Mackenzie of Devlin – who was also factor to the Earl of Moray. He was successful in recovering the debt, but the Frasers were furious at his intervention and determined to avenge their clansman. As Mackenzie travelled north at set times of the year, a plot was devised to ambush and dispose of him at Sloch-Muice. This plot was overheard by the minister of Kiltarlity in Fraser country, who was anguished to know what to do for the best. If he were to write directly to Mackenzie, his letter might well be intercepted which would mean the end of his job, if not his life. He decided, therefore, to get in touch with his friend John Morrison in Perthshire, and ask him to come north, stressing that the matter was urgent.

John accordingly visited the Aird and as soon as he heard of the plot, travelled straight to Edinburgh to warn Mackenzie not to go north without a strong bodyguard. The lawyer took his advice, and when the Frasers found him so well protected they retreated without attacking.

Mackenzie, as Lord Moray's factor, was able to recommend

Morrison's removal to Petty. The letter offering him the job arrived during the middle of Sunday worship. John pocketed it in spite of the curiosity of his congregation. When, later, he read it he was heard to say, 'I thank thee, O Lord God Almighty, for having opened up a place for me from which I shall not be removed while it is thy will to leave me in the world.'

John was, like his father and grandfather before him, a poet and a musician. Indeed he was often called a bard. In gratitude for his preferment, he composed a Gaelic eulogy in praise of his patron, Lord Moray, and christened his eldest daughter Devlin after the name of the lawyer's estate. According to other sources, he was chosen out of four candidates for Petty, a compliment to the fact that 'he was a highly gifted and orthodox preacher, and was believed to be gifted with the spirit of prophecy in a wonderful manner.' He soon settled down to life in Petty Manse and after a few years met and fell intensely in love with a young girl called Mary Hagart, forty years his junior. They married and it was said that he cherished her as fondly as if she had been a child. Their married life was exceptionally happy, but too short. Mary was never strong and after the birth of her third daughter, her health declined rapidly.

John did all in his power to help her and was heart-broken when she died in 1772, aged only thirty-three. So great was the loss that he never really recovered. Though he continued to preach and care for his three little girls, Devlin, Margaret and Janet, the joy had gone out of his life. Within two years he also was dead, at the age of seventy-two. The two graves stand side by side in the east end of Petty kirkyard to this day.

Over the years many have testified to his gifts of preaching and prophecy. The Revd John Grant, one of his successors in Petty, wrote in 1841:

All that is related of Mr Morrison indicates that he was a man of great sagacity, much humour and fervent piety. There is to this day a prevalent belief in the North Highlands that he was endowed with the gift of prophecy, and anecdotes in confirmation are related.

The Revd Donald Corbet of Kinlochbervie in Sutherland wrote in 1876:

Father and son (the Morrisons) were eminent in their day . . .
Their success in the ministry both in the conversion of sinners and
in the edification and comfort of the household of faith, was, I may
say, extraordinary . . . After his settlement in Petty his church was
day after day literally crammed to the door with crowds hungering
for the Bread of Life. That continued to the termination of his
course.

Good preacher and pastor though he was, his fame today rests on his
prophecies and predictions. There are many, of course, who disregard his gifts as a seer. Morrison himself never laid claim to it, and
there are still those in the kirk who believe that prophecy belongs
firmly to the Old Testament – in spite of the fact that St Paul in his
first letter to the Corinthians lists it specifically as one of the gifts of
the Spirit. There is, it would seem, a very fine line to be drawn
between Bible prophets and those who have second sight: F. C.
Burkett in an article entitled *Prophets of Israel* states that Samuel was
not a prophet but a seer, 'the wise man who is believed to have what is
called in Scotland – second sight.'

John Morrison's deeds and words were the talk of the district for
many years before they were collected and published in 1894 by
A. B. Maclennan, author of other short vignettes of Highland personalities and contributor to Alexander Mackenzie's *Prophecies of the
Brahan Seer*. As he says, those who read the stories about John
Morrison 'will have an opportunity of judging correctly whether
those who heard Mr Morrison's wonderful utterances were justified
in ascribing a gift to him which he did not claim, and of which he
himself said he was wholly unworthy.'

Picture then Morrison's first few Sundays in the pulpit. The
church was as bare as it had been in Episcopalian times, for the
inventory records that there was no Communion table, no sandglass,
no mortcloth, only two Communion cups, one handbell and 184
Communion tokens. The congregation was equally poor when it
came to spiritual clothing: John found them so wild and incorrigible
that he declared he had never met or seen such ignorant people in all
his ministry – they knew nothing of God or of his Church.

Sunday worship was disrupted by the presence of dogs who sat by
their masters at the ends of the pews. John, who had to preach against
the continual 'snarling and uproar', was outraged by such disrespect

170

to the House of God. He counselled, cajoled, and ordered his flock to leave their dogs at home, but no one listened to him. In the end he resorted to cunning. 'I am at a loss to understand, my dear friends,' he declared from the pulpit, 'why you bring your dogs with you to church, unless it be that they gnaw the bones of your relatives as they pass out and in through the churchyard. If that is so, it is truly horrible to think of it.' The congregation listened in silence, but the words struck home. From then on no dogs were allowed through the kirkyard gate.

Animals were not the only disturbance in the church. The fisher-folk from Fisherton about a mile up the coast used to sit together in the gallery. They would usually arrive late and leave early, making a great clatter in the process. One Sunday when the noise was overpowering, John waited till they had settled, then he told them off: 'The fishers of Petty come and go from the church like a parcel of goats, when they choose themselves, but God will sweep them down to hell when he chooses.' The words had the desired effect.

In spite of the noise, some of his parishioners managed to doze during the sermon. One man was particularly annoying for his stentorian snores. The minister spoke to him privately, but the man instead of showing shame, was outraged. 'Time enough for you to correct me when your own family is perfect. Speak first to your wife. She sleeps all through the service.' John answered mildly that no one was perfect and that he would be greatly obliged if the man would wave his handkerchief next time his wife dozed off, for he could not see her as she sat directly under the pulpit.

Next Sunday, accordingly, during the sermon the man began to wave his handkerchief vigorously. John stopped preaching and peered down over the pulpit. 'Waken, Mary. I did not receive a large dowry with you, and if you are without grace, you are a poor penny-worth.' From then on, the man was too busy keeping an eye on the manse pew to sleep himself.

Illegitimacy was considered a great sin in the eyes of church and parish. John was always particularly tender to those young girls who in desperation were driven to contemplate infanticide. One winter's night during a snowstorm he had a premonition that he must go out. His servant protested, 'Can you not wait till daylight?' But John shook his head. He knew that these impulses of his must be obeyed;

they were part of his gift of vision. Although the object of his journey, Lochandunty, was a long way off, he set out alone in the teeth of the gale. As he neared the stretch of water he overtook a woman, shawled and huddled against the elements. Dismounting, he walked beside her for a while.

'What's that you are carrying?' he asked.

'Nothing, sir.' She held her bundle tighter. Her eyes were wide and scared.

'Don't lie to me. I know well what you have, but before you part with it, give it a kiss and say, "God bless you".'

Tears poured down the girl's cheeks as she opened her shawl. She embraced the infant and by her kiss proclaimed her love. No doubt the minister set her on his horse and took her home.

'How did you know?' he was to be asked time and time again. 'You must have the second sight.'

'I am no prophet,' he answered, 'nor the son of a prophet, but you must admit, it is a poor servant to whom his master will reveal nothing of his mind.'

The same impulse came over him on another occasion. Towards dark one evening, while on his way to the east end of his parish, he came to a wood. Instead of keeping to the path, he dismounted, tethered his horse and walked off through the trees. There he came across a young couple digging a hole.

'What are you doing, my friends?' he asked.

Not having heard him approach, the woman fainted with fright.

'Don't be afraid,' he said, raising her gently. 'Thank God you have not yet committed the crime you intended.' He then told the young man to carry the mother who, having just given birth, was weak and ill. He himself took the baby and together they all went back to the girl's home. As they approached, the young man set the girl down and would have bolted if John had not collared him. When they were all indoors he made the woman sit down and without another word, married them.

Tender though John could be with the weak and the victims of adultery, he did not condone the sin. In the neighbouring parish of Croy, the farmer at Easter Leanach was believed to have fathered a child on his servant but would not admit it. He was summoned before the Session but no one could make him confess. Just before the meeting closed John stood up. Directing the full force of his personality

172

on the man he asked, 'You are a farmer, you have a wife and children, horses, cattle, and sheep, have you not?'

The man agreed.

Mr Morrison then requested him to swear a solemn oath by all his possessions that he was innocent.

'I will not take that oath,' the man shouted. 'I am guilty. The bairn is mine.'

On two occasions the minister himself was to become the victim of gossip in the parish. When his servant found a babe abandoned on the manse doorstep, John declared, 'We'll keep him until he's claimed.' Months passed, however, and when no one came forward to claim the child, the minister himself was thought to be its father. This was scandal indeed. Two elders were appointed to find the child's true parents and hand the baby back. The only problem was where to look. If John knew, he was not telling. However, he agreed to help: off they set with the child and its nurse on a mystery tour, first to Inverness, then across the Kessock Ferry to the Black Isle. By the road to Drumderfit, they met three men digging peats.

'Go to the middle of the three,' said John to the elders, 'and tell him to claim his child.' The labourer ran over and, full of gratitude, took the babe, explaining to the elders that his wife had died in childbirth and as he was too poor to look after the child himself, he knew that it would be well cared for at the manse until he had earned enough to look after it. No doubt the minister, who knew his flock, had known the facts all the time.

John was again the object of scandal when his servant Kate became pregnant. One of the elders informed the minister but he seemed indifferent and made excuses for the girl. 'Woman is the weaker vessel. Human nature is fallible, is it not?'

The elder agreed but insisted nevertheless that Kate be summoned before the Session. There she was duly asked the name of her seducer. 'I know neither his name nor where he stays,' she answered boldly. 'All I know is that he's a drover.'

No one believed her. She was repeatedly questioned, even threatened with bodily punishment, but still she stuck to her story. The elders were very angry, and thought John should make her confess, but all he said was: 'I am more sorry than any of you for the poor, fatherless girl's folly, but she must not be treated too harshly. Her crime is not so black as to send her from my protection and sympathy, provided she behaves in the future.'

173

The elders were not satisfied. Already they suspected that the minister himself must be implicated. Next Sunday one of the congregation who had misbehaved was ordered to stand up at the pillar, but as the kirk officer proceeded to put the sackcloth over his shoulders, he threw it off and no one could make him wear it. Uproar followed, until the minister cried out to leave him alone. Next Sunday, he declared, the sinner would have a companion. A rumour flew round the parish that the companion would be Mr Morrison himself, and one of the elders repeated it to him.

'Ach, well,' said John, 'the Great Judge will at the last day free me from that charge.'

Kate, however, put her own interpretation on the minister's prediction. She hurried round to see her lover, a certain married man in the parish, and told him there was no need to keep their secret any longer – 'For you yourself told the minister all about it.'

'What do you mean?' demanded her lover. 'I have said nothing to the minister. He's the last person I would tell.'

'I tell you he knows all about it,' Kate argued. 'You had better confess at once. You may get off more lightly if you do.'

Reluctantly the lover agreed. Next Sunday he was sack-clothed together with the first offender, as the minister had foretold.

In accord with his tolerance of sinners – if not of the sin – the minister was also particularly gentle with simpletons. Jamie Petty was just such an innocent, whose parents had died when he was a child. Supported by neighbours, he lived on in the family hovel making paper windmills – his passion – and saying his prayers. Sundays were special to Jamie. Without fail his was the first fire to be lit in the parish on that morning. The minister, also an early riser, could see the coil of smoke from his study window.

One Friday previous to a Sacrament Sunday, Jamie came to the manse and asked for a token of admission to Communion. John hesitated, not sure if Jamie understood the meaning of his request, so he questioned him. To his delight, he found Jamie's answers to be clear, full of the understanding of true Christianity. It occurred to him that Jamie might receive some extra blessing from the sacrament so he put the token into his hand. 'Now Jamie,' he said, 'I give you this on condition that if you hear or see anything particular when you are at the Communion Table, you will tell me on Monday.'

Jamie promised, and true to his word appeared at the manse as arranged. 'You were at the Lord's Table yesterday, were you not,

Jamie?' the minister prompted. 'Did you see anything while you were there?'

'Yes I did,' said Jamie. 'I saw a beautiful man in a white robe. He came in at the head of the table and as he came along he put his hand on the heads of all the people. When he came to me, he stroked my face and said, 'Be a good lad till I come for you a year from today and take you to the beautiful place where I live.'' '

John was deeply moved. 'Go now, Jamie,' he said to him, 'and remember what you were told. Be ready for the good Lord when he comes.'

A year passed to the day and when John entered his study early as usual he noticed there was no smoke from Jamie's fire. He waited a while and looked again. Smoke rose from all the other cottages in the parish, but not from his, so he sent his servant to inquire. The man soon returned with the news that Jamie was dead. His body was lying peacefully and it was obvious he had died without pain.

John was always humble in the face of goodness and able to recognize sanctity when he saw it. William Main from Ardersier, generally known as Willie Teetee was just such a man. One Sunday, John overtook him on the road to Inverness where he had been invited to administer the sacrament. 'Where are you off to?' he asked, halting his pony.

'I am told there is to be a market in that big town west of here [Inverness] and I have a deal of copper [sins] which I am wishing to be rid of. I am also told that a man [God] will attend the market [Communion service] who will be glad to give me good coin [grace] in exchange for my worthless copper. I am going to strike a bargain with this man.'

John, whose quick wit had followed the allegory, immediately dismounted.

'Willie Teetee, you are far more worthy of having a horse to carry you than I am,' he said, setting his companion on his pony, and he walked beside him all the way to Inverness.

Although drunkenness revolted the minister, he did not object to a dram. When one of his parishioners called to arrange baptism for his child, John offered him whisky, which they both enjoyed. After an hour of relaxed conversation, the farmer rose to go. 'You'll take a dram for the road?' said John, knowing the man had a distance to ride.

'Better not. I might get drunk.'

175

'One glass of whisky won't make you better or make you worse,' was the reply. 'Two will better you and won't make you worse; three won't make you better but will make you worse.' So the farmer took the dram.

Tolerant though John was, he could be firm when needful. Donald Macrae was a youth whose delinquent habits were the trial of the parish. His most annoying trick was to wait till the people were in church on a Sunday then set the water on to the mill wheel. John did his best to improve the lad but with no effect. One Sunday, bent on mischief, Donald decided to go to church. As the place was packed, he could only find room at the front of the gallery. Fidgeting and fooling, he overbalanced and fell down on the congregation below. John stopped preaching, and after making sure no one was hurt, tried a new tactic. Pointing at him sternly, he recited in Gaelic:

> Donald Macrae, who's aye astray,
> A day will seize thee yet
> You scared all those who were awake
> And wakened those that slept.

This was interpreted as meaning that Donald would be a reformed character. No doubt the boy glowered and flushed at being the centre of such attention from the pulpit. The following Sunday he went to the salt-water mill close by the church in order to do mischief, but just as he was about to open the sluices, he thought he saw a large open hand coming out of the water to grab him. Terrified, he ran home, and from that day on he improved. Later he too was to become an eminent Christian poet whose work was reviewed glowingly in the *Inverness Advertiser* of 1882.

John's methods of dealing with petty crime were reminiscent of those of the Mikado: when one of his parishioners was discovered to have stolen a pot from a neighbour, he decreed that he should stand at the church door with the same pot on his head for three successive Sundays. His ways of exposing fraud were certainly unorthodox. On the death of one of his elders, the Session put forward the name of a certain innkeeper from Newton. John, who knew the man better than the others, objected to the appointment, believing that the proposers had been bribed by free drinks at the inn. On this occasion, however, he could not win over the Session, so he resorted to cunning. Before the day of ordination, he held a party in the manse to which he invited all the church officials, including the elder-elect. Standing at the door, he welcomed each one with a warm handshake. Behind his back, however, there stood a jug of dirty water. When the new elder arrived, instead of a handshake, he received the contents of the jug full in his face. The outraged publican broke into a tirade of imprecations against his minister in language unheard of in the manse.

John turned to the others. 'Do you observe, gentlemen, how the one kind of filth brings out another? Give me your candid opinion now: do you consider this man to be fit to rule in God's house?' Shamefacedly, they dropped their candidate to a man.

In the story of the crooked cripple, John was shown as equally unorthodox. In those days it was the custom for the handicapped to be carried about in crude little carriages from house to house for charity. At the first house he would be taken in and entertained, then carried or drawn to the next, where he would be similarly entertained, then taken on to a third. He would remain overnight at the house he reached by sunset, and on the next day would start on his travels again. Such was the extent of good-neighbourliness in the Highlands. On this occasion John happened to meet two men carrying a third whom John believed to be a fraud. They were on the point of crossing a river in spate at the time.

'Let him down in the water,' John ordered.

Thinking he must be joking, the bearers refused to obey, but John insisted. Reluctantly they dropped both carriage and man in the river. To their surprise, the cripple rose up and was on the opposite bank before them. There was nothing the matter with him: he had just pretended to be lame in order to live off the backs of his neighbours.

Above all John Morrison had a sense of humour. One of the most delightful stories told of him records an encounter with the wives from Fisherton. After a long exhausting day selling fish at the doors of Inverness, they had stopped at an inn for refreshment on the way home. John watched them staggering all over the road, and so amused was he that he ran out with his violin. One of the wives persuaded him to play them a reel and soon they were all dancing on the road. Needless to say, the episode was seen and disapproved of by an elder who complained of the minister's unseemly behaviour.

'How could I refuse to play for the poor woman who asked me?' John replied. 'The holy angels themselves are already tuning their harps for her. It would be better than a thousand worlds to hear the sweet music in the midst of which her soul will pass into glory.' The woman died a few days later.

A similar story is told of the drunken postmistress. It was her job to carry letters from Petty to Inverness, and being too fond of the bottle, she occasionally slept on the job. Once the minister found her drunk and exhausted by the road.

'Come along, woman, it's time you were home,' he urged her, but she would not move until he had promised to sing to her. Accordingly, he struck up a tune called 'Dunken Maggie' and the poor woman got up and danced till the minister's servant came out and ordered her off.

'Let her alone,' John said. 'This is the last reel she'll ever dance.'

It was true. She died soon after.

Because of these anecdotes John was to become a legend in his lifetime. He emerges as a strong man, secure in his own beliefs and his position, eccentric perhaps, but gifted with humour, common sense and kindness, no different from a thousand unsung godly parish ministers. It was his predictions that set him apart.

Although the spirit of prophecy imbued all the deeds and words of the minister, many of the recorded instances indicate no more than that he was deeply intuitive and knew his flock so well that what seemed prophetic to some was simply common sense to him. The story of the importunate beggar illustrates this point. This particular pauper was so persistent in his demands for charity that the day came when John had no more to give him. 'Be patient a while,' he reassured the beggar. 'The Devil is preparing something for you in the east end of the parish. I can't tell what it will be, only that in time you'll get it.' Some time later a young girl gave birth to an illegitimate child. The father, a man of means, was fined heavily by the Session, and part of the fine was given to the beggar. Though this was considered to be a genuine prediction, it seems more likely that John knew of the girl's plight and made a shrewd guess.

The following tale falls into the same category. John and his wife Mary were paying an overnight visit to Mrs Knowles of Milton of Connage, a prosperous farmer's widow with a reputation for saintliness, and in the morning John was unusually restive, pacing up and down the sitting room in a fever of impatience. 'I hope I've done nothing to offend him,' Mrs Knowles whispered to Mary, who was as ignorant of the cause as she.

'Are we to have any breakfast here today?' demanded the minister testily.

'Breakfast is quite ready,' replied his hostess. 'I'm just waiting for a good friend of mine whom I would like you to meet. I think you will like his company.'

John frowned. 'I know you've sent for him and I know you think him honest, but good as you think him now, within six months you will shun him like a viper. If you want to wait for him, we will leave without breakfast.'

Hastily Mrs Knowles insisted he sit down to his food, and as soon as the meal was over, the Morrisons left. When they had gone, the friend arrived and made himself so pleasant that Mrs Knowles could not help reproaching the minister in her heart. Yet within six months that friend had disgraced himself and Mrs Knowles was so shocked by his conduct that she never spoke to him again. Here, too, it is probable that the minister knew more than he was prepared to say. Ministers usually do.

The prediction regarding the ungodly fisherman, though, would seem to be genuine. The man, whose name was Patience, had a reputation for drunkenness and cruelty. Though John repeatedly remonstrated with him, he refused to repent. One day, the minister was talking to a friend on the manse doorstep when suddenly he exclaimed, 'That poor man, Patience, has had so many opportunities to heed the gospel, but now he has lost them for ever.' Later it was learned that Patience had sailed that day to Inverness to sell his fish. On the way home, he had fallen overboard and drowned.

The following story, which seems to come straight from the realms of superstition, is so uncharacteristic of the minister that it sounds apocryphal. One of his servants had gone to the well on the far side of the churchyard to fetch a jug of water when he saw a ghostly apparition in the dusk. According to the superstitions of the time, he turned up his cuffs and ran back to the manse, banging the door behind him. John, disturbed by the commotion, came into the kitchen where he saw the poor boy with his folded cuffs. After hearing the story, he turned to the lad. 'Why were you so foolish as to turn up your sleeves. Did you not know that you should have turned them down as soon as you saw the ghost? Then it would have left you alone.'

Trembling, the boy shook his head.

'Prepare, my child, for eternity,' the minister continued. 'Within

179

eight days you will appear before the great white throne on which sits the judge of all.' He died with the week, and it was supposed locally that the boy had seen an apparition of himself.

Another tale connected with the same well would seem to be a case of clairvoyance. One evening the minister requested a glass of fresh water, so one of the maids ran off to oblige her master. Time went by and when she did not return, John called the other girl. 'Where is the water?' he asked.

'Coming,' she told him.

'No, it is not,' he answered, 'for the jar is broken and the water spilled. You had better go out quickly and help your friend out of the grave in the churchyard.' The girl ran off and found her companion, no doubt hysterical, trying to climb out of a newly dug grave.

Somewhat similar is the story about his cattle which were grazing on common land on the Braes of Culloden. One day he sent his servant up to see how they fared. On his return, he reported that they were all doing well.

'Did you see each one of them, Willie?' the minister asked.

'I did,' said the lad.

'Well, William, you will just have to return as fast as you can with a horse and cart and bring the dun stot home. He is lying at this moment on his back in a watercourse with two of his legs broken.'

The servant stared at him in disbelief.

'You have lied to me, Willie, for you never saw the poor dun stot.'

Immediately the servant confessed he had lied. Telling the tale later to his friends, he admitted, 'I was stupid to hide anything from the minister, for he knows everything before it happens. I went to the ditch and found the beast just as he had described.'

The following prophecies appear to be genuine predictions. One concerns an old miser called M'Glashan, living near Castle Stuart, who was wealthy enough to leave his wretched hovel, but who, in spite of repeated offers from Lord Moray's factor promising him better accommodation, refused to move. While preaching on the sins of his flock one Sunday, John proclaimed: 'It is more difficult to wean you from your cherished sins than to induce M'Glashan to leave his hut. But I can say regarding him what I dare not utter regarding some of you, that the day will come, and it is looming in the near future, when he will be driven out of his home and the *feith diach* will run through its present site.' This prophecy was considered extremely

180

unlikely by those who heard it, but soon afterwards M'Glashan was evicted to make way for a large draining ditch which was known as the *feith diach*.

On another occasion while John was riding to Inverness he turned to his servant, who was walking beside him to order to ride the horse back to the manse, and said, 'Do you see that crowd of people ahead of us on the road?'

The servant nodded.

'I am telling you that only six of them will go to heaven. As proof that I speak the truth, the innkeeper at Milton of Culloden, who is now in good health, will be dead before you return with my horse to Inverness.' The lad was so impressed that two days later on his way to meet his master he stopped at the inn. There he heard that the innkeeper had fallen down his own stairs and broken his neck. His body was being laid out for burial.

In common with other seers, John Morrison foretold the Highland Clearances: 'Large as the Ridge of Petty is and thickly as it is now peopled, the day will come, and is not far off, when there will only be three smokes in it, and the crow of the cock at each will not be heard at either of the other owing to the distance. After a time, however, the lands will again be divided, and the parish of Petty become as populous as it is at this day.' At the time the prediction was uttered, there were fifteen well-to-do tenants in the district described, but by the late nineteenth century there were only three 'smokes', at Kerrowaird, Morayston and Balmachree.

He also foresaw the day when the evictions would leave only cattle and sheep on the Braes of Petty. This too came to pass.

With reference to a piece of wasteland in the heights above Morayston which was overgrown with broom, he predicted the day would come when corn would grow there, and that later the corn would give place to broom and woodland, and then again to corn, by which time the parish would be populated and the people flourishing. Mr Maclennan, when collecting the prophecies, was assured that at one time there had been a village nearby and that the hill was cultivated until the evictions. During the Maclennan's time it was wooded but now that Ardersier has become the centre of an oil rig construction industry, it is once again populated.

John's most famous prediction, which was probably genuine, concerned the Abban Stone, a conspicuous object on Petty beach. After his morning sermon, he was so depressed at the lack of response that he cried out vehemently, 'Ye stiff-necked, sinful people, Good will, unless you repent, sweep you soon into a place of torment, and as a sign that what I say is true, the Abban Stone, large though it is, will be carried soon without human interference a long way out to sea.'

Vain words, it would seem, for the stone weighed at least eight tons, and even if it could be moved, no one would think of doing so, for it marked the boundary between the Moray and Culloden estates. And yet on the night of 20 February 1799 it was lifted and carried out to sea some 260 yards from its original site. George Anderson, in his *Guide to the Highlands*, wrote: 'Some believe that nothing short of an earthquake could have removed such a mass, but the more probable explanation is that a large sheet of ice, which had collected to the thickness of eighteen inches round the stone, had been raised by the tide, lifting the stone with it, and that its motion forward was aided and increased by a tremendous hurricane which blew from the land.'

A poor prognosis for the unfortunate parishioners of Petty!

Apart from his prophetic utterances from the pulpit, John experienced private visions too. At one time he proposed preaching on the Book of Revelations to the people. However, he found it hard going, and after a day in his study he went off for a walk along the shore. There he saw a stranger digging a hole on the beach and asked him what he was doing. 'Building a trench to hold the sea,' was the man's extraordinary answer.

'But you can't do that,' protested John. 'You must be out of your mind. Go home and forget such a crazy notion.'

The man looked at him gravely. 'I shall accomplish my task before you succeed in making Revelations more plain than it is. God's word is so plain that he who runs may read it.'

So saying, the stranger vanished. John believed he had experienced a vision and gave up the idea for his sermon: a salutary vision indeed!

But John was human, after all, and never more so than in his last prediction which is redolent with sorrow at the thought of handing his flock over to another pastor. 'When John Morrison is laid in his grave,' he announced, 'you will get a stammering Lowland minister who will neither have English nor the Gaelic.' The prophecy was fulfilled to the letter, for John's successor, William Smith, was a native of Rafford whose Gaelic was as incomprehensible as his English. It cannot have been easy for him to follow in the steps of such a

182

saintly and well-loved minister. One of his new parishioners was said to have remarked, after hearing him preach. 'When I used to come to Petty, I was always given well filled oatcakes with butter on both sides, but I find now that there is only a small supply of rye bread with a take it or leave it as you please.' But William Smith was a worthy successor, nevertheless, and was described as second to none 'in strength of mind, ecclesiastical knowledge, and methodical habits.'

At first glance, it would seem that John Morrison was not a seer in the traditional, spectre-haunted sense of the word. His utterances were certainly prophetic, particularly the prediction concerning the Abban Stone, but many of the anecdotes would seem to have been exaggerated, honed to fit the memory of a godly man and capable of natural explanation. Certainly there are one or two stories that may have been genuine psychic experiences, such as the predicted death of the innkeeper and the sighting of the dun stot in the ditch. His followers believed that they were, and, although Morrison made no claim to the faculty himself, there were plenty to do so on his behalf.

At first glance, too, there would seem to be little in common between the minister of Petty and Columba, its first evangelist. Yet the links are there. Both were poets and musicians, men of high artistic talent. Both were passionate and compassionate, both could be harsh and tender. Both were evangelists in the true sense of that word, charismatic preachers, true Celts, and both were credited with the gift of second sight.

Ministers throughout the history of the faculty have always been its main chroniclers. This is because they were often the only educated men in the isolated parishes throughout the Highlands who were concerned to observe the beliefs and customs of their race. There may have been another reason: in spite of the several reformations of the church, there existed in the hearts of these Highlanders a deep and abiding belief-in the 'waking dream' so gloriously manifested in Columba. Just as Columba heralded an upsurge of Christianity among the northern Picts who had only been lightly touched by the mission of Ninian, so John Morrison was one of the first of a breed of ministers and laymen who were to evangelize the Highlands for almost a century, great men many of whom were credited with the gift of vision.

Second sight throughout the ages has been the object of curiosity and research by churchmen, as we have seen, whatever their denomination. During the five centuries of the Columban church, the gift was taken for granted. Roman rule equated second sight with superstition. The Reformed Church demonstrated an intellectual approach, enjoyed theorizing and research. The church in decline during the eighteenth century took its cue from the scientists and tended to disbelieve. It was not until the late eighteenth century that second sight took on a fresh and unexpected image in the north. By this time, the Parliamentary Church – the religion of the Yellow Stick, as it was called – or the lairds' church, was no longer satisfying the need of its members.

The reason? Patrons or heritors controlled both building and minister. Because the lairds refused to spend money on repairs, the churches were in ruins, and the clergy, not wishing to lose their jobs, were afraid to insist. Dr Johnson in his *Journey to the Western Isles* wrote in 1773, 'Through the few islands we visited we neither saw nor heard of any house of prayer, except on Skye, that was not in ruins.' Dr John Kennedy in *The Days of the Fathers*, published almost a century later, described his father's church in the Black Isle from the time of his induction to within two years of his death as 'almost as bad as it could be. Built in the form of a cross, with the pulpit at one of the angles, its barn-like roof unceiled, its windows broken, its doors all crazy, its seats ill-arranged, and pervaded by a dim uncertain light, it was a dismal, dingy-looking place within.'

Parishioners were poor, with no vote in ecclesiastical, parochial or political affairs. During the time of the Clearances when the ministers were in a position to speak up for the cottars and crofters, most of them sided with the lairds and taught their flocks to believe that eviction was a punishment from God for their idleness, fornication, and general sinfulness.

However, the established church may have been sinking fast but revival existed, as Dr Kennedy wrote, 'in the hearts and closets of the people'. In 1771, the Revd John Smith was appointed successor and assistant to the minister of Kilbrandon. His inspired evangelical preaching caused a religious revival and when Mr Smith was appointed to Campbeltown and the congregation at Kilbrandon could not find another evangelical minister, they seceded to become the first Reformed Presbyterian Church in the Highlands. In Ross-shire the reform was just as dramatic, if not so immediately final. Rather than secede, the dissatisfied congregations flocked to the churches of evangelical ministers who, with 'an intense aversion to unsoundness, formality and unwatchfulness', rekindled the faith of the people.

It was just before 1792 (which was known as '*bliadhna nan caorach*', the year of the sheep, when the lairds exchanged so many of their tenants for 'four-footed clansmen') that a congregation of hundreds gathered from far afield and met to take Communion and hear the preaching of Dr Fraser of Kirkhill. These were the early days of the great open-air Sacrament Sundays where people walked miles to hear their favourite preachers, many of whom were not ministers at all but acknowledged laymen. The order of 'the Men' as opposed to ministers, though recognized, was never official. These loyal supporters of the 'good' ministers became known as the 'Friday men', since traditionally they were to become the principal speakers at the Friday Fellowship, gatherings where they sought to answer questions such as 'Am I in Christ?' or 'How can I be born again?'

Some of 'the Men' were fanatics, railing against ministers and indulging in extravagant displays of exorcism and faith-healing, but most were holy men who led prayer groups in private houses, who did not seek to secede but remained loyal to such ministers as Dr John Macdonald of Ferintosh known as 'the Apostle of the North', Dr Charles Mackintosh of Tain, the Kennedys, father and son of Killearnan and Dingwall, Donald Sage of Resolis, and many others. Among the gifts credited to them was that of second sight. Dr Kennedy recorded many instances as 'indubitable facts', and in anticipation of the 'sneers of some as they read them' he added:

> A little careful thinking on the subject might help one to see that, by means of the written word, under the guiding hand of His Spirit, the Lord may give intimations of His will in a way very different from the direct inspiration of prophecy, and that ends are served by such communications of His mind that make it far from improbable that the Lord may have given them.

One of these men 'eminent for godliness' was Mr Mackay of Hope, a member of Dr Kennedy's father's first parish in Eriboll. Though ill and aged, he insisted on his entire household attending church. On their return, one of the family told him that they had heard 'a precious sermon'. 'My soul knows that,' said the old man, 'for while I was lying here, my mind was following the preacher as he was engaged in his work.' To the astonishment of the household, he told them both text and substance. Dr Kennedy adds, 'This story, seemingly so incredible, is perfectly true, and furnishes a most remarkable instance of the mysterious fellowship of the saints.'

Another of the 'Men' was 'the godly Donald Macpherson still alive when my father was minister in Eriboll,' wrote Dr Kennedy, 'of whom he has often said that of all the Christians he had ever known he was the man who lived nearest the Lord.' He looked like the traditional seer with long hair, a handkerchief tied round his head, and old-fashioned eccentric clothing as he strode over the hills. When he prayed for a particular person, 'there was scarce a thought or feeling of the party prayed for hidden from him by the Lord.'

He had a disciple, Robert Macleod, who was to become one of the most noted 'Men' of the time. One day Donald asked Robert to lead the prayers at family worship. Robert dared not refuse such a request so he fell to his knees. 'Thou knowest, O God, that though I have bent my knees to pray to Thee, I am much more under the fear of Donald Macpherson, than under the fear of Thyself.' Donald promptly tapped him on the shoulder. 'That will do, Robert. You have honestly begun and you will honourably end.'

Robert then declared he would never be any use in public testimony. 'Yes, Robert,' said Donald, 'the Lord will open your mouth to speak the praises of free grace, and, as a sign of this you will be called thrice to speak, on the very first day you are called to speak in public.' When some time later, Robert heard that Communion was to be dispensed at Lochbroom, he decided to go, but arrived late. Just before he came, the minister announced that he expected a new preacher that day. Robert had scarcely sat down when he was called to 'speak to the question'. He was so embarrassed that he could only mutter a few words. Later the minister called him again. 'As you had only just come you were taken by surprise. Rise again,' he was bidden. This time Robert stood up and delivered such a fine address that he was called upon a third time to raise the concluding prayer. Thus at his first appearance, he was three times called to speak, in fulfilment of the prediction.

Women too were endowed with the same gift. Mary Macrae,

186

'retarded and ignorant', who had lived for fifty years in Lochbroom, felt called to go to Killearnan in the Black Isle when Dr Kennedy's father was the incumbent. She had never heard of the place and the journey was long and hard, but eventually she arrived. 'Foolish Mary' was kindly treated by Mr Kennedy who took pains to explain the gospel to her in simple terms. Her particular way of communicating her views or feelings was strange, and seemed to those who did not know her as if she was recalling a dream. To one young minister on the eve of his licensing, she declared, 'I saw you lately in a bog with a fishing rod and you were sinking fast. You cried out as if you would never rise again. Then I saw you on the banks of a broad river and the joy in your heart was in the smile on your face, and you were coming home with your rod on your shoulder and a basket of fishes in your hand.' This symbolic vision she then interpreted to the young man.

On another occasion she felt compelled to visit the manse of a minister she liked. 'What is the matter with him?' she asked at the door.

'I don't know,' she was told, 'but I never saw him in greater distress.'

'I know that,' said Mary 'and I know that he is tempted not to go to church today, but he will go in the end. The snare will be broken and he will get on the wing in his work today.' The minister, who had overheard the conversation, was in his pulpit as usual.

Once she visited Dr Kennedy himself and with an anxious expression asked him about a certain minister whom she had seen 'fixing a wing to each of his sides and rising on these wings into the air till he was very high, and then suddenly he fell and was dashed to pieces on the ground. I think that this minister has but a borrowed goodness, and that his end is near.' The man in question died later that week.

One of the most celebrated of 'the Men' was John Munro, known as 'the caird of Kiltearn'. On a stormy winter's day he was obsessed with the need to visit a friend in a nearby parish. The journey was exhausting, and as soon as he arrived his friend burst into tears. This was not the welcome he had expected. 'I had hoped you would be pleased to see me,' he remonstrated.

'What grieves me is that you have come so far on such a stormy day, and I have no food to give you.'

'I know now why I was impelled to come,' said the caird, laying some bread on the table. On his journey home he called in at every house and spoke of the family's hardship. Next day horses and creels laden with stores called at the cottage with enough provisions to last for a year.

Alister Og, the weaver of Edderton in Easter Ross, another of the celebrated 'Men', admitted a stranger for the night, against his wife's judgement, and gave him the best that his lonely croft could provide. Next morning his irate wife found that he had gone off with her husband's best web.

'Didn't I tell you not to let that man in!' she cried.

'I let him in because the Lord commanded me, and I promise you that he will send back the man who stole the cloth.'

Meanwhile the thief found himself lost in the heavy mist that had fallen over the Hill of Edderton. He spent the day walking in circles and at nightfall called on the house with the nearest light. It happened to be Alister's croft.

Probably the most famous of all the 'Men' was Hugh Ross, known as Hughie Buie, who up to the age of twenty had been a powerful, handsome youth, proud of his looks, his strength, and his skill at shinty and dancing. Dressed up in a fine new plaid he decided to show himself off to the congregation at Fearn in Easter Ross, and chose the most conspicuous seat at the front so that all could admire him. During the sermon he was converted, and thereafter each Sunday he would be found alone and desolate outside the church, sometimes with icicles hanging from his hair, not fit in his own eyes to go inside. One of the elders took pity on him and pushed him sharply through the door and locked him in. Thereafter he became a catechist and a famous preacher throughout Ross-shire. When he was ninety, he was seen by the congregation at Resolis in the Black Isle surrounded by a radiant aura. Later in the manse, after saying grace in his own clear way, he leaned back in his chair and died.

Among the ministers who shared, like the Petty Seer, the gift of vision was John Kennedy himself, whose life is so vividly described by his son, Dr Kennedy of Dingwall, in *The Days of the Fathers.* Born in Applecross in 1771, young John had a reputation for goodness from the age of four. A story is told of a woman who, passing by his window, happened to overhear his childish prayers and became converted. At the age of six he caught smallpox, the killing disease of the age, and while on the point of death was visited by a neighbour who had the reputation for being a seer.

'What do you think of my John?' his mother asked.

'Ere the tide that now ebbs shall have touched the shore again, your child shall be no more,' the seer solemnly predicted. The sick child heard him but was unafraid, sensing that the man's motives were evil. Then his father came in and ordered the seer out. 'That messenger of Satan lies,' he told his weeping wife. 'The Lord had given me the life of my child, and blessings shall rest upon his head and he shall serve the Lord in the gospel of his Son.'

The boy recovered, and the seer, who was a close neighbour, kept well out of his way until years later he lay in wait for him on his return from college. Suddenly appearing from a narrow gorge, he thrust some money into the young man's hand and disappeared. A peace-offering perhaps, or an indication that the future is not as fixed as is generally thought by seers, but is reversible in the hands of a greater power.

John's education was as thorough as such isolated conditions allowed and after a spell at Aberdeen University, he was, among others, licensed to preach by the Presbytery of Lochcarron when he was twenty-four. The presiding minister was heard to remark, 'The others are preachers of our making, but the Lord made a preacher of John Kennedy.'

One incident recalled by his son reveals not only the nature of the man but also the impoverished condition of the times:

Called to see a dying woman [his son recorded] I found on reaching the place to which I was directed, a dark filthy attic, in which I could observe nothing till the light I had carried in had quite departed from my eye. The first object I could discern was an old woman crouching on a stone beside a low fire who, as I afterwards ascertained was unable to move except on all fours. Quite near the fire I then saw a bed, on which an older woman still was stretched, who was stone blind, and lying at the very gates of death. The two women were sisters, and miserable indeed they seemed to be; the one with her breast and face devoured by cancer, the other blind and dying. They were from Lochbroom; and we had spoken but little when one of them referred to the days of my father's labour in their parish, and told of her first impression of divine things under a sermon he preached at the time. The doctrine of that sermon was as fresh in her mind, and as cheering, as when she first heard it half

189

a century before. Such was the humble hope of both of them, and their cheerful resignation to the will of God, that I could not but regard them in their dark and filthy attic, as at the very threshold of glory.

In 1802, John Kennedy was appointed missionary in Eriboll in Sutherland, and the young man, fair-skinned, well-proportioned and athletic, soon pleased his new parishioners. From Eriboll he was moved to Assynt to become the assistant of 'Parson William', described as a drinker and 'stipend-lifter'. There was little contact between the two, with John doing the bulk of the work in an extensive and at that time populous parish. After his marriage there he was translated to the parish of Killearnan, and it was during his ministry here that he was credited with second sight.

One Sunday he pronounced from the pulpit, 'There is one here who has been bargaining about his cattle regardless of the Sabbath and the eye of the Lord. He knows I speak the truth and I tell him this, that if the Lord has mercy on his soul, he will yet be reduced to beg for his daily bread.' Next day one of his young parishioners came up to him and asked how he knew that he had been selling heifers to the rover on the Sabbath.

'Did you do so?' John asked him quietly.

'I can't deny it,' the farmer replied.

'Remember then the warning that was given you, for you will lose either your substance or your soul.'

'But will you not tell me how you knew?' the young man persisted.

'The secret of the Lord is with them that fear him,' was all the minister would say. Years later the farmer lost his substance and applied for charity to many of those who had heard the prediction.

Another Sunday, Kennedy paused in his sermon and declared, 'There is a sinner in this place, ripe for destruction, who shall this night be summoned to the judgement seat.' Next morning, neighbours saw that the hut of a woman, notorious for immorality, was on fire. They arrived too late to save her.

While officiating at a Communion gathering at Contin, John Kennedy declared, 'There is still a communicant here who has not come forward, and till that person takes his seat at the table, I cannot proceed with the service.'

A hymn was sung but the merchant from Kiltarlity did not move.

'I implore you to come forward, for this is your last chance of showing forth the Lord's death till he come, for, if I am not greatly mistaken, you will not reach your home alive today,' urged the minister. Reluctantly the merchant then went forward, and as soon as he had taken his seat at the Communion table, the minister declared, 'We may now proceed with the service.' On his way home, while crossing the ford of the River Orrin, the poor man was carried downstream and drowned.

News of the sudden death of the minister of Kirkhill, a close friend of Mr Kennedy, was brought to the manse too late to be delivered, for the minister had already left for service. To everyone's surprise he declared in prayer that 'a breach had been made in the walls of Zion in the north by the removal of one of the most eminent servants of the Lord'. As he came out of church, he was told of Mr Fraser's death. 'I was prepared for it,' he declared.

Often he predicted the Disruption when the Church of Scotland became officially divided in 1843. While preaching at Ferintosh in 1829, he sadly declared, 'This crowded church shall yet become a place into which none who fear the Lord will dare to enter. Not long before this change takes place, I shall be removed to my rest, but many who now hear me shall see it.' From that date, his visions became increasingly vivid, and the prospect of the Disruption 'wrung more groans from his heart, than the actual experience of the trial from the hearts of many who survived it'.

His last pastoral visit was paid to a pious couple who were both close to death and anxious to see him. The husband was one of his elders, but less bright both spiritually and intellectually than his wife. 'Do you believe that your affliction was appointed by God in the everlasting covenant?' he asked them both.

'I believe it is permitted by God in his providence, but I have not attained to believe that it was ordered in the covenant,' declared the wife.

'I cannot even say what my wife has just said,' declared her husband.

'You are a step behind her, Donald,' said the minister, 'and as surely as she is before you in this, she will be before you in heaven.' And so it happened. Though the husband was the older and more ailing, his wife died first.

191

Like Columba, Kennedy was aware of the approach of his own death. He would start on a course of sermons, then lay it aside for another, while entreating his flock to observe how the Lord was urging him to fulfil his ministry with all haste, for the end was near. His last sermon in church was preached on the Tuesday evening before his death and it closed a series of sermons on the text, 'We are come to God, the Judge of all'. The congregation were then dismissed, persuaded they would never see him again on earth, while he stood at the door exclaiming, 'My poor people, my poor, poor people.' All this time he was in excellent health, yet on the following day he developed a sore throat. Inflammation increased but he complained little, and his family was not unduly alarmed. He went to bed and laid himself down calmly to die. His one reply to all queries was, 'I'll be soon quite well'.

While his wife and a friend were sitting in his sick room, not really alarmed by his illness, they heard music, soft, strange and unearthly. They listened, rapt, in silence. When the music ceased, Mrs Kennedy turned to ask her husband if he had heard it, but he did not answer. His expression was absorbed and radiant. Alarmed at last, she sent for the doctor, but there was nothing he could do. By Sunday night, Kennedy was dead.

Although these incidents are common to periods of religious revival throughout the ages, and superficially at least would seem to have little to do with what we understand as second sight, yet there are connections that could be seen as links between the manifestations described above and the earliest interpretation of the gift. The predictions of the ecstatic religious man from pulpit or open hillside would seem to parallel the utterances of Druids in their sacred groves and the visions of that older priesthood, guardians of the burial mounds. Both seek to convey the message of a god, whether Christian or ancestral spirit of the tribe.

Methods used to reach the ecstatic state were not dissimilar. Druids probably fasted, chanted and practised ritual worship before reaching the state of waking dream. The 'Men' and ministers of the nineteenth-century Highlands also fasted and prayed mightily before preaching to the assembled crowds. Ecstasy is not common to one faith, or confined to one generation: it is part of the religious history of mankind. One of its manifestations is the ability to see through space and beyond time.

Today ecstasy can be induced in the laboratory by a series of repeated sounds and movements, a further proof, if such be needed, that what is so often thought to be supernatural is a normal talent in mankind. This is not, of course, to say that all ESP is produced in a state of ecstasy, but as we try to understand the nature of the faculty, it is worth bearing in mind that for some this is the only way.

THE HELMSDALE SEER

A native of Sutherland, John Macdonald was born about 1800 'tongue-tied', and had to be operated on before he could feed. His father was employed as a ground-officer for the Duchess of Sutherland, and John was brought up in Brora. At school he was nicknamed '*an ciobair*', the shepherd; and at the age of thirteen he was taken on as a shop assistant in Gartymore. However, John was a scholar and he eventually managed to win a place at Aberdeen University when he was twenty-one. He must have been a frugal lad for his total expenses for the whole of the second-session amounted to only £15 8s. During the holidays and after he had taken his degree he worked as a school teacher at Farr, and it was not till 1837 that he was appointed by the patrons – the Duke and Duchess of Sutherland – to the church at Helmsdale, at a stipend of £50 a year (which was raised by the fishermen) and a free house.

Helmsdale at that time was a busy fishing-port with 200 boats, which had been created by the Sutherlands to employ crofters evicted from the glens. Every stick and stone of it, including the church and manse, belonged to the patrons.

John was a busy, dedicated minister preaching four long sermons every Sunday. He soon was much in demand at the great Sacramental gatherings throughout the north; he was passionate, outspoken, and known as a seer of some repute. Perhaps because he saw so much injustice in the treatment of humble folk during the Clearances, he decided to leave the Established church at the time of the Disruption and join the Free Kirk. To do this in the heart of Sutherland was a brave act, and for a time he was churchless and homeless, for sites for a new building were continually refused by the Duchess and her factors. James Loch, MP and Commissioner for the Duke and Duchess, obviously regarded the elders who had broken away with John Macdonald as the Bolshevists of the day, for he wrote in reply to a petition from them:

There is one assertion in your petition which cannot be passed over without observation and animadversion; and if you had been aware of its import and its tendency, it would never have been adopted by you; for you would never have used such words as these. That, from a love of peace, your petitioners implore as a favour what the law of Britain and the law of the Proprietor of all entitle them to demand as a right. Now, this is not the law, nor was it ever the law. It is at variance with all law, and is subversive of every right of property.

But John was a strong man, confident in his beliefs, who was eventually to gain his church and manse and a reputation for godliness throughout the Highlands.

His first known prophecy was made in the street at Helmsdale when he and a friend were walking past a partly finished house. 'That house,' he declared 'built in part at least with the gains of Sabbath profanation, will be built but not inhabited by the owner.' While preaching the next Sunday he named those whom he thought to be the offenders. They were so angry that John predicted that one would be drowned and the other stoned. Shortly after one of the two was drowned, as foreseen, and the other had his right arm amputated. Neither was to inhabit the house.

On another occasion some Helmsdale fishermen petitioned the Dunrobin estate office to remove a sandbank which had accumulated at the mouth of the river and which was blocking the harbour. The factor told them scornfully to go to their minister and ask him to pray for a spate to take it away. This they did; within a few days the spate came and the sandbank was removed.

While preaching in Caithness in 1849, Macdonald saw a woman shearing her corn in full view of the Sunday worshippers. 'Now,' he declared, 'I will give you my thoughts about that woman. The Lord has so much regard for his own work, that He will keep her longer from her work than if she had given him all the days of this feast to his service.' It was not for another year that the woman referred to was fit enough to attend church or work in the fields.

While preaching at Halladale, he mentioned by name several of the chief sheep-farmers who were actively trying to suppress him and the Free Kirk. 'I shall preach the gospel in Sutherland after the last of these men are in their graves.' And so it turned out.

At that time there were rumours of war with France, but John predicted from the pulpit, 'This country has nothing to fear from the French, but unless the Lord puts a hook in the nose of that Leviathan, the Emperor of Russia, the danger will arrive from that quarter.' This he said at least three years before the outbreak of the Crimean War.

Once he called to see a close friend who was later to become his biographer, and found him feverish and unconscious. After prayer he told the sick man's wife, 'Now Mrs Mackay, don't be in the least afraid, for your husband will soon be as well as ever.' And so he was.

John Macdonald died in Glasgow in 1854. At his funeral in Helmsdale at least 1,200 attended, and his reputation lived on, both as a seer and a preacher, into the twentieth century.

These stories match closely those told of John Morrison of Petty and John Kennedy of Killearnan, and one might be forgiven for thinking them at least partly apocryphal. But Highlanders are not fools, nor are they credulous – particularly when it comes to a subject on which they are expert, such as second sight. The style 'seer' is not lightly bestowed. At the time of the Disruption there were dozens of preachers as great, and greater, in reputation who were not so styled.

What stands out when studying the lives and talents of these men is the reverential attitude of Highland Christians to 'the gift'; that it is viewed as God-given in order to reveal God's purpose for his people. Bound to the Old Testament, the patriarchs and prophets as the Free Kirkers undoubtedly were, prophecy had a noble precedent, yet their visions and predictions were not wholly characteristic of those of the Jews. These Christian seers would seem to owe at least as much to Columba, their foster-father in the tradition, who himself was a product of the ancient culture of the Celts.

The psychic ability of these men would seem to have put on the faculty a further seal of respectability, which lingers on in the Highlands to this day. And yet there is a difference. The gift which Columba gloried in, and which was accepted and used by the ministers and the 'Men' during a period of evangelization in the Highlands, is today regarded either as a holy affliction better not spoken about, or as a superstition and therefore sinful. No area of Christian life and teaching, whatever the denomination, produces more muddled thinking than in the field of psychic talent to this day.

7 *The Brahan Seer*

THE LEGENDARY COINNEACH ODHAR

Lewis is an island of moods dictated by the sky. Black pools, black peat hags, and black houses reflect depression. Wet rocks lie greyly lichened in the rain. Machair grasses cower under howling winds. But there are days when the sky is blue and benign, the white crofts sparkle, the sea is gentle on sands as white as ivory, and then there is nowhere on earth more magical.

Lewis is also an island of history, where ancient men planted monoliths and duns, where Celtic princesses bred with Norse Vikings, where clan succeeded clan in bloody conflict, and natives were uprooted from their ancestral soil.

The land is poor to cultivate but rich with waterhorses, fairy washerwomen and the *sithean*. Winters are harsh and long, but brightened at the *ceilidh* hearth with stories and music and poetry. In Lewis the second sight is commonplace. Some say it was here, in the early half of the seventeenth century, that Coinneach Odhar Fiosaiche, Sallow Kenneth, the One who Knows, was born.

A church still stands on the grassy hillock crowning the township of Baile-na-Cille on the northern arm of Uig Bay. You can still find the ancient burial ground right on the edge of the sea next to the manse. Small, round (as was the custom) and overcrowded, it had recently been cleared of weeds when I went there in 1982, and it was possible to read some of the names on the old stones: Mackenzies, Macaulays, Macraes, Macleans. In the centre, a large unmarked, undressed slab had fallen. Every available space was crammed with smaller unmarked stones. Perhaps the weather had eroded the inscriptions; perhaps none had ever been chiselled. A cat streaked past me as I entered, reminding me of the legend that cats had haunted the

196

burial ground for many generations, though no one remembered why. Mine was sleek and grey, and probably came from the manse.

This was the kirkyard where, according to legend, Coinneach's mother, a young crofter wife, encountered a well-born ghost. One night as she was herding the township cattle on a grassy ridge above the burial ground, she saw in the light of a full moon the graves each open. One by one old men, warriors, wives, and bairns rose and disappeared into the dark. Fearfully she waited until just before dawn the ghosts returned, each to its own grave which closed over it as before. All were filled save one. Curiosity gave her courage. Down she crept and stole into the graveyard. Remembering an old belief that no spirit could cross rowan wood, she placed her distaff over the mouth of the hole and waited.

Soon she saw a beautiful woman rushing through the air from the north. She wore white with a band of gold in her hair and she was in a hurry.

'Lift your distaff from my grave so that I may return to the land of the dead,' she implored.

'Who are you?' the woman whispered. 'What made you so late?'

'I am the daughter of the King of Norway, drowned long ago. My body was found on these sands and buried in this grave.' Once a year, the ghost explained, the dead were permitted to return to their homes, but her journey was so long that she was always late back. Coinneach's mother lifted her *cuigeal*, but before the ghost disappeared she took a stone from her breast. 'Give this to your son when he is seven years old. It will give him the gift of prophecy.'

When Coinneach reached that age his mother sent him to call in his father from the fields. At first the child refused so she bribed him with the promise of the stone. He took it, looked through it, and 'saw' a whale stranded outside a distant cave – riches, indeed, for the crofter-fishermen of Uig, and the foundation of his reputation as a seer.

Another Lewis tale of Norse origin says that Coinneach found the stone in a raven's nest. Many of his future predictions were to feature 'Odin's bird' who, according to Norse mythology, possessed the power to prophesy victory in battle. To the Celt, on the other hand, the raven was a bird of ill-omen and death.

Quickly Coinneach's fame as a seer spread abroad. He was sought after by lairds and chiefs throughout the Highlands and Islands, and no gathering or feast was complete without him. Kenneth, third Earl of Seaforth, laird of Lewis and most of Ross-shire during the second half of the seventeenth century, and who commuted between his three castles at Lewis, Brahan, and Fortrose (or the Chanonry, as it was then called) soon came to hear of his gift. He took a fancy to the outspoken youth and gave him employment on the Brahan estate on the river Conon not far from Strathpeffer. Perhaps fame went to the young man's head, or perhaps his foreknowledge made him impatient with ordinary folk, for he was to become arrogant, shrewd beyond his years, and afraid of no one. If any attempted to laugh at him, he soon turned the joke against his tormenter.

All this Alexander Mackenzie tells us in his *Prophecies of the Brahan Seer*, first published in 1877.

A Black Isle version, repeated by Mrs R. Higginbottom in 1984, is as follows:

Kenneth's father and mother were a fine young couple who lived on a croft in Lewis. The young wife was expecting her first child when her husband died. It was the custom in those days to watch the grave at night for a month, for some people would rob the graves and take parts of bodies to use in making witchcraft. The widow took her collie dog with her, and every night at twelve she saw spirits of the dead leave their graves and return before cock-crow, but the spirit of a young girl was always late, and the collie would lie on her grave. The girl's spirit asked the widow to keep the collie off her grave, so the widow asked her why she was late, and the spirit told her that she was the spirit of a princess from the north who had been coming on a ship to marry the son of a king but had died of fever. The sailors had taken her ashore and buried her there. 'I have a long way to go to visit my home, and if I am not back in my grave by cockcrow, I cannot leave my grave again.' So the widow kept the collie off the grave. When the month was up, she told the spirit who said she would give the son the widow was carrying a gift, but it was not to be passed on to him until he was a man. She told the widow to pick two white stones off her grave; they would bring luck to her son if he used them wisely in helping others. Also he must use them to help a red-haired woman. Then the spirit looked at the stones in the widow's hands, and an expression of terror came over her face. 'What have I done to you

198

who have been so kind to me? He will help a red-haired woman, and she will repay him with hell-fire.'

When Kenneth was born, the widow, remembering the terror in the spirit's face, threw the stones into a deep well that never went dry. But the year Kenneth became a man the well went dry, and he found the stones. His mother told him the story and warned him. He did help a red-haired woman, the Countess of Seaforth, and she had him burned in a barrel of tar.

Hugh Miller's version is somewhat different. While labouring for a wealthy Mackenzie farmer who lived near Brahan Castle, Coinneach made himself so unpopular with the farmer's wife by his sarcastic tongue that she was driven to get rid of him. After mixing some poisonous herbs with his dinner bannock, she took the food to where he was digging peats in a lonely place. Finding him asleep, she left the food by his side and hurried home. When he awoke, he saw the food and would have eaten it had he not felt something pressing heavily against his heart. On opening his waistcoat he found a beautiful smooth stone resembling a pearl, but much larger, which had apparently been dropped into his breast while he slept. When he gazed at it, he found that not only could he see the future as distinctly as the present, but also that he could detect people's real designs and motives as clearly as their deeds. Thus he knew what his employer's wife had done.

A similar version from the Black Isle gives Coinneach a wife. After a morning spent cutting peats, he sat down to wait for her arrival with his dinner. After a while he fell asleep, with his head on a fairy mound. Later he was wakened by the pressure of a round stone with a hole through it, which was hurting his head. Picking it up, he looked through it and 'saw' his wife approaching with a dinner of sowans and milk 'unspeakably' polluted. To test the truth of his vision, he gave the dinner to his dog, which died in agony. Thereafter Coinneach found that he had exchanged the natural sight of that eye for supernatural vision.

Each version describes Coinneach's stone differently, from small and white to jet-black and shining, from blue and spherical to round with a hole in it like a spindle-whorl. All versions are agreed, however, that he had a stone. Whether it was, like a crystal ball, essential to his vision, or whether he used it merely as a symbol of power is not important. What is also of interest is that in each version Coinneach received his gift from the *sithean*, those ancestral spirits or fairies who haunted burial mounds and graves, and within whose bounty the gift of second sight lay.

After his fame as a seer became established, an enthusiast from Inverness sent for him in order to record his predictions. He wrote down several, but when Coinneach told him that the day would come when ships would be led round the back of Tomnahurich Hill in Inverness, the writer gave up and, believing that Coinneach was mad, tore up his manuscript. Nevertheless that prophecy eventually came true with the opening of the Caledonian Canal in 1822.

From then on, Coinneach's prophecies were to range over Ross-shire and to cover a host of happenings both great and small. Many were to forecast the doom of local Mackenzie lairds, the landlords of the day, and it was these prophecies above all that were to endear Coinneach to the Highlanders and to turn him, in spite of some unpleasant characteristics, into the folk-hero and anti-Establishment figure he has now become. In those days it was not easy for sub-tenants and cottars to criticize their masters; there was no hint of equality in society at that time. But within the private warmth of the *ceilidh* hearth, such stories repeated again and again soothed injuries and helped to heal the memory of injustices. They were the common folks' revenge.

Chief of these lairds was Kenneth Mackenzie of Kintail, third Earl of Seaforth, who in spite of his wife's disapproval continued his patronage of the controversial, gifted young man. Perhaps it amused his lordship to see him stand up to the Countess, for Isabella was as sharp-tongued and shrewd as the seer himself. Certainly, Coinneach made no effort to please her. During a gathering at Brahan Castle where the flower of the clan was assembled, including Isabella's eight children, some sycophant remarked in the seer's hearing that such a gathering of gentlemen's children was rarely seen. Coinneach answered that he preferred the children of gillies to that of the gentry, and made dark insinuations about the paternity of some of the Brahan guests. Isabella was so annoyed that, according to one story, she ordered his arrest. While attempting escape he was seized, so he quickly threw away his stone which fell in a cow's hoof-print that was full of water. While his captors scrambled in the mud to find it, he predicted that it would eventually be found by a child with two

200

navels, four thumbs and six toes, inside the belly of a pike. At that point, water oozing through the mud, hid the stone and spread rapidly to become Loch Ussie. Alexander Mackenzie states that during his lifetime a child was born nearby disfigured as predicted, but whether he found the stone is not recorded. It is rumoured currently (in 1984) that there is a man fishing the loch who has two navels.

The better-known version of how Coinneach came to be arrested describes how the Earl was sent to Paris by Charles II on an affair of state. Taking into account the lengthy journey, Isabella finally decided he had stayed away too long. Suspicious and uneasy, she summoned Coinneach from his home in Strathpeffer and asked if he could give her any information. The seer, confident and no doubt gratified that the great lady had condescended to consult him, told her that he would certainly be able to find Seaforth if he were still alive. He lifted his stone and laughed at what he saw.

'Fear not for your lord,' he told her with a smile. 'He is safe and sound, well and hearty, merry and happy.'

Isabella was both relieved and annoyed. She asked Coinneach to describe the Earl's surroundings. What was he doing at that precise moment?

'Ask no more questions,' he told her. 'Be content with the knowledge that he is well and happy.'

'But where is he? Who is he with? When is he coming home?'

'I see your lord in a magnificent room,' said the seer, 'in fine company and far too agreeably occupied to think of leaving Paris.'

Isabella's curiosity was now thoroughly aroused. There was a knowing gleam in Coinneach's eye which she distrusted. She was also jealous. Why should she have been left out of so much luxury and pleasure? She demanded to know more, but he would tell her nothing.

As time passed, she continued to bully the seer with threats and bribes and taunts. He resisted them all until at last, during her birthday feast at Brahan, he finally gave in. 'Since you insist on knowing what will only displease you, I will tell you the truth. Your lord has little thought of you, or of his children and his home. I saw him in a gay gilded room, grandly dressed in velvet, silk, and cloth of gold. He was on his knees to a fair lady, his arm round her waist, his lips pressed to her hand.'

This was what Isabella had secretly dreaded. She was hurt and angry with her husband certainly, but far more so with the seer. He had humiliated her, doubtless deliberately, in front of her children, her relations and her servants. She had never approved of him and his occult gifts. The man was in Satan's thrall. It was her duty to make an example of him. Slowly she rose to her feet.

'You have spoken evil of dignities. You have defamed a great chief in the eyes of his servants. You have abused my hospitality and outraged my feelings. You have sullied the good name of my lord in the hall of his ancestors. You shall suffer the death.'

Coinneach, not as knowing in the ways of women as of the future, was astonished. He had expected to be rewarded for his vision. Surely the Countess was not serious? He soon saw that she would never change her mind, and the clan, loyal to their chief and his lady, also turned against him. He was arrested.

Now it was his turn to be angry. He shook off his captors and for the last time raised his stone to his eye. No one interrupted him, no one moved as they listened awestruck to Coinneach's final prediction.

I see into the far future. I read the doom of my oppressor. The long descended line of Seaforth will, ere many generations have passed, end in extinction and sorrow. I see a chief, the last of his house, both deaf and dumb. He will be father to four fair sons, all of whom will go before him to the tomb. He will live careworn and die mourning, knowing that the honours of his line are to be extinguished forever and that no future chief of Mackenzies will rule at Brahan or Kintail. After lamenting the last and most promising of his sons, he shall sink into the grave, and the remnant of his possessions shall be inherited by a white-hooded widow from the East, and she is to kill her sister.

As a sign by which it may be known that the things are coming to pass, there will be four great lairds in the days of the last deaf and dumb Seaforth – Cairloch, Chisholm, Grant and Raasay – one of whom will be buck-toothed, another hare-lipped, another half-witted and the fourth a stammerer. Chiefs thus distinguished will be allies and neighbours of the last Seaforth; and when he looks around him and sees them, he may know that his sons are doomed, that his broad lands shall pass to strangers and that his race shall come to an end. And of the great house of Brahan not a stone shall remain.

202

Uproar followed. There was no hope for the seer now. He was seized, bound, and taken to Chanonry. On the way he cast his stone into Loch Ussie and declared that whoever found it would be gifted with second sight. After a hasty trial he was condemned to be cast head first into a burning tar barrel thickly studded with long sharp spikes. On his way to the stake, Isabella taunted him that he would never go to heaven, but Coinneach was once again to have the last word.

'I will go to heaven but you never shall, and this shall be a sign for you. After my death, two birds – a raven and a dove – will circle the sky above my ashes. If the raven alight first, then you have spoken truly; but if it be the dove, then my hopes are well-founded.'

And so it happened. Watchers by the seer's cooling ashes saw the dove, that harbinger of hope, alight, while the bird of ill-omen flew away.

Ironically, on the day of the burning the Earl came home. At Brahan he was told of the seer's fate. Without stopping for food or rest, he saddled his favourite horse and set off for Chanonry. Riding like the wind, he out-distanced his companions and saw the thick black column of tell-tale smoke on the horizon. Spurring his steed too harshly, he was thrown as the poor beast collapsed beneath him, dead. So he ran the rest of the way, but by the time he arrived it was too late.

'I tried to save you,' he cried to the dying man.

'I saw you coming,' Coinneach answered from the pyre, 'but I knew you would be too late. For what your lady has done this day, your race will end but mine will begin. After I am dead, a child of my seed will be born on Brahan land and will be called the Brahan child, and from his seed there will be a Brahan child in every generation who will see as I have seen, and let those beware who would do them harm, for my shadow will be watching over them.'

So saying, he was consumed.

Of the Brahan child we know nothing, but ten years ago there were living in Inverness two women who believed themselves to be descended through their father from Coinneach Odhar. Both claimed to have inherited the second sight.

A stone slab laid on Chanonry Ness to mark the site of the burning has long ago been obliterated by sand. Eighty years ago, however, the site was known, fenced off and children were warned not to go near.

In 1969, Fortrose Town Council erected another stone, thus perpetuating into another century the legend of Coinneach Odhar.

WHO WAS COINNEACH ODHAR?

In 1982 a party of lively eleven-year-olds from a school in Dingwall visited the small museum of Groam House in Rosemarkie in the Black Isle. Their primary interest was in the Pictish Symbol Stone housed there, and they had done their homework well. They knew the latest theories, the dates and the historical facts, such as there are, about the Picts. The museum also contains an audio-visual film about Coinneach Odhar. When the children were asked who he was, every hand shot up. When questioned as to how he received his prophetic stone, there was a forest of waving arms, and again a tattoo of clicking fingers when they were asked how he died. They all knew the legend and could repeat many of the predictions.

Again in 1982, some half-dozen young teenagers attended a talk on the Brahan Seer in Ness in the north of Lewis, the birth-place of Coinneach Odhar according to the *Bannatyne Manuscript History of the Macleods*. Curious to know how they had first heard of the seer, and hoping to find that the stories had been told to them in the old oral tradition, I was at first surprised to learn that they had read about him in a comic book.

The oral tradition may have gone, but the legends continue in newspapers, radio, conversation, and even in comic-strips. Such is the power of myth.

Whether the old tales would have survived even if Alexander Mackenzie had not seen the decline of oral transmission and, in 1877, collected them into his best-seller *The Prophecies of the Brahan Seer* is arguable. My belief is that they are indestructible. Folklore is no dead science. Like a tapestry continually woven with the threads of events – some significant, others of no apparent importance – it enriches the life and memory of mankind.

No one was more aware of this than Alexander Mackenzie. In his book, he divided the prophecies into three sections: those which might be attributed to natural shrewdness, those as yet unfulfilled, and those wholly or partly fulfilled. Since the publication of his book many more predictions have come to light; some are still emerging and will probably continue to appear as long as the Highlands survive.

A prophecy, to be worthy of the name, has to be written down before its fulfilment. A handful of Coinneach's predictions were well known before fulfilment, notably part of the Seaforth doom. Those not yet fulfilled are now recorded, but the vast majority cannot be proved to have existed before the event. They have entered the realm of myth. This is not to say they are lies and that those who still believe in them are deluded. There is perhaps more intrinsic truth in folk-lore, more knowledge and more wisdom in myth, than can ever be gleaned from the pages of a history book. The fascination of Coinneach Odhar does not depend upon where or whether he existed in fact, nor that his name has become inextricably linked with prophetic history in the Highlands; his story clearly demonstrates how legend is born, grows, and survives into the present generation. The truth of Coinneach Odhar is this, that he is as alive and well in the Highlands today as he was 300 years ago.

So who was he, this elusive figure who still dominates the folklore of the north?

The earliest literary reference to him comes, as we have seen, in Thomas Pennant's *A Tour in Scotland* written in 1769. When describing Sutherland he says, 'Every country has its prophets . . . and the Highlands their Kenneth Oaur.' The *Bannatyne Manuscript History of the Macleods*, 1832, which contains many references to his prophecies in Lewis and Skye, places him as a native of Ness on the Isle of Lewis, born in the sixteenth century. Hugh Miller in his *Scenes and Legends of the North of Scotland*, 1834, has him a field-labourer working in the vicinity of Brahan Castle in the mid-seventeenth century. Alexander Mackenzie also places him in the mid-seventeenth century, a native of Uig in Lewis. The only historical reference so far known exists in two Commissions of Justice ordering the Ross-shire authorities to prosecute a certain Keanoch Owir for witchcraft in the sixteenth century.

The single *fact* to emerge from these references is that the Keanoch Owir accused of witchcraft in the sixteenth century could not possibly have been the seer burned by Isabella Mackenzie a hundred years later.

Let us look first at the seventeenth-century seer, the Coinneach we think we know, whose story has just been recounted. That period in

Highland history is well documented. Top people were the Mackenzies, powerful lairds whose influence was wide-spread. Owing to the brilliance of Rorie Mor, the Tutor of Kintail who died in 1628, Clan Kenneth owned vast tracts of the north including most of Rossshire and the Isle of Lewis. Rorie's nephew Colin, chief of the clan and second Lord Mackenzie of Kintail, was created the first Earl of Seaforth in 1623, taking his title from the sea-loch of that name in Lewis. Colin was popular and handsome, called 'my Highlander' by the beautiful Princess Elizabeth, daughter of James VI and I, soon to become Queen of Bohemia. He was responsible for building Castle Brahan, for setting up a church in every barony of his land, and for leaving a donation to the town of Chanonry for the support of a grammar school.

Colin died predeceased by his only son, and was succeeded by his brother George. Though George had a reputation for political wavering during the troubled times of the Covenanters, he was to die loyal to the throne, in exile in Holland, after hearing of the defeat of the loyalists at the Battle of Worcester in 1651. (Elizabeth of Bohemia gave 'her speciall direction of the forme and order of his burial'.) George's wife Barbara, daughter of the tenth Lord Forbes, made her home and brought up her nine children in Chanonry in the Black Isle.

Their eldest son, Kenneth, called 'Mor' for his height, was born in 1635 and educated at the age of six by the Revd Farquhar MacRa, minister of Kintail and keeper of Eileandonan Castle, who ran a seminary for the children of local gentry. Later Kenneth left for Elgin school, 'where he gave great evidence of his abilities'; and in 1651 he had just joined Aberdeen University when news came that he had inherited the clan. Rather than settle to his studies, he rode straight to Kintail to raise men for the King's service. The clansmen refused to ride with him, considering him to be too young, and he soon found himself with a price of £200 on his head. His estates were bankrupt and in the hands of 'four prime gentlemen of his own kindred for satisfying creditors and paying off debt . . . Brahan was deserted', we are told by the Revd James Fraser, a contemporary diarist who chronicled the history of Clan Fraser in the *Wardlaw Manuscript*. James Fraser was to get to know the Seaforths well, for Kenneth's sister was married to Lord Lovat.

In 1655, Kenneth was arrested by General Monk and imprisoned in Cromwell's citadel in Inverness. Life there was not too hard, for James Fraser tells us he was allowed out on bail, taking 'the flower of all the youth in our country, with a hundred pretty fellows or more' including the minister and the English prison governor, on a hunt to Kintail where 'we got sights of six or seven hundred deer and sport of hunting fitter for kings than country gentlemen.' By 1658, Kenneth was out of prison and married to Isabella (or Isobel as she signed herself), a daughter of Lord Tarbat and a grand-daughter of Rorie Mor.

James Fraser disapproved of the match: 'After all men's hopes of him, [he] debases himselfe mean spirited to marry below himself, getting neither beauty, parts, portion, relation.' This is a spiteful remark and it would be interesting to know why James Fraser disliked Isabella so much. Though her portrait by David Scougal (to be seen together with other paintings of the Seaforth Mackenzies in Fortrose Town Hall), shows that she was not beautiful in the conventional sense – *jolie laide*, perhaps – she had a lively, intelligent expression. Probably she had very little dowry, being the ninth out of eleven in her family, but to write that she had no 'relation' is untrue. She was Kenneth's second cousin and her brother George, a brilliant lawyer, was later to be created the first Earl of Cromartie.

However, Isabella was not popular. Brodie of Brodie, in his diary for 1676 writes,

> July 31: my Ladi Seaforth cald; and we being from home, she went to Darnaway.
> Aug 1: my Ladi Seaforth went by and cald not. I reveranc the Lord's providence.

Perhaps she was too clever, too sharp-witted, to make herself likeable to her acquaintance.

In 1663 Kenneth was asked by Charles II to go to Court. James Fraser writes that Kenneth expected some favour from the King in recompense for 'ruining his father's interest in the civil wars, though all he had was bad success . . . Yet all Seaforth gained at Court was the King's countenance and the compliment of carrying the Sword of Honour before the King upon some solemn holy day from the presence to the Chappell Royall, and, after service, back again. A farthing of the King's money he never saw, not so much as to repair his castle of Brahan, which the rebells spoiled.'

207

Fraser does not mention that King Charles sent Kenneth to France, nor that he stayed away too long, for barely a year later we learn that Kenneth and Isabella were at Beauly acting as god-parents to Lord Lovat's daughter. Alexander Mackenzie, however, in his *History of Clan Mackenzie* mentions that Kenneth visited France on two occasions, once as a boy to see his exiled father and later on the King's business.

Both Brodie and Fraser suggest that Kenneth was a drinker. Fraser tells us that while in Lewis, Isabella gave birth to one of her eight children.

> His lady being brought to bed there, the Earle sent for John Garve M'kleud, Laird of Rarzay, to witness the christning; and after the treat and solemnity of the feast, Rarzay takes leave to goe home, and, after a rant of drinking upon the shore, went aboord off his birling and sailed away with a strong north gale of wind; and whither could not manage the strong Dutch canvas sail, the boat wh'lm'd and all the men dround in view of the coast. The Laird and sixteen of his kinsmen, the prime, perished . . . One Alexander Macleod in Lewes the night before had voice warning him thrice not to goe at all with Rarzay, for all would drown in ther return; yet he went with him, being infantuat, and drowned with the rest; drunkness did the Mischiefe.

Brodie writes sanctimoniously in his diary entry for 5 July 1673: 'I heard of great drinking betwixt the Earl of Seaforth and Aboin. Alac! God dishonoured and not in al ther thoghts.'

That Kenneth was also fond of women we can guess, for he had an illegitimate son, John, who married the daughter of Colin Murdoch Mackenzie of Logie. He died in 1679 and was buried in the family tomb at Chanonry Cathedral. His life was not particularly distinguished and he seems to have made little impact on public affairs.

Dr Hickes, in his letter to Samuel Pepys dated 1700, writes: 'It was commonly reported when I was in Scotland, that Lord Seaforth, then living, had the second sight and thereby foretold a dreadful storm to some of his friends in which they had like to have been castaway. Once I heard the Duke of Lauderdale rally him about it, but he neither owned it nor disowned it.' It seems likely that this was the occasion of the tragic drowning of the Laird of Raasay and his kin, foreseen not by Kenneth but by Alexander Macleod of Lewis. Either way, it is not surprising that the Earl refused to comment.

Isabella lived on until 1715 and was buried on 18 February in the Church of Holyroodhouse in Edinburgh, 'on the north side, betwixt the fourth and fifth pillar from the west, opposite to the fourth glass window from the west, lying on the south side of these pillars.' That she was a strong-minded, intelligent woman is demonstrated by the interest she took in her children's affairs. Margaret, her eldest daughter, married James Sutherland, the second Lord Duffus, who got into trouble by slaughtering William Ross of Kindeace in the Invergordon area in 1686. His excuse was self-defence, though judged by the papers of the prosecution this sounds improbable – Lord Duffus' hagbutter (musket-bearer) pursued the victim with his gun until he dropped dead off his horse, and William Mitchell, Lord Duffus' foot-man, hindered the victim's escape out of reach of the sword which killed him by holding his horse by the bridle till the deadly wound was given. Whatever the reason, Lord Duffus was obliged to escape. He went to court in London and stayed at the Cross Keys, Pall Mall, where he received the following letter from his mother-in-law, dated 6 April 1688 and written in Chanonry.

My dear Duffus,

We are mightily afraid of your health and have sent this express to conjure you to be carefull of yourself. As for what is done, Lord pardon you the sin of it, but no man thinks you could have done less or that you could have borne that which you met with. I pray you have a care of yourself, and go to your business, and let us know where and to whom we shall direct your letters while you are at Court; I think to my Kenny [the fourth Earl of Seaforth] when you are in London. You may write to Meg with every occasion to give her assurance of your health, which she shall be doubting. We all think, and so does Suddy who has better skill in such affairs, that after all the provocation you met with, yet that it was in your own defence that you did, for certainly you had been killed had it not turned out as it did. So your business will not cost much trouble to get it done. Be careful of yourself for Meg's cause and the babie's. Many a man has fallen out on such an accident worse than your circumstances was, yet has been at peace with God and the world, and lived happily for all that.

209

The Lord's peace be with you and direct and preserve you from all ill.

I am your affectionate mother.   Isobel Seafort.

Isabella was right. The criminal proceedings against Lord Duffus came to nothing.

Suddie, mentioned in the letter as 'Suddy', is thought to have been Sir George Mackenzie of Rosehaugh, known as the Bluidy Mackenzie for his prosecution of the Covenanters. As we have seen on page 36, he was not only a brilliant lawyer but also a seer himself. Kenny, also mentioned in the letter, was Isabella's eldest son, the fourth Earl, and adored by his mother. Born in 1661, he became a Roman Catholic on his marriage to Lady Frances Herbert, daughter of the first Marquis of Powis, thus causing great upset in the family. Kenny remained loyal to James VII after his English abdication in 1688, and James was to create him Lord Fortrose and Marquess of Seaforth. He died in Paris, an exile for his loyalty and his religion, in 1701. Isabella wrote to Duncan Forbes of Culloden, a great family friend, 'He was the great joy of my lyf and the suport of my age.'

Her grandson, William Dubh, was only fourteen when he inherited the clan, and Isabella, who must have been a formidable mother-in-law, proposed that he should be brought up by Culloden. 'I am fully persuaded the boy will be better a great deal with you than here [Brahan]' she wrote to Culloden, but Frances, William's young and beautiful mother, made it clear that he should 'not meddle derectly or inderectly with her son except he disobleidge her exceedingly'. She had her way, and the fifth earl was 'carried out of the kingdom to be popishly bred' against his grandmother's and the government's wishes.

William grew up to be a staunch Jacobite, and as a result the Seaforth title was attained and his estates were forfeited in 1716, a year after Isabella's death. He spent the rest of his life in Lewis where he died in 1740.

This, then, was the Isabella who allegedly burned Coinneach Odhar. She appears through the eyes of her contemporaries as a strong-willed woman, possibly harsh towards her tenants, formidable to her family and the clan, capable of making important decisions. Her dominant manner may have been responsible for her husband's weaknesses, or perhaps his inherent faults turned her into a forceful partner. But a murderess? Robert Bain in his *History of Ross* 1899 maintains that her letter to her son-in-law, Lord Duffus, is 'characteristic of the virtual murderess of the Brahan Seer'. Yet the text is tender and supportive, far more indicative of a loving mother whose tenet was 'my family, right or wrong' than the complicity of an evil woman.

The main events in the Coinneach Odhar story match those in the lives of the Seaforths. They did spend much of their time in Lewis, where Coinneach was allegedly born. The Earl did go to Court and cross the Channel. He certainly gave Isabella cause for jealousy on at least one occasion.

Perhaps Hugh Miller's version of the story comes closest to the truth when he writes: 'Coinneach derived little advantage from the faculty, for he led, it is said, till extreme old age, an unsettled, unhappy kind of life – wandering from place to place, a prophet only of evil, or of little trifling events, fitted to attract notice when they occurred merely from the circumstance of their having been foretold.' Though he goes on to add that shortly before his death Coinneach was said to have flung his stone into Loch Ussie, he makes no mention of his arrest, let alone his burning as a witch. Unfortunately the records for Rosemarkie Parish were destroyed by fire in 1737, but there is no record of a trial or execution, or even of an accusation of witchcraft, in the Dingwall or Inverness Presbytery records, which survive in great detail.

James Fraser goes into explicit description of a particularly unpleasant witchcraft-tester called Paterson,

> who had run over the kingdom for triall of witches, and was ordinarily called the Pricker because his way of triall was with a long brasse pin. Stripping them naked, he alleadged that the spell spot was seen and discovered. After rubbing over the whole body with his palms he slipt in the pin, and, it seems with shame and feares being dasht, they felt it not, but he left it in the flesh, deep to the head and descried them to find and take it out. It is sure some witches were discovered, but many honest men and women were blited and broak by his trick . . . this villan gained a great deale of money haveing two servants; at last was discovered to be a woman disguised in man's cloathes. Such cruelty and rigure was sustained by a vile varlet imposture.

How Fraser would have relished Coinneach's punishment at the hands of the unpopular Isabella, had it ever happened. Living no further than twelve miles from Brahan, he would certainly have known all about it.

But such a seer as Miller describes Coinneach to have been might certainly have escaped notice in contemporary records.

As we have seen in the first part of this book, Isabella's brother Sir George Mackenzie of Tarbat, created Earl of Cromartie in 1703, was a man of great learning and well-versed in the law, being at one time Senator of the College of Justice, Clerk Register, one of the Privy Council and Justice General. He was particularly interested in second sight as is indicated in his long and detailed letter to the chemist, Boyle (see page 66). It is not to be supposed that a man of his stature would have tolerated such punitive behaviour from his sister without some sort of public protest.

Yet the Seaforth prediction remains as evidence that there *must have been* a seer. It was known at least in part by men as eminent as Walter Scott, and its realization was not to be finally fulfilled until the twentieth century.

After William Dubh's death in 1740, his eldest son Kenneth, Lord Fortrose, who would have been the sixth earl but for the attainder, inherited the clan. He was born about 1718 and brought up a Protestant, after which he sat in Parliament as a commoner for Inverness and latterly Ross-shire. Gradually he recovered his estates and the family once again began to prosper. During the Jacobite Rebellion the old family friendship with Forbes of Culloden prevailed, and when Lord Cromartie took part of Clan Mackenzie to support Prince Charles Edward Stuart, Kenneth did not support him. He lived in London at the end of his life, and was buried in Westminster Abbey.

He had one son, Kenneth, who made his name as a soldier having raised the 72nd Highland Regiment known as Seaforth's Highlanders. He recruited 500 men from his own estates and 400 more from other Mackenzie property who, on their final inspection, were 'found so effective that not one man was rejected'. Kenneth was created Earl of Seaforth in the peerage of Ireland, and sadly died while sailing to India with his regiment, without leaving a son.

On his death there were no male descendants left of the fourth, fifth, sixth and seventh (but for the attainder) Seaforths, so the chieftainship went to a second cousin, a direct descendant of Kenneth and Isabella by their fourth son.

Having first bought the family estates, Thomas Frederick Mackenzie was to hold the chieftainship for barely two years before he was killed on board the *Ranger* in action with the Mahratta fleet in

1783. As he had no son, his brother, Francis Humberston Mackenzie succeeded to the clan.

At last the prophecy was about to unfold.

Francis was born in London in 1755. At Eton he had an extra-ordinary experience which was told to Alexander Mackenzie by Colonel John Stanley, husband of Susan Mary, a great-grand-daughter of the last chief. When Francis was about sixteen, scarlet fever broke out at Eton. Those who were ill, including Francis, were nursed together in a dormitory. One night Francis woke to see in the doorway a hideous old woman with a bag around her neck. She shuffled up to the first bed, stared at the sleeping child, and then moved on. At the foot of the next bed, she paused for a moment and then crept up to the head. Opening her bag, she took out a peg and mallet and viciously drove the pin deep down into the boy's forehead. Francis could hear the crunch of bone, though the boy never stirred. She continued her journey slowly round the room, passing some of the boys, stopping at others to hammer home her nail.

Transfixed with terror, Francis waited his turn, unable to move or cry out. As she approached him, she reached down into her bag, then fumbled for his ears. After the longest moment of his life, she put back the peg, shuffled off, and slowly completed her progress round the room.

As soon as she had gone, Francis cried out. The night nurse laughed at his story and told him to go back to sleep, but shortly afterwards when the doctor heard of it, he was impressed by the vividness of the dream and took detailed notes. Days passed. Some boys recovered, others died, and a few were afflicted for life. The doctor noticed with amazement that those whom the old hag had nailed were the ones who died, those whom she had passed recovered, and those whom she had touched, like Francis, were afflicted. He became stone-deaf. Though he continued to speak a little, communication became increasingly difficult and by the end of his life he was virtually dumb.

In spite of his disability he led a distinguished life and was created a British peer in 1797 as Baron Seaforth and Lord Mackenzie of Kintail. He raised a second battalion of the Seaforth Highlanders, the 78th, magnificent soldiers later to be known as the 'Saviours of India'. After a period in Parliament he was appointed Governor of Barbados, where he put an end to slave killing. In 1808 he was created a Lieutenant General.

It was said of him by the Honourable Henry Erskine, Scots Dean of Faculty, that 'Lord Seaforth's deafness was a merciful interposition to lower him to the ordinary rate of capacity in society,' meaning that he was so brilliant that his intelligence might have otherwise been oppressive – a pretty compliment. He was known for his patronage and lively interest in the arts, and when Sir Thomas Lawrence, then a young man and in debt, wrote to him, 'Will you be the Antonio to a Bassanio?' he gave him £1,000, for which he was repaid with a magnificent portrait now hanging in the museum at Fort George. He also patronized Benjamin West whose huge canvas representing the royal hunt at which Alexander III was rescued from a stag's attack by Colin Fitzgerald, now hangs in Fortrose Town Hall.

He modernized Brahan, altering it from a castle to a country mansion by removing the castellation, which was not to everyone's approval – but his landscaping of the gardens was exceptional. He married Mary Proby, daughter of the Dean of Lichfield, and together they spent some time in Seaforth Lodge, their Lewis home. Lady Seaforth encouraged the women to knit, spin and weave, while his Lordship interested himself in fishing and road-making. He also recruited as many of the male population as were suitable to swell the ranks of his regiment. The Seaforths had ten children, four of whom were sons. It looked as if the clan was safe at least for another generation, but one by one the four boys died. The eldest, William, died in infancy. The second, George, also died young. Francis, the youngest, grew up to be a midshipman but died at Brahan in 1813.

William, the third son, was already a distinguished young man, MP for Ross-shire, when he became ill. Ordered south for his health, he seemed to rally. A visitor to Brahan remarked on the cheerful news to Seaforth's piper. 'Na, na,' said the old man unhappily, 'he'll no' recover. It's decreed that Seaforth will outlive his sons.' And so it happened. A few posts later brought the news that William had died in Edinburgh.

Unfortunately too, the family fortune was in decline. Mismanagement of Seaforth's West Indian estates forced him to put Kintail on the market. The tenants and clansmen wanted to buy the 'giftland' for their chief, but could not offer enough. Kintail was sold. As a friend of the Prince Regent and a man of wide interests, Francis became involved in expense beyond his means, and when he died barely two months after his last surviving son, great tracts of land had

214

to go. His death saw the end of the House of Kintail, for the clan was entailed in the male line. There were no male descendants left out of all the younger sons of the first earls.

The prophecy predicted that his heir would be a white-coiffed (hooded) widow from the east. Mary Frederica was Francis' eldest daughter. Her first husband was Sir Samuel Hood, Vice Admiral of the White. They had become acquainted in Barbados where he was Admiral when Seaforth was Governor. After their marriage, he was appointed chief commander of the Indian Seas. He died in India a month before his father-in-law, so Lady Mary returned to mourn not only her brother and her father but also her husband. Later she was to remarry a grandson of the sixth Earl of Galloway who assumed the name Stewart-Mackenzie. The prophecy was even more strikingly fulfilled when the Stewart-Mackenzies were forced to sell Lewis to Sir James Matheson.

How did Lady Mary kill her sister? It was an accident, of course. They were driving together in a pony carriage near Brahan when the horse took fright and bolted. Both sisters were thrown out. Mary was bruised and hurt, but Caroline died of her injuries. A monument commemorating the tragedy may be seen on the road between Contin and Brahan. The inscription reads:

'Hic fato ut fertur praedicto abrepta est Francis Baron de Seaforth filia Carolina Mackenzie cujus soror eusdem pericli particepts domus suae redintegrandae spes ultima super fuit. MDCCCXXIII' (At this point, according to the prophecy uttered, Caroline Mackenzie daughter of Francis, Baron Seaforth, was snatched [from life]; her sister who shared the same hazard was the last surviving hope of restoration of his house. 1823.)

But Francis was not the last Lord Seaforth, although he was the last of the Mackenzies of Kintail. His great-grandson, James Stewart-Mackenzie, who died in 1923, was created Baron Seaforth of Brahan. Once again he had no male heir and Brahan went to a great-nephew, Francis, who adopted the name Stewart Mackenzie of Seaforth. Sadly both he and his brother Michael were killed in the Second World War within twenty-four hours of each other, and were buried at Salerno.

Brahan was then inherited by a cousin, Madeline Tyler, who in accordance with the late Lord Seaforth's will, took the name of Stewart-Mackenzie. It was she who had to decide the fate of the castle which by that time was full of dry rot and woodworm. As the cost of reconstruction was beyond the means of the estate and no one would buy it, the old house was demolished and the Georgian stables were designed as a new Brahan. The site where the old house had stood for so many years is now a great green lawn. When eventually Mrs Stewart-Mackenzie had to leave the Highlands for health reasons, Brahan was handed over to the next heir designated by Lord Seaforth's will. It is now owned by Mr Andrew Matheson, son of the late Captain A. F. Matheson and of Mrs M. Matheson of the Little Scatwell Mackenzies.

As for the disfigured lairds mentioned as a tailpiece to the prophecy, Sir Bernard Burke in his *Vicissitudes of Families* maintains that the four men were blemished as predicted, but states, 'I am uncertain which was which.'

James Fraser recalls a similar prediction which states that there would be 'some alteration upon families when there was a black-kneed Seaforth, a black-spotted Lord Lovat, squint-eyed Mackenzie and a Chisholm blind of an eye; and these four are just now contemporary.' A prediction from Raasay (see page 324) involved 'a fair haired Lochiel, a red-haired Lovat, a squint-eyed, fair-haired Chisholm, a big deaf Mackenzie and a bow, crooked MacGillechalum'. Pennant, writing in 1768, states that, 'Whenever a Macleane with long hands, a Frazier with a black spot on his face, a Macgregor with the same of his knee and a club-footed Macleod of Rasa should have existed . . . oppressors would appear in the land, and the people change their own land for a strange one. These predictions, say the good wives, have been fulfilled, and not a single breche in the oracular effusions of Kenneth Oaur.'

The above would seem to have forecast the Clearances, and it would look as if these tailpieces were added, like some sort of doxology, to round off the major prophecies and give them added authority, if it were not for a curious entry in Elizabeth Grant's *Memoires of a Highland Lady* for the year 1815.

My last year's friend, the new member for Ross-shire, Mr Mackenzie of Applecross, was at this Meeting [the Northern Meeting] more agreeable than ever, but looking extremely ill . . . He was a plain man, and he had a buck tooth to which someone had called attention, and it was soon the only topic spoken about, for an old prophecy ran that whenever a mad Lovat, a childless —, and an Applecross with a buck tooth met, there would be an end of Seaforth. The buck tooth all could see, the mad Lovat was equally conspicuous, and though Mrs — had two handsome sons born after several years of childless wedlock, nobody ever thought of fathering them on her husband. In the beginning of this year, Seaforth, the Chief of the Mackenzies, boasted of two promising sons. Both were gone, died within a few months of each other. The Chieftainship went to another branch, but the lands and the old Castle of Brahan would descend after Lord Seaforth's death to his daughter Lady Hood – an end of Cabarféidh. This made everyone melancholy, and the death of course kept many away from the Meeting.

A prediction to be valid must, as has been said, be known before the event. Alexander Mackenzie maintains that the Seaforth prophecy was well known long before 1815 and it would seem that Elizabeth Grant and her friends also knew of it, or part of it. Lockhart in his *Life of Sir Walter Scott* says that the prophecy was 'quoted in the Highlands at a time when Lord Seaforth had two sons alive and in good health, and that it was certainly not made after the event.' He goes on to state that Scott and Sir Humphrey Davy were most certainly convinced of its truth. In 1878, Duncan Davidson of Tulloch, Lord Lieutenant of Ross, wrote personally to Alexander Mackenzie as follows: 'Many of these prophecies I heard upwards of seventy years ago and when many of them were not fulfilled, such as the late Lord Seaforth surviving his sons and Mrs Stewart Mackenzie's accident, near Brahan, by which Miss Caroline Mackenzie was killed.' The Davidsons were regular visitors at Brahan and often heard the predictions referred to among members of the family.

But proof that the prediction existed does not necessarily mean that it was made by the Coinneach Odhar of the legend. So far there is *no* contemporary written evidence that the seventeenth-century hero of the legend was born in Lewis, lived near Brahan or was burned at Chanonry by Isabella Mackenzie.

And yet, in spite of the lack of evidence, the legend of Coinneach Odhar lives on, as if constant repetition cancels out the lack of documentary proof. In July 1977 the *Sunday Times* headlined an article '*Has the Seer Struck Again*?' The reason was to be found in the Royal

Burgh of Fortrose, once known as the Chanonry where Coinneach was allegedly burned. According to the local registrar, there had been forty-two deaths so far that year, twice the average number for six months, or roughly the same as the total for the whole of 1976. 'Anywhere else this statistical bump would be no more than a cause for mild surprise,' wrote the correspondent, 'but to the residents of Fortrose . . . it marked the fulfilment of yet another prophecy of the Brahan Seer.'

This prophecy apparently stated that if a wedding were ever held in the ruins of the town's thirteenth-century cathedral, then 'the cemetery of Fortrose would overflow and Fortrose become a town of widows.' There had been just such a wedding two years earlier which had used the ruined cathedral as a setting, a rather grand affair which had not met with the approval of all the local inhabitants. Coincidentally, the cemetery at Fortrose was full, and another was being prepared on the edge of the town. It was a fact that there had been more deaths than usual. The cathedral, too, had featured in one of Coinneach's unfulfilled predictions: that it would fall 'with a fearful crash when full of dead Mackenzies'.

The new prophecy originated, it is thought, in one of the busy hotel kitchens where a group of women, talking together, added the facts and somehow came up with a prediction. Nobody lied deliberately. Nobody was directly responsible for the invention. It grew out of the fears, dislikes and traditions of the area. When in 1982, the new Kessock bridge was opened linking Inverness to the Black Isle, journalists did their utmost to dig up a prophecy. Some, inevitably, succeeded!

It seems, perhaps, that Highlanders, seeking an explanation for momentous events, find it in prophecy. People searching for answers to sorrow and tragedy find comfort in the fact that they were pre-ordained. On one hand, it is soothing to know that all was foreseen; conversely, we have only ourselves to blame if we disregard the warning. It is all very Biblical, and Highlanders are a religious people. Coinneach Odhar is both scapegoat and prophet, the man crying in the wilderness who ended up not on Herod's platter but in Isabella's fire. He was created out of a need and he is kept alive for the same reason.

What is so extraordinary is that there *was* a real Coinneach Odhar, that we know at least as much about him as we do of the legendary figure, and yet we persist in promoting the legend. How and why this should have happened makes an intriguing study.

THE HISTORICAL COINNEACH ODHAR

The *Bannatyne MS History of the Macleods*, written about 1832 and based on older writings, places Coinneach Odhar as a native of Lewis prophesying disaster to the Macleods in the sixteenth century. This does not prove his existence any more than the writings of Alexander Mackenzie or Hugh Miller which place him in the seventeenth century, but it is a step in the right direction.

The first clue to what was probably his true profession lies in his name, for the old Gaelic tradition does not connect Coinneach with second sight. 'Brahan Seer' was a style invented by Alexander Mackenzie as a title for his book. Having a fine ring, it appealed to the Highland imagination, but it is no older than 1877. As we have seen, there are many Gaelic words for second sight and seers, the most common of which is probably *taibhsear*. Coinneach was never known as this. His style was always *fiosaiche*, which, according to *Dwelly's Gaelic Dictionary* can mean fortune-teller, soothsayer, augur, diviner and – most significantly – sorcerer. The clue to Coinneach's identity, ignored by collectors of folklore including Alexander Mackenzie, lies in the definition of this word.

The first critical approach to the legend came from Donald A. Mackenzie writing in *The Encyclopaedia of Occultism*, 1920, edited by Lewis Spence. In his entry on Coinneach Odhar, he states that the legend regarding the raven and the dove which alighted on the seer's ashes was also told of the wizard, Michael Scot. He also points out the lack of evidence that the seer was ever burned, and refers readers to the find of his brother, Dr William M. Mackenzie, among the Scottish Parliamentary Records of the sixteenth century.

This was a Commission of Justice from Holyroodhouse, dated 25 October 1577 and issued to Walter Urquhart, Sheriff of Cromarty, and Robert Munro of Foulis, among others, to seek out and apprehend six men and twenty-six women charged with 'the diabolical practices of magic, enchantment, murder, homicide and other offences' within the bounds of the Earldom of Ross, the Lordship of Ardmannach (the Black Isle), and other parts of the Sheriffdom of

Inverness. Among those to be arrested were Thomas McAnemoir McAllan McHenrik, alias Cassindonisch; Mariota Neyn McAlester, alias Loskoir Longert; and Christina Milla, daughter of Robert Milla. The last name on the list is that of Keanoch Ower – Coinneach Odhar, as spelt by a non-Gaelic-speaking clerk – who is described as 'the leading or principal enchantress' [sic], no doubt due to the same clerk's inability to distinguish between a male and female Gaelic name.

Donald A. Mackenzie in the *Encyclopaedia* points out that the Commission was issued many years before the Seaforth title came into existence in 1623. Probably this Kenneth was caught and burned, though there is no record of it, and through time his name became attached to the many floating prophecies and sayings current in the Highlands, including those attributed to Thomas the Rhymer and Michael Scot. 'The sayings of "True Thomas" ', wrote Mackenzie, 'were hawked through the Highlands in Gaelic chapbooks, and so strongly did the bard appeal to the imaginations of the eighteenth-century folk of Inverness that they associated him with the Fairies and Fingalians of the local fairy mound, Tomnahurich.' (Thomas the Rhymer, known as Thomas of Ercildoun, who lived in the thirteenth century, was alleged to have received the gift of second sight from the Queen of the Fairies and to have spent seven years in Elfland.)

Some years later a second Commission was discovered among the Foulis archives and it follows in full.

1577 January 23
Commission under the Quarter Seal appointing Lauchlin Mackintoshe of Dunnachtane, Colin Mackenzie of Kintail, Robert Munro of Foulis, Walter Urquhart, Sheriff of Cromartie, Hugh alias Hugheon Ross of Kilraok, and Alexander Falconar of Halkartoun, or one, two or three of them conjunctly and severally, justiciaries within the bounds of the Earldoms of Ross and Moray and Lordship of Ardmannach, and other parts within the Sheriffdoms of Innernes, Elgin, Forres and Narne, to apprehend, imprison and try Kennoth, alias Kennoch Owir, principal or leader in the art of magic, Neyeane McAllester alias Loskoloukart and Marjory Miller, daughter of Robert Miller, smith in Assint, and all other men and women using and exercising the diabolical, iniquitous and odious crimes of the art of magic, sorcery and

incantation within said bounds, who shall be named by the ministers within the bounds foresaid each for his own parish.

At Halerudehouse.
(Seal appended, slightly damaged)

Here at last was the documentary proof that Coinneach was a historical figure, if not in the person or century expected.

And now unfolds a whole new story involving two other clans of Ross-shire, the Munros of Foulis and the Rosses of Balnagown, a tale quite distinct from, but just as intriguing as, the legend, and with a heroine equally capricious. The important difference lies in the fact that this tale is true.

Catherine Ross was the daughter of Alexander, ninth laird of Balnagown in Easter Ross and of Janet, a sister of the notorious George, fourth Earl of Caithness. Not an auspicious start, for Alexander and George were cruel men, not typical of Highland chiefs even in those days. Alexander Ross, who inherited the clan in 1528, was one of the most unscrupulous men alive at the time. Fighting was his passion. In 1553 he bought an eighteen-pounder cannon and coats of mail for his private army, who ransacked the surrounding countryside.

These were the troubled times of the Reformation, and Alexander was determined to seize the forfeited church lands and property. He forced three monks at sword-point to sign a deed handing over Fearn Abbey lands, and though they later rescinded, Alexander treated the property as his own. He feuded with his neighbours, destroyed Cadboll Castle, raided cattle, stole corn and stores to such an extent that the Regent Morton had him arrested and imprisoned in Tantallon Castle. Only by promising to pay compensation to those he had robbed was he released, but he had no intention of keeping his word. In 1583 letters of fire and sword were issued against him, and his son George, who was now chief at Balnagown in his place, was one of those ordered to capture him. This did not stop the old man from levying rents at sword-point and using the Chapter House at Tain for his personal store-house. He died in 1592, lawless to the last.

Earl George of Caithness was also known as a hard and violent man who imprisoned his son in a dungeon at his castle at Girnigoe for six years, let him eat salt beef, refused him water, and when he went mad, let the jailers strangle him to death. This, then, was Catherine's pedigree.

Her husband, Robert Mor Munro, the fifteenth Baron of Foulis, was as upright in character as he was in stature. Served heir to the clan in 1548 when he was twenty-one, he was respected and honoured – a complete contrast to his next-door neighbour at Balnagown. Nevertheless they managed to keep the peace, Robert no doubt believing that it was wiser to have the old warrior friend than foe. This may have been one of the reasons why he chose Catherine as his second wife. Or perhaps it was Catherine's brother, George, who arranged the marriage during their father's absence in prison, either as a political move or at Catherine's request. As we shall see, George and Catherine were always very close.

Robert Mor was a good deal older than Catherine. His first wife, Margaret Ogilvie, widow of Mackintosh of Mackintosh, had given him three sons and three daughters, who on his remarriage came under Catherine's care. She was to have six children of her own, and great were the half-sibling rivalries. Some time between 1576 and 1577, when Robert Mor's eldest son, Robert the younger, was about twenty-four and already married for two years to Margery Mackenzie of Kintail, and Catherine's eldest son George was about fourteen, jealousy flared into conflict.

Catherine was accused by her step-family (though not, it seems, by her husband) of employing certain witches, warlocks and gypsies to get rid of her three stepsons, Robert the younger, Hugh, and Hector, by enchantment so that her own son George might eventually inherit the clan.

But there were complications. George Ross, Catherine's brother, who was married to Marian Campbell of Cawdor, had fallen in love with Robert the younger's pretty young wife, Margery Mackenzie. Catherine, or Catherine in collusion with her brother George, decided that if Marian and Robert the younger were both out of the way, then the laird of Balnagown would be free to marry the widowed Margery.

According to Pitcairn's *Criminal Trials*, Catherine's first contact with the occult world was William MacGillivray, whom she 'feed' with a piece of linen and some money. When he was found to be a fraud, Agnes Roy, another witch, was dispatched to find Marion Mackean Macalister, a notorious sorceress better known by her

222

nickname of Loisc na Lotar, meaning 'Burn the Ladle' or 'Burn the Castle'. She duly arrived at Foulis and lodged with Christian Ross Malcolmson, who was sent to Dingwall to bring to Foulis John Macmillan, Thomas Mackean, and various others – including, though the name is not mentioned in Catherine's subsequent trial, Coinneach Odhar.

The witches, twenty-six of them, assembled in a barn at Canorth where they made images of Robert the younger and Marian Campbell out of butter. Loisc na Lotar shot at them three times with elf arrows – prehistoric flint arrowheads – and missed. Clay images were then set up and were also missed, so the dolls were wrapt in linen and hidden under the stank bridge at Foulis. This too was ineffectual.

Catherine and George then met at a kiln on a nearby farm where, it was alleged, they decided to try poison. Catherine, according to the fifteenth point in the indictment against her, sent 'to the Egiptians, to haif knawledge of thame how to poysoun the young Laird of Fowles and the young Lady Balnagoune'. Eventually ratsbane was procured from 'Thomas Roiss, merchant in Aberdene, in Elgne'. A stoup of poisoned ale was prepared and set aside, but it leaked and allegedly killed a servant who had tasted it. Catherine was then accused of procuring a 'pipkin' of ranker poison' from Loisc na Lotar which she sent by her nurse to Robert the younger. Unfortunately the nurse took a sip and died on the spot. It was said that the 'place where the pipkin broke, the gerse that grew upon the same was so heich beyond the nature of other gerse that neither cow nor sheep ever tasted thereof of it; whilk is manifest and notorious to the haill county of Ross.'

With regard to her sister-in-law Marian, Catherine was supposed to have said 'she would do by all kind of means of God in heaven or the devil in hell, for the destruction and down-putting of Marian Campbell'. By corrupting the Balnagown cook, Catherine allegedly arranged to poison a dish of kids' kidneys; and a certain Catherine Niven who had obtained the poison 'was scunnerit with it sa meikle that she said it was the sairest and most cruel sight that ever she saw seeing the vomit and vexation that was on the young Lady Balnagown and her company'. No doubt the vomiting saved her, but Marian was recorded as being an invalid for the rest of her life.

So notorious were these events to become that the law intervened

223

and, as a result of the first Commission of Justice quoted, Christian Ross and Thomas Mackean were caught, brought to trial, convicted and burned at Chanonry in November 1577. Because the relevant documents are missing, it is not known if Coinneach Odhar was arrested as a result of the second Commission, but if he was, then as 'principal enchanter' he would no doubt have been burned too. Thus he would have suffered the same ordeal by fire at Chanonry as the legendary Coinneach Odhar, though in a different century and for different reasons.

Catherine was sent by her husband to stay with her uncle, the Earl of Caithness at Girnigoe Castle, where she remained for nine months until Robert Mor considered it was safe for her to return. Robert Mor must have kept a firm hand on his family for it was not until he died in 1588 that the matter flared up again. Robert the younger, having succeeded to the clan, obtained a commission for the trial of his stepmother but died before it could be carried out. He was succeeded by his younger brother, Hector, Hugh having also died at an earlier date.

Hector was the clever member of the family. He had attended St Andrews university, become a minister in the Reformed Church, and was also Dean of the Diocese of Ross. He arranged that Catherine should be brought to trial in Edinburgh in July 1590; but by that time Catherine's beloved son George had also died in mysterious circumstances for which she in turn blamed Hector, so that he too was ordered to stand trial, on the same day, for 'sorcery, incantation and witchcraft'. He was accused of consorting with a witch called Marian Macingarroch, and the story told in the trial is truly extraordinary considering that he was both minister and clan chief.

When ill himself, Hector had allegedly been told by the witch Marian that there was no cure for him unless 'the principal man of his blude' should suffer death for him. Hector decided that this must be his half-brother George, so on the witch's instructions he sent for him from the hunting-field and, obeying the spell, put his left hand into George's right hand without uttering a word.

That night, Marian and her accomplice (who was Hector's foster-mother) left the house with spades and dug a grave on a piece of no-man's-land near the sea. Hector was to lie in it for 'his relief and for the death of his brother'. Hector pointed out to Marian that if George were to die suddenly, he would be blamed, so she promised to delay the death until April. Hector was then laid in a blanket and carried by his servants to the grave into which he and Marian descended together. The servants covered them with turf held up by staves. The foster-mother was then told to run the length of nine rigs. When she came back, she called down to Marian in the grave, asking who should die. Marian replied that Hector would live and George would die. After this bizarre ritual was performed three times, Hector was allowed home to his bed. Considering the ordeal, it is amazing that he recovered. However, poor George became ill as predicted – auto-suggested, perhaps? – and soon afterwards died.

Both trials were prosecuted by Mr David McGill of Cranston Riddell, and although James VI was at the time in Falkland Palace, he was to show keen interest in the case. A packed jury of Rosses and Munros acquitted them both.

It is perhaps interesting to note that Catherine Ross was related to the notorious Francis Stewart, Earl of Bothwell, who was himself to stand trial for witchcraft and treason the following year. Catherine and Bothwell must have often met at Balnagown where Bothwell would stay on his visits north to his Caithness kin. George Ross, Catherine's brother, was charged with high treason in 1592 for having sheltered and assisted the Earl.

These strange events are almost impossible to unravel these days, yet are of interest in that they reflect not only the eternal passions of love, jealousy, and revenge, but also the fact that witchcraft was not confined to the uneducated but proliferated in all classes of society. One of the reasons for this may lie within the Reformed Church itself, which, having done away with mystery, ritual and colour in religion, failed to satisfy the needs of the people so that they turned to the Devil instead.

For the purpose of this book, the trials are of supreme interest in that they give an indication of the true profession of Coinneach Odhar and a reason why his name has survived above all others in the Highland occult scene. The style – *fiosaiche* – finally makes sense.

A further clue to his identity may lie in his other name. The adjective '*odhar*', according to *Dwelly's Gaelic Dictionary*, means 'dun-coloured, drab and sallow'. When written '*odharaidh*' its meaning changes to 'dark and swarthy', which would be descriptive of a man who leads an outdoor life. We are told in Pitcairns' *Criminal Trials* that Catherine sent to the 'Egyptians' for advice as to how to get rid of her stepson and her sister-in-law. It seems, then, that Coinneach might have been a gypsy.

The origin of Scottish gypsies is still not fully understood. Some maintain they are descended from the Romany race who were first mentioned as Egyptians' in 1505. Others believe that they are in direct descent from the cairds and tinklers – the ancient Celtic tin-smiths – first documented in the twelfth century in Perth. Lewis Spence maintains that the two races fused and united during the sixteenth century because they shared a similar way of life.

In the earliest days the cairds were regarded as entertainers. In Fr James Dalrymple's translation of Bishop Leslie's *History of Scotland*, 1575, we read of an early Scottish king said to have reigned in AD 600 who 'compelled cairds and bards, gamesters, gluttons and such kinds of men . . . to seek their living with all hardship and drudgery.' Note the association of cairds with bards, both of direct Celtic origin.

From the earliest records it is evident that gypsies, whether descended from the Romanies or from the cairds and bards, were fortune-tellers. Dekker, writing in 1609, states: 'Young men and bachelors . . . do flock after them and they then profess skill in palmistry and (forsooth) can tell fortunes.' By the second half of the sixteenth century, the Scottish Parliament had passed an Act 'for the staunching of masterful, idle beggars . . . That it may be known what manner of persons are meant by idle and strong beggars' the act included 'the idle people calling themselves Egyptians, or any other that feign themselves to have a knowledge of physiognomy, palmistry, or other abused sciences, whereby they persuade the people that they can tell the weirds [destiny] death and futures, and other fantastical imagination . . . shall be taken, adjudged, deemed and punished as strong beggars and vagabonds.'

The Act had little effect, for in 1576 an edict proclaimed that gypsies continued to abuse 'simple, ignorant people with sorcery and divination to the great offence of God and contempt of the King'. A further Act proclaimed that they would henceforth be treated as thieves and murderers, and ordered all sheriffs and law officers to root them out.

The Commissions of Justice ordering the arrest of Coinneach both mention the name of Mariota Neyn Macallester. Neyn was a known gypsy name and is mentioned in a writ signed by James V in 1540. That gypsies were linked with witchcraft is evidenced in other trials of the period. In 1588 an accused witch stated that she had learned her craft from a certain William Simpson who 'was taken from his father by a man of Egypt, a giant, being but a child, who led him away to Egypt with him'. By the early seventeenth century, gypsies were generally regarded as witches, and Presbytery records give instances of penances levied on those who consorted with them.

It would seem possible, therefore, that Coinneach might have been descended from the dispossessed Druidic bards who turned nomad, linked up with the tinsmiths, and became classed as gypsies in general. He would have inherited knowledge of the old Celtic ritual and religion which was classed by outsiders as sorcery and magic; of divination and augury associated with fortune-telling – and he might well also have inherited the faculty of second sight.

The link between second sight and sorcery in the person of a gypsy is a first clue to the connection between the legendary Coinneach Odhar and the historical figure who appears in the sixteenth century Commission of Justice. And, considering how folklore evolves, there are others. Assuming that the historical sorcerer was caught, both Coinneachs would have been burned at the stake. Both met their fate through powerful, unpopular women. Catherine and Isabella were probably totally dissimilar, yet both would have appeared to clansman and cottar as dominant, demanding, and evil. Poison features in both stories, though in the legend the seer is the victim rather than the perpetrator, as the documents state.

And there is a strong clue in the stone.

From the earliest times Druid ritual included the use of stones. Pliny records that the Emperor Claudius condemned to death a Gallic knight for carrying a serpent stone while engaged in a lawsuit. He explains how the stone was made from the sweat and saliva of a mass of wriggling, intertwined snakes (creatures of great significance to the Celts): as the stone was thrown up from the hissing, writhing mass, it had to be caught in a piece of cloth for fear it should touch the ground. The possessor had to escape quickly before the serpents could follow him and destroy him. The test of the validity of the stone was its ability to float upstream.

The Cruban Stone was said to cure diseases of the joints. It could be loaned out to the people of Breadalbane in exchange for two cows, and if the stone were not returned the cows were forfeited. The Ardvoirlic Stone in Perthshire was used for the cure of cattle diseases;

and a round stone with circles carved on it found its way to Tiree where it was used for the relief of colic and stomach pains. There were stones called after the saints, most famous of which was St Mary's Nut. Mary Macintyre, a witch from Barra, had a blue stone called Clach na Leig, with a hole through which she thrust her tongue before making a prediction. By using it thus, Mary could give young women news of their lovers, and secure good sales for the fishermen.

A larger stone, said to have been used in Druidic rites, is kept in the garden of Arpafeelie Rectory in the Black Isle. It was supposed to have been removed from some Celtic sacred site by a certain Canon Paterson, nicknamed 'the Devil Incarnate,' who used it as a feeding trough for his poultry. When the hens all died of a mysterious disease, he used it for his pigs. These too died almost immediately, so the Canon, believing the stone to be responsible, threw it away. Next day it had returned, so he tried to give it away, but always it returned overnight. The present tenant kept it in a shed but found that the animals who shared the building died untimely. Now it is kept in a wire-netting enclosure where it can do no harm.

Coinneach's stone has been described by the legends in a variety of ways, ranging from black and shining to white and translucent like a pearl. It was also thought to have been round with a hole in it, perhaps similar to the serpent bead handled by J. G. Campbell who described it as being about 1¼″ long, shaped like a bullet, with a hole through it from end to end and depressions on either side as if it had once been soft and moulded between finger and thumb. It was made of translucent material akin to, but different from, modern glass, with brilliant streaks of colour. It was thought to have originated in Egypt and to have been obtained by the Druids from their religious counterparts. A similar bead found at Thebes was dated to 1500 BC.

The fact that Coinneach possessed such a stone would mark him as being more a member of the Druidic priesthood than a spectre-haunted *taibhsear*. It indicates that he must have been a man of considerable power and knowledge, well entitled to the style of 'principal enchanter', and more in character with the historical Coinneach Odhar rather than the legendary Brahan Seer.

The location of seer and sorcerer is apparently a problem, as there is no solid evidence (prophecies apart) that Coinneach ever existed in Lewis. Historical evidence places him in Ross. But the Revd William Matheson has an ingenious and credible theory to explain the

228

connection, which he elaborated in a paper to the Inverness Gaelic Society in 1968.

When, at the beginning of the seventeenth century, the Mackenzie wrested Lewis from the Macleods, a certain George Mackenzie was made tacksman of Baile-na-Cille, that same district where the ghost legendarily appeared to Coinneach's mother. George Mackenzie's mother was a Munro of Kaitwell in Easter Ross, closely connected to the Munros of Foulis. She spent her latter days living with her son in Lewis, and no doubt the stories she took with her centred round Catherine and the 'principal enchanter' himself. So popular were these stories to become, so often repeated at the *ceilidh* hearth, and so colourful, that it must have seemed as if both the tales and the character originated in Lewis itself.

One thing is certain. The historical Coinneach, the gypsy sorcerer, could not have made the Seaforth predictions. The title did not exist until 1623. In the Gaelic tradition the chief of Clan Mackenzie was always – until the end of the line – styled MacCoinneach or Cabarféidh, and there is no Gaelic equivalent for the word 'countess'. There is an argument among some Gaelic scholars today that the stories about the legendary seer derive not from the Gaelic tradition at all, but from someone using English, possibly Alexander Mackenzie himself, who had a lively imagination when it came to translating and handling the original legends.

And yet the prophecy that there would be a deaf Cabarféidh is of ancient origin. Someone must have made it. The other prophecies also exist. Though it is possible that where some are concerned (like the 1977 prediction about the wedding) events decided the embellishments, others were well established long before their fulfilment.

When we come to examine the prophecies in detail (in the Appendix, page 314), we will find that they range over so wide a period of history and so wide a range of geography that they would appear to be the work of many seers. The compelling conclusion must be that Coinneach Odhar is no more than a collective name for a number of *taibhsears*, a magnet that has drawn to itself the whole of Highland prophetic history. There was a man called Coinneach Odhar; there are a host of prophecies. From these two facts, folklore has woven its own rich and colourful tapestry, a living, growing mystery that cannot properly be explained. And this is the wonder of Coinneach Odhar, that although he may not have uttered one of the predictions ascribed to him, he has drawn the whole of prophetic history in the Highlands to his name; that although he may only have existed historically as a shadowy sorcerer, he is a folk-hero today; that in spite of science, modern technology, and education, Coinneach is almost as whole-heartedly credited now as ever he was.

8 The Mantle of Coinneach Odhar

THE HIGHLAND SEER

The peninsula of Easter Ross, bounded by the waters of the Cromarty and Dornoch Firths, is ancient in history, varied in scenery, and remote from the cities of the south. From the flat plains of the seaboard villages to the Ardross Hill, thatched with forest, and up into the heights of Ben Wyvis where snow lingers from one winter to the next, Easter Ross is mysterious and magic. Here, in hidden glens, Neolithic men built chambered tombs. On the sea links, Picts carved symbolic monoliths and Celtic saints settled, some say to write the Book of Kells. St Duthac's shrine at Tain drew pilgrims from all over the world, including a barefoot king. The great earls of Ross ruled and hunted and kept court. Descendants of the first Munro chiefs still live at Castle Foulis.

This was the land of the historical Coinneach Odhar and of Catherine Ross of Balnagowan. This is the land of Swein Macdonald, and well suited to a contemporary seer.

It was February – the dead month of the Celtic year – when I crossed the heights of Struie. Below, the silver coil of the Dornoch Firth wound between patches of forest black against the grey mountains of Sutherland beyond. Snow fell like feathers from a pewter sky, a few hens poked in the slush, and three cats watched as I parked outside the croft on Kincardine Hill.

As Swein was out at the sheep, I was left alone to warm myself by a huge fire in the living-room. Ornaments of every description jostled for space: willow-pattern dishes, Chinese plates, and a painted mandarin; a Celtic cross, a Buddha and a head of Christ; a kettle, brass bells and a black skull. Books were piled high everywhere, *East Lynne* beside *Chinese Creeds and Customs*, Alexander Mackenzie's *Highland*

Clearances, a textbook on ESP, a Burns encyclopaedia and a pile of *Scots Magazines*. There were family photographs and signed pictures of the stars, including Larry Grayson and Isla St Clair; a portrait of Swein by Coia; and a series of bird-prints on the wall. Dominating all was a large *No Smoking* sign. Somewhere through the cottage a telephone began to ring. Its muted call continued more or less ceaselessly all afternoon, but with a commendable sense of priorities Swein managed to ignore it.

As soon as he had coped with the sheep, changed from his working clothes into a smart tweed jacket and cavalry twills, Swein came in, fresh-cheeked from the fields, his sturdy figure bursting from the confines of conventional dress. Though he looks the part of prophet, with flowing whitening hair and beard, with deep-set, dominating blue eyes, Swein is very much a man's man, has described himself as hard, and has been called a great earth father. Capable of inspiring trust, affection and respect from his clients and friends, he admits to having little time for layabouts, cheats and uninformed critics.

He was born on 17 July 1931 into a local family whose roots go back 500 years. His maternal grandfather carved the croft out of some twenty acres of barren land, one of a number of tenants who founded a small township above the church at Kincardine. He should have been born on the croft but his mother (one of thirteen) had travelled to Elgin for the weekend and he was in a hurry – an indication, perhaps of his character, for throughout his life he has driven himself hard.

After attending the local school, he served his time as a stonemason with Alexander Corbett and Sons of Tain, a firm which has long since closed. On his return from National Service he found that trade was poor in the north, so like many a Highlander before him he went south to Glasgow, where he found employment with the Clyde Navigation Trust, 'working seven days out of the seven'.

It was here that he met and married Isabelle, also from Easter Ross, and it was she who was to nurse him through an all but fatal accident. This happened one Sunday. Swein wanted to check on some work before taking his family for a picnic in the Campsie Hills. As he was walking down a narrow passage between two buildings, the swinging jib of a crane deposited a load of bricks on the back of his head. After a long spell in hospital, where he was given eighteen months to live, he gradually recovered sufficiently to return to the family croft. The accident left him with a form of tunnel vision which means he cannot drive and finds crowds difficult.

After a period of depression he found a new mission in life, the use of his psychic talent as a means of benefiting the public. But acceptance of his incapacity did not come without much heart-searching and bitterness, and it took time for him to believe, as he now does, that his destiny was in the hands of God.

His second sight was not, as might have been supposed, the result of his accident. It was, he believes, inherited from his grandfather John, who also saw visions. Once he and a friend watched a neighbour ride down the road in a horse and cart.

'Where is he off to?' asked John.

'He's away to the station,' replied his friend.

'No,' said John, 'he'll never get there. He'll be brought back himself on that cart.'

'Never,' said the friend, 'a big strong man like that.'

Sure enough, the neighbour took a bad turn and was found lying on the side of the road. He was put on the cart and brought home.

As a child Swein often saw sights that others could not share. When he was about ten years old he was standing outside the croft at twilight one summer when he saw a tall man pass up the road in a tail-coat, with a black veil hanging from the back of his hat. Thinking it was a visitor he called out to a neighbour, 'Who's that strange-looking man on the road?' The neighbour shook his head and told him that there was no one on the road, that he must have been reading too many stories. Later he told his mother, and she recognized the stranger from the description.

'You couldn't have seen him, son. News is just through that he died in London within the hour.' The stranger was an undertaker who had been born and reared in the house next door.

Swein often senses the presence of his grandfather about the croft, through a strong smell of pipe tobacco which is particularly notice-able in the back shed. As he actively discourages smoking, Swein has no doubt that he is sensing his grandfather. He finds the presence comforting.

Throughout his youth, Swein continued to have telepathic experiences, and saw unaccountable lights and visions. In Glasgow his friends often asked him to predict their futures, but it was not a faculty he relished. Work then was all-important; he preferred to leave the psychic side of his life alone. Then in 1970 came the accident and with the closing of one door, the opening of another. His wife wrote to the Society for Psychical Research, who sent him a letter. There was nothing written in it except a name – J. Potts. Swein sensed the writer so strongly that when, three weeks later, the result of his reading came back, he was 98 per cent correct. Blind psychometry – the power of divination by contact with an object belonging to the subject – turned out to be one of Swein's special skills.

Gradually thereafter Swein came to terms with the accident, his changed existence, and his gift. In time he was to turn from being a hard man with high expectations and little tolerance for the idle and weak, into a compassionate person with a new insight and understanding of his fellow man.

'Do you regard your faculty as an affliction or a gift?' I asked, mindful of old beliefs and traditions connected with second sight.

'As a chosen gift to be used wisely, not frivolously, and never for personal gain,' he answered firmly. 'By continual use, it has developed in the same way as a muscle. The more you work at it, the more you get out of it.'

His visions are seen with the 'second eye' somewhere in the middle of his forehead, in a series of moving pictures like a film, and all the time he talks about what he sees. Like a dreamer, he seldom remembers afterwards what he has said or seen unless the vision is particularly dramatic – such as a car accident, strong grief, or pain. If he is interrupted during the flow of vision, he may well lose the thread, as in one instance when he was describing the Edinburgh flat of a client who was having trouble with her lawyer. He found himself in his vision walking up a tenement stair, turning left, and entering the flat where he described the walls, furniture and fitments in detail down to a threadbare patch on the carpet. Then he said, 'I'm looking at a black coin-operated telephone –'

'No,' interrupted his client, 'you're wrong. You must be in another flat.' And then suddenly she remembered that at one time she had decided to let the flat to students and had arranged for the telephone to be installed, though she had never actually seen it *in situ*. That interruption broke the flow of the vision. Swein was unable to get back into the waking dream, in spite of the client's pleading.

Sometimes he 'sees' in symbolic form. Three stepping-stones might imply three weeks, or even three years. The number five might indicate the number in a family, a date, or even the number of a house. In the interpretation of such symbols he admits he can make mistakes. For example, he predicted some time before his engagement that Prince Charles would marry an English girl who would soon give him a son and heir. The child's name would begin with the letter M. Only a week out with his dates, he believes that he saw the letter W for William upside-down. Such mistakes are possible in the interpretation of signs and symbols. The vision itself is never wrong.

'I know that whatever I see or sense in my mind has either happened or will definitely come to pass,' he assured me solemnly, though on one notable occasion he was mistaken. He sensed then that Margaret Thatcher would never come into power. 'This was because I built myself up strongly that she would not succeed, because I knew that if she were to become prime minister, trouble would lie ahead.'

He needs no gimmicks to focus his concentration and sees nothing in the crystal ball. 'With the tarot, you are reading what the cards say. In palmistry you follow the lines of the hand. With astrology you have to research.' Use of the ouija board he actively discourages. 'I wouldn't touch it. You can contact spirits, entities, evil forces. My advice to youngsters who want to meddle is, cut it right out.'

He likes to spend a few moments in quietness before a client enters his small 'consulting-room', and he always starts and ends the session with private prayer. Sometimes he gets a little tired, but after a short rest is able to continue again. Often visions and revelations come to him in moments of calm and in the open air. He wishes he could write them down, as he forgets them almost immediately.

'So what is second sight?' I asked him.

'Just a vision, an inner vision, a waking dream,' he answered. 'Mind-reading is not second sight. Telepathy is not second sight. You can't measure it. You can't judge it by modern experimentation.'

'Where does it come from, do you think?'

'It goes back to the dawn of time. In prehistoric days most people had it. Minds were not so cluttered in those days.'

He knows no one else with genuine second sight, nor does he believe it can be learned or acquired, 'But if you are born with it, you can develop it.'

Swein is deeply interested in history, and one of the figures whom he senses strongly is Coinneach Odhar. He sees him as a hard-working man, with longish brown hair, going white. He gets the impression of a man of five foot six or seven inches, ahead of his time and of everyone else in the area, who has no desire to improve his status. He places him in the sixteenth century against a primitive background with no roads or bridges, no carts with wheels, only pack-horses and litters for transport.

'When I think deeply about him, I sense him as a misjudged man. Fair to his fellows, but if anyone tried to double-cross him he would use his powers to keep those people in their place. A stern man who answered to only one power.' Unconsciously Swein has given, perhaps, a portrait of himself.

Although Swein, too, believes in God, he considers that the church has much to answer for in its persecution of those with psychic power, and thinks that he himself would have been burned at the stake a few hundred years back. The church is still muddled in its thinking, he contends; it accepts the Petty Seer but condemns Swein himself. He has been told by ministers that his gift converts people to the Devil while ministers like the Petty Seer converted people to God. 'Is there one power for me, then, and one for ministers?' he argues. 'Prophecy is a gift of the spirit. Certainly you can abuse the spirit and get drawn into darker things, but I am a Christian and always will be.'

If Swein feels some bitterness towards the churches in Scotland, it is hardly surprising. He was told by one insolent young man – who has since become a family friend – 'My church keeps a dossier on you.' On another occasion he was seen in a local graveyard where, as a favour to the bride whose wedding he had just attended, he was putting her bouquet on her grandmother's grave. He was reported to the minister who hurried over to accuse him angrily of necromancy.

After a broadcast Swein had made, a minister complained that he never mentioned Jesus Christ. 'I deal with Jews and all religions, and I also deal with atheists, so I use the word God,' he told him.

'Why do so many people come to you?' another minister complained. Swein, who believes that the established church can be biased and condemnatory, replied, 'Maybe it's because I make no judgements.'

Though Swein is no black practitioner, his gift has led him into confrontation with darker forces. Witchcraft exists in Easter Ross as elsewhere, and he knows of at least two covens in the area. Most people indulge in it for kicks and power, and Swein is particularly anxious to warn youngsters not to dabble. 'It usually starts with the ouija board. I say it's the work of the Devil, that you can't control.' A woman from a coven boasted to him that she was going to sell her soul to the Devil. She wanted to be important, to gain money and power. Not long afterwards he had a phone call from her in tears: she had lost her car, her job, her house, and her health.

'A black magician once cursed me,' he said soberly. 'He thought he was Aleister Crowley.' A young woman had come to Swein in a frightened, unhappy state, saying that she was in the power of this man who was using her for indecent sexual rites. 'Make a break,' Swein had advised. 'Tell him you're finished. Tell him Swein Macdonald says so.' In due course the woman was summoned to the coven, but she refused to go, and, as a result, Swein was contacted by a friend who warned him that he would be cursed to death. 'The magician will do his best to kill you,' the friend warned.

For two nights in succession, the 'Horsemen' (of the Apocalypse) were sent to Swein and he had no sleep. So, 'I sent them back,' he said. Eventually the black magician himself called at the croft. 'He was the most pathetic man I ever saw. I felt sorry for him. He begged me to raise the curse I'd put on him.'

Swein explained that he had put no curse on anyone and asked why he was so troubled. 'Everything I do now goes wrong,' the magician explained. His wife had lost her job. He had had to sell his house, and that morning his son had been taken away from him.

Swein was not surprised. 'If you dabble in witchcraft, Satan gives you everything – money, position, travel – to begin with. But in the end you lose the little you ever had.'

I asked him if he was ever afraid of the power of evil. 'You've got to be strong mentally to cope with that sort of thing, but I've never been afraid of my own gift. I've seen things, heard voices, been brought up with ghosts, but I've never been afraid.'

Though Swein can be a good and loyal friend, compassionate and understanding with his clients, he can also be an implacable enemy to those whom he considers to be false, unfair or dishonest. A regular columnist of the *Northern Times*, who used the pseudonym of 'Sentinel', had incurred Swein's contempt by making snide comments about local people who could not hit back. For example, he had complained in print that it took less time to build the Great Wall of China than for three particular workmen to complete a certain small job. And when Sentinel turned his attention to Swein himself, his wrath was roused as well.

> Our front page, [wrote Sentinel] has been head-lining the Seer of Ardgay. For myself, I have no great confidence that there are people endowed with that kind of psychic vision, and, indeed, in the past I frequently watched the efforts of fortune-tellers' allegedly remarkable powers, not one of whom I found convincing . . . It seems much more likely that what is claimed as success in the reading of the future is in reality educated guessing arising from information subtly extracted from the subject, who is, in the nature of things, already conditioned to talk . . .

Swein's anger was roused, not because he had been criticized, but rather because he had been condemned by a journalist who had not bothered to research his subject properly by finding out for himself whether Swein was gifted or not. He contacted Jim Henderson, the editor of *Northern Times*, who pointed out that there was little he could do about it. Free speech entitled the Sentinel to his opinion. Nor would he reveal the identity of his contributor, which was known only to him and one other in the office.

Letters to the editor followed. Donald G. Macleod of Scourie wrote:

> I would like to say a few words in defence of Swein Macdonald as it seems that he is getting the big stick from Sentinel in your paper and from the church. I went to see Swein and he told me the name of my mother, my ex-wife, the name of the man she married. He described the house where my uncle had recently died, and told me many personal things as well as naming my next-door neighbour . . . No, no, Sentinel, there are more things twixt heaven and earth than are dreamt of in your philosophy. If Swein Macdonald has an unusual gift, well that is all right with me. If you believe it, you believe it, if you don't believe it, you don't believe it. That does not prove that he has not been gifted.

Swein's wife also wrote to the paper:

> I would like Sentinel to know that no information is ever extracted from callers by my husband, Swein Macdonald, or myself. How can Sentinel try to judge the seer when he has never met or talked

238

with him? . . . I issue a challenge to Sentinel to meet the seer publicly when all can hear and judge for themselves what is the truth. Surely that is not too difficult a task for one who would appear to be so certain of his facts. We give him fourteen days to accept our offer to meet, because our days are precious and not to be spent idly but constructively . . .

The hall in Golspie was duly booked. The announcement of the challenge naturally aroused much public interest, for Sentinel was generally unpopular. One man called at the croft with an offer of £100 to any charity supported by Swein, if he could name the columnist, and came back twice, each time with the offer doubled. He too had suffered from Sentinel's pen.

Meanwhile Swein began to concentrate.

The story is now taken by Jim Henderson, editor of the *Northern Times*, who told me that over the next few days his telephone rang regularly as Swein fitted together another piece of the puzzle. At first he sensed water and sand, possibly a village . . . Jim had laughed. 'That could be almost anywhere in the British Isles.'

'No,' said Swein, 'it's in the Dornoch region.'

An hour or so later, he had called again. 'I see a Bible. I sense that he is involved with religion.'

The next call produced a description of the village, followed by its name. Jim became uneasy. He was still more surprised when Swein's next call produced a description of the man. Finally, to Jim's incredulity, Swein told him his initial, his job, described his house, and finally gave the name.

'It was an uncanny experience,' said Jim. 'I had always admired Swein as a man, was maybe a bit doubtful of his claim to be a seer; but this convinced me that he undoubtedly has powers.'

He wrote in the *Northern Times*:

Swein Macdonald, the Kincardine crofter, gave another dramatic demonstration of his powers of second sight this week, when he named, described, provided the locality and occupation of our columnist Sentinel . . . Now Swein is challenging our writer to public debate to prove he is no fake. 'I am able to do these things with the help of God and the spirit, and it angers me that a man can say I am a charlatan without first testing me out himself,' said the bearded Mr Macdonald . . . On guard, Sentinel!

239

The meeting duly took place. Two hundred folk crammed into the hall. At last Swein stood up. 'I see the man is not in the audience,' he announced. 'I know where he is, and I also know that none of you will be bothered by him again. He will never write as Sentinel any more.'

Sure enough, the following week a paragraph in the paper stated that owing to pressure of work, Sentinel would no longer be continuing his column. Shortly afterwards he left the district.

It would be easy for sceptics to say that someone must have told Swein the identity of Sentinel, if it were not for the evidence of Jim Henderson, a level-headed newspaper man who knew both sides of the matter and who, having done his own research, was convinced that Swein's part in discovering the identity of the columnist was genuine.

But Swein is not a vindictive man. Some who have come to scorn have gone away close friends and believers. It is the uninformed or prejudiced critic, the closed mind that rouses the wrath of his powerful personality. When a young boy asked in good faith, 'Are you a fake?' he was treated to a courteous, honest answer. I have seen Swein deal with a group of women as gently as a family doctor. To one who had the courage to ask if she would have another heart attack, he told that she would be fine provided she rested, dieted and did all that her doctor had told her. No magic in that, only common sense. Another, whose grandson was missing abroad, he satisfied with the promise that he was alive and would be in touch in the near future. Both women went home comforted and reassured. Whether he had used his powers of vision or played the part of a psychologist, it is impossible to say.

'What happens', I asked, 'if you see something bad for your client?'

'You have to tell them,' he answered seriously, 'but you tell them in such a way as to prepare them and to warn them.' Some come to him on the verge of suicide and despair. Often he can see an end to their unhappiness, or advises them to change tactics and start on a new path altogether. His clients are often women who have had unhappy love affairs. To be able to foresee a new friendship, possibly marriage, gives them and him great satisfaction. Often he gets asked to the wedding.

He frequently foresees accidents. He told one man who called on a certain Tuesday that he saw him driving south from Invergordon and warned him to take extreme care, for his car would be severely damaged and he would hurt his hand. On the following Friday the man telephoned to say that his car had crashed a mile from the end of the Struie road and that he had sustained a hand injury.

On another occasion, four youngsters called in. Swein felt particularly drawn towards the last but could not see much of his future. He warned him to take special care with his motor bike, sensing that a high wind might blow him off the road. Shortly afterwards, the lad's transport to work failed to appear so he took out his bike and, just a mile from his home lost control, hit a dyke and was killed. The boy's parents still visit Swein on the anniversary of his death.

'Is there any way you can stop an accident once you've predicted it?' I asked.

'All you can do is warn. If the boy on the bike had remembered my prediction he might have survived.'

A local farmer had been warned to be particularly careful on his tractor for Swein had seen it roll right over on the hillside. The farmer admitted that he had not as yet fixed an anti-roll bar, that he felt guilty about it and would see to it immediately. A few weeks later the accident happened as foreseen, but the new appliance saved the farmer's life. Swein warned a Golspie woman not to interfere with an outdoor light. She in turn warned her husband who was about to replace a shattered bulb, so he used rubber gloves to unscrew the lamp. The wires crossed and shorted in his hand.

An Aberdeen journalist with little respect for Swein's powers was amazed when Swein told him on the phone that he had a green car which would soon be involved in an accident. With the receiver in his hand, he glanced out of the office window and saw another driver reverse into his car.

Not all lives, however, contain dramatic incidents and gloomy prognoses, and Swein is as accurate in the small domestic details, the day-to-day events of ordinary lives, as he is with accidents and disasters.

Alex Main writing in the *Scottish Daily Express* on 28 December 1977, stated:

He asked for my watch and clutching it in his right hand he stayed silent for a few moments and then started to speak. He told me of some of my inner feelings, of my hopes for the future, of a stone-built house by water and rocks where I found peace and satisfaction

– he even described the staircase and, to a degree, the relative who lives there. Later he mentioned a name . . . it was amazingly accurate. There were other things. He pinpointed a recurring illness, and he touched on a family situation and how I believed, and he, that it would be resolved. It was almost as if it was myself speaking.

An important side of Swein's gift is his ability to trace those who are lost, for the police, for anxious relatives, or even for pet owners as far away as London. With some article belonging to the missing person, or a photograph, he can be uncannily accurate. When consulted, he sensed that a certain local woman, thought to be in London, was dead and that her body would be found face downwards in a loch, entangled in weed, by a man with a sheep and a dog. A search was mounted by helicopters and skin-divers, but no trace of her was found. Eventually a shepherd discovered her body in a loch not half a mile from her home, just as Swein had predicted.

In a case of suspected murder, Swein predicted to the distraught parents that the victim, a young lad, was still alive, that he would be found in Glasgow in 'a building where pigeons fly in and out, near water,' and that he would have a sore on his face. The police had set up an incident caravan near his home and were searching the mine shafts, afraid of foul play. The parents contacted Swein again to say that the boy had sent them a postcard from Newcastle, but Swein still insisted that he was in Glasgow and that he would turn himself over to the police in a week's time. Sure enough, a week later the boy walked into Maryhill Police Station in Glasgow. The left side of his face was swollen by a gum-boil. He had been squatting with a friend in a condemned building, and the postcard had been sent from Newcastle by the two boys who had made the trip to conceal their true whereabouts.

Perhaps the most extraordinary case occurred in Inverness in March 1983. Stephen Clunas, aged twenty-four, had gone to Aviemore for a short holiday from Inverness. During the weekend the barefoot body of a young man was found by hill-walkers on the banks of Loch Einich halfway between Glenfeshie and the Lairig Ghru. A full-scale search was mounted in the hopes of finding the dead man's shoes, or some clue to his identity.

On the Monday morning, Mrs Clunas, Stephen's mother, read

about the dead man and was horrified to find that the description matched that of her son whom she knew to be in Aviemore and who had not yet returned. She contacted the police and eventually identified the body. Later Mr Clunas, the boy's father, also identified the body. The obituary was printed in the paper and the funeral arranged. Then Stephen turned up, alive and well.

Meanwhile Swein had been contacted by the relative of a young arts graduate from Chesterfield who had disappeared and was thought to have gone to London. Swein sensed darkness and coldness, and asked for an article of clothing to be posted. The young man's mother herself contacted Swein, and again he had a strong impression of darkness, coldness and loss. All he could tell the distraught mother was that he was sure her son was not in London. Knowing Swein's gift better than most, his wife contacted the police to find out whether anyone had been reported missing in the mountains, and was told about Stephen Clunas. Eventually the body turned out to be that of the arts graduate, an inexperienced, ill-equipped climber who had been overcome by the weather.

Another of Swein's gifts is the ability to predict over the telephone. He listens to the voice and gradually an image builds up. He gets calls from all over Britain and features regularly in a phone-in programme on local radio.

'What do the scientists and psychologists say to you?' I asked.

He roared with laughter.

'I'll tell you what one distinguished gentleman said – "When I get you into my hospital I'll keep you there for life. I'll see to it you never get out." ' The reason for this was that Swein had seen too much. After his interview, the psychiatrist had handed him a gold charm bracelet and asked him to describe the owner. 'As I held it,' said Swein, 'I saw a jeweller's shop. There was a fair-haired girl talking to him and a darkish girl across the counter.' He felt angry. 'You bought that bracelet this morning to give to your mistress. You're trying to trick me and I don't need that kind of test.' Seemingly, the psychiatrist was not pleased.

Swein's long-term predictions tend to be fairly general. In 1982 he accurately foresaw a scandal involving a Member of Parliament (thought to have been Cecil Parkinson who resigned in 1983) and increased violence leading to a bid to bring back capital punishment, which would be outvoted in Parliament. He foresaw conscription of young people into community projects; further tension between Russia and America; petrol up to £2 a gallon; more unemployment in the Highlands and elsewhere; more IRA bombing in the major cities. Most remarkable was his correct prediction that the Invergordon Smelter would close. Unfulfilled so far is his forecast of a U-turn by Margaret Thatcher and an assassination threat to a visiting celebrity.

In 1983, he saw more dark days ahead. He particularly warned northerners who care about the railway to fight now for its survival, foretelling that trains would be cut to one a day in the north and gradually all be axed in the Highlands. Construction of the Dornoch bridge would start ahead of time, but he warned that bridges like those at Kessock and Invergordon would not only bring people into the area but would also take them out.

Looking further into the future, he sees the end of industry at Nigg, where the shore will turn back to a beach again. He also warns against the buying and sub-letting of crofts to form big units for holiday visitors. To be properly cared for, a croft should be let to the family who has always run it, not sold. He warns too of Coinneach Odhar's 'black rain', which he sees as acid rain and predicts will certainly fall. Another of Coinneach's prophecies has meaning for him: 'When there are seven bridges over the Ness, the city will fall into the sea.' On a visit to Inverness in 1983 he 'saw' the castle waver, crumble and fall. This might tie up with another long-term prediction where he 'saw a great wallop of water swamp the north-east coast of Scotland'. Like a great tidal wave, it will wash in and destroy the coast. He does not see a nuclear explosion, but rather a tidal wave caused by some undersea disturbance, possibly an earthquake.

'How do you regard your vision?' I asked finally.

'As a force for good,' he replied firmly. He believes his gift comes from the subconscious and may be instinctive. 'Nine times out of ten you are guided in this life by instinct. But there is no guesswork, no coincidence, about what I tell people. It has happened or it will happen some time in the future.' He believes his purpose in life is to help others to the exclusion of personal gain, and thereby he has found the key to contentment. His gifts of hindsight and foresight have also given him insight, not just into the minds of those who consult him about their fears and troubles, but also into his own life. In 1983 he met and fell instantly and overwhelmingly in love with one of his clients, Lindsay MacKinnon, a young mother of twins. It was a case of love at first sight for both of them and they subsequently set up a home together in the Barn near his family croft. When on 5 November 1984 Lindsay gave birth to a son, she told reporters, 'Swein predicted it would be a son. That was nine months ago and it has come true.'

Talking to those who consult him, I find they divide roughly into three groups.

There are those whose minds would seem to be wide open to his seeing eye and who are amazed at the accuracy of his judgement of their character and situation. He told one young man, 'You are one of the modern magicians,' – an apt description of an electronic engineer. He is particularly good at predicting accidents with cars – perhaps the modern equivalent of the old-time sightings of phantom funerals.

Another group finds that he gets the occasional detail right, but are not convinced that this is more than coincidence. A young woman with a strong talent for piano-playing who was told that he sees her working with her fingers, perhaps as an artist, was not sufficiently convinced of his powers, particularly as he had little else to tell her.

There are lastly the few with whom he fails completely. One of two sisters who visited him in succession found that he laid her whole life before her in incredible detail, the other, who admitted to closing her mind deliberately and giving nothing away, learned nothing.

It would seem, perhaps, that Swein is strongly telepathic and depends for his success – like hypnotists – on the conscious or unconscious co-operation of his clients.

Swein's claim to second sight in the Highland tradition has been disputed by purists who argue that the gift should be involuntary, never deliberately cultivated, and that the vision seen should be external, in the form of a *taibhs*, rather than within the mind. Yet Swein has fulfilled both these conditions, for he has had many involuntary visions throughout his life and continues to experience them. A recent example occurred when he was walking down his road with a neighbour one dark December night. His tunnel vision caught sight of a bobbing light moving this way and that on the road ahead, which he could not account for and his neighbour could not see. Three weeks later, on 2 January, he and his wife first-footed the last of the friends who lived close to where he had seen the light.

'Thank goodness you've come,' cried their neighbour. 'My man's taken a bad turn.' The doctor was sent for, but as he was new to the district and not sure how to get to the croft, Swein went out to watch for him. After a while he saw the bobbing light at exactly the same place as he had seen it in December. It was the doctor, who, having parked further down the road, was searching by torchlight for the right path.

Cultivation of the gift is a natural progression in those who have it to the degree that Swein Macdonald has. The legendary Coinneach Odhar is just such an example: we are told that a 'gentleman from Inverness' wrote down his predictions and that Isabella Mackenzie consulted him herself. We know, too, that Columba was consulted from time to time. Looking back into the remote past, it would seem to be more in the tradition of Celtic second sight actively to encourage the gift than to suppress it. As an inheritance from the Druids and earlier tribal priests who communicated with the *sithean*, the gift, it must be supposed, was there to be used. Even in Christian terms, the word 'gift' implies usage in the same way as 'talent'.

There are, of course, many people who have the gift but who choose deliberately to suppress it. Fear of the future, of religious condemnation, of mental distress, and of awakening occult powers, would seem to lie at the root of such suppression, and for those who hold such views it would be well for them to leave the talent buried. However it is surely invidious to suggest that their gift is 'traditional second sight' and Swein's is not.

Like Swein, I do not suppose that his faculty is spooky or even supernormal, but as natural as any function of the mind, if less well understood. His gift is a creative talent to be compared with art or poetry, and probably originating from the same source. All can draw a shape or rhyme a sentence, experience a precognitive dream or a premonition, but few can rise beyond the amateur status. Swein has that touch of genius which sets him – like all true artists – apart.

THE CELTIC CLAIRVOYANT

Since the days of the Industrial Revolution when the Celts from Ireland and the Highlands overwhelmed the elegant houses, broad streets and 'oderiferous orchards' of the tobacco lords, Glasgow has suffered a contemptuous press. The myth persists: this is the city of pallid people in sunless closes, the breeding ground of psychopaths, sectarians, and street gangs, of social and cultural wastes in great ghetto housing schemes, of violence, vandalism and puny-chested hard men.

Take a closer look. The sooty tenements of the east end are fast being replaced with elegant landscaped buildings. Motorways have made Glasgow the easiest city to traverse, throughout Europe. Festivals flourish in the unlikely soil of Easterhouse. Gregariousness, generosity, and courage dominate the meanest streets.

Yet all myth contains a grain of truth, and certainly hardship and hard men exist in these hard times; but for those who appreciate humanity, Glasgow is rich. Humour, kindness, music, and poetry abound in this city which contains more Celts than ever left the north and west.

One of them, whose origins, beliefs and skills are Celtic to the core, is the clairvoyant, Henderson Lynn. Though not, perhaps, a seer in the conventional Highland sense, Harry Lynn's faculty would seem to owe its origins more directly to the Druid cult of divination. He makes no secret of the fact that he belongs to the old Celtic religion, and though he is not a practising ritualist and is fairly contemptuous of those who degrade and debase the ancient knowledge of 'wicca', he still celebrates the feast of Samhain at Hallowe'en with wine and a round of shortbread (symbolic of eating the sun) and he is steeped in the lore and legends of pre-Christian days.

Like Swein Macdonald he is an admirer of Coinneach Odhar, but where Swein could be said to embody many of the characteristics of the legendary Brahan Seer of the seventeenth century, Harry – as we shall see – has more in common with the sixteenth-century Coinneach Odhar, who was indicted for witch-craft and styled as a leader in the art of magic. I doubt that Swein would have been burned as a witch 300 years ago, but I have no doubt at all that Harry Lynn would have been put to the test and suffered the death.

Like Swein, too, he has – probably unconsciously – fleshed out the historical figure with some of his own characteristics. He sees Coinneach as a labourer who preferred to keep a low profile in spite of exceptional powers, and who was clever enough to cheat the authorities of his execution. He senses strongly that the true Coinneach escaped the fire and that someone else died in his stead. His admiration for that shadowy figure is genuine.

247

Harry is a neat, thin, pale man who looks a decade younger than his fifty-nine years until you see his eyes. Grey and full of knowlege, they are sombre, the eyes of a man who sleeps too little and knows too much – until they lighten with humour. Harry has all the quick-witted patter of a Glaswegian, and a keen sense of fun. 'Clairvoyants are often thought of as serious people, but we're not. I'm a very down-to-earth sort of man. I enjoy life, and I like the punters who come to see me.'

Although in his own quiet, comfortable home in the south side of the city Harry could be mistaken for any conventional businessman, his office in one of the city's busiest thoroughfares betrays his pro-fession. A cross between a fairground booth, an alchemist's den and 'Frankenstein's Grotto', this dark, ground-floor tenement room must have caused many 'a wee girl' (as he calls his female clients from seventeen to seventy) to shiver. Indeed, one arrived for a reading with five crucifixes stitched to the lining of her coat.

The reason for the skulls, the zodiac clock, the Hand of Fatimah, the statue of Da Magdalena, the planchette board, the books, and the beads may be found in Harry's past. Of gypsy – or *gadjie* as it is called in the Highlands – extraction, Harry's forebears, Boyds, O'Briens, and Lynns, came from the Highlands and Ireland. Gypsies, as we have already seen, are of confused origin in Scotland: some may be descended from the nomadic cairds or tinklers, tinsmiths and horse dealers; others are thought to have originated in the bards and Druids themselves, dispossessed and outcast by the Christians, who formed into wandering groups and later joined up with the other 'travellers' but whose lore and knowledge was passed down to successive genera-tions. Coinneath Odhar himself (see page 226) may well have been a gypsy. We know, too, that from the earliest days, all those classed together as the Egyptians practised fortune-telling, divination, and prediction.

The name 'Lynn' is of Gaelic extraction meaning 'pool' and has strong occult connotations: the Linn of Tummel between Killicrankie and Pitlochry is a long, deep, peaty, dark-brown pool, and Loch Linnhe is similarly named. Harry's parents were fortune-tellers who sometimes worked from fairground booths, but not constantly. Clair-voyance – and Harry repeated this several times – is exhausting, draining, not something you do continually. His father would rather have been a gardener, having a passion for roses, and Harry himself

248

would rather have been an artist. He spends much of his time designing displays for industrial companies, and makes a living out of entertaining at pubs and clubs with a mental act which has nothing at all to do with his life as a clairvoyant. Yet like his ancestors before him he is always drawn back to the small dark room to practise the art of prediction which is so much part of his background and tradition.

The relics that adorn his office were once part of his wider family's tools of trade, possessions which he has inherited from those who have died. He showed me his mother's teacup for reading the leaves. She was a spae-wife who toted round the tenements a small case containing cup and leaves. Spae wives are rare these days, but he has a sister who still reads the cups. On the table, in the place of honour directly in front of his chair, stands his father's crystal ball, a delicate, beautiful object with which his father, who was a scryer – one who practises crystal-gazing – used to make predictions.

Harry belongs to Glasgow and is proud of the fact that he was born in the same close where De Quincy once lived. He was eight years old when he realized he had second sight. On a visit to his grandmother, an old lady with a face like a wrinkled apple who frightened him considerably, he heard her say, 'He's one of us.' Although so young, Harry understood what she meant. 'Knowing' is perhaps a better name for his faculty than 'vision'. Even at that early age he could tap minds; found himself one step ahead of his contemporaries; had an insight and knowledge that he could not account for. He still finds the faculty hard to describe. Part image, part telepathy, part intuition, a touch of *déjà vu*, a click of the mind – all these add up to knowledge both of the future and of the client which he believes to be totally accurate.

Harry did not attend school very often, not because his family travelled (though occasionally they moved) but rather because his people believed that conventional education was mentally crippling. Once or twice the law caught up with them, but the family genuinely believed that school turned children out to a pattern and they were against indoctrination of the individual. Nevertheless, Harry reckons he had a good education. He was taught arithmetic with a pack of cards, which is possibly one of the reasons why he can win large sums of money for charity by gambling on the turn of a card. His extensive library contains many valuable and rare books, and his knowledge of history and literature is daunting.

During the war, he served for four years in the Western Desert. Calling himself a 'display agent' he was posted as a camouflage expert, but his true profession was soon discovered. One fortune-teller can create havoc in a barrack, so he and eleven others, all in the same game, were posted to a small outpost in the desert which contained a temple built by Alexander the Great and not much else. Forgotten about by the authorities, he spent most of his time reading everything he could get hold of, but Frazer's *The Golden Bough* made the deepest impression on him, and it was here that he developed a passion for Alexander the Great. After the war he 'borrowed' a truck and treated himself to a private tour of all the famous Egyptian sites. Nobody missed him. Nobody even realized that he was gone.

After demobilization, he decided to go to London and set up as a clairvoyant. It was all too easy. Harry soon found that he was in a position of great power over gullible people. He freely admits he misused his talent and as a result found he was going blind. He strongly associates that spell of incipient blindness with 'playing the occult game' for himself. 'You have to use the faculty to help other people. No doubt about that.'

He believes that he cured himself by working for charity. When I talked to him there were two collecting boxes for blind children on the settee in his office, and he told me with a certain amount of pride that he had made some £40 the previous night by taking bets on the turn of the cards. Harry has a theory that seers who abuse their talent are punished through the eyes. He knows of at least one clairvoyant in Glasgow who is going blind, and pointed out that Coinneach Odhar was said to be blind in his 'seeing' eye.

Not long after the war Harry met his wife, Margaret. He calls her his 'pearl of great price' and it is obvious that they have a strong and happy marriage in spite of – or perhaps because of – the fact that she dislikes and avoids anything to do with the occult. Margaret is a strongly practical person who works for a leading firm of chartered accountants in Glasgow. She worries about Harry and his fortune-telling, the fact that he can slow his heartbeat until the pulse is no longer detectable, that he sleeps for only three hours at night. They have no family. Harry knew this would be the case, just as he knew whom he would marry before he met his wife. This was what he wanted. He is thankful that at his death his line will come to an end.

'Your children can call you back,' he explained seriously, 'just as I can call my grandmother or my parents back. I don't want to be called back. When I die, I want to go for good.'

'What do you think happens to you when you die?' I asked.

'You go on. I don't want to be called back.'

'Do you know when you are going to die?' I asked.

'Certainly I do – but I'm not going to tell you.' Doctors have warned him about his health in the past. He has walked through a minefield smoking his pipe because he has an unshakeable belief in his ability to predict for himself. His mother knew the date of her death just as his father knew his, long before it happened.

He also believes that his forebears watch over him. They help him with his predictions, therefore he calls on them and uses their tools of trade to assist him. Although he does not actually see his ancestors, he is continually aware of their presence in his life. On the table in his office there are two coloured, amber-like stones, very old, that had at one time come from Naples. These were once used by his great-aunt – Touchstones she called them – who handed them to her clients to hold for a while, then took them back so that she could predict. He also showed me a small brass chalice, charred inside, which he called a pyromatic. His clients write their birth date, or a name perhaps, on a scrap of paper which he burns in the cup. He watches the flames and calls on his grandmother for assistance. Images often come to him through the smoke. (This is in full accord with the old Highland belief that seers receive their best images through fire.)

Contrary to Swein Macdonald who believes that only some have the gift of vision and that it cannot be acquired, Harry is convinced that the faculty is entirely natural, that all of us have it to some degree, and that it can be encouraged and brought out. He will not have it called a gift, which implies that it was specially given and that there must be a giver. He insists that it is part of the human psyche, and can be developed by practice.

'So you can learn clairvoyance?' I asked.

'Yes,' he answered, 'depending upon your age. The younger you are the easier it is.'

Sometimes parents have brought their children to him in the belief that they have the ability. Often these children are handicapped in some small way – illness, perhaps, has kept them out of school. These are the children who are easiest to teach.

After his spell in London, Harry returned to Glasgow. At the same time he was beginning to realize just what a responsible position he was in. Most of his clients only want to know who they are going to marry and how many children they are going to have, but sometimes they have more profound problems and he feels bound to help them.

'It's not because I like it, specially, but because it's my job.'

'Do you look on your faculty as a curse, then?'

'Oh no, no. But I'd rather have done something else with my life. I'd rather sit down with a couple of beers and a Rangers' scarf, watching television. As it is, I hate that scarf, and beer I don't like at all: I'm not like these people, but I wish I were.'

'If you see something distressing in a client's life, what do you do?'

'I have to tell them. I'm dealing with some wee guy or some wee girl's life. I can't screw it up. I can't play about. It's not ethical.'

'Why do you feel you have to tell them?'

'Because it's my job,' he insisted. 'If I don't tell the truth, I'm not doing my job properly.'

'Could you programme people to act in a certain way?'

'It's possible. Punters come here year after year, and ask me should I take this job or that line of action. I give them an answer.'

'You don't try to help them think out the answer for themselves?'

'No. They come here with a question. It's my job to give them an answer. I act as a sort of father to them. Some just come to talk. For example, I get a lot of homosexuals. Who else can they talk to in Glasgow? If they're married, they can't tell their wives. They need someone.'

I suggested that perhaps he saw himself in the role of priest or psychologist, and he admitted that it could be so. He is a great admirer of Freud. 'I love that man. I love his interpretation of dreams. He's spot on.' But Jung, in his opinion, wrote a lot of nonsense. 'Jung took weeks to find out what a fortune-teller could tell you in two minutes.'

'So you see your faculty as a way of helping people?'

'No doubt about that at all. You have to tell people what's in front of them. If you see something bad, you have to tell them. You have to prepare them for it.'

'Can you always get through to your clients? Or is it possible for them to put up a barrier?'

'It's possible, but very unusual. There are very few I can't predict for. If that happens I ask them to come back another day. Punters get worried if you say, "Sorry, I can't predict for you today." It implies they have no future.'

'Can you put up a barrier yourself?'

'Certainly I can – and have.'

He told me a story about an old fortune-teller who must have been about seventy when she came into his office and sat down in his chair. She pushed aside his gimmicks and opened an old-fashioned carpet-bag with amber handles. Then she took out a stick of rhubarb and with it proceeded to give him a reading. He was a bit put out to begin with, then amused, and finally full of admiration. 'It was a fantastic experience.' He put up no barriers that day.

Harry believes the future is firmly fixed. 'If the future can be changed, then it is a paradox: my family hammer this into us at a very early age. Our work as seers only prepares folk for the future, it does not mean you can escape it. Sometimes I have folk who makes notes and vow mentally to avoid what was predicted. It can't be done. You must keep your appointment in Samara. Everything in life is laid down. You're going to take certain actions and there's no choice at all. There's no such thing as free will.'

When I suggested that a prediction might give the client an extra dimension of choice of action, he wouldn't hear of it. 'The future is fixed. If you can change it, then it can't be the future. There can be no mucking about with it.'

'You say the future is fixed,' I continued, 'but do you also say that what you see is absolutely right?

'Yes, I think so.'

'If you see in pictures and images and symbols, is it not sometimes possible to misinterpret what you see?'

'I suppose it is possible,' he admitted, but with obvious reluctance. 'Although the future happens the way I see it, sometimes it doesn't work out the way you think it will.'

'With your ability to see into the future of so many lives, do you think that things tend to work out for the good of individuals?'

'What is good and bad? I don't understand those terms.'

'Do you think there is a purpose in life?'

'That's a bit twee, isn't it?'

'What do you see as the purpose of your life?'

'Just to live. Maybe to help some people. Life is never dull. I enjoy life and I like people. There's a wee punter comes here sometimes

253

who's buried five husbands, and has fifty-four grandchildren; I love her coming here. I meet show-biz people from time to time, but they are just like cardboard cut-outs compared with that wee girl. She's real; like the student who came to me because she couldn't pass her exams. I used the psychologist's jargon, which I shouldn't have done, and told her she had a mental block. Back she came, quick as lightning, "Yes, I know, but I love him." '

From time to time Harry has a visit from an old Jesuit priest who comes to borrow some of his books. He enjoys their discussions. One of their arguments is about Judas Iscariot. 'If your God is so great,' Harry argues, 'he would know that Judas would be born and would betray this Christ, as you call him. So why do you blame Judas?'

I asked if he thought the priest was trying to convert him.

He laughed. 'Maybe. But he hasn't a chance.'

I was beginning to understand why Harry was continually drawn back to that dark little tenement room, in spite of the fact that he would rather have been an artist.

'I may see the funny side of life,' he said, 'but I never laugh at people. I'm very sympathetic towards them. So many come for comfort, often the same faces again and again.' They bring him gifts, they send him postcards, and ask him to their weddings. He always goes to their funerals as a mark of respect. Although I interviewed him in March, his evenings were booked up till the end of November.

So you see your profession as a way of helping people?'

'Don't get me wrong,' he said hastily, 'I'm not a do-gooder.'

'What's wrong with doing good?'

'It's a bit of an ego trip, isn't it?'

I was interested to know how he prepared himself for a reading. Did he concentrate first?

'No, that's the worst thing you can do. If you start concentrating you get sidetracked. You wonder why the punter is wearing a certain ring, or acting in a certain way. It has to come right off the top of the head. An intuitive thing.'

'If you're interrupted in the middle of a reading, can you get back to where you were?'

'No bother.'

'Do you think that your knowledge comes from your mind or from somewhere outside?'

'I don't know where it comes from, but I don't think it's the subconscious.'

After using the pyromatic, Harry gives his clients a reading of the tarot which he keeps fanned out in front of him under his father's crystal ball. The pack has a well-worn appearance, and Harry told me he had been using it for twenty years. Something about the touch of the old cards appealed to him.

'The tarot is amazing. Do you know there are 3,200 different designs?'

I suggested that, like the Ouija board, the tarot were capable of influencing as well as predicting, and he did not entirely deny it.

'The tarot are not good or bad in themselves. What makes them good or bad is the motivation of the person using them. Money or a gun can't be good or bad, they're just things. It's the person using them that matters.'

I told him I had known people have bad experiences with the tarot. Again he did not deny it.

'I'm protected,' he told me. By the spirits of his ancestors, I presumed.

'Do you really need all these gimmicks to help you predict?'

'I can work without them, but they are a help,' he answered.

Although Harry takes no active part in the ritual of modern witch-craft, believing the cult to be thoroughly debased these days, he is a believer in the old Celtic faith which includes in its cult the practice of 'wicca'. He is known by, and knows of, eighteen covens that exist in Glasgow today, and he is visited from time to time by some seeking initiation. One of the tests involves the use of a gin trap which he has a special permit to keep. He set the powerful spring, triggered it with a pencil which was instantly snapped in two. Then he set it up again and – to my horror – put his own hand in the trap; touched the spring and, a second later, removed it, mercifully unharmed. The trick with this particular trap was not to pull away and the point of the exercise is to test the trust of the novice.

His father's test was equally alarming. He would produce six small shot glasses, fill five with water and one with sulphuric acid, and shuffle them around. He would then choose one, which he handed to the novice to drink, and would invite him to pick another for himself. If the novice backed down, he failed the test. The point is, if you can't trust your teacher you're in trouble. These were merely ways of proving absolute loyalty to the initiator.

Harry showed me other symbols of witchcraft, including the athame, or ritual knife; but he laughed when I asked if he possessed an ankh and told me it was corny. He preferred his own medallion made for him by a family who came from the Black Isle when he was thirteen years old. (In his youth, he admits to being a 'tearaway, a bit of a swinger', which earned him the family nickname of Beelzebub: one of Lucifer's lieutenants, Beelzebub was supposed not only to have been cast out of heaven, but also out of hell, for he created chaos wherever he went.) The medallion, made of pewter and set with one yellow and two blue stones said to have come from Torridon, caused him some embarrassment as a boy, but he is very fond of it now and always wears it in his office.

Also said to have come from Torridon is the sinister-looking 'curse stone', kept in a jar of water to neutralize its power. Harry believes in its ability to cause harm in the wrong hands and keeps a careful watch over it.

One of his possessions which I felt I could genuinely admire was a heavy, cast-iron black cat standing about eighteen inches high, with lapis-lazuli eyes and a sleek enigmatic expression. He told me it came from the cottage of a relative, an old herbalist or wise man who lived in the country. 'It's the custom in our family that when a member dies I go round and pick out something to keep. It's a job I hate, but I have to do it. When I arrived at the cottage I found the old man's daughter had cleared everything away. She had loved her father and she didn't at all like what I had to do any more than I liked doing it. Anyhow, there was nothing at all to be seen until I put my hand behind the fireplace and found the cat. He was "wicca", the old man, what you would call a witch.'

He pointed out a goat's skull and horns – symbols of the Devil – fixed to one of the walls, and hanging behind it a small leather pouch. It looked familiar, and presently I recognized it as the exact replica of the picture on the dust-jacket of my novel about Coinneach Odhar, *The Seer of Kintail*.

'Strange, isn't it?' he said, his grey eyes serious. 'That was there long before your book was published.'

'One of Jung's "meaningful coincidences", perhaps,' I suggested, but he didn't smile. I remembered other coincidences which singly

256

amounted to little, yet when added together seemed significant. He had written to me several years ago to tell me that during a visit to the Black Isle he had strongly sensed one of the characters out of *The Seer of Kintail*. Not so much Coinneach Odhar, though he had sensed him too, but a character invented by myself, the priest who was responsible for the death of Coinneach and who took the role of Devil in the local coven. 'You can't have got him from history,' I pointed out. 'He came straight out of my imagination.'

And again, a couple of years before I met him, a young schoolteacher after reading his New Year card which came to me at Hallowe'en, or Samhain, asked if she could contact him for a reading. 'It's up to you,' I told her, 'but I'd rather you didn't mention my name.'

I heard her make the telephone call, noted her disappointment at being told there was a five months' waiting list, her elation when Harry suddenly changed his mind and said he could fit her in the next day. I well remember her incredulity when she returned from her visit the following night, full of his opening words: 'What,' he had asked her, 'have you to do with someone called Elizabeth Sutherland and the Brahan Seer?'

'Did she also tell you,' Harry said as we recalled the event, 'that I had two of your books lying here on the table?'

Again, at Hogmanay later in that year, I was watching a film on television when for no good reason I rose, switched channels, and found the usual New Year *ceilidh* which I normally avoid. There was Harry's face – though I didn't know it until the end of the programme – dominating the screen, predicting for the coming year.

Coincidences? Or a measure of Harry's ability to 'tap minds'?

Remembering that broadcast, I asked him about his ability to make general predictions and he admitted it was not one of his skills. With his telepathic and intuitive powers, he prefers to make personal forecasts, and perhaps needs the proximity of another mind to trigger off his faculty. As his predictions are so personal he was not willing to talk too much about them, but he had some strange tales to tell about hauntings.

He pointed to a £5 note on the table under one of the Touchstones. 'That has a curious history behind it,' he told me. 'A man came in one day and I was immediately aware of a strong scent of perfume – Lily of the Valley, – quite unmistakable. The man reminded me that I had once predicted that he would marry a certain girl, that they'd have a daughter, but that his wife would leave him. They had even called the child Valerie, as I had predicted. The man then took out the £5 note, which was reeking of the scent, placed it on the table and asked if it was enough.

' "Fine," I told him. "It doesn't go to me anyhow."'

'Then something clicked in my mind and I said to him, "Why didn't you go to the funeral?"'

' "Don't you know?" he asked me.'

' "I do now," I told him.'

'I was able to tell him that after Valerie was born his wife had left him, as foreseen. She had given the child into the care of her mother, and though she always remembered its birthdays and Christmas, she had never come back. After a while she took ill and died in hospital in Doncaster. When they found his address, the police contacted him; he sent a cheque to cover the funeral expenses, but he had not attended the burial.

'Then he told me that on the night she died, he had been aware of the smell of perfume on the sheets. It was so overwhelming that he had changed the bed, and eventually burned the linen. It made no difference. He could not get rid of the scent. It was the same perfume that his wife had used to sprinkle on the bed when they were living together. He was literally haunted by the smell.' (Martin Martin mentions the psychic sense of smell possessed by the Gaels in the seventeenth century (page 85), and Swein Macdonald also possesses the faculty (page 233).)

On another occasion he was called in to do some psychic research in a haunted house on Kirkwall Road that was shortly due to be demolished. He arrived at night with some fine talc to dust for inexplicable draughts, and a thermometer to test for changes in temperature, and was shown into a small room with a bed, but no light or heating. He sat down on the bare springs and prepared to wait. Suddenly he was surrounded by children's voices. Annoyed that he had no tape recorder, he listened with enjoyment to the lilt and chatter until after a while the sounds faded away. He left the room, filled in the research form, and was offered a lift home by the local minister who had been waiting outside.

'Do you know how long you were in there, Mr Lynn?'

He supposed about half an hour.

'I was in there for only two minutes, and it scared the life out of me.'

Harry was surprised that the minister should have been so afraid. As far as he is concerned there are no such things as evil ghosts, though he will admit to the existence of inexplicable entities.

One Hallowe'en he was invited by the TV and radio personality Paul Murricane to take part in a phone-in programme from a haunted shop. A couple of women had set up a business there, making wreaths. Those wreaths left in the shop overnight were always found in tatters in the morning. During earlier reconstruction of the shop, the builder had removed a wall which had hidden an oven at least 200 years old and packed with debris (it is now to be seen in the People's Palace). It was reckoned that its removal had released some entity, for there had followed a number of inexplicable events including a suicide and the destroyed wreaths.

What particularly interested Harry that evening was the response he received to his story about how his grandmother used to whiten her doorstep with pipe-clay at Hallowe'en, and in so doing would make strange patterns on the stone. Many listeners telephoned to tell him that either they or their mothers had followed the same custom; some sent him patterns of the designs, which he has preserved with care. He believes they date from the pre-Christian era and that the patterns were runes designed to ward off bad luck in the coming year.

Superstition is still rife in Glasgow, as elsewhere. Because there are no mirrors in his office, one client was convinced he was connected with Dracula. 'We all have tales in our minds, no matter who we are. At certain times in our lives, under certain conditions, the primitive in each one of us is aroused.' Then his whole face lightened with humour. 'They're all mad out there – except me. I'm all right!'

But clairvoyance is taken seriously by some, including the police who have consulted him on several occasions. The most recent was in connection with the murder of a taxi driver.

'Were you successful?' I asked.

'Unfortunately they never let you know.'

Finally I asked him if there was anything that made him angry.

'Frauds and cheats. There's plenty of them about in all walks of life.' He had once been interviewed by a minister who wore a scarf to hide his clerical collar. 'I didn't like that. We didn't get on at all well together.'

Particularly he dislikes people who cheat at clairvoyance. 'People like me are in a position of great power over those who are very dependent. You can't screw up their lives.'

He often meets people who try to con him at cards and dice. 'They never get away with it. One thing I'm good at is cards' – again that gleam of humour – 'I'm modest, me! But seriously, there are a lot of crooks in this business and I like to find them out.'

How does Henderson Lynn, the Celtic Clairvoyant, fit into the traditional image of Highland second sight? At first glance it would seem not at all, that there is as little in common between him and Swein Macdonald as there is between the historical and legendary Coinneach Odhar.

Harry uses the tarot, the crystal ball and the pyromatic where Swein has no gimmicks. Harry is content to call himself a fortune-teller where Swein prefers the style of seer. His predictions 'come off the top of his head', where Swein concentrates for a short period first. Harry believes that the faculty is common to all and that it can be learned, where Swein sees it as a gift, God-given to a few, which cannot be acquired. Harry is not a Christian and does not find Christian doctrine acceptable. Swein is a member of the Church of Scotland, though not accepted, perhaps, by all its adherents.

It is often assumed in the Highlands that those who use the crystal ball, the pyromatic, or the teacup, are somehow lesser seers in that they are dependent on gimmicks and aids. Not true. For those who have the psychic ability, the touchstone, or the stone with a hole in it such as Coinneach allegedly used, is probably as good a way of externalizing the ability as any other. It may even facilitate the faculty and enhance it.

Harry Lynn maintains that crystal-gazing and clairvoyance may be taught, but I would suggest that this is true only to a limited extent. Any music-master can teach his pupil the mechanics of piano-playing, but whether that pupil can make music or merely a performance depends upon his temperament and talent. Seers vary in ability and performance just as pianists may vary in technique and musicality. The true seer, whether or not he uses a gimmick, is not dependent upon it.

Of particular interest is Harry's mystical contact with his forebears, his ability to call upon dead ancestors for guidance, his awareness of their unseen but potent presence in his life. This would seem to date back directly to that primitive priesthood which must have existed in Scotland as far back as Neolithic times. It is hinted at in an ancient Irish fragment known as Fiac's Hymne, which says: 'On Erin's folk lay darkness; the tribes worshipped the *sith*.' As we have seen, the *sithean* who became known as fairies, according to the folklorist Eleanor Hull may have been part of an older pantheon of deities supposed to reside in the ancient burial-mounds and standing stones, and still an important part of our folklore to this day. A priesthood was probably employed to keep in touch with the *sithean*, or spirits of their ancestors. They 'saw' them, received advice from them, and consulted them about the fortunes of the tribe or individuals in the wider family group. In return they received from them the power of vision. This second sight may have been part of a large body of magical practice developed in connection with the cult of the dead. The great cairns and henges that still adorn the countryside today are a constant reminder of the strength and importance of ancestor-worship in the Highlands.

The cult of the dead was also an important part of Druidic ceremonial. Many of the great Celtic festivals such as Lammas were held at burial mounds. Samhain, particularly, was a feast that commemorated the dead, which is why it is of such special importance to Henderson Lynn and his family. That was the night when the great cairns opened and the spirits of the dead wandered freely. No doubt it was Samhain when Coinneach Odhar's mother allegedly watched the spirits from the burial ground at Baile-na-Cille fly away from their graves. Dis, the Roman name for the Celtic earth-god, was regarded as Lord of the Dead. In Ireland, food was laid out for those who returned to their homes on that most important night of the year.

Just as the first Christian missionaries – themselves Celts – transformed old Druid festivals into Christian feasts and turned the sacred groves into Christian sites, so the cult of vision – with the example of Columba, the first great Christian seer – was transformed into the involuntary, unrelished 'gift' of second sight. Never persecuted, and finally raised to the heights of inspired prophecy in the mouths of such fine men as the Petty Seer, second sight has maintained a respectable image in the Highlands to the present day.

But the coming of Christianity did not entirely eradicate the old cult and beliefs of the Celts and their Neolithic forebears. At about that time, secondary vision must have split into two paths, one continuing the old art of divination and sooth-saying, where the descendants of the Druids became 'wise' men and women, sorcerers and prophets such as the historical Coinneach Odhar; the other, followed by Columba, branching off into what is now properly called second sight.

It could perhaps be said that Swein Macdonald exemplifies the followers of the second road, whereas Henderson Lynn's forebears kept to the ancient highway.

Although so different in background, tradition, and belief, there are some points on which the two seers might agree. Both have a strong and sincere belief in, and admiration for, the predictions and person of the one they consider was the true Coinneach Odhar. Both believe that the faculty is natural rather than supernatural, proceeding from some latent sense in man that is not as yet fully comprehended. Both, curiously, support charities for the blind.

It is possible also that both men might agree in the matter of motivation. That which is able to teach us more about ourselves, our powers and our potential; that which may strongly influence not only our own lives but those of our fellow men; that which demands a responsible and mature judgement and approach, is not to be used for personal gain and aggrandizement, nor for idle amusement to pass the time, and particularly not as a weapon to hurt or harm any individual.

9 A Spectrum of Seers

THE LADY OF LAWERS

Although early researchers into second sight maintained that women were not generally seers in the grand sense, the exception – whose predictions are as remarkable as those of Coinneach Odhar and whose life was contemporaneous with the Brahan Seer of legend – must be the Lady of Lawers. Mystery shrouds her person, and though her prophecies were said to have been recorded in the Red Book of Balloch, bound in a barrel with hoops of iron and long lost from Taymouth Castle, they too depended for survival on oral transmission until late in the nineteenth century.

A' Bhantighearna Labhuir is thought to have been a Stewart of Appin who married a younger brother of the impoverished Sir James Campbell, sixth Laird of Lawers, a cadet branch of the Campbells of Glenorchy, soon to be created the Earls of Breadalbane. The couple rented a two-storey thatched house, whose ruins may still be traced on the northern banks of Loch Tay half-way between Kenmore and Killin. In those days Lawers was a busy port with a growing population, which supported a new church erected next door to the House of Lawers in 1669.

One of her predictions concerned the building of this church, when she told the workmen: *The ridging stones will never be placed on the roof. If they are, then all my words are false.* Scorning her, they unloaded the sandstone blocks which had travelled by barge and left them overnight on the shore. A great storm swept them out into deep water where some can still be seen today, half buried in shingle.

An ash tree which she is said to have planted by the church featured in three of the prophecies. She must have loved the tree, for she is thought to have been buried beneath it, and it is pleasant to picture her tending it, watching it spread to inspire her visions.

The tree will grow and when it reaches the gable the church will be split asunder, and this will also happen when the red cairn on Ben Lawers falls. By 1833 the tree had grown as high as the gable, when a storm destroyed the loft causing it to fall and ruin the rest of the building. More significantly, when the red cairn toppled in 1843, the Church of Scotland 'split asunder' symbolically in the Disruption, and the congregation at Lawers joined the Free Kirk.

When the ash tree reaches the ridge of the church, the House of Balloch will be without an heir. This was fulfilled in 1862 when the second Marquis of Breadalbane, owner of Taymouth Castle, died without a son.

The third prophecy concerning the tree stated simply: *Evil will come to him who harms it.* Rashly, a certain John Campbell of Milton Farm and a neighbour cut the tree down in 1895. John was gored to death by his own bull, his neighbour went mad, and the horse who had dragged away the trunk fell down dead.

Trees were to feature in the prophecy the Lady uttered in 1680 which stated: *The lands of Macnab will be joined to those of Breadalbane when two trees join together on Inchbuile and grow as one.* In 1820 a branch from a pine tree growing in the Macnabs' burial island at Killin fell and grafted on to another tree. When the two were literally 'growing as one', the Chief of Macnab fled bankrupt to Canada and his lands were bought by his chief creditor, the first Marquis of Breadalbane. The trees continued to grow as one until 1948 when Archibald Corrie Macnab, the twenty-second chief, bought back his ancestral estate. Thereafter the grafted branch began to die.

A clutch of predictions which closely resemble those of Coinneach Odhar, and which must be part of Highland prophetic history disseminated both orally and in the cheap chapbooks eagerly bought from pedlars at croft and cottage doors, concerned the economic and social changes of the times. *There will be a mill on every stream and a plough in every field, and the two sides of Loch Tay will become a kail garden,* foretold improvements. *The jaw of the sheep will drive the plough from the ground,* and *The land will first be sifted and then riddled of its people,* and again *The homesteads on Loch Tay will be so far apart that a cock will not hear its neighbour crow* all looked to the changes brought about by the Clearances and modern methods of farming.

A neat prediction which deals with the passing of the oral tradition states concisely *The feather of the goose will drive the memory from man.*

The most important of the Lady's predictions uttered about 1680 centre on the Breadalbane Campbells, a family as powerful in and around Loch Tay as the Mackenzies were in Ross-shire. Just as the famous Seaforth predictions were to be known as the Doom of the Mackenzies, so hers were to be called collectively the Curse of the Breadalbanes. She is thought to have been alive when John Campbell of Glenorchy, her kinsman by marriage, took over the estate of Lawers in 1693 and was created first Earl of Breadalbane. Of him she prophesied, *John of the three Johns, the worst that has come, or will come, but nothing will be right until Duncan arrives.* That John was undoubtedly the 'worst', for he is believed to have taken part in the notorious massacre led by Campbell of Glenlyon in which thirty-eight MacDonalds were slain at Glencoe. He disinherited Duncan, his eldest son, in favour of John, his second-born, and as Duncan did not come back, nothing to do with the succession prospered thereafter.

The rest of the predictions concerning the Breadalbanes are as follows:

> *The earldom will not descend beyond a grandson in one line. Great and perplexing doubts will arise as to an heir.*
>
> *The House of Glenorchy will attain its height of glory when a boulder is covered with trees.*
>
> *In time the estates of Balloch which were put together in hides will fall asunder in lace.*
>
> *In time the estates of Balloch will yield but one rent, and then none at all.*
>
> *The last laird will pass over Glenogle with a grey pony leaving nothing behind.*
>
> *A strange heir will come to Balloch when the boar's stone at Fearnan topples over.*

So far all except the last section has come to pass. The first Earl's grandson died without an heir. In 1782 the title went to a relative whose son became the second Marquis. He too died without an heir, in 1862. Thereafter the predicted 'great and perplexing doubts' arose, and it took five years to decide which claimant should inherit. Eventually John Campbell of Glenfalloch succeeded and his son, the

265

third Marquis, also died heirless in 1922. The earldom again passed to a cadet branch, whose son is the present holder of the title and who is unmarried.

The Breadalbanes reached the heights of glory with the second Marquis who entertained Queen Victoria in 1842. His estates comprised some 500,000 acres 'put together in hides' or large lumps gained by marriage or sometimes by more dubious means. Disintegration started in 1922 when many acres had to be sold off to pay death duties. By 1933 about half the land had gone in small pieces, or 'lace' as the seeress pronounced poetically. In 1946, this great landowning family was reduced to Kinnell House at Killin, and one farm paying rent. The Countess of Breadalbane was seen at this time by a retired gardener on her way from Killin Station in a trap drawn by a single grey pony. In astonishment he recognized the vision of the Lady of Lawers. By 1984 even Kinnell House had gone to the Chief of Macnab.

Apart from the tailpiece to the Breadalbane Curse, only two prophecies remain unfulfilled. *A ship driven by smoke will sink in Loch Tay with great loss of life.* Up till 1939 pleasure-steamers used to frequent the loch and many who knew of the prophecy, including the last Marquis, refused to travel on them. And, last and most fearsome, *The day will come when Ben Lawers will become so cold that it will chill and waste the land around it for seven miles.* Just as Coinneach's black rain is thought by some to predict nuclear fall-out, so the Lady of Lawers might be witnessing the nuclear winter.

As with Coinneach Odhar, so the predictions of this shadowy woman which foresee every aspect of Highland social, economic and religious history, would seem to reflect the deep anxieties of mankind. The forecasts of lack of children, loss of land, changes not only in the church, in social customs and livelihood, but also in the earth itself, seem both to mirror the neuroses and offer a panacea, in that the disaster is somehow lessened by the fact that it has been predicted.

These thoughts do not necessarily detract from the validity of prophecy. On the contrary, they support it as the backbone does the body, for what the seers witness in vision must also reflect their own deep anxieties and needs.

As we have seen, apart from the Lady of Lawers, Highland history has recorded significantly fewer women seers than men. This is not because they did not exist, for it would be true to say that where psychic experience is concerned, sex is irrelevant. There are several reasons which might perhaps account for the lack of records. The general neglectful attitude towards women through the ages must certainly be one. Secondly, women with psychic powers were generally dubbed witches and suffered as such. That early priestly sodality, trained by fasting and ritual to cultivate the waking dream, may probably have been predominantly – if not exclusively – male.

If second sight could be said to predominate in any class of society, it might be found in those who are creative in other fields. At a week-end for Scottish writers held in 1983 in a sundrenched Pitlochry, forty-one out of the fifty I questioned had experienced the paranormal to some extent, ranging from an isolated precognitive dream to a wide range of phenomena. This is an indication, perhaps, that those who are continually using their creative talents may have easier access not only to their own subconscious minds but also to what Jung called the Collective Unconscious. Outstanding among these experiences were those of Alanna Knight, painter, novelist and biographer. Alanna's ancestry is part Celtic, part Orcadian; she is tall, red-haired, with extraordinarily expressive eyes. A delicate child, she was typical of those described by Henderson Lynn as possessing psychic ability, spending long periods of her childhood out of school and without the company of her peers. As a young child she became accustomed to 'seeing' places invisible to adults and was often punished for telling lies. She took it for granted that grown-ups were unable to see in the same way as children and that the latter were disbelieved on principle.

She inherited the faculty from her grandmother who 'knew' when a person was going to die and had seen many deathbeds – in the tradition of Columba – flooded with light; and also from her mother who was particularly critical of Alanna in the hopes of suppressing what seemed to her to be an unacceptable gift.

At the age of ten, Alanna had a particularly vivid experience. Her family was living in Newcastle at the time, close to Jesmond Dene Park, and one sunny summer day while she and her dog were walking home along a quiet street that bordered the secluded gardens of some fine old houses, she noticed, to her surprise, a gap in the railings of Deep Dene. Being a curious child, she slipped through and found herself in a large garden full of marble statues, with an ornate, rustic summerhouse. Creeping nearer, she saw what looked like a woman's cloak hanging there with a tricorn hat.

After exploring for a while, she slipped back through the gap and found her dog waiting for her. Strangely, he had not followed her inside; usually they were inseparable. Calling him, she ran home to tell her father that she had found a way into Deep Dene and that he must come and see for himself. Her father, who was gardening, protested that he couldn't be bothered, but eventually relented, told her to wait till he'd changed his shoes, and then together they returned to the street. There was no gap in the fence, no way of entering let alone of seeing inside the garden, and the gate was locked as usual.

'You were mistaken,' he told her, no doubt regarding the episode as childish fantasy. He promised not to tell her mother. He was sufficiently curious, however, to question an elderly local inhabitant about the house, and learned that in Victorian days the garden had been full of naked statues which had so shocked the subsequent tenants that they had destroyed and removed all traces of them.

An incident which happened when Alanna was thirteen illuminates the psychic relationship that existed between her and her mother. Their home in Newcastle was a modern semi-detached villa, with nothing, one would have supposed, of historic interest in its past. However one afternoon, while sitting in front of her bedroom mirror, Alanna was aware that the reflected room had changed. It seemed bigger and there were great wooden beams across the ceiling. At the same time she could distinctly hear the creak and grind of wood and the rush of water. Her mother came running upstairs demanding to know why she was moving her furniture about and running off all the hot water. Instantly, the reflected room changed back to normal, and Alanna protested that she had not been near the bathroom. 'I distinctly heard you,' her mother argued, 'and I heard the water.'

Later Alanna confided in her father, who consulted the same local inhabitant. He told him that their house had once been the site of a mill. The sounds heard by both mother and daughter would seem to have been the grinding of the wheel and the rush of the stream.

If her psychic link with her mother was close, it was equally so with her father. As a child she experienced a recurring dream in which she was walking up the path of a terraced Georgian house. A huge conservatory surrounded the front door, and inside she could see conch shells and a ship encased in glass. All she could make out of the ship's title were the first and last letters, both of them 'A'. The floor was tiled and contained a pool of flickering coloured light. Just before her father died, while they were chatting together about the old days, she told him about the dream. He laughed. 'I know why you couldn't see the full name. I couldn't read it either.' As a boy he had stayed with his grandfather, a sea-captain, who had brought the conch shells back from one of his voyages. The ship in the glass case was called AURORA, and the coloured light on the floor came from a stained-glass window on the stair. The house and street had since been demolished, but he had very clear memories of staying there when a boy. Alanna believes that somehow she had had access to her father's memory pattern.

Later, at one of the Romantic Novelists' Association dinners, a fellow-writer who was also psychic described to Alanna the figure of a small grey-haired man standing close to her. 'Tell her about the ship in a glass, and she'll know who it is,' the man told the medium.

When she was sixteen, Alanna and her parents were visiting Edinburgh at the time of the Festival. During a trip to Holyrood House Alanna became bored with the official tour and slipped off by herself. Beyond the stone-flagged kitchens she found a side door that was not locked, opened it, went through, and entered a walled garden with grass and a flower border. To her left, railed off, was the Abbey and burial ground. Above the wall, she could see the tops of trees, but what intrigued her most was the hump in the centre of the lawn where the grass grew rank and sparse. It was undoubtedly a grave, and not that old by the look of it. A piece of curved wood like the back of a kitchen chair had been planted behind the mound and on it was written the name, *D. Riccio*.

Alanna had heard of David Riccio, private secretary to Mary, Queen of Scots, stabbed to death in 1566 by over fifty dagger-wounds, and she wondered why he had been buried here. Why not in the proper cemetery. When she caught up with her parents she told them, 'I've seen Riccio's grave. Come and have a look.'

By this time her parents had seen enough; it was a hot day and they were tired. It did not seem important to them, or to Alanna, for that matter. The incident seemed trivial, but later she would often advise friends planning a trip to the capital to be sure to visit Riccio's grave. One of these, a sculptor, gave her a strange look, she remembers, but nothing was said until she suggested to the American novelist, Elizabeth Byrd, who was taking a party of friends to Holyrood, that they look out for the grave. Miss Byrd, whose historical novel *The Immortal Queen* is based on the life of Mary, Queen of Scots, turned to her in surprise. 'But, my dear, no one knows where he was buried. He was put in an unmarked grave.'

Alanna herself went back to Edinburgh, found the side door in Holyrood House, and opened it. There was the Abbey of course, but no sign of the garden, only some overgrown rhododendron bushes. Instead of trees, she could see the outline of the city. She was astonished: surely in thirty years it could not have altered so much? She did some research of her own. Riccio had been murdered in early March, 1566. Her visit had been in August – just enough time for grass to grow rank and sparse, if you ignored the passing of four centuries.

Alanna has given much thought to her ability to enter the past. She believes that when her physical strength is low, her psychic powers are intensified. As a child she suffered three times from pneumonia, and when she entered the gap in the Newcastle fence she was still weak from illness. Her experience at Holyrood was probably tied up with puberty. Her strangest experience of all came when her body was partially paralysed by a crippling attack of polyneuritis, a virus-related disease which affects the arm and leg muscles.

The incidents which took place in 1968 are fully recorded by Elizabeth Byrd, herself a psychic researcher, in *A Strange and Seeing Time* published by Robert Hale in 1969, which describes among other incidents Alanna's experiences at Leith Hall.

The Leith family was established in Aberdeenshire in the thirteenth century, and in 1650 James Leith built the Hall which remained with the family until 1945, when it was presented to the National Trust. Divided into apartments, the east wing was, at the time Alanna knew it, rented by Miss Byrd. By this time married to a scientist, Alasdair, Alanna had two sons, Chris and Kevin. Alasdair believes that Alanna has the ability to move backwards and forwards into other time-levels. He encourages her to keep written records of all her 'waking dreams' and other paranormal experiences. Thus the incidents at Leith Hall were factually recorded as soon after the events as possible.

Having made friends with Miss Byrd through the Aberdeen Writers' Workshop, Alanna was first invited to Leith Hall in 1968. During the car journey, as soon as she and her husband had passed through Pitcaple (about ten miles from the Hall) she became strongly aware that she was riding in a coach and that she was going home. Later she had an odd experience in the drawing-room: while sitting in an armchair before lunch talking to a fellow guest, she saw the room flatten out into a picture of itself. Nor could she see it clearly; it was almost as if she was seeing it through a network of shattered glass, or cracked oil paint. Physically she felt strange, drained, almost as if she had come out of her body and was observing the scene. Aware of what was happening, she forced herself to stand up and move with difficulty across the room. She had to fight against a desire to be absorbed into the room's past, for she was afraid that unless she did so, she might never be able to return to the present.

On her next visit, Alanna slept in the old nursery on the third floor of the east wing which had once been a spacious room but had subsequently been divided. It was in the larger of these two rooms that she was to experience the first of a series of waking visions. In her 'dream' she woke up as a child in her nursery watched over by a tall woman dressed in black, with brown hair drawn back in the Victorian fashion, and exceptionally fine hands with long slender fingers. She knew she was a child because the woman who bent over her and told her to go back to sleep seemed so large, even her smile. Then the woman walked across the room towards the window and Alanna could hear her weeping. Still in her 'dream', Alanna then woke up to a different time of day, possibly a different year. The room was cold, the window open. Dead leaves blew in and she could hear their rustle on the floor. She had the strong impression that the woman who had been her governess, had fallen or perhaps jumped out of the window.

In June 1968 she again slept in the nursery, a room where she always felt safe and cherished. Again she had a 'dream' that she was walking with her governess by a pond surrounded by formal gardens. Ahead she could see other people playing on a small hill planted with pine trees. She ran forward to pick up some cones, and fell and grazed her knee. The scene changed and she found herself in very ornate stables: she and her governess were looking at a newly born foal lying on some straw in one of the stalls. When they came out, a handsome young man was lounging against a wall, leering at them. Alanna instinctively disliked him.

When she was sufficiently recovered from her polyneuritis to walk, her hostess showed Alanna the grounds. As soon as they reached the lake, she exclaimed, 'There it is, only it was much smaller in my dream – and the gardens have become a wilderness.' Elizabeth Byrd told her that in 1904 the pond had been extended into a lake, and confirmed that there had been gardens there at the time. Alanna also recognized the hill and the pine trees, and asked if there were stables on the estate. Her hostess took her to an old coach house dated 1754. That too she recognized: 'It's exactly as I saw it, and there's the stall where the foal was lying.'

On 4 July of the same year she recorded; 'Retired to nursery and slept soundly till dawn. Then in the state of "between sleep", during which I was conscious of the birds singing outside, I saw myself looking out of the window towards the entrance just below me.' Her governess wrapped her in a shawl and warned her not to lean out too far. Below she could see a performing bear with its wizened old owner and a monkey dressed in a scarlet hat. Other children were also watching. She was aware of their voluminous clothing and their delight in the performance. The scene changed to winter. A carriage was leaving and the child Alanna was waving good-bye to a man and woman in a coach. She felt sad, and even more alone and unwanted when she saw her beloved governess coming round the side of the house in the company of the leering young man.

By 7 July, Alanna was recording that she no longer needed to visit Leith Hall to 'dream' of it. Part of her mind was conscious of a milk-van in the Aberdeen street while at the same time she experienced her dream. She was a child again sitting in the nursery when a great golden-coloured dog bounded in. Through the open door she could see two servants weeping and whispering at the top of the stairs. She was aware of impending disaster. After a break, she found herself at the door of the main bedroom. There was no four-poster bed, but she could see an elderly woman sitting there, dressed in a green bonnet. It seemed to Alanna that she had just arrived.

After her next vision, she was to record: 'At last I've made some progress. I know I'm a young girl.' She had always suspected as

272

much, but on this occasion she had seen herself reflected in the window of a cottage in a cobbled yard. She was wearing a big flat hat tied under the chin with ribbon, had very dark hair, dark eyes and a pale face, and was aged somewhere between six and eight. As she turned away, her governess who had been knocking on the cottage door, put her hand on her shoulder. When the vision departed, Alanna could still feel its warmth and pressure on her left arm.

At this point Alanna's story takes an extraordinary twist. Elizabeth Byrd had an American friend, Carole, who had once slept in the smaller part of the old nursery, and had reported that she continually heard noises of someone turning in bed. Elizabeth believed that Alanna's description of her governess matched that of Carole, so she showed her a photograph. 'That's her,' Alanna cried. 'That's the face of the governess! It's like seeing an old friend whom I've missed for a hundred years.' When Carole in America saw Alanna's picture she too recognized her, though she could not recall ever having met her. From Alanna's description she also 'knew' the leering young man, though she had no idea who he was. She wrote to say that she had once thought of becoming a governess herself, and that she too had experienced strong feelings of *déjà vu* at Leith Hall; she had stood at the window and thought about jumping out, not to commit suicide but out of curiosity. When Alanna and Carole eventually met they were both aware of a feeling of rapport and a certainty that they had met before.

Alanna's grandmother finally made some sense out of the story. She told her – for the first time, and Alanna is quite certain about this – that her grandmother (Alanna's great-great-grandmother) had been a Miss Leith from Leith Hall. She had been the youngest of four daughters, who had run off with the coachman between 1816 and 1820. When she became pregnant, her family disowned her and had her name erased from the family Bible. Sadly she died in childbirth; the coachman remarried and had four other children, but he always used to boast of his first wife's grand connections. Alanna's grandmother must have inherited her own grandmother's looks, for Alanna writes: 'Gran looked very aristocratic. My great shock was to see a painting of Major Leith and his four daughters in the museum at Leith Hall, one of whom was exactly like Gran. When Miss Byrd rented the east wing, there was a picture of the last Leith heir who was killed in 1940. He was fourteen at the time of the painting and was the

273

image of our son Chris, who was about the same age when we first visited Elizabeth.'

Alanna is the first to admit that her Leith Hall experiences could not be called conclusive evidence of paranormal phenomena, but she adds, 'The coincidences are too strong to be ignored completely. Nothing in this world would make me go back and investigate further. My psychic side is something I treat with caution. The only explanation I can offer as to what happened at Leith Hall and on other occasions when my physical strength was low, is an intensifying of awareness. My waking dreams were the resurgence of a racial memory rather than anything so dramatic as ghosts.'

But Alanna has seen a ghost too. While working on the ground-floor office of a Regency house, she used frequently to see a red-haired young man with a white face, dressed in a green corduroy jacket. He was always in the same position looking anxiously over the bannisters. Alanna could see the whites of his knuckles. When her employer told her he was thinking of opening up the whole house, she said, 'But what about the man upstairs? What will happen to him?' There was no young man, the rooms were uninhabited, and she never saw him again.

Precognitive dreams are also part of Alanna's experience. On one occasion she had a spectacular vision of an aircrash in a cornfield: the plane fell in a ball of fire from the sky and she could see the bodies tumbling. It was a terrifying experience which she interpreted as being anxiety for her husband who was due to travel by air that morning. Not long after he had gone, the television news announced an air disaster in Yugoslavia. Later she saw in the newsreel the same cornfield and the plane burning as she had witnessed it in her dream. When she told her mother, the latter confessed that she too had precognitive dreams that occurred regularly three days before the event.

Since Alanna made a full recovery to health, she has experienced little in the way of psychic phenomena and she is happy to have it so; but she does find that her easy access to the subconscious mind where time is not governed by months and minutes has helped her beyond measure with her writing. In *The Passionate Kindness*, her biography of Robert Louis Stevenson, she wrote a chapter without knowing that she had done it. It came purely from her subconscious and she retained no conscious memory of how she came to write it. She believes that writers are particularly intuitive and that most share a common bond.

It would be easy to dismiss Alanna's experiences at Leith Hall as the fantasy of a talented romantic writer, or even as self-deception, if it were not for several facts. Alanna disliked and feared her experiences, always associated in her mind with illness. Nothing would have induced her to go back to Leith Hall after her first visit if her husband had not been with her at all times. She has never sought to cash in on her faculty either as a writer, a researcher, or a clairvoyant. She had no motive to invent the experiences. Elizabeth Byrd, herself a shrewd investigator into the paranormal, would have been quick to detect any suspicion of invention, whether deliberate or unconscious. Alanna's husband would have been even quicker. Alanna is a dedicated, devoted Christian, well aware of the Church's attitude to the paranormal. By principle, she is not a liar.

More important, the totality of her experience matches up to that of seers throughout the ages, and includes the dream vision received in a period of disassociation; the old Druidic belief that such sightings were experienced between waking and sleeping; the ability to see apparitions, to communicate telepathically; the inherited faculty, the unacceptable gift, the involuntary vision.

Perhaps her husband's theory that she suffers from 'a dislocation of time' is near the truth. Perhaps through the collective unconscious she was able to enter her great-great-grandmother's thought patterns and experience her life and feelings as a lonely child. Perhaps she is the reincarnated spirit of her great-great-grandmother. Theories abound, as to the why and wherefore, but elements in the experience remain the same.

THE SOLDIER SEER

William Kirk was described by his colonel, Douglas Lyall Grant, as 'a Celt of the Celts with the vivid imagination that peoples the howes and knowes of Celtdom with brownies, sprites and wee folk'. He served with the London Scottish until his retirement before the First World War but was one of the first to re-enlist when hostilities broke out. Turned down by a medical officer of his former regiment who knew his age, he joined the Seaforth Highlanders, was promoted to corporal, and sent to France. His tales of supernatural experiences

275

were first published in the regiment's gazette and proved so popular that they were issued in book form under the title of *Stories of Second Sight in a Highland Regiment*, published in 1933.

One of these instances occurred in September 1915 when Kirk was ordered to watch a piece of land set aside for landing aircraft in Picardy, close to the Mailly woods. For three days he enjoyed the lull in fighting and used his time to read, write letters and reflect, until a thunderstorm of spectacular energy forced him to look for shelter. On one side there was a roofless wreck of a windmill, and on the other he could just see through the trees the red roof of a farm. Gathering his equipment, he ran down a grassy track which led to a high barred gate. Shouldering it open, he entered an overgrown yard clogged waist-high with weeds.

In spite of his need for shelter from the hissing rain, Kirk could sense the eeriness and an air of menace all round him. The main door of the farmhouse and all the windows were bolted and barred, but one side door remained unsealed. It yielded to his elbow and led to a carpenter's bothy, full of rusted tools and dusty benches, but dry. With the storm still raging outside, Kirk fell asleep to dream of gunfire, warfare and destruction.

Suddenly he woke. Shouts, screams of women, and the whinny of tortured horses clamoured around him. He opened the door. Outside the sounds of riot raged, and above the midden he could see the red glow of a fire, 'as if some gigantic opening in the heavens threw down some malignance on the earth and here it centred.' Even the lightning paled against the flare. Yet there was not a living soul in sight.

Kirk's immediate thought was that the French must be stationed nearby, and that someone there had frightened the horses and woken the camp. Satisfied by this conclusion, he went back to his bench and fell into a profound sleep. Next morning he decided to look for the allies, but in vain. Not a soul had been near the place for years, and the woods were impenetrable with undergrowth. He noticed that no birds sang, and the smell of tragedy hung heavily on the air.

Later that day a French officer called in at his post and asked how he had survived the storm. When he heard the answer his expression changed: 'Good God, you slept there!'

He went on to explain that during the war of 1870 a raiding party of Uhlans had arrived at the farm on the day of the marriage of the proprietor with the local *belle*. Rape and murder had followed. Later, while the Germans slept 'in drunken depredation', the French had surrounded the place, chained horses and men together, poured oil over the lot and roasted them to death on the midden.

Not a Frenchman within 100 miles would now go near the place.

THE MAN FROM THE RIG

John Graham calls himself a sceptic when it comes to belief in second sight. Nevertheless he has found his life to be full of inexplicable coincidences. 'Since adolescence,' he writes, 'I have been aware of something within myself, a knowledge of what is about to happen, someone about to arrive before you hear or see them.'

He experiences strange feelings about places and buildings – 'To use a modern term, I get vibes from them.' During a period of research into his family background he found many odd incidents, nothing much in themselves but together adding up to what Jung called 'meaningful coincidences'.

As an oilman working offshore and based on Brae Alpha Platform, he often feels 'different from his fellow workers; '*not* better or worse', but apart. He also has a talent for writing which manifested itself recently in an article relating to life on Brae Alpha, which won first prize in a competition organized by the company magazine. John is intuitive, creative, and with a Highland background that can be traced back to Islay. He describes the thoughts, feelings and occurrences that are to him inexplicable, as 'rather spooky'.

Certainly his experience connected with the Kieland disaster in 1980 gave him a fright. 'I don't remember much about the day I flew out to the Murchison Platform on the day the Kieland capsized, except that it was rough weather, not an unusual feature in the North Sea! I don't believe anyone who doesn't admit to being somewhat afraid of flying, especially in a helicopter in a force seven gale. However I arrived safely and settled down to my evening meal at seven. There was to be a good film showing that evening in the cinema and, knowing this, I decided to go in early to be sure of a seat.

'In fact, the cinema was quite empty when I entered and I sat idly gazing at the blank screen, turning over the events of the day in my mind. For what must have been only a second or two, I thought of the cinema packed to capacity with about eighty to ninety men sitting in the darkness watching the film. All of a sudden, the whole room lurched to one side, the right-hand side, where the emergency door was situated. There were men screaming in panic tearing at each other to get out of the door, but it was jammed shut. A shiver ran through me in that instant, and almost immediately my thoughts returned to more comforting illusions of home, out in the hills, etc, and the impression was gone.

'I sat through the film and enjoyed it, and on my exit from the cinema I saw lots of men standing in small solemn groups, and soon I heard the whisper that a rig had capsized. Rumours are rife on these platforms and this news had not been verified at the time. Dismissing the story as such, I went for supper and a shower before retiring to my cabin where I switched on the news at eleven.

'Of course the first item was the Kieland story. The newscaster said, 'It is believed that about fifty men are still trapped in the cinema.' It was then that the vision came back to me and the hair on my head rose up at the back, and I could not speak to my cabin mates for about twenty minutes or so. The shock was real.'

Although John still maintains that he is sceptical where the paranormal is concerned, he has worked out a theory about second sight. 'It is like a transmitter and receiver. Since thought is a condition produced by electrical impulses, which, due to the nature of the power of the electron, produces electromagnetic energy, this energy radiates from the source in all directions. If we could build equipment sensitive enough or sophisticated enough, we could transform the electromagnetic energy into sound or vision and display it on audio-visual monitors. I understand the technical aspect of what I am saying because of my technical education, and what I describe is understandable, I think.'

Another theory – but, alas no more provable than any other. Popular at the end of the last century, the theory of electromagnetism is thought today by most physicists to contain too many paradoxes and to be based on too shaky a conceptual foundation to be credible.

THE ORGANIST AND THE TAMHASG

Linnhe Gobby, an organist from Leeds, would seem to be a *taibhsear* in the true tradition of Highland second sight, in that he has been from time to time haunted by a *tamhasg*, the spectre of a person alive and

278

well. J. G. Campbell tells of a soldier from Coll who while on active service in Africa frequently caught glimpses of, and was touched by, the wraith of the woman he eventually married. Mr Gobby is haunted by the spectre of someone he might have married. Between December 1979 and March 1982 he experienced six sightings of a woman he had not seen nor communicated with, or even heard of, for over thirty years.

'All of these incidents occurred in my home,' he writes. 'I did not at first recognize the wraith. I was only aware of her identity when I heard her voice . . . As you will agree, over a long period people obviously change physically, but the human voice rarely changes its character.

'In all six appearances the lady appeared as she is now. She was definitely solid in appearance. On three occasions, she moved. On termination of the visions, she faded away slowly. The texture of her face and skin were normal. I witnessed the apparition on three occasions before I made contact with her. I witnessed the apparition on three occasions after I had contacted and visited her.

'On the first and second visitations, she spoke the words, "Len, I have something to tell you." These words enabled me to recognize her as she has been the only person in my life to address me as such . . . . On the third visitation, she said, "You are coming to see me." This was at the time when I was deliberating as to whether to go and visit her at her home, or not. It seemed to me that she was aware of this and that her remark could be interpreted as a request or a command.'

Mr Gobby was greatly disturbed by these 'visitations', though not afraid. He felt that something was wrong and that his old friend was distressed in some way. He still had her address from 1947 and it was not too hard to obtain her present whereabouts, not more than fifty miles from his own home, so he telephoned her. 'The voice was the same. I would have recognized it anywhere,' Mr Gobby wrote. 'She was twenty-three when I last saw and spoke with her . . . and is now sixty one.'

She told him that she was just recovering from a serious illness. 'That in itself was sufficient proof to me that I had not imagined all that had occurred . . . She said that I would not know her now; although I did not enlighten her, I could have, in detail, fully described her present physical condition. That was proved when I eventually met her.'

279

They reminisced about old times when he had been in the RAF and she in the WAAF, where they worked together as MT drivers in Harrogate, and the conversation ended with her invitation to him to call. Meanwhile Mr Gobby had told his sister, with whom he lives, all that had happened, including a full description of the lady so that when she met her she would be able to confirm that the apparition was true. He also told his vicar, and a friend who is a psychologist. He did not, however, tell the lady his reasons for contacting her again, nor did she ask. 'I just didn't know the manner in which I could explain.'

He and his sister visited her several times, the last occasion being in May 1980. Although she said little to him about her illness, she confided in his sister that she had been so ill that she thought her end had come. Since then he has written to her occasionally but, apart from Christmas cards, she has not replied. However the apparitions have not ceased. On the fourth occasion, she did not speak at all, just stood facing him with an 'appealing expression'. On the fifth visitation, 'she stood facing me, lifted up her arms in an embracing position and said, "Thank you".' The sixth sighting was rather different. 'On this occasion I observed her seated on a chair in what I assumed was the living-room in her home . . . and directly opposite her, a younger lady was seated. They both appeared to be in conversation, and it was as if I was seated between them watching them, but neither of them was aware of my presence. I can describe both physically, their articles and colour of clothing.'

This was in March 1982, since when he has not seen her again. But he is convinced that he will and that there must be some reason for these sightings. He accounts for them thus; during their period in the Forces, he was very much in love with her and that love remained unchanged in spite of her marriage to another man. They both shared a love of music and the countryside, and other interests. He feels that because of the love and trust that existed between them, she is in some way calling for help and he is aware of it. They are in some way telepathically linked. As a Christian, he sees God's hand in it. 'Such power that has been exhibited to me does exist,' he insists, 'however mysterious it may be, and no one will ever persuade me to think otherwise.'

Like John Graham, Mr Gobby is also susceptible to atmosphere, particularly in the Highlands which he looks upon as his spiritual home. One evening near Loch Etive, his dog ('a mongrel with the characteristics of a pointer') refused to leave the caravan for a walk, and later that night he refused to settle. Outside there was a moon, a light haze on Rannoch Moor, no wind or movement anywhere. 'One could hear the silence.' Then 'Myself, my sister, and my elder brother distinctly discerned a medium-pitched wailing sound. Quite eerie and unexplainable.' This was only one of many similar experiences.

Linnhe Gobby's theory that we are all linked to each other through the love of God, which accounts for his particular experiences, is one that is widely held and certainly no less credible than many put forward by scientists. It would be easy for the latter to dismiss the 'visitations' as romantic fantasy, the wish-fulfilment dreams of an aging man if it were not for several facts. Mr Gobby saw his apparition not as a girl but as the woman she had become thirty-eight years later, so altered that all that was recognizable to him was her voice. Three witnesses to his character and his account, his sister, his vicar and a psychologist friend, see no reason to doubt the truth of his story. His visions are firmly in the tradition of Highland second sight, and his character is sensitive, intuitive, and creative (he is a musician) which is typical of those with psychic ability. There is no reason for him to lie, no financial motive, and, as a practising Christian, every reason why he should be concerned to tell the truth.

THE TEACUP READER

It started as a party joke. As a young woman from the Black Isle during the last war, Mrs A. picked up her brother's teacup and told him that he would go to Australia, fly over Sydney harbour, go on to Japan, and land at a port there. The incident was forgotten until a few months later when her brother wrote to tell her that everything she had predicted for him had come true.

Pure coincidence. Certainly she thought so. The so-called reading had come straight off the top of her head. However her reputation as a fortune-teller grew from that moment, and later as a married woman and teacher living in Sussex she was in constant demand at every fund-raising organization in the area. A caravan, booth, or tent was set up for her and there she would either read the cups or palms and give the money to charity. For her, both the cups and the hands were unnecessary, nor had she any knowledge of palmistry or teacup reading. They were merely a means of contact. Her readings were spontaneous. Like Henderson Lynn she found concentration killed the faculty. Like Swein Macdonald she found she had no memory of what she said, unless there was some discussion with the client afterwards.

Mrs A. tended not to take her faculty seriously, but as time passed she collected a following of people who turned up at every event. One incident she does remember involved a woman whom she told that she was being accused of something she hadn't done and that she was greatly hurt. There was nothing in the woman's expression to betray her feelings, but at the time she was in fact being accused by her brother-in-law of conniving with her sister in the sister's extra-marital affair. A lucky guess, perhaps – but Mrs A. had never made this particular prediction to anyone else as far as she could remember, and there were too many lucky guesses.

In spite of the spontaneity of the act, she found predicting to be utterly draining and exhausting. She said she was happier to retire from that side of her life than she was from teaching.

She has also had numerous telepathic communications with her family. One afternoon she had a strong vision of her sister-in-law with her hands held to her head as if she were in great pain. That night she telephoned and learned that a stack of chairs had fallen on her sister-in-law's head.

She admits to being 'terribly frightened' of her ability and knows that if she were to encourage it she could have stronger experiences, which might hurt and disturb her family. They are very much aware of her psychic abilities and it was one of her daughters who persuaded her to talk of her faculty.

In common with the other seers mentioned in this chapter, Mrs A. is creative, with a strong urge to write poetry. She is also constantly aware of her roots as a farmer's daughter on the Black Isle. Part Celt, part Norse, she feels that she can trace her ancestry right back 'to the very bugs that came out of the Black Isle bogs'. She is a believer in Jung's theory that all humans share some common memories and experiences, and that these are stored in the collective unconscious. The precognitive mind in action, she thinks, is in touch with the spaceless, timeless collective unconscious which contains our dreams, urges, mythologies, and artistic creativity.

It is not possible to give more than a handful of examples of the dozens of psychic incidents reported to me over the past year of research. The following are typical of those experienced by men, women, and children in every walk of life, some of vital importance to the seer, others apparently meaningless.

A nursing officer in Inverness had a precognitive dream that she would have an accident in a white car. Accustomed to experiencing premonitions, and to telepathic communications, she did not dismiss the warning but she could not understand why the car in her vision was white, as she owned a blue vehicle. However while driving a car belonging to a close friend she did have an accident, and the car was white.

An anaesthetist in Inverness has had four strong premonitions which on each occasion have saved his life. The most dramatic was at Dunkirk where he and some other men were waiting on the beach to be transported across the Channel. Suddenly he knew urgently that he had to move. Calling to the others to shift, he took to his heels and ran. The others paid no attention. Within seconds they were blown up.

A young healthy Uist man told his sister over a dram at New Year that he would not be alive the next Hogmanay. He died in March.

A woman living in Achiltibuie on two separate occasions saw a young child running round an isolated croft on one of the Summer Isles. On going to investigate she found the place derelict with no close neighbours and no sign of a picnic party.

The mother of a woman in Avoch saw the funeral of a local laird pass through the village weeks before the man died.

The Revd Douglas Macroberts when aged six was holidaying in Ayr with his parents. As they walked past the Gaiety Theatre he told them that round the corner a lorry would run over a crate of oranges. He could not understand why his parents were so shaken when they turned the corner and witnessed the event.

A lady from Tranent had a strange experience on 10 July 1984 in Room 23 of Aultguish Inn, which is situated about six miles from Garve on the Ullapool road. She was wakened from sleep by an unseen force shaking her, 'not the bed, just me'. She sat up, and though the curtains were closed and there was no moonlight, it was sufficiently light to see three disembodied clenched fists, one ahead of the other two, moving towards her 'in what looked to me like a threatening manner'. She lifted her left arm and kept repeating, 'Go, go!' using her left arm all the time. When they disappeared, she saw on her right side about six disembodied faces of what looked like clansmen. They were beardless with unusually white skins and they were wearing black tam o'shanters adorned with black feathers. The leader alone was wearing a gold-coloured metal headband. Again she told them to go and when eventually they disappeared she heard a male voice say from somewhere in the room, 'Lie down, breathe deeply as if asleep, but keep your eyes open.' This she did, and after a while she drifted into sleep. 'At no time did I feel scared, which I thought unusual and I wondered, Were my visitors trying to tell me something?'

A young boy from Tain on a family picnic refused to go near a certain well where they had planned to eat. He could give no specific reason for his reluctance, only a strong premonition of revulsion and fear. Shortly afterwards a man committed suicide at the well.

N.C., when aged about four, looked up and saw the image of a tall woman dressed in blue to her ankles, standing in the passage of Rosehaugh, a mansion house in the Black Isle that was demolished in the late fifties. Later she learned that her hostess's mother had died at that precise spot, and had looked and dressed as described many years before.

A young girl was asked by an older friend to exchange seats on the school bus. 'No,' she thought, 'because I'll be next the window when the accident happens.' Within minutes the bus collided with a coal lorry. She was unhurt.

The son of a minister in Inverness was bicycling home to the manse when he had a terrifying premonition that he was about to witness an accident. Frightened, he pedalled home as fast as possible – in time to witness the result of an accident outside his home. When the police asked him why he had been riding so fast, they were astonished at his answer.

During the black-out of the last war, a woman from Achiltibuie had to walk home in the pitch dark, having forgotten her torch. Seeing a bobbing light on the road ahead, she followed it thankfully, believing it to be the torch of someone else out late. Suddenly the light went out, but fortunately the moon came out just in time to reveal that she was on the very edge of the harbour wall. Though she peered anxiously into the water there was no sign of anyone, nor were any of the villagers missing. Shortly afterwards a child was drowned at the precise spot where the light had disappeared.

Part Three

Second Sight Today

The Terminology

As we have seen, the Gaels have ancient names for all aspects of psychic phenomena. So today, in step with the slow advance of knowledge in this field, a new lexicon is gradually evolving. The experiences – dreams, visions, premonitions and hauntings – remain the same, but as new theories proliferate there is a need to describe them in scientific terms.

ESP – extrasensory perception – is a blanket phrase used to cover any phenomenon outwith the range of our five senses and beyond the scope of memory. It covers all aspects, including dowsing, mediumship, faith-healing and others not within the remit of this book.

Parapsychology and the Paranormal. These widely used terms are not entirely satisfactory, in that they imply that the study deals with the abnormal. Psychic phenomena, although unpredictable and inexplicable, are so common that they should perhaps be considered within the range of normal experience.

Psi. The twenty-third letter in the Greek alphabet is used as the newest word to cover all aspects of the paranormal. Suggested by Thouless and Weiser in 1947, it occurs both in physics and in parapsychology, and from the practical point of view is a useful short word. 'Psi World' is a term widely used to describe all that may happen in a fourth dimension.

Telepathy – the communication of one mind with another – is probably the commonest aspect of ESP. Invented by Frederick W. H. Myers, a founder of the Society for Psychical Research, the word comes from Greek roots, *tele* meaning distant, and *pathos* for feeling or happening.

Biocommunication is the Russian equivalent of telepathy.

Clairvoyance, Clairaudience – seeing and hearing through space – are words that have been debased by unscrupulous operators. *Distant viewing* is used in preference to clairvoyance these days.

Premonition is a warning or strong feeling that something is about to happen.

Pre and retrocognition – the ability to see forwards and backwards in time – should not be confused with *Prediction* which is a statement that may be made following a premonition or precognition.

Prophecy may be interpreted as inspired utterance or 'telling forth' in a Biblical sense. Where 'prediction' suggests a reasoned revelation, 'prophecy' hints at the ecstatic.

Metachoric experiences include all dreams and out-of-body occurrences.

A waking dream happens when the seer's natural environment is replaced by a different one, as if he were experiencing a dream except that he is awake. *Lucid dreams* occur when the dreamer knows he is dreaming.

Out-of-body experiences happen when the seer is able to watch himself from another point of view, usually from above.

SOURCES

Do second sight and psi phenomena come from a faculty within ourselves, latent in some, advanced in others; or do they come from an outside agent? Are the visions and messages received imposed upon us from entities apart, or are they the products of our own minds? Is it, as Freud believed, a vestigial sense that was once useful to primitive man as a means of communication, or, as Professor C. E. M. Joad thought, a new sixth sense towards which we are gradually evolving?

These are the questions which continually perplex philosophers, scientists, and parapsychologists like Professor Archie Roy of the Department of Astronomy at Glasgow University who is keenly interested in researching the paranormal. He is an admirer of Carl Gustave Jung who believed that psychic experience was more common in primitive men, and still is in children, than it is in adults today. Never doubting that psi experience existed, Jung's ambition was to understand how it worked. His theory of the Collective unconscious is certainly convincing and attractive.

Jung saw the Collective unconscious as a repository of everything that has ever happened to anyone from the beginning of time. All thoughts, fantasies, and beliefs are there and can be tapped on occasion by the individual human mind. Easterners called this theory the Akashic Record; Jung saw it not as a passive 'library', but as a living entity with its own drives and needs which may be satisfied by the occasional invasion of the conscious mind by the subconscious. Events that may seem coincidental could be brought about by the working of the common subconscious – this idea he called the Theory of Synchronicity.

By synchronicity, Jung means what we would call coincidence; and he makes a clear distinction between 'chance' and 'meaningful coincidence'. When you buy a raffle ticket which happens to be the same number as your telephone, that is chance. Professor Roy's example of meaningful coincidence occurred shortly before my visit to him.

'Two weeks ago I had a sitting with a medium in Leicester. I then had a letter from a Mrs Drake about an experience in Banbury, quite near Leicester. Shortly after, I had a phone call from a Miss Drake whose home is in Banbury but who studies in Leicester. She told me she bred Pekingese dogs. My secretary also breeds Pekingese. These,' says Professor Roy, 'are a constellation of singularities that make no sense from a surface point of view. Each event is totally independent of the other, yet below the surface there is perhaps some reason why they should all be pushed into the conscious.'

John Graham (who had a vision of the Kieland disaster, see page 277) experienced a host of coincidences when researching his family

291

history. In January 1980 he commissioned the Research Society to plot his descent. Almost immediately he made friends with a man who was living in Islay and discovered he was married to a girl who shared John's great-great-grandmother. John has a keen interest in photography. While searching in the Mitchell Library in Glasgow, he came across a reference to 'the Graham Collection' and found this to be a portfolio of some 3,000 photographs by a certain William Graham who had a studio near where John's great-grandfather had set up house after leaving Islay.

More sinister is the coincidence recorded by a retired police sergeant who in 1972 was investigating the murder of a woman whose body was found covered with leaves in Renfrewshire. The murderer was a man called David Couborough. At the same time, one of the constables on the case was leafing through old police records when he discovered that in 1872 a woman's body had been found in exactly the same circumstances near Stirling, some twenty-four miles distant from the 1972 murder. The killer in this case was called William Couborough whose age, description and height was identical to David.

Writers, too, know that these strange coincidences crop up only too frequently in the publishing world. How often do we read of two biographies published within months of each other about the same – often obscure – personality? How often do we come up with the idea for a novel, only to find that someone else is working on the same theme?

Perhaps the analogy of the archipelago best illustrates Jung's theory. Each of us is an island. We may perceive each other across the sea, with our conscious minds, as being safely separated by the spread of water. Below the surface, however, we are not only joined to the earth, but joined to each other by the earth. The thoughts, ideas, and beliefs which may be formulated by our conscious minds and then communicated, may owe their origin to a common source. If this is the case then the puzzle as to whether we are evolving away from or towards a sixth sense is irrelevant.

In one sense, however, it could be said that we would seem to be growing away from the psi world. Professor Roy believes that the greatest con trick played on human beings was by the nineteenth- and early twentieth-century scientists who maintained that we were all electro-chemical-physical mechanisms that die when the brain dies.

We have been brainwashed into believing that what we cannot see, touch and feel does not exist. To that extent it could be said that our civilization is evolving away from experiencing the paranormal.

In fact, most people believe in the psi world to some extent. Archie Roy finds that 10 to 20 per cent of students will tell him of some inexplicable experience, and the stories they tell are strangely similar. In my own questioning among Highlanders, I found the percentage far higher. In fact there are very few people who have not had psychic experience either in the form of coincidence, premonition, or telepathic communication.

If we believe that science has conquered 'superstition', we should take a closer look at the world. We don't burn witches these days, but there are still covens in Glasgow, eighteen of them according to Henderson Lynn, which is more, I should imagine, than existed in the days of Jamie Saxt. Belief in the occult, if the number who flock to fortune-tellers, clairvoyants, astrologers and spiritualists is any guide, is on the increase. Faith-healers and folk-medicine are now on the fringe of respectability. The charismatic movement within the churches, which looks to miracles rather than theology, is part of the occult explosion. So perhaps Professor Joad was right to suggest that we are evolving *towards* a sixth sense and that it has never been more evident than it is today.

Some people claim to have had no psychic experience in their lives, felt no premonitions, had no hunches, but even they are constantly in touch with their own subconscious when they dream. Although Swein Macdonald believes that it is impossible to acquire second sight, yet all can learn something about themselves and about the world and their relationship to it by the study of their dreams. The psychotherapist who claimed to have taught herself to dream precognitively is not all that different from the person who, faced with a decision, decides to 'sleep on it'. Professor Roy knows many academics who, when faced with a problem in their work, will find the answer after a period of dissociation. A woman told me she solved crosswords by taking them to bed with her. Such answers as are provided would seem to come from our own subconscious minds, though there are scientists who, faced with extraordinary problems, would claim that the answers were 'given'.

Dreams, however, that warn of a great disaster or of some striking event within the family would seem to come from a deeper source. On

293

these occasions it would seem that we are able to reach a deeper unconsciousness than that which lies within ourselves, the deep sea bed, perhaps, that connects each island to the other. Such dreams are, for some, a personal doorway into the psi world.

Perhaps the ability to dream is the most important faculty we possess. Everything we dream is of importance to us. A dream can enhance a relationship, renew belief, improve work problems and better our mental health. It can also, it would seem, see beyond the present state and warn of what may lie ahead.

Dreams are perhaps the most important clue to the totality of life, but though theories abound the question still remains unanswered: Are we in nightly communication merely with our unconscious selves, or is there a greater force that lies beyond? God, or the collective unconscious, or our own – as yet – unfathomable minds?

THE PARADOX OF TIME

Of all the facts of ESP, the hardest to credit is undoubtedly precognition because of the problems it raises regarding free will and a fixed future. Mediums, seers, and mystics say there is no such thing as time. It is an unnatural distinction made by the conscious mind grooved to a certain course. Outside the conscious state, there is only *now*, which extends over past, present and the future.

How dominated we are by clocks and time checks; yet at the same time few can fail to be aware that time is not always measured with the accuracy of Greenwich. Three hours at my desk passes in a flash, while five minutes at a Glasgow bus stop on a wet night seems forever. Time changes with our personal metabolic rates. Remember, when we were young, how an eternity stretched between one Christmas and the next? As we grow older, and our metabolic rate slows down, a year is gone before we know it. If we were to be shut up in a dark room for too long, we would lose our sense of time altogether.

The first researcher into precognition and time was J. W. Dunne, an aeronautics engineer born in 1875. In his book, *An Experiment with Time* published in 1927, he proposed a theory which he called Serial Time.

He started from the premise of self-awareness, that if part of you is busy reading these words, there is also part of you aware that you are reading these words. This small example shows that there are two dimensions of awareness. In Serial Time, he suggests that there are several dimensions of time. It is all a matter of perspective. Thus an event which takes place in Time A could be seen differently from the dimension of Time B, which in turn might be seen from yet another dimension, and so on back to Absolute Time, which would be God's point of view. Time A is what we are conscious of here and now, and when we are asleep we have access to a higher time dimension. It should therefore be natural for us in that state to witness an event which might not yet have happened in Time A. Awake again, we would see our dream as being of a 'future' event because it did not lie within the conscious perspective.

One of the early researchers into psi phenomena, William James, decided that the 'present moment' had certain dimensions, and held that everything perceived as 'now' was within the specious present and had some sort of dimension. H. F. Saltmarsh in *Foreknowledge* suggested that the specious present of the unconscious is of greater duration than that of the conscious, and therefore, extends partly into what seems to the conscious mind to be the future, or possibly the past. The specious present of the unconscious therefore includes what is going to be seen and what already has been seen. This, Saltmarsh thinks, might explain precognition: if the unconscious already perceives the future, and if that future includes some dire disaster, then the unconscious would communicate to the conscious mind in dreams, and the conscious mind could then decide what action to take.

Saltmarsh, like others, did not relish the idea of a fixed future, so he suggested that the future was essentially malleable, but became more difficult to mould as it neared the present, until when it actually happened, it was fixed. Too contrived a theory, perhaps, to be credible?

Professor Roy thinks that the future depends literally on our point of view, in the sense that from our position in time we can take decisions and decide what path to take, but if we could stand outside time, then we would know what decisions we had made. The trouble, he suggests, lies in words. The English language is built on the idea of a future which has not yet happened. If we could see the whole picture, there would be no way of distinguishing past from the future.

The whole panorama of events exists. We superimpose past, present and future on time because our conscious minds are designed to travel in that direction. If the faculty of precognition exists, the future must be now. If the event 'seen' is a something that has happened in history, then the past is now. Both have happened.

Or perhaps it might be that the seer does not experience the whole event, or necessarily the true event, but only his future perception of that particular event. He is witnessing in vision what he himself will one day see in the flesh. This would mean that the events foreseen must necessarily occur within his lifetime. For example, when the Brahan Seer precognized black rain, that event must have been fulfilled within his lifetime. It is a theory that what he actually saw was water dripping from the sodden sooty thatch of a Highland black house after a particularly heavy precipitation. In the Gaelic this has been described as black rain. If the seer is limited to his own perception of future events, his interpretation of these events must therefore be subjective. Dr J. C. Barker discovered, when comparing the predictions made for him by many different seers, that those whom he felt to be genuine often picked on different events to emphasize, a variety of aspects to describe. It would seem therefore that a seer's vision is affected by his own personality, by what seems important to him, by his interpretation of what he sees.

Most predictions are fulfilled within a short time of their having been made. When Swein told one of his poorly sighted visitors to watch out for a small table by the stairs, she presumed he meant in her own home and was puzzled because there was no such table. Within minutes, she would have walked into just such a table in Swein's house had she not been prevented by the foresight of a friend.

E. H. Walker in *Consciousness and the Quantum Theory* suggests that the conscious act of looking into the future has the effect of creating the very event foreseen. Human consciousness has the power to bring about its own predictions. When the Brahan Seer uttered the Seaforth Doom, he was, in effect, creating it. A frightening thought.

The quantum physicists have, says Professor Roy, somersaulted the theories of the late nineteenth-century and early twentieth-century scientists who saw the world as a hard, material, billiard ball with no place for psi phenomena. Far from disproving the paranormal, quantum nuclear physicists have now shattered the 'billiard ball' and many have come to accept the psi world. They see the universe in terms of an equation which tries to predict the probability of entities that are neither physical nor particles nor waves. In fact, says Professor Roy, the whole universe has very little resemblance to anything material. The electron is at one and the same time a particle and a wave which may be anywhere. Everything in the universe is linked. Nothing is separate and there is cohesion everywhere. A particle here may be influenced by a particle on the other side of the world. Quantum mechanics state that if an atomic particle breaks and gives out two particles, they are co-related. One will be spinning this way, one that way and this will *always* be the case; no matter if they are a billion miles apart, the two particles will always take up the same co-relation.

This conflicts with Einstein's theory that light is the fastest moving entity. According to Einstein, if two particles are a billion miles apart it will take time for them to relate, but the quantum physicists say modern experiments have proved it happens instantaneously. Thus, objects that seem to be separate are somewhere part of a wholeness. This is not dissimilar from the idea that psychic phenomena demonstrate that there is a part of us that is independent of time and space. Mystics, too, believe that the universe is a whole and that we are all connected in some great plan.

Certain psi researchers have tried to explain the paranormal by invoking quantum physics. Dr Ninian Marshall, an American psychiatrist, suggests that the disturbed electron throws out feelers towards its own future. These feelers simultaneously work out all the futures possible for the electron, and it can then decide which to choose. Maybe the mind works in the same way – has glimpses into all its possible futures and then decides how to act.

Another theory suggested by the American physicist, Gerald Feinberg, and entitled *The Remembrance of Things Future*, holds that it should be possible for the brain to receive information from the future as well as the past. This could be done by comparing what is common to both precognition and short-term memory. By regarding precognition as memory in reverse, it might be possible to understand how it could work. All of us have long- and short-term memories though we don't know exactly how they function. Long-term memory consists of things remembered from a few hours before, or right back to infancy. Short-term memory records what is happening now, the brain acting as a sort of processing machine to take or reject the immediate past. Information is passed through the brain as electrical impulses bounced from neuron to neuron by charges fired between nerve endings. The results are thoughts and images, which may later be recalled. So then, if there were stimuli from the future as well as from the present and the past, the seer might also 'remember' events from the future. Future memory, far from being the paradox it sounds, would seem to make sense of precognition. A quirk in the individual brain's memory system might make it easier for some to 'remember' the future and the remote past as easily as the present. A fascinating thought.

This could account for the fact that a surprising number of seers have acquired psi ability as the result of an accident. Peter Hurkos, the Dutch seer, was a hard-headed man of the world until he had an accident with a ladder, after which he found he was psychic. Swein Macdonald, though professing psi powers since childhood, only developed his faculty after an accident to the head. The Brahan Seer was said to be blind in one eye. American psychiatrists have noticed that ESP among hospital patients is often more evident in the dissociated state induced by a mild concussion.

THE IMMENSITY OF SPACE

If precognition is the ability to see through time, then clairvoyance can be said to be the aptitude for seeing through space. One of the most intriguing and recent theories is Guy Playfair's conjecture of hyper-space, which he expounds in *The Infinite Boundary*.

We live, he tells us, in two worlds, one world of matter which we may not understand but which supports us comfortably, the other being non-physical, made up of psi elements. The physical world seems to have three dimensions of space and one of time; but the psi world has at least four of space and two of time. The two worlds can and do inter-act – in fact, life is impossible without their interaction. But psi matter can exist in its own world and is not subject to physical laws. Communication between man and beings of the psi world is possible, though rare and confusing. But 'rarity has nothing to do with reality', says the astronomer, V. A. Firstoff. 'One elephant is just as real as a hundred elephants, and quite sufficient to establish the existence of elephants.'

The theory of multi-dimensional space was first suggested by a German physicist-astronomer called Johann Zoellner in 1877 when he came to the conclusion that intelligent beings, who could communicate with us, did not appear to come from earth, and must therefore belong to another special dimension. Einstein stated that we are living in a four dimensional space-time continuum where the three dimensions of space are joined to one of time. What if there were a fourth dimension of space?

To understand better what there are no words to describe, Playfair suggests that we look at a two-dimensional world, a moving picture where flat forms slide like shadows without any means of moving off their surface, not suspecting that it might be possible to do so. Imagine the flat shadow coming in contact with a spherical object that moves in a different dimension: the shadow could neither describe nor comprehend it. Now imagine ourselves as shadow men, faced by beings that move in another dimension which Playfair calls hyperspace.

His own experience of what this dimension could involve occurred in 1973 during his investigation of a poltergeist. Sleeping downstairs, he woke around seven in the morning to see and hear the girl who slept upstairs leave the house to go to work. She had shut her bedroom door as she always did. When she had gone, he fell asleep again. A few minutes later he awoke to see a stool slide downstairs. It had been placed on top of the girl's wardrobe and had somehow come through a closed door to get to the stair. This was only one of a number of similar incidents that had plagued the girl's family for years. There were no normal explanations, but Playfair has given two possible paranormal ones. Either some power can dematerialize an atom and put it together again elsewhere, or some intelligent force can move objects in and out of a fourth dimension.

Where is this fourth dimension, or hyperspace? The answer is that it exists all round us here and now. Just as the shadow picture is a two-dimensional representation of a three-dimensional man, so the man is a three-dimensional representation of something that exists in a four-dimensional world.

Matter is composed of atoms. These are the basic building-blocks of physical matter, each with its nucleus and orbiting electrons. If physical matter has an atomic structure, so then should psi matter. This was Hermani D. Andrade's theory, which he demonstrated by looking at the single cell protozoon, the most elementary form of life that exists. It has the three essential characteristics of life – vitality, perception-memory and intelligence. Andrade then ascribed an elementary psi particle to each characteristic to demonstrate that each physical body also has a psi body, a body that is at least partly in hyperspace all the time. We are insulated against its effects, or as Gardner Murphy put it 'We are incapsulated entities,' probably for our own protection. It is more important to be able to cope with the present moment than with the crisis that may happen next week. But when we have flashes of ESP, we are emerging from the capsule to contact something greater.

If we have psi bodies, and a psi counterpart to the atoms that compose our bodies, it is logical to believe that we would also have psi genes. Jeno Miklos, a chemist from Romania, suggests that the study of psi genetics should be given a prominent part in the area of psi biology. Psi ability, he says, probably appeared at an early stage in our evolution and has been preserved by inheritance. Why should psi genes not obey the same laws of dominance, recession, and crossing-over that govern our physical genes? This theory would fit in with the fact that second sight is so often inherited. It would also fit in with the theory that psi ability is believed to have been possessed more fully by our ancestors. More interestingly, it would fit in well with the Gael's belief in the 'double', the *sith* (or psi, as we would now say) possessor of our bodies who can appear independent of space and time.

Frederick Myers reckoned that about one person in ten has seen the apparition of someone supposed to be dead and buried, or at the point of death, and that this was probably one of the commonest psi experiences. What is a ghost? The psi body, according to Playfair, does not leave the dead physical shell immediately. It takes its time. As it emerges from the dead shell, it takes with it some of that stuff called ectoplasm which it uses to become visible. Where and when it appears depends on who is polarizing its psi atoms at the time. This could be a parent or lover, someone close in spirit to the dying person.

Although Professor Roy feels that these theories are perhaps a little too easy, he himself had an experience which, if true, indicates that – like hyperspace – the other world is as close to us as the air we breathe. A medium was brought to his attention recently who appeared to have astonishing powers, so he asked if he could attend a sitting. There were five in the room: himself, an American woman, a husband and wife whose sixteen-year-old son had been killed in an accident, and the medium. The seance was conducted in total darkness – an immediate cause for suspicion, one would think. But Professor Roy said that his hand was taken about twelve times during the three hour session. On each occasion his hands were in a different position, either folded apart, on his knees or across his chest, and yet the hand that touched his in the dark found it unerringly every time. One of the 'communicators' was the grandmother of the medium, as she had been as a young woman. When she was there, the room was pervaded by a strong scent of hyacinth perfume. When she left, the scent immediately disappeared without a lingering trace – an impossible feat in the physical world, one would think. Strangest of all, his hand was on one occasion drawn down to touch the warm knee of a young child. He could feel the bony knee-cap, the flesh of the calf.

It was hard to believe that he was not the victim of a hoax, and yet he could find no reason why this should be the case. The medium had not contacted him herself. She took no money, not even expenses. She professed herself to be as perplexed as everyone else and was eager for him to form a committee of investigators to bring in paper, ink-pads and other testing equipment.

So, if hyperspace exists, it would seem to be present here and now, and to be a timeless repository for our psi selves. We may be insulated against it, but it is constantly in contact. What is the nature of this fourth dimension, what is its purpose, who created it?

HEAVEN AND HELL IN HYPERSPACE

Those who have had out-of-body experiences either in meditation or at the point of death hint at a paradise. Spiritualists talk somewhat naïvely in terms of a Utopia. Can good and evil exist in the psi world?

It is generally thought that the personality does not alter at death. A wicked man will not become a saint because his body dies. We know that the power of evil is potent in our three-dimensional world. From the mass of evidence that records the mischief of poltergeists, the misery of occult possession, the power of a curse, the effect of black witchcraft, we can only conclude that the fourth dimension has its own hell. Contact with it is all too easy for those whose motives are self-seeking, or those who foolishly knock at dangerous doors. Archie

Roy as a parapsychologist believes that the paranormal is not a safe subject in the hands of the ignorant or those whose motives are for thrills. Using the ouija board is rather like taking a telephone directory, opening a page at random, sticking a pin on a number and calling it: you don't know who you are going to get.

Death may be more bewildering for some than for others. A minister friend of Professor Roy, whose wife is a medium, is often called out to examine houses that are haunted. His wife encourages the spirit to speak through her, and he then helps it to rest. On one occasion, the spirit was that of an elderly woman who spoke in an anxious voice, 'I'm not looking forward to my operation tomorrow.' Further inquiry revealed she had died on the operating-table. The minister was then able to persuade her that she had died and that it was time to move on. Whatever the explanation, the proof of the pudding was in the eating – the house was no longer haunted.

On another occasion, at which Dr Roy was present, he heard the communicator say in an angry, ugly voice, 'They gave me a terrible time when I was alive and I'm going to give them a terrible time right now.' Dr Roy cannot help feeling that people who have led gross, materialistic lives in this dimension will want to do so in the next.

No body is more aware of the dangers that may be encountered in the next world than the Christian Church. In constant contact with that world through the power of prayer – itself a doorway into the other dimension – the Church knows only too well the results of uncontrolled and idle search. The Revd John Richards in *But Deliver us from Evil* insists that there is a basic incompatibility between Christians and psi researchers. The latter search for truth in the hidden or occult areas of life, but for the Christian, the truth about the next world has been revealed in the life, death, and resurrection of Jesus Christ. The best way to find what you are looking for, they believe, is in the life of Christ.

The Jewish God clearly ordered his followers to avoid occult practices, for in Deuteronomy we read:

When you come into the land which the Lord your God is giving you, do not learn to imitate the abominable customs of those other nations. Let no one be found among you who makes his son or daughter pass through fire, no augur or soothsayer, no diviner or sorcerer, no one who casts spells or traffics with ghosts and spirits, and no necromancer . . . The nations whose place you are taking listen to soothsayers and augurs, but the Lord your God does not permit you to do this.

The Christian faith, though rooted and grounded in the psi world where the organizing model is God and where contact is by prayer and union through the sacraments, wisely protects its children from the psi forces of evil.

Dennis Wheatley, that expert on the psi underworld, concludes in *The Devil and all his Works* that psychic research should only be undertaken under licence. June Johns in *Black Magic Today* states that the people most at risk of being recruited and initiated into black magic groups are the young and inexperienced, the lonely, the social climbers, sexual deviants and the mentally disturbed. Rollo Ahmed, an authority on the black arts, says 'spiritualism wrongly conducted forms an excellent channel for the forces of black magic'. 'Superstition,' says John Richards, 'psychic experimentation and attempts to manipulate the future are likely starting-points for the occult journey.'

The big difference, says the Christian Church, lies between unsought psi experience – the dreams and visions of seers and saints like Columba, which are direct revelations from God – and those deliberately cultivated by people using the tarot, the ouija board and the stars, who seek to gain power and wealth by tapping the resources of hell.

The church is wise to point out the dangers and protect the weak, but among is devout members there are those who seek to study the paranormal in relation to their faith. For them, the Churches' Fellowship for Psychical and Spiritual Studies was set up in 1953. The field of study includes psi phenomena, mysticism, creative meditation and spiritual healing. The psi phenomena include telepathy, clairvoyance, clairaudience, precognition and psychokinesis.

Dr Martin Israel, chairman in 1979, wrote in his report, 'It is important that we should involve ourselves in the problems of psychical research and the survival of death with the proper use of the mind. This is where our faith and a great deal of popular literature fail to impress those of sound mind and professional status. We want our Fellowship to be of such a calibre that, while it does not lose the common touch, it can also attract intellectually cultivated people

303

when they realize that the rational mind is not the end of reality. There has to be a proper balance between the cerebral, the psychical and the spiritual.'

Beryl Statham, writing of the Fellowship, states, 'Probably well over 50 per cent of the population have experienced some sort of supernatural happening, good or bad, in the meeting of someone who has died, in true dreams, in spontaneous or sought examples of mediumship, in shuddering coldness in some place later found to be haunted, in a flash of foresight, a moment of illumination or in conjuring up more than they bargained for in playing planchette. They rarely speak of these things, for who is there to understand them? It is our role to make ourselves available, after qualifying to the best of our limited abilities, and to seek for training to be given within the theological colleges and Christian groups.'

It would seem, then, that the forces of good and evil exist in this world and in the next. There are channels whereby both forces may be contacted, and while it is enriching and enlivening to contact the good, it is dangerous to contact the evil. Just as goodness and beauty and the power of love in the fourth dimension is probably much greater than in the third, so too is the force of evil. Both are literally inconceivable. The aura that surrounded Columba in thrall to a vision, the ecstasy that sometimes floods our minds at the sight of a starry sky or a golden dawn, are only glimpses of what may lie beyond. Only one of countless experiences of the forces of evil is the story of a girl called Judy who was possessed by an evil entity. She spoke in an alien voice through the mouth of the child saying, 'I am not Judy. I want to kill Judy,' and challenged the child's minister by saying, 'You don't believe in Satan, do you? I'll prove him to you.' The voice then proceeded to give intimate details of his private life that he alone knew.

The question remains, however: Who is in control? Who created the universe, the dimensions of time and space, the atom, the human mind? The true religions of the world all seek to comprehend underlying reality, and perhaps the Book of Genesis is nearest to the truth in stating that God created man in his own image. God, then, is the sum total of reality, the great organizer of creation whose ultimate purpose is as obscure to us as the dimension he inhabits.

In its oldest and narrowest meaning, second sight is the ability to see ghosts. Throughout the centuries, thick in the files of the SPR, within the experience if not of ourselves then of many of our acquaintance, ghosts appear and re-appear, but so far no satisfactory conclusion as to their nature has been produced.

As we have seen, there are ghosts of the living, of the dead, of those who have reached a crisis point in their lives, and ghosts with a purpose. Theories abound. Frederick Myers suggested they might represent the dreams not only of the living but of the dead; might be urges created by some mental act, manifestations of 'persistent personal energy'. G. M. N. Tyrell concluded that they were thought-patterns produced in the subconscious of the seer with or without the co-operation of the 'seen'. Edmund Gurney, also a founder member of the SPR suggested they might be hallucinations created by seers in response to telepathic impulses sent by the 'seen'. Others believe that ghosts of the dead are their spirits not yet come to terms with death, or the astral bodies of the 'seen'.

Andrew Mackenzie, ghost investigator and author, outlines in *Hauntings and Apparitions* the two main propositions contained within the theories. Firstly, ghosts are semi-*substantial* in that they can be seen, felt, and heard; their details of features and clothing are often accurate, although previously unknown to the seer; they may be reflected in mirrors; and they are often seen by more than one person at the same time. Secondly, they are *semi*-substantial in that they can pass through walls and locked doors; can rise in the air, glide; appear and disappear involuntarily; and commuicate telepathically.

Ghosts, according to the physicist Dr Raynor C. Johnson in *The Imprisoned Splendour*, are confined to a single idea or act, a touch, a gesture or appearance in a certain place, 'having done which the sustaining subsistent thought (or object) has expended the impulse which gave it birth, and it fades away'. Ghosts share certain characteristics such as extreme pallor of complexion. Details of features or clothing may be abnormally vivid to the seer. Their behaviour is usually meaningless and automatic. Women are more apt to appear than men.

Frederick Myers also believed that certain places could be haunted. He called these 'phantasmogenetic' centres, or points in space 'so modified by the presence of a spirit that it becomes perceptible to persons materially present near it.' Others believe that there is something in the building or place itself that can cause ghosts to be seen.

Ghost researchers suffer from two great handicaps. Stories about apparitions are so deeply entrenched in the myths and horror legends of our race that we are naturally inclined to disbelieve them. Secondly, although ghosts are harmless they create a strong element of fear in most people, which causes them to run to exorcists or to suppress evidence. The day will no doubt come when ghosts will be regarded as relics to be cherished, as glimpses into and evidence of another dimension of space and another concept of time. Just as we in the third dimension cast shadows that are flat and colourless, perhaps ghosts are shadows from a fourth dimension where time and space are entirely beyond our comprehension.

CAN THERE BE PROOF?

For most people, the answers provided by religion and materialism are insufficient to explain all the phenomena of the unseen world. This was the conclusion reached by Frederick Myers who, with a group of eminent friends, set up the Society of Psychical Research in 1882. Committees were started to investigate the different categories of what Myers called the supernormal. Throughout the years, some of the most distinguished men and women in the various fields of science were to become members, and today the Society continues to attract physicists, psychologists and theologians ready to examine the mass of evidence that accumulates each year.

As yet, however, there are no clear answers and it is fair to say that no seer or scientist, medium or minister has yet produced hard and firm facts to demonstrate the existence of the psi world. All we can do is continue to gather evidence, test it, experiment and look for the truth. How, then, should we react to all the instances of spectre-haunts, precognition and prediction that make up the bulk of this book?

Certainly we could assume that all the examples given are deliberate falsehoods or self-delusions. Alternatively we could believe them all to be true, from the Mackenzie Doom down to the devastating black rain. Or we could study the abundant evidence and conclude that some of the stories are fantasies, some myth, some fraudulent, some exaggerated by the oral tradition of the Gael, and some genuine.

And if only *one* were true, what then?

In the *Journal for Psychical Research (4)*, Professor G. W. Lambert suggests some guidelines when judging a prediction. Firstly, it should have been written down before the event. The interval between the prediction and its fulfilment should not be too long. The connection between seer and prediction should be improbable. The outcome should be literal rather than symbolic, and the details should correspond exactly with the details of the event.

In the following example, Professor Roy shows how carefully he follows up a new case. Recently one of his students brought him a photograph taken of a lopsided room decorated for Christmas, with a man's face superimposed in the centre. The man looked about fifty and wore Edwardian clothing. The student, an American, explained that when his sister and her husband had been staying in a farmhouse in England a year or two before, the camera had jammed during a photographic session. While the husband was trying to fix it, the shutter had clicked by accident. This accounted for the lopsided view of the room, but not for the man's small but recognizable face in the centre. Other incidents had impressed them. The family dogs had a habit of clustering round an empty chair and looking up eagerly as if someone were sitting there. The whole atmosphere of the house was noticeably friendly and warm, and the family was happy there.

One night, when they were back in America, the sister was taking off her jewellery to put back in its box, and found a brand-new gold sovereign worth about £400 sitting there. No one could account for its presence. No one claimed it, or confessed to having put it there. She consulted an Anglican priest whose father was a medium; the father went into a trance, and the communicator said, 'I gave you that coin. I was the man whose photo appears in the snap you took in the farmhouse where you were happy. I owned that house and I was so pleased that you liked it that I thought the coin would be a token of my appreciation.'

What, the student asked Professor Roy, did he make of the episode?

Archie Roy's first task was to establish whether the student's story was genuine or an elaborate hoax, so he asked for his sister's address and wrote to her for confirmation. Her letter back was reassuring, and she added that she had traced the name of the man who had previously lived in the farmhouse and found out that he had died in 1911 as the result of a tractor accident. So far, then, the story would seem to be genuine. The student and his sister had nothing to gain by inventing such a story. Indeed, if the gold coin had some sinister explanation, they would most certainly have kept quiet about it. On the other hand, the supernatural appearance of the gold coin is not easy to account for, so the professor's next task is to contact the priest and learn from his father just what happened at the seance. He will also subject the photograph to rigorous tests. So there is a great deal more work to be done before the case can be pronounced genuine.

Many are satisfied with the sort of proof collected by Dr J. C. Barker who set up an investigation into the precognitive dreams and visions that foresaw the Aberfan disaster in 1966. When the coal-tip set on the mountain-side above the village slipped and crashed on to Pantglas Junior School, killing 144 people, most of whom where children, Dr Barker appealed through the London *Evening Standard* for people who had precognized the tragedy. Out of seventy-six answers, he judged sixty worth further investigation. As many as thirty-five of these seem to have been genuine precognitions. The saddest was the dream of a ten-year-old victim, Eryl Mai Jones, who told her mother, 'I dreamed I went to school and there was no school there. Something black had come down over it.'

Perhaps the most potent proof of all is the fact that from the beginning of recorded history, people have experienced the psi world and in much the same ways. When Spiritualism took the Victorian world by storm, writers like Ruth Brandon suggested that it was based on a need for proof of immortality by people whose faith had been shattered by Darwinism and the science of the day. The fact of its newness troubled researchers, who thought it unlikely that a new set of phenomena should suddenly appear in the nineteenth century. In fact, it was not new. A group of Neo-Platonists in the first centuries AD were interested in a cult called theurgy which Professor Roy defines as 'the wish of the people to contact the gods'. They used the same paraphernalia and even the same Greek word for medium, believing that the best were young and simple persons. In the seances, the mediums were controlled by the gods – the Greek name for spirit beings – and the communicators were the same mixture of nonsense and genuine personalities as they are in modern sittings.

Not only have people experienced the psi world from the dawn of time, but we find that the same sorts of experience come from every part of the globe. Highlanders have no special claim to second sight, as the early explorers soon found out when they first visited the remoter corners of the globe. Shamans and witch doctors share gifts similar to those of mediums, seers, prophets and saints. From the start, primitive people singled out members of the tribe with psychic abilities in order to contact ancestors, spirits and gods. It seems unlikely that the same experiences shared throughout the world and from earliest recorded history could all be fraudulent.

Let us look briefly at two typical contemporary examples. Professor Murdo Ewan Macdonald told Professor Roy that when he was a student he went for a walk with an elderly Highlander (at least forty years old!) who had stopped suddenly. Great beads of sweat appeared on his brow as he declared, 'My son Hamish is dead.' Later a telegram arrived from Canada, where his son had been working, to break the tragic news.

On another occasion, a vet went by car to a remote hillside farm to attend to a cow. The owner, an old lady, asked him in for a cup of tea. 'Isn't it terrible about Colin Campbell being knocked down and killed in the village?' she said.

'But that's impossible,' said the vet. 'I was only speaking to him an hour ago in the village.'

'Oh no, he's been knocked down and killed. I am sure of it,' insisted the woman.

As soon as the vet returned he found out that it was true. He also knew there was no way the old lady could have heard the news, for she had no telephone and no callers.

In both cases the Highlander and the old woman had nothing to gain by their knowledge, and no reason to lie. Their experiences are only two of countless similar tales, as we have seen elsewhere in this book.

In fact, says Professor Roy, there is abundant evidence from psi research that at the very least there is a part of the human being that exists independent of time and space and that the whole question of survival is completely open. From the evidence available, two hypotheses may be deduced: firstly that a sort of super-telepathy exists by which means psychic persons can receive information; and secondly, that when we survive death, we keep our wits, our memories, and our consciousness, and on occasions we can come back. However, the fact that since Neolithic times belief in an after-life has been the basis of every creed does not constitute hard 'scientific' proof, nor does the credibility of seers and witnesses. Second sight remains the enigma it always was to those of us living in this three-dimensional plane. Possibly it always will do – and yet, as Charles Richet once said, 'The improbabilities of today are the elementary truths of tomorrow.' Because there is no laboratory proof today does not mean that there never will be any.

On the other hand, current research may be altogether off the right rail. Perhaps it is impossible to judge psychical ability by physical experimentation. The psi world and the realm of matter are not comparable. Precognition may already be a psychic fact, but it may never be a scientific fact.

WHAT MAKES A SEER?

As with other creative talents, second sight produces the professional and the amateur. As with other artists, the professional attempts to make a living out of his talent where the amateur does not. Where second sight is concerned, the amateur often actively disapproves of taking money for what he considers a God-given gift. He disapproves, too, of encouraging and forcing a gift that in his opinion should be involuntary and not instigated.

It is not surprising that the professional seer is treated with wariness. Just as the writer has the power to pollute the mind by turning to pornography to make a living, so the clairvoyant literally has power of life and death over some of his clients. Auto-suggestion is a dangerous weapon, and, as Dr Barker has said, some people are literally 'scared to death' by negative prognoses. His remedy for a fatalistic forecast is, 'Go and consult another fortune-teller as quickly as possible. You will probably be told a completely different story, or the emphasis will be different and you will then see things in another perspective.' The woman who was told by one seer that her husband would be dead within a year was told by another that she would have an addition to the family during that time. Both predictions may well have been true, so it would seem that what the seer sees is coloured by

310

his own personality, attitude to life, and beliefs. Swein Macdonald has a preoccupation with cars, which feature in many of his readings. Maybe this is because he would enjoy owning a powerful car himself but is prevented from driving by his damaged eyesight.

If the seer's predictions are coloured by his own personality, then there are bound to be frauds, cheats and manipulators in this field as in any other. Equally, there are scruplous, highly motivated men and women who look upon their talent as a means of helping rather than exploiting their fellows.

So what constitutes a professional seer? As with other creative artists, he was probably born with the talent. The medium Doris Stokes knew she was different when, as a child, she saw three people standing outside a church whom her friends could not see. Henderson Lynn knew it even before he heard his grandmother say, 'He's one of us.' The chances are that the gift was inherited. Most seers, amateur and professional, will admit to a mother or forebear who 'had the sight'. The Dutch clairvoyant, Peter Hurkos, did not develop his faculty until after a head injury. Though Swein Macdonald believes he inherited the talent from his grandfather, he did not use it professionally until after his accident. Dr Barker found that seers tended to be elderly, extrovert and outspoken. I have found them to be strong personalities. Too much knowledge can breed mental disorders. Too much power can be equally damaging.

What of the amateur? Just as we can all tell a story, sing a note, or draw a line, we are all psychic to some extent. Press the hard-headed, practical man to look back on his life and the chances are that he has experienced something he cannot account for in practical terms. Those more gifted would seem to be creative in other fields, sensitive, intuitive and imaginative. Age, sex, and background are unimportant. Those who are most able to enter a state of dissociation, whose doorway to their own subconscious is thinner than that of others, are the ones who can slip out of time and space. It could be anyone.

CONCLUSION

Why, when the evidence seems so strong, are there still many people like the Cromarty man who told me with a wink and a grin after I had finished a lecture on Coinneach Odhar, 'Second sight? It's all a load of rubbish, isn't it?'

There are some like Professor John Taylor who after careful investigation come to the conclusion that paranormal phenomena do not exist. Every seemingly authentic case he examined turned out to be fraud, self-delusion or fantasy. The paranormal, he states, is to be found within our own minds and bodies. Sir John Eccles, Nobel Laureate in Physiology, would agree – he told a convention of parapsychologists in 1976, 'The most paranormal thing of all is how I can move my finger when I so will it.'

Yet there are just as many men of intellect, integrity and scientific training who do believe in another dimension, our ability to contact it, and the immortality of souls. For them the question is not whether ESP exists, but rather how it works.

Human beings on the whole are remarkably dishonest in their attitudes to concepts and faculties that lie on the fringe of what is considered to be normal. Our opinions are governed by current fashion, inherited prejudices, and by what we want to believe. Belief and disbelief would seem to share a common dual root: fear and prejudice.

On one hand, we are afraid of there being no after life, no psi world, no further existence. The deep need for immortality produces in some an unquestioning gullibility, but in others a strong reluctance to be thought naïve or to commit themselves to a belief that may ultimately be proved wrong. Scepticism is safer than faith. Conversely, though we may long for immortality, we may also be afraid of all that it entails. Afraid of the act of dying, certainly, and of the unknown, but also afraid of breaking free from the capsule of our flesh or showing too much of ourselves, of facing what lies beyond. We fear losing our identity, that part of us that is 'me'; of meeting those we have wronged. So many have been indoctrinated with a fear of hell that the thought of immortality arouses feelings of guilt and dread.

Thus the many-pronged fork of fear makes some deny the evidence of centuries, of the saints, and of our own experience. Only the blindest put their trust in faith. Only the boldest are not afraid to say so.

Prejudice, equally, colours our attitude. We see what we want to see, what we have been conditioned to see, accept what seems acceptable to us, condemn what we cannot tolerate or what we cannot

312

'scientifically' prove. Yet the very fact that, as we have said, belief in an after-life has been the basis of every creed since Neolithic times is indubitably significant.

Perhaps fear is the right instinct. Arthur Koestler pointed out in *The Roots of Coincidence* that the paranormal is not a playground for superstitious cranks.

One reason why many have been reluctant to spend more time and money on researching the paranormal is the seeming pointlessness of the exercise. For Neolithic man, clairvoyance and precognition played an important part in personal and tribal communication. There are more reliable methods these days.

And yet it would seem that ESP still has its uses. According to BBC Television's *Horizon*, screened on 25 September 1983, 'remove viewing' is becoming big business in the United States. Psychics can do better than satellites, for they can see inside buildings, therefore they can be used as spies. Clairvoyants are of practical use when it comes to mineral, oil, and gas exploration. The police turn more and more to seers for help in detecting crime or finding missing persons. Experimentation in and encouragement of precognition would surely have some value when it comes to averting, or at least mitigating, the effects of great disasters. In the States, it is already used to predict market trends, with some success.

This may all seem far from the *taibhsear* at his twilit hearth visualizing the future through the peat-fire flame. Yet nothing in life is static, nothing remains the same. If I may be allowed a prediction of my own, which needs no psychic gift and comes from no occult source, I will suggest that the day will come when it will be an accepted fact that the human mind is not confined to the limitations of the flesh, and when that happens there will be no boundary to the achievements of mankind.

Appendix

General

The day will come when a king will be born but never crowned. Be sure there will be troublesome times at hand. This is thought to refer to Edward VIII who was proclaimed king in 1936 but abdicated before he could be crowned. The prophecy was known in Skye in 1918.

When there are three queens in Scotland there will be snow in every month. Queen Mary, Queen Elizabeth the Queen Mother, and Queen Elizabeth II were all alive for nine months in 1952. The prophecy is also from Skye. *When there are three queens in Britain, summer will be turned to winter and winter to summer.* Well known in the Outer Isles, this prophecy was quoted in the *Bulletin* of 26 March 1953, when, apart from a January storm, the weather had been exceptionally mild.

When two women are in power in the land there will be a bad summer. The two women are sometimes thought to represent Queen Elizabeth II and Mrs Margaret Thatcher, and this prophecy has been ascribed to Swein Macdonald. But it is of a much older vintage, and has been reckoned by some to refer to Mary, Queen of Scots and Elizabeth I of England. *When England is ruled by two women, there will be conflict.* Also thought to refer to Elizabeth II and Margaret Thatcher, this vision of the above prophecy has been known for at least fifty years in the Lochalsh area.

The day will come when the hills of Ross will be strewn with ribbons.
There will be a ribbon on every hill and a bridge over every stream.
The hills of Ross will be crossed with shoulder-belts.
There will be a road through the hills of Ross from sea to sea and a bridge over every stream.
There will be a mill on every river and a white house on every hillock.
The time will come when dram shops will be so plentiful that one may be seen at the head of every plough furrow.
Policemen will become so numerous in every town that they may be met at the corner of every street.
Travelling merchants will be so plentiful that a person can scarcely walk a mile on the public highway without meeting one.

The above prophecies collected by Alexander Mackenzie look forward to the modernization of transport and communication in the Highlands. Roads and bridges were few until Field-Marshal George Wade became Commander-in-Chief in Scotland in 1724 and began his programme of road-making which was to extend to about 250 miles, necessitating forty-two bridges. (Many military roads of a later date were wrongly ascribed to him.) Today there are still vast tracts of the Highlands unreachable by road, but those that do exist are well-maintained, and look remarkably like grey ribbons or shoulder-belts across the countryside.

The white house was so called in contrast to the traditional black house of the Highlander, low-thatched, with central hearth, blackened inside and out by peat reek. Today the brilliant white-washed cottages of the Islands and Wester Ross, often adjacent to the ruins of a black house, are a striking feature of the landscape. Meal mills were at one time very common and certainly the most useful and busy industrial institutions in the north. Their ruins may still be traced on the banks of most rivers. Though the travelling merchants referred to the hawkers, chapmen and hucksters of another age, the prophecy is particularly apt today where the Highlands are largely served by travelling shops. There was a time when each community had its local policeman, a well-kent and comforting figure in the street. Today they serve a wider area and are rarely to be seen outside their cars.

The clans will become so effeminate as to flee from their native country before an army of sheep.
The people will degenerate as their country improves.
The day will come when the big sheep will over-run the country until they strike the northern sea.
Sheep shall eat men, men will eat sheep, the black rain will eat all things. In the end old men shall return from new lands.
Many a long-waste rig will yet be seen between Uig and Ness of the plains. The day will come when the jaw-bone of the big sheep will put the plough on the rafters. When sheep shall become so numerous that the bleating of the one shall be heard by other from Conchra in Lochalsh to Bun-da-Loch in Kintail, they shall be at their height in price, and henceforth will go back and deteriorate, until they disappear altogether, and be so thoroughly forgotten that a man finding the jaw-bone of a sheep in a cairn will not recognize it, or be able to tell what animal it belonged to. The ancient proprietors of the soil shall give place to strange merchant proprietors and the whole highlands become one huge deer forest. The people will emigrate to islands now unknown, but which shall yet be discovered in the boundless oceans, after which the deer and other wild animals in the huge wilderness shall be exterminated and browned by horrid black rains. The whole country will be so utterly desolated and depopulated that the crow of a cock shall not be heard north of Druim-uachdair.
The people will then return and take undisturbed possession of the lands of their ancestors.

These prophecies foresee the whole of Highland history from the Clearances and evictions of the eighteenth and nineteenth centuries right up to the present and into the future, and are perhaps the most relevant to modern times of all Coinneach's predictions.

The big sheep represents not the deer, as is sometimes thought, but the Cheviot which was brought into the glens in the eighteenth century to replace the cattle and small wiry sheep previously owned by Highlanders. During the early nineteenth century, the Sutherland estates were exporting 200,000 lbs of wool annually from land that had once been farmed in small crofts. To make way for the sheep, local inhabitants were forced out of the glens and thousands emigrated to Nova Scotia, Prince Edward Island and others. Although many were to prosper in the New World, the enforced separation of

Celt from his beloved soil caused a wound that has still not healed. Highland history is permanently scarred by the memory and it is little wonder that the approach of such a traumatic event was so often predicted.

'The ancient proprietors of the soil' – the lairds – after Culloden were impoverished in many cases, and forced to sell their estates to 'strange merchant proprietors'. These were Germans, Dutch, English and Arabian, many of them absentee landlords, and also major industrial companies who use vast tracts of land as leisure ground. Far too much of the Highlands is today deer forest, and available only to those who can afford to fish, shoot and stalk.

The 'black rains' have so far not descended which means that this is a prediction known before its fulfilment, and therefore important. The image is clear and startling, typical of a genuine instance of second sight. Some see it as a blow-out of oil in the future when the wells beneath the North Sea are dried up and new supplies found on land. Others believe it will be a nuclear fall-out, or else possibly acid rain. On the other hand, Gaels use the term 'black flood' to describe a deluge, so it may simply refer to heavy rains which perhaps fell many years ago. Time will tell!

The tail-piece of the prediction, which describes how 'people will then return' was thought to refer to the employment of Highlanders, dispossessed in the past by eviction and lack of work, in the paper mill at Corpach, the smelter at Invergordon and the oil-related industries at Nigg, Ardersier, Kishorn and elsewhere. If so, the prophet did not see far enough, for Corpach and Invergordon have now both closed. Others believe the prediction refers to devolution and the success of Scottish Nationalism.

The prophecies pertaining to the clearances have been ascribed to Coinneach Odhar, the Petty Seer, a seer from Isla, and Thomas the Rhymer. They are part of Highland history.

The Islands of Lewis and Harris

The day will come when the Lewismen shall go forth with their hosts to battle, but they will be turned back by the jaw-bone of an animal smaller than an ass. The Revd Colin Mackenzie, minister of Fodderty near Strathpeffer, was one of the first to hear that Bonnie Prince Charlie had landed in 1745. He set off at once for Brahan Castle to inform the

Earl of Seaforth. It was late at night, but he managed to creep through the Earl's bedroom window without waking the Countess and whisper the news. He managed to persuade his chief that it would be wise for him to 'disappear' for a while, so they set off together for Lewis. Eventually they reached Poolewe and while they were dining on a sheep's head, two ships full of Mackenzie clansmen armed for battle, drew into the bay. Waving the sheep's jaw-bone, Seaforth ran down to the pier to order their captain, another Colin Mackenzie, to return to Stornoway. This they did, thus fulfilling the prophecy.

However unlikely it may now appear, the Island of Lewis shall be laid waste by a destructive war, which will continue till the contending armies, slaughtering each other as they proceed, shall reach Tarbert in Harris. In the Caws of Tarbert, the retreating host will suddenly halt: an onslaught led by a left-handed MacLeod called Donald, son of Donald will then be made upon the pursuers. The only weapon in this champion's hands will be a sooty-black caber (rafter) taken off a neighbouring hut: but his intrepidity and courage will overpower their pursuers. The Lewis then will enjoy a long period of repose.

The translation of the original Gaelic is given by the Revd William Matheson of the Department of Celtic Studies, Edinburgh, as follows:

Donald of the three Donalds
Son of Clan Macleod, a left-handed man,
Using a sooty rafter from his neighbour's house,
Will repulse the enemy in the Cadha

Mr Matheson suggests that there is good evidence to suppose that this prediction has already been fulfilled. In 1544 and 1545 there was a feud between the Morrisons of Ness and the Macleods of Harris when Domhall Dubh was contesting the Lordship of the Isles. Although Alexander Mackenzie classes the prediction as 'unfulfilled' and ascribes it to Coinneach Odhar, it must have been uttered by a seer predating even the historical Coinneach, or else invented after the occasion.

It is on the day of Allt nan Torcan
That injury will be done to the women of Lewis:
Between Eidseal and Aird a 'Chaolais
The sword edges will be struck.

318

They'll come, they'll come, 'tis not long till there
Will come ashore at Portnaguran
Those who will reduce the country to a sorry state.
Alas for the woman with a little child –
Everyone of Clan Macaulay
Will have his head dashed against a stone
And she herself will be slain along with him.

Translated from the Gaelic by Mr Matheson, this prophecy, he believes, might describe a battle in which the MacAulays were mass-acred on the road between Stornoway and Uig. The only survivor was the chief's youngest son, Iain Ruadh, and his illegitimate half-brother. Iain was the grandfather of Domhall Cam, chief of the MacAulays in the early seventeenth century. This would place the massacre as long ago as the early sixteenth century, yet the people of Uig still remember and talk about it.

In Raanish of Lochs will be done fell work indeed: in the shadow of the rocks there will be a cleaving of heads. This prophecy, also recorded by Mr Matheson, is thought to have been fulfilled in 1616 when a band of Macleods attacked and killed a certain Iain Og, an incomer to Raanish. His widow complained to the Privy Council that her hus-band had been murdered 'in his naked bed'.

In Harris a cock will crow on the very day it is hatched and a white calf without a single black hair will be born.

A large stone will roll up a hill turning over three times.

On the top of a high stone in Scaristavore Parks, the raven will drink its fill of men's blood and the tide of battle will be turned back by Norman of the three Normans at the steps of Tarbert. The Revd J. G. Campbell relates that this stone, about ten feet high, is in Harris and is one of three fragments broken by an old woman who used it to hammer limpets off the rocks. The other two fragments are at Uigh-an-du-Tuath and the Isle of Tarnsa. An old legend states that at the spot where all three fragments can be seen at once, there is a crock of gold and silver. It is easy to find the place where two of the fragments are visible, but almost impossible to see all three. A herdsman once found it, but just as he was about to dig, a cow fell into a stream. When he'd rescued the beast, he could no longer find where the gold was hidden.

When the Gael begins to wear the garb of the stranger, a dark-haired man in white hose and a green plaid will cross and recross the Sound of Scarpa, a thing which has never been done and never will be done again. Quoted in the *Bannatyne MS History of the Macleods*, this prediction was fulfilled in 1784 when the Disarming Act forbade the wearing of Highland dress. A certain Philip Macdonald, dressed as foretold, crossed and recrossed the Sound one Sunday in August when the tide was low 'for a frolic'. A hundred people were witnesses.

The Island of Skye

In the days of Norman, son of the third Norman, there will be a noise in the doors of the people, and wailing in the house of the widow; and Macleod will not have so many gentlemen of his name as will row a five-oared boat round The Maidens. Recorded in *A summer in Skye* by Alex Smith.

When Norman, the third Norman, the son of the hard-boned English woman, will perish by an accidental death; when The Maidens become the property of a Campbell; when a fox will have young ones in one of the turrets of Dunvegan; and particularly when the enchanted fairy flag should be for the last time exhibited; then the glory of the Macleods shall depart; a great part of the estate shall be sold to others so that a small 'curragh' [boat] will carry all the gentlemen of the name of Macleod across Loch Dunvegan. In times far distant another John Breac will arise, who shall redeem those estates and raise the power and honours of the house to a higher pitch than ever.

These prophecies are reckoned to be fragments of longer Gaelic sayings of Coinneach Odhar, now lost. The above is part of the reminiscences of Dr Norman Macleod and may be found quoted in the appendix of his biography written by his brother, Donald. Dr Macleod gives an extraordinary account of its fulfilment.

In the summer of 1799, the English smith employed at Dunvegan, swore him to secrecy and then told Dr Macleod that the iron chest which contained the Fairy Flag was to be forced open the next day.

Dr Macleod asked the factor if he could witness the event, and he was given permission provided he agreed not to tell the chief or any of his kin. Next day, accordingly, he joined the smith and the factor in the east turret where the chest was kept. There the lid was forced open 'with great violence,' we are told. Inside was a wooden box of strongly scented wood which contained the Fairy Flag, a piece of rich pale-brown silk embroidered with crosses of gold thread and 'elf spots' stitched here and there.

Within days, news came of the death of Norman the third Norman, who was the chief's heir and a lieutenant on the *Queen Charlotte* which had been blown up at sea. During the same week, 'Macleod's Maidens' – well-known nearby rocks – were sold to Angus Campbell of Ensay. At the same time, a fox belonging to a certain Captain Maclean cubbed in the west turret: Dr Macleod handled the offspring himself.

'I'm glad,' he wrote, 'the family of my chief still enjoy their ancestral possessions and the worst part of the prophecy remains unverified. I merely state the facts of the case as they occurred, without expressing any opinion whatever as to the nature of these traditionary legends with which they were connected.'

Strangest of all, perhaps, is the fact that the 'three Normans' were each the result of mischance. The son of Rory, the seventeenth chief died in infancy, so he was succeeded by his brother Norman. The latter's eldest son John also died young, so his second son inherited the clan. He too was called Norman. *His* eldest son John predeceased him, so the 'third Norman', the twentieth chief, inherited from his grandfather. The prophecy was well-known long before its fulfilment, and those who knew it placed Coinneach in the sixteenth century.

The raven will drink its fill of men's blood from off the ground on the top of the high stone in Uig in Skye. According to J. G. Campbell, this prediction probably was fulfilled centuries ago, for the 'high stone' alluded to has already fallen on its side.

> *Thou Well of Ta, and Well of Ta,*
> *Well where battle shall be fought,*
> *And the bones of growing men*
> *Will strew the white beach of Lacras;*

And Lachlan of the three Lachlans be slain
Early, early.
At the Well of Ta.

The Well of Ta is at Cill-a-chro in Strath on Skye. It is safe to assume the prophecy was fulfilled many years ago.

When the front doorstep is levelled, the Skye Gathering Hall will fall into the sea with all the people dancing inside. This old prophecy, still well known locally, has not as yet been fulfilled.

At Neist Point by Waterstein, a rock called Cnocan, known as the Rock of the Large Dog-whelks, will fall into the sea with as many Stewarts as could get a footing on it. The rock has already fallen into the sea with no harm to the Stewarts, but it might yet overturn, for it is said that anything could happen in *Camus nan Sithean*, the Bay of the Fairies.

The Uists and the Island of Benbecula

When the black horseshoe is seen, a frightful disaster will overtake the world. Recorded by Frances Thompson in *The Supernatural Highlands*, this prediction claimed to foresee the Second World War before which the North Uist ring road was left untarmacadamed on its northern side, thus presenting a bird's-eye view which looked like a black horseshoe.

The day will come when North Uist will be encircled with steel. This foresaw the advent of electricity cables and wires.

When a road runs up Eaval the second clearance will come and the island will be populated by green men and grey geese.
The day will come when the islands will be full of bent grass and big grey geese.
The day will come when North Uist will be inhabited by Chisholms and big grey geese. Although a road up Eaval (347m) would seem to be impossible, other mountains in the islands are now crowned with radar and other installations. 'Green men' aptly describes soldiers from the Royal Artillery Range Hebrides stationed in Benbecula, and the 'big grey geese' are thought to be aeroplanes. These predictions are still remembered and quoted locally.

Aird nan Ceann, Aird nan Ceann,
I am glad I will not be there,
At the head of Clachan a Deas
Where the men will be faint,
And the hot hard battle will be fought.

The Revd W. Matheson, who was brought up in North Uist, states that although Coinneach's name is known in the Uist tradition, the above prophecy from Benbecula is the only notable prediction he can recall. Presumably it was fulfilled in the distant past.

A priest will never leave Benbecula. Although this prophecy has been ascribed to Coinneach Odhar, local belief is that it was probably made at the time of the Reformation when a group of nuns were savagely cast out of Nunton House (Baile nan Cailleach) by a local family. It is believed that no priest has been ordained from Benbecula. One who offered himself went mad before he could be priested.

The day will come when the old wife with the footless stocking [cailleach nam mogan] will drive the Lady of Clanranald from Nunton House in Benbecula. Recorded by Alexander Mackenzie, the above prophecy predicted the end of the Macdonalds of Clanranald, the great family of Benbecula for many generations. 'We are informed', writes Mackenzie, 'that this was fulfilled when the Macdonalds took the farm of Nunton, locally known as 'Baile nan Cailleach'. Old Mrs Macdonald was in the habit of wearing these primitive articles of dress!'

When the Bornish Stone falls in South Uist, little green men will over-run the island. It is said that when the Army wished to establish a base in the area, the prophecy was remembered and local opposition was strong. The 'little green men' were thought to be soldiers in uniform. Certain officials one dark night used a jack to try to dislodge the stone in order to facilitate the military takeover. They were not successful, however, and the ancient monolith still stands.

The Island of Barra

When the big-thumbed sheriff and the blind man with twenty-four fingers shall be together in Barra, Macneil may make ready for a flitting. Well-known in Barra for generations, this prediction was literally fulfilled when a blind man with six fingers on each hand and six toes on each foot left Benbecula to beg for charity in South Uist. He was so successful that he decided to visit Barra before returning home. Arriving at the ferry, he met '*Maor nam ordagan mora*' – the sheriff with the big thumbs – and they crossed in the same boat. The sheriff was on his way to evict the laird of Barra, so MacNeil had indeed to prepare for a flitting.

The Island of Raasay

When we shall have a fair-haired Lochiel, a red-haired Lovat, a squint-eyed, fair-haired Chisholm, a big deaf Mackenzie and a bow-legged, crooked Macgillechallum, who shall be the great-grandson of John Beg of Ruiga, that Macgillechallum will be the worst that ever came or ever will come. I shall not be alive in his day and I have no desire to be. An octogenarian from Raasay gave this prophecy of Coinneach Odhar to Alexander Mackenzie, and his explanation was as follows: Ruiga is the name of a place in Skye. When the last Macleod of Raasay was born, an old sage in the district called upon his neighbour, and told him, with an expression of great sorrow, that Macgillechallum of Raasay now had an heir, and his birth was a certain forerunner of the extinction of his house. Such an event as the birth of an heir had been hitherto, in this as in all other Highland families, universally considered an occasion for great rejoicing among the retainers. The other old man was amazed, and asked the sage what he meant by such unusual and disloyal remarks. 'Oh!' answered he, 'do you not know that this is the great-grandson of John Beg of Ruiga whom Coinneach Odhar predicted would be the worst of his race.' And so he undoubtedly proved himself to be, for he lost forever the ancient inheritance of his house, and acted generally in such a manner as to fully justify the prediction; and what is still more remarkable, the Highland lairds, with the peculiar characteristics and malformations foretold, preceded or were the contemporaries of the last Macgillechallum of Raasay.

Note the allusion to the deaf Mackenzie.

The day will come when the island of Rona will be desolate and totally uninhabited. The island of Rona is situated just north of Raasay. When its lighthouse became automatic in 1975, the island was left full of ruined crofts and classified defence installations.

Wester Ross

A dun, hornless cow [ship] will appear in the Minch and make a 'geum' [bellow] which will knock the six chimneys off Tigh Dige. Gairloch House was called 'Tigh Dige', the House of the Ditch, because the original dwelling was made of wattled twigs and thatched with turf surrounded by a deep ditch which could, if necessary, be flooded with water from the river. The house built on its foundations was also called Tigh Dige, and it was the proud possessor of six chimneys. The prophecy is thought to have been fulfilled during the search for Prince Charles Edward Stuart, when a man-of-war entered Gairloch Bay and the captain invited Sir Alexander Mackenzie, owner of Tigh Dige, on board. He received a rude answer for his trouble, and angrily fired a broadside at the house. Although there is no specific mention of the chimneys, an eighteen-pound cannon-ball was found lodged in the gable end. This story is told in Osgood Mackenzie's book, *A Hundred Years in the Highlands*.

Another possible explanation of the 'dun, hornless cow', was given in Lochinver in 1983: it might have been a German submarine seen in the neighbourhood of Tigh Dige in 1917.

A white cow will give birth to a calf in the garden behind Gairloch House. A black hornless cow will give birth to a calf with two heads in Flowerdale. Both these predictions were well known to local inhabitants before they were fulfilled in the last century.

A bald black girl will be born at the back of Gairloch church. During one of the large, open-air services common to the last century, a well-known young woman gave birth to the child so described.

When the Ullapool Ferry crosses to Stornoway, it will sink with all lives lost. In current circulation in Ullapool in 1982. One local inhabitant refuses to travel by the ferry for fear of the prediction.

A severe battle will be fought at the Ardelve market stance in Lochalsh, where the slaughter will be so great that people will be able to cross the ferry on dead men's bodies. The battle will be finally decided by a powerful man and his five sons, who will come across the Achmore district. Probably fulfilled in the distant past.

A Lochalsh woman shall weep over the grave of a Frenchman in a burying place at Lochalsh. There are two explanations for this prediction. A Lochalsh girl was said to have married a French footman who died soon after and was buried in the kirkyard, thus leaving his widow to mourn at his grave. Although the prophecy may seem trivial, Scotland was not friendly with France during the Napoleonic wars when the marriage was said to have taken place, and thus it was a notable event. More interestingly, there is in Lochalsh graveyard a flat stone carved in the shape of an armed figure with crossed or praying arms. Known locally as 'the Crusader', the figure is supposed to represent the Frenchman of the prophecy.

The time will come when houses on wheels will pass over the Aird ferry. Contributed by Mrs M. Mackay of Lochalsh, the prediction was said to have been realized with the building of the Dornie Bridge over which caravans continually cross in the tourist season.

A pinnacle of rock in Reraig will fall and kill a red-haired woman and child. Also contributed by Mrs Mackay. This strange rock, left stranded on the raised beach between the cliffs and shore, stood 30ft high and in two parts, one piled dangerously upon the other, on the Balmacara/Ardelve road between Seaforth Cottage and Mo Dhachaidh. The prophecy had always been well known in the area, and it was generally supposed that the red-haired woman referred to one of the 'Royal Stewarts of Plockton', a family of gypsies famed for their red hair and the fact that they were constantly on the road. During the recent construction of the new road it was necessary to remove the pinnacle, and local workmen continually reported sick for no one wanted to be responsible for interfering with the prophecy. All that remains now is the base, which can be found among the grass and gorse at the edge of the road.

The day will come when the Macraes of Kintail will become so scarce that a crippled tailor of the name will be in such demand among the ladies as to cause a desperate battle in the district between themselves and the Maclenans, the result of which will be that a black fishing-wherry will carry back to Ireland all that remains of the Clan Macrae, but no sooner do they arrive than they again return to Kintail. Before this is to take place, nine men of the name of Macmillan will assume their bonnets [arrive at manhood] in the district, assemble at a funeral at Cnoc-a-Chlachain in Kilduich and originate a quarrel. At this period exactly, the Macraes will be at the height of their prosperity in Kintail, and henceforth begin to lose their hold in the country of their ancestors. According to Alexander Mackenzie, the Macmillans met at Kilduich and originated a quarrel as predicted, although 'nothing could have been more unlikely, for in the seer's day there was not a single one of the name in Kintail, nor for several generations after. It is somewhat remarkable to find the Maclennans are at this very time actually supplanting the Macraes as foretold, for the last two of the ancient stock – the late tenants of Fernaig and Leachachan – who left the district have been succeeded by Maclennans; and other instances of the same kind, within recent years, are well known.'

The Macraes, who formed the traditional bodyguard of Mackenzie of Kintail, were originally known as 'Mackenzie's Coat of Mail'. They first became Constables of Eilean Donan castle in 1509, and eventually took control of the area. During the Jacobite risings the castle was destroyed, and remained a ruin until 1912 when Lieutenant-Colonel John Macrae-Gilstrap, grandfather of the present Constable of Eilean Donan, rebuilt it according to the vision of Farquhar Macrae, who had seen it restored to its former glory. Today it is probably the most photographed castle in Scotland.

Duncan Macrae of Kintail will die by the sword. During the Brahan Seer's lifetime, an old man, Duncan Macrae, consulted a fortune-teller who told him he would die by the sword. This appeared so unlikely – Duncan was an old man who had escaped injury in many a skirmish – that he decided to consult Coinneach Odhar. The seer agreed with the fortune-teller, but still Duncan refused to believe them, calling the prediction the Gaelic equivalent of 'a load of rubbish'. However, the Revd John Macrae, minister of Dingwall, who wrote the *Genealogy of the Macraes* and who died in 1704, stated that in 1654 Duncan was discovered hiding by a band of General Monk's soldiers on the look-out for plunder. They questioned him roughly in English, which he did not understand, so he bravely drew his sword and was promptly killed. The story is remembered because, as the Revd John Macrae writes, 'This was all the blood that General Monk or his soldiers, amounting to 1,500 men, had drawn, and all the opposition he met with' on that occasion.

When a holly bush shall grow out of the face of the rock at Torr-a-Chuilinn in Kintail to the size large enough to make a shaft for a 'cairn-slaoid' [sledge-cart], a battle will be fought in the locality. Recorded by Alexander Mackenzie, it seems likely that this prediction was fulfilled in the remote past.

When Loch Shiel in Kintail shall become so narrow that a man can leap across it, the salmon shall desert the loch and the River Shiel. Alexander Mackenzie writes: 'We are told that the loch is rapidly getting narrower at a particular point, by the action of the water on the banks and bottom, and that if it goes on as it has done in recent years it can easily be leaped at no distant date.' So far this prediction still awaits fulfilment.

The day will come when a river in Wester Ross shall be dried up.

A large stone standing on the hill opposite Scallisaig Farmhouse in Glenelg will fall and kill a Macrae on a white horse. The stone still stands in a precarious position above the Glenelg road.

A white elephant will be built in the shadows of Ben Nevis and the deer will be inside houses looking out. Contributed by Calum Maclean of Fort William, who heard the prediction as a child from his grandfather, the prophecy is thought to represent the Pulp Mill at Corpach. Built of aluminium sheeting, the mill could be compared to a huge white elephant – which indeed it turned out to be, for it is now closed with great loss of employment in the area. The second part of the prediction might relate to the houses left empty by the workers.

Beware, beware of Lochiel's fair hair. This snippet, contributed by Calum Maclean, seems to be all that remains of a longer prophecy connected with the Camerons of Lochiel. Note the allusion to a fair-haired Lochiel in the prophecy on page 324.

The day will come when the Mackenzies will lose all their possessions in Lochalsh, after which it will fall into the hands of an Englishman, who shall be distinguished by great liberality to his people and lavish expenditure of money. He will have one son and two daughters. After his death, the property will revert to the Mathesons, its original possessors, who will build a castle on Druim-a-Dubh at Balmacara. On the death of Sir Hugh Innes (who had bought Lochalsh from Francis Humberston Mackenzie, 'the last Lord Seaforth', in 1801) the estate passed to his great-niece, Kathleen Innes Lindsay. She was married to an eccentric Englishman called Isaac Lillingstone, a nephew of William Wilberforce, whose passions were the Bible, good works and sailing. Convinced that the Second Coming was scheduled for 1837 after a week of spectacular Aurora Borealis, he would sail up and down Kyle Rhea in his yacht, *Elizabeth*, inundating passing craft with religious tracts. Apart from two rooms, he turned Balmacara House into a hospital where he would dose the inmates with mercury and Epsom Salts and any pills he could get hold of. Some traded on his generosity, but most realized it was probably safer to stay well!

Local people were ready to acknowledge him as the Englishman of the prophecy, but he had no children. However, after seventeen years of marriage, Kathleen eventually gave birth to a son and two daughters, thus satisfying all that the prediction was valid. On Lillingstone's death, his son sold Lochalsh to Alexander Matheson, MP for Ross and Cromarty. A castle was built at Duncraig, some distance from the predicted site, which is now a domestic college. The Lillingstone graves, with impressive monuments, may be seen in Lochalsh graveyard.

The day will come when Ben Liathach in Torridon will fall and destroy a village, and the only survivor will be a woman in a red petticoat carrying two red cockerels. There are several variations to this prophecy, which is known in Kintail and Lochcarron. All mention a village, a woman or child and a red cockerel, but the situations vary: both Fasag and Morvich have been linked to the prediction.

When the black rain falls in Lochcarron, all the men will run away to leave twenty women to go after a crippled tailor. This would seem to be an amalgam of several other similar prophecies, and was repeated in Lochcarron in 1983.

The one-legged monster will leave Loch Kishorn and will go twice below the water breathing fire and the third time will spell disaster in the German ocean. Contributed by Mr John Graham, the above prediction was heard among the oil-rig workers on Loch Kishorn recently. It would seem to refer to the Ninian Central Platform built there. Mr Graham writes: 'It is a monolithic structure (most rigs have four or more legs), it was submerged twice before its final positioning, and it does indeed "breathe fire" from the flare stack.'

When a spade of turf is removed from Kishorn, there will be a mast of gold. Known in Lochcarron in 1983, this prophecy would seem to refer to the building of the Ninian Central Platform at Kishorn. The 'mast of gold' is a symbolic description of the great rise in prosperity that has come to the area.

When the iron horse is seen at Strome Ferry, Dornie will run with blood. This predicted the coming of the Highland railway. When the line reached Strome Ferry, a bad harvest and hard winter forced the crofters to 'bleed' their cattle for sustenance.

When the people of Dornie can walk dry-shod to Kintail, a battle will follow. This prediction said to have been fulfilled when Dornie Bridge was completed. The battle is thought to have been with some government department.

Caithness and Sutherland

The northern land will be desolated and black-hooded figures will cover the landscape. Contributed by Henrietta Munro, folklorist, this prediction is said to be connected with the Dounreay nuclear power station in Caithness. The workmen, issued with navy and black duffle coats, were thought to be the hooded figures. The prophecy is not taken seriously by local inhabitants.

330

Whenever a Maclean with long hands, a Frazier with a black spot on his face, a Macgregor with the same on his knee, and a club-footed Macleod of Rasa, should have existed: whenever there should have been successively three Macdonalds of the name of John, and three Mackinnons of the same christian name; oppressors would appear in the country, and the people change their own land for a strange one. Recorded by Thomas Pennant in 1769, the above prediction has a familiar ring to it. The tail-piece would seem to be a genuine forecast of the Sutherland Clearances.

The day will come when there shall be such dire persecution and bloodshed in Sutherland that people will be able to ford the River Oykel dryshod on dead men.
The day will come when a raven, attired in bonnet and plaid, will drink his full of human blood on Finnbheinn in Sutherland three times a day for three successive days. It is reasonable to suppose that these prophecies belong to the remote past.

The natural arch of Clach Tholl near Storhead in Assynt will fall with a crash so loud as to cause the Laird of Ledmore's cattle, twenty miles away, to break their tethers. Hugh Miller, who recorded the prophecy, writes: 'It so happened that some of Ledmore's cattle, which were grazing on the lands of another proprietor, were housed within a few hundred yards of the arch when it fell.' In 1841 when the arch fell, the cattle heard the crash and fled home in terror, tearing everything in their path.

The day will come when a fox, white as snow, will be killed on the west coast of Sutherland. Also recorded by Hugh Miller.

The day will come when a certain Baraball Mackenzie will die of the measles. Baraball lived in Baile Mhuilinn in West Sutherland and was born, according to Alexander Mackenzie, about 1750. From her position, history, and personal peculiarities it was reckoned she must be the woman of the prediction. However, time passed and she grew so old that the prophecy began to lose credit in the township. Then, during the course of an epidemic in the area, the poor old lady finally caught and died of the disease. She was in her ninety-fifth year!

Horses dripping with blood will herald a great disaster. Heard in Achiltbuie, this prophecy is a fragment remembered of a longer prediction

331

which the Brahan Seer was reckoned to have made in Inchnadamph. It was thought to have been a vision of slaughter on the battlefields of the First World War.

The bridge over the railway station at Dunrobin will collapse and kill the Duke of Sutherland. Heard in Brora, this prophecy was evidently known by the fifth Duke who invariably got off the train at Golspie and drove to Dunrobin Castle.

The old bridge at Bonar Bridge will go down with a red-headed fishwife on it. The old bridge was washed away by floods in 1892. Whether the red-headed fishwife was on it at the time is not recalled. This prediction was recounted in Bonar Bridge in 1984.

Invershin railway bridge will collapse with a flock of sheep on it. So far the bridge still stands, and a local inhabitant told me it would be hard to find enough sheep to constitute a flock in the area nowadays.

The day will come when there will be a stable for war horses in the church at Reay in Caithness. Told in Wick, this prophecy was said to have been fulfilled during the last war when tanks were housed in the old church.

When the big sheep reach the northern ocean the deer will deteriorate and disappear. The big sheep here are thought to be the deer, and the northern ocean the Pentland Firth. In 1963 the exceptionally hard winter drove the deer to the coast. Soon afterward acres of forest were planted, thus driving out the deer in their thousands. They are, however, beginning to return to their old haunts.

Birds will pick the bones of Caithness folk. A fragment of prophecy thought to predict the outcome of nuclear installations at Dounreay.

The day will come when a war will end at Loch Eriboll. Remembered by Professor T. L. Marr of Emory University, Atlanta, and quoted in the sixth edition of the *Blue Guides Scotland*, this prophecy was literally fulfilled when the German Navy U-boats came to the deep inlet of Loch Eriboll to surrender in May 1945.

Strange as it may seem to you this day, the time will come, and it is not far off, when full-rigged ships will be seen sailing eastward and west by the back of Tomnahurich Hill.

The day will come when English mares with hempen bridles shall be led round the back of Tomnahurich.

Both these prophecies – the second a translation of the idiomatic Gaelic – predict the construction of the Caledonian Canal, designed by Thomas Telford and completed in 1822, which runs behind Tomnahurich and opens the Great Glen to shipping.

The day will come when Tomnahurich [the fairy hill] will be under lock and key, with spirits secured within. In 1846, the first recorded burial took place at Tomnahurich which was eventually to become a great cemetery surrounded by a fence and locked gate.

The day will come when two false teachers shall come across the seas who will revolutionize the religion of the Highlands. It was suggested by Alexander Mackenzie – somewhat invidiously – that the two false teachers were the evangelists, Moody and Sankey, who from the Brahan Seer's point of view (probably Episcopalian) would no doubt have been considered false.

The day will come when fire and water shall run in streams through the streets of Inverness. An apt description of the coming of piped gas and water.

The Ness Bridge will be swept away by a great flood while crowded with people and while a man riding a white horse and a pregnant woman are crossing. People will pick gooseberries from a bush growing on the stone ledge of one of the arches.

The Ness Bridge will fall when there are seven females on it in a state in which ladies who love their lords wish to be.

Although no people were drowned in 1849 when a great flood destroyed the old bridge, the gooseberry bush did exist. It grew on the south side of the bridge near the grating which lit the old Inverness prison; it flourished there and bore fruit.

It is also recorded that a certain Matthew Campbell, riding a white horse, was on the bridge when it crumbled. Seeing a woman ahead of him, he caught her up on his saddle and leapt to safety just in time. Whether or not she was pregnant is unrevealed.

A man called Maclean writing in the 1820s repeated the prophecy in his *Memoires of a Nonagenarian*, so it was known before the event.

When it is possible to cross the River Ness dryshod in five places, a frightful disaster will overtake the world. In 1937 the suspension bridge at the foot of Bridge Street became unsafe, so the Town Council agreed to erect a temporary bridge alongside to relieve the strain of traffic and as an alternative crossing while the old bridge was being dismantled. It was pointed out that if both bridges were in use at the same time, there would be five places where it would be possible to cross the river dryshod. However the construction was carried out and in August 1939 both the temporary and original bridges were open for traffic. A few weeks later Hitler marched into Poland.

When there are seven bridges over the Ness, Inverness will be consumed with fire from the black rain and tumble into the sea. In 1978 Highland Regional Council's Planning Committee were considering the construction of another bridge which would bring the total to seven. An anxious rate-payer rang one of the committee members to warn them of the prophecy, which he interpreted as being a nuclear disaster. The story was recorded in the *People's Journal*, 23 September 1978. Counting the three bridges that link the Ness Islands as one, the proposed new construction would have been the seventh bridge. Building did not start until 1984. In the following prediction, the islands are counted as three.

When there are nine bridges in Inverness, the streets will be full of ministers without grace and women without shame. This prediction, first recorded by Alexander Mackenzie, again aroused the interest of Invernessians in 1984 when on 4 September Mr John Young started the pile-driver to begin construction of the 2.6m Friars Bridge – the ninth to span the River Ness. The other bridges are as follows: Railway Bridge, Greig Street Bridge, Black Bridge, Ness Bridge, Infirmary Bridge and three smaller bridges that link the Ness Islands. The prophecy was recorded in the *Glasgow Herald* for 5 September 1984.

Built by Edmund Nuttall and Sons, the bridge is expected to take just under two years to complete.

When the Loch Ness monster is captured, Inverness will be engulfed in flame and flood. For many years now people from all over the world have unsuccessfully tried to trap 'Nessie', that 'monstrous wurm' first calmed by St Columba, according to his biographer St Adamnan. The latest monster-catchers in 1984, Vladivar Vodka and Steven Whittle, with their huge underwater cage, have so far not succeeded. Although known locally for some years, this prophecy was recorded in the *Glasgow Herald* on 5 September 1984, probably for the first time.

Culloden

Oh Drummossie, thy bleak moor shall, ere many generations have passed, be stained with the best blood of the Highlands. Glad I am that I will not see that day, for it will be a fearful time; heads will be lopped off by the score, and no mercy shown on either side.

The day will come when the wheel at Millburn will be turned for three successive days with water red with human blood; for on the Lade's bank a fierce battle shall be fought in which much blood will be split.
These two predictions are vivid, frightening images of the Battle of Culloden fought about five miles east of Inverness. In 1746 the Hanoverians under the Duke of Cumberland, with 9,000 men, defeated the 7,000 Royalists under Prince Charles Edward Stuart. The English lost 50 killed and 200 wounded. Two thousand Highlanders were killed and many more wounded or taken prisoner. It was the last battle to be fought on British soil.

There is a shadow over Culloden. That shadow covers Scotland, but that shadow will rise and the sun will shine over Scotland brighter than it has done before. Contributed by Mrs Higginbotham in a letter to the *Scots Magazine* in 1982, the above prediction was allegedly spoken by Coinneach from his funeral pyre. Some would claim that the prophecy has yet to be fulfilled and that Scotland – particularly the Highlands – has not fully recovered from the disaster of Culloden. Others suggest that, with the establishment of the Highlands and Islands

Development Board, and with the discovery of oil in the North Sea, the prophecy is slowly coming to pass.

Beauly

When the River Beauly is dried up three times and a scaly salmon or royal sturgeon is caught there, that will be a time of great trial. The river had dried up at least twice before a 'bradan sligeach' or royal sturgeon measuring 9 ft was caught in the Beauly estuary, about 1875.

A loch above Beauly will burst its banks and destroy in its run a village in its vicinity. In 1967, heavy rain caused the hydro-electric dam at Torachilty to overflow, thus flooding the river Conon. Many buildings, cattle and crops were destroyed and havoc created in the village of Conon Bridge, five miles north of Beauly. The prophecy was well known before its fulfilment.

The day will come, however distant, when Cnoc na Rath will be in the centre of Beauly town. At the time of the prophecy, Beauly stood south of the railway station at least a mile from Cnoc na Rath. At the turn of the century, a new school was built near the Cnoc. Today it is part of the town.

The day will come when a fox will rear a litter of cubs on the hearthstone of Castle Downie. Castle Downie or Dounie was the old name for Beaufort, the seat of the Lovat Frasers. The original building was burned by the Hanoverians in 1746, which no doubt accounts for the prophecy. The present Beaufort Castle was built in 1878 in the 'Field of Downie'.

The following are fragments of old predictions concerning the Lovat Frasers:

> *A claimant will come from the south*
> *Like a bird from a bush.*
> *He will grow like a herb,*
> *He will spread like seed*
> *And set fire to Ardross.*

Mac Shimidh (Lovat), the black-spotted, will leave the estate without the rightful heir.

Chisholm, the squint-eyed, who will leave the estate without a rightful heir. The buck-toothed laird who will leave Gairloch without the rightful heir. Alexander Mackenzie writes: 'We do not know whether there has been any Chisholm with the peculiar characteristics mentioned by the seer . . . we are aware, however, that Sir Hector Mackenzie of Gairloch was buck-toothed, and that he was always known among his tenants in the west as "an tighearna storach".'

Hugh, son of the tenth Lord Lovat, was born in 1666 with a large black mark on his upper lip which gave him the nickname of *Mac Shimidh ball-dubh*, black-spotted Lovat. With his death in 1696, his daughter – he had no sons – was to have been married to the son of Lord Saltoun, chief of all the Frasers. The male heir, Simon of Beaufort, would not allow it. He seized Saltoun and threatened him with death unless he promised to go no further with the matchmaking; and Amelia was married instead to a Mackenzie who took the name of Fraser of Fraserdale while Simon was in France. When Simon returned to help oust the Jacobites from Inverness, he was given the title, but promptly lost it and his life by double-dealing in and before 1745. The succession passed to the Strichen line in 1815, and later the title too was restored. The present Mac Shimidh is the fifteenth Lord Lovat, outstanding both in stature and as a hero in the Second World War.

These prophecies should be compared with the Seaforth prediction which has a similar tail-piece.

Dingwall and district

The day will come when the ravens will drink their fill of Mackenzie blood three times off the top of the Clach Mor, and glad I am that I will not live to see that day, for a bloody and destructive battle will be fought on the Muir of Ord. A squint-eyed, pox-pitted tailor will originate the battle; for men will become so scarce in those days that each of seven women will strive hard for the tailor's hand, and out of this strife, conflict will grow. Clach Mor or Clach an t'Seasaidh (Stone of the barren cattle) stands at Windhill between Beauly and Muir of Ord, and is all that remains of a prehistoric chambered cairn. It is sensible to suppose that this prophecy dates from the far-distant past.

337

The red-headed laird of Ord will be carried home, wounded, on a blanket.
The Mackenzies were lairds of Ord from about 1580.

> *When there shall be two churches in the parish of Ferintosh,*
> *And a hand with two thumbs in I-Stiana,*
> *Two bridges at Conon of the gourmandizers,*
> *And a man with two navels at Dunean,*
> *Soldiers will come from Tarradale*
> *On a chariot without horse or bridle,*
> *Which will leave the Muir of Ord a wilderness,*
> *Spilling blood with many knives;*
> *And the raven shall drink his three fills*
> *Of the blood of the Gael from the Stone of Fionn.*

There have been, since the middle of the last century, two churches at
Ferintosh, two bridges over the river Conon, and Alexander Mackenzie knew of a man from the Black Isle with two thumbs, and a man
with two navels. Soldiers were stationed at Tarradale during the First
World War and rode on trains. The last two lines of the prophecy
would seem to date from another age.

*When a wood on the Muir of Ord grows to a man's height, regiments of
soldiers shall be seen there drawn up in a battle order.*

*I would not like to live when a black, bridleless horse shall pass through
the Muir of Ord.* Local tradition suggests that this prediction was
fulfilled when the Duke of Portland travelled north by a steam-driven
car before the railway was built.

*After four successive dry summers, a fiery chariot will pass through the
Muir of Ord.*

*The day will come when long strings of carriages without horses shall run
between Dingwall and Inverness, and, more wonderful still, between
Dingwall and the Isle of Skye.* There are many variations of the prediction of the railway – not surprising, as it revolutionized life in the
Highlands.

*The day will come when there will be a Laird of Tulloch who will kill four
wives in succession, but the fifth will kill him.* Duncan Davidson, Laird

338

of Tulloch by Dingwall, known locally as 'the stag', had five wives who bore him eighteen children, and he was said to have had at least thirty illegitimate offspring in the district. One of his wives was the youngest sister of his daughter-in-law, which, as both had children, caused immense family complications! He died of pneumonia in Edinburgh and was survived by his fifth wife. It was his letter to Alexander Mackenzie, dated May 1878, that helped to authenticate the Seaforth prediction. Tulloch Castle is now owned by Highland Region.

When the River Conon floods three times, the river will go back to its old course by the church.

When a tree on the River Conon grows to the height of a full-grown man, there will be three bridges and one will fall.

When there are three bridges over the Conon, a coachload of school children will go down when the bridge collapses. There are now three bridges over the Conon, one which holds a pipe line, a second which takes the railway and a new one that has replaced the bailey bridge which stood for many years. It is authentically recorded that within the last few years one school bus-driver made the children get out of his bus and walk across the bridge while he drove across alone and picked them up again on the other side. The fact that there are so many predictions concerning bridges emphasizes their importance to the Highlands. Not so long ago fords and ferries were the norm and such bridges as existed were often precarious erections.

The stone which covers Fingal's Well on the top of Knockfarrel Hill hides a crock of gold.
If ever the stone that covers Fingal's Well on Knockfarrel is removed, Loch Ussie will ooze up through the well and flood the valley below to such an extent that ships could sail up to Strathpeffer and be fastened to Clach an Tiompain: this will happen when the stone has fallen three times.
When the Tympane Stone falls three times, the waters will come up so far that ships will be moored to the stone. Knockfarrel is one in a line of three great Pictish defence sites, the other two being at Craig Phadraig in Inverness and the Ord Hill, Kessock. It is a fine example of an Iron Age vitrified fort, built before the use of lime as a matrix.

When excavated in 1774 the walls were 23ft high, but today only the foundations may be traced. In Alexander Mackenzie's day a large stone covered the well, which was clearly hollow underneath. Today the well is no more than a depression on top of the hill surrounded by rushes.

The old site has attracted many legends over the years, one being that it was the stronghold of Fingal and his Celtic heroes. On one occasion Fingal was challenged, by a giant of remarkable strength who loved 'putting the stone' to a stone-throwing competition. Fingal refused, but offered to match his dwarf against the giant. The hour of the contest arrived and the giant picked up Clach an Tiompain (the Eagle Stone) and flung it right across Strathpeffer. The dwarf then picked up two huge standing stones, the gate posts to the fort, and flung them even further.

The Eagle Stone, like the fort itself, has gathered a host of legends over the centuries. One states that it marks the site of a battle between the Munros and Donald of the Isles in 1411, and should more correctly be called Clach an Tuindain, the Stone of the Turning. Another legend records that it was erected by the Munros and inscribed with their crest – the eagle – after they were defeated in a battle with the Mackenzies. It is in fact of far greater antiquity, inscribed with Pictish symbols of the first period, dating from about AD 600, and has probably been moved at least four times over the centuries.

The Gaelic scholar W. J. Watson, in *Place Names of Ross and Cromarty*, writes of Ardival House near Strathpeffer that there was a mill there in 1487 called Le Tympane de Ardovale. In 1681, it is mentioned as the Tympane Mill, near Clach an Tiompain or the Tympane Stone. Watson repudiates the idea that the stone was ever called Clach an Tuindean, though this would have made good sense considering its proximity to the mill. He believes that the misunderstanding arose over the two meanings of the word *tiompain*, one of which is a musical instrument and the other a hillock. This would suit the position of the stone as it is today, but the old records state that stone and mill were close to each other.

J. Clarence Finlayson, author of *The Strath*, who spent most of his boyhood in Ardival House, states that 'tympane' was also the English form of a local Gaelic word meaning gully. He writes:

At the junction of Ardival road with the main road there was a pond, formed by damming up the burn which runs (nowadays

340

mostly underground) through the Strath. This is on all the old maps. The water then flowed down to turn the wheel of the Tympane Mill which was situated at the bottom of our old garden. It was still standing in 1850, more or less on the site of a modern craft shop today. Watson apparently did not know that the Eagle Stone nowadays occupies at least its fourth site and that while it is now nowhere near the Tympane Mill, once upon a time (including the seer's) it was located in its precincts . . .

So in the seer's time the stone was somewhere near the mill. He knew the place well and possibly spent his last night there before his final summons to Brahan Castle, and this has considerable bearing upon his prophecy about the Eagle Stone.

When I was a small boy in Fodderty School, the mistress was Miss Campbell who was steeped in local legends. The story she had to tell was that the seer foretold that when the stone fell for the third time, the waters would come up the Cromarthy Firth and ships be anchored to it.

In view of the present high location of the stone, the story always seemed so improbable that one wondered at the persistence of the legend . . . I put myself (metaphorically!) into the shoes of the seer and tried to imagine the scene. It was now not so difficult to accept for the water in the burn at the foot of our garden flowed quite gently down to the sea. Could a small model boat somehow satisfy the enquirer? As I thought it over, I could almost feel it was large, almost menacing, and loading and unloading passengers! Then suddenly I was back in my boyhood at the bottom of the garden and there bearing down upon me and stopping only a few yards away was this great hulk – only we didn't call it a ship, we called it a railway train.

So one thinks of the seer familiar with the mill, ever busy with customers and hangers-on some of whom treated the curiously carved Eagle Stone, then nearly a thousand years old, very roughly; and perhaps as a warning related his prediction to their conduct with the impression always with him of some great object bearing down upon the locality.

When five spires rise in Strathpeffer, ships will sail over the village and anchor to one of them. Recorded by Otta F. Swire in *The Highlands and their Legends*, this prediction was fulfilled in an extraordinary way.

341

The five spires were in existence when St Anne's Episcopal Church was completed. Soon after the First World War, a small airship attended the Strathpeffer Games and dropped a grapnel which caught in one of the spires. Thus the prophecy was safely concluded.

Uninviting and disagreeable as it now is, the Strathpeffer Well, with its thick crusted surface and unpleasant smell, the day will come when it shall be under lock and key, and crowds of pleasure and health seekers shall be seen thronging its portals in their eagerness to get a draught of its waters. The medical history of Strathpeffer as a spa stretches back nearly 200 years when local people first discovered the healing properties of the waters. The springs produced natural hot water from both iron and sulphur wells, which when mixed produced a black fluid which stank vilely and gave rise to the legend that the de'il washed in the Strath.

Dr Thomas Morrison of Elsick in Aberdeenshire was the first to establish the health resort. Through his personality and enthusiasm, the village soon became famous. Though the pump-rooms have been closed now for some years, Strathpeffer is still a favourite place for tourists.

If any man harms the Whispering Rock at Brahan and if his hair be fair, he will die a lingering death within six months. Quoted in the Dingwall district and recorded in local newspapers, this prophecy concerns a strange rock formation situated in the Brahan estate. When it was found to be in the way of the new Ullapool road, the contractors were petitioned locally to site the road round the stone. Workmen from the area were also unwilling to touch it. In the end explosives were used, and in August 1984 the famous rock was blasted out of the way. The rock had a long folk-history and in ancient days was thought to be the haunt of fairies.

The Black Isle

The day will come, however distant, when the sandbanks at Findon will form the coastline. When this happens, know for a certainty that trouble-some times are at hand. With the building of the Cromarty Firth causeway which extends the A9 from the Black Isle to Easter Ross, this prediction is said to have been fulfilled. The closure of the aluminium smelter at Invergordon in 1982 has indeed brought trouble to many families and a blow to the growth of industry in the north.

When a magpie shall have made a nest for three successive years in the gable of the church of Ferintosh, the church will fall when full of people. In the days of the Revd Dr John Macdonald, 'the Apostle of the North', a magpie nested in the church gable as foretold. There was also a dangerous crack between the church wall and the gallery. One particular Sunday the congregation was so large that it was necessary to join the ends of the centre and side pews with planks to accommodate everyone. Suddenly in the middle of the service one of these benches snapped with a loud report. Mindful of the seer's prediction, all crowded to the door. Many fell, were trampled, and seriously injured. The church, however, did not collapse.

A variation of the prophecy maintains that it was Fearn Abbey, not Ferintosh, that the seer mentioned. Bishop Forbes in his *Journal* of 1762 recounts the following incident that befell this ancient building, once the site of a thirteenth-century Premonstratensian monastery. 'The roof of flagstones, with part of a side wall, was beat down in an instant by thunder and lightning on 10 October 1742 and so crushed and bruised forty persons that they were scarcely to be discovered, who or what they were, and therefor were buried promiscuously without any manner of distinction . . . the church had been a large and lofty building, as the walls are very high, and still standing.'

Extensive though the possessions of the land-grasping Urquharts of Cromarty may be, the day will come, and it is close at hand, when they will not own twenty acres in the district. The Urquharts were hereditary sheriffs of Cromarty since the days of Robert the Bruce. Their most distinguished son was undoubtedly Sir Thomas Urquhart born in 1613, and a contemporary of the first three Earls of Seaforth. He was a literary genius who translated the first three books of Rabelais, wrote a treatise on arithmetic, and invented a universal language. He was also a fierce loyalist and was taken prisoner at the Battle of Worcester in 1651, where he was said to have lost a hundred manuscripts on the battlefield. Imprisoned in the Tower, he eventually died in a fit of laughter at news of the Restoration.

True to the prediction, by the end of the eighteenth century the family had lost most of its possessions and the great castle at

Cromarty was razed to make way for a new house and a new owner. The present chief of the clan is an American, and all he owns on the Black Isle is the ruined Castle Craig.

The day will come when the Chanonry of Ross, when full of dead Mackenzies, will fall with a fearful crash. The Chanonry here refers to Fortrose Cathedral built in the thirteenth and fourteenth centuries and already in ruins by the seventeenth century. Kenneth, third Earl of Seaforth, was brought up in the Mackenzie castle at Fortrose and was responsible for setting fire to what remained of the roof, for Alexander Brodie wrote in his diary for 6 November 1662: 'I heard that Earl Seaforth by a shot of a gun had burnt the Kirk of Canonry, other houses there being at the same time burnt by the accident.' The Earl had been shooting pigeons on the kirk green.

Only the south aisle remains still roofed and standing. It is here that the Mackenzies are buried, including Francis Humberstone, the last Lord Seaforth, and his four sons. Some believe that the prophecy has yet to be fulfilled.

When there is a wedding in the ruins of the cathedral, Fortrose will become a town of widows and the cemetery full to overflowing. As has been seen (page 218), this prediction probably originated after the event.

The day will come when a deer will be caught alive at Chanonry Point in the Black Isle.

When an iron chariot is seen between Avoch and Fortrose, a rock will fall on the road below. The Black Isle railway was axed in the early fifties, but the rock still stands.

In the parish of Avoch is a well of beautiful clear water, out of which whoever drinketh, if suffering from any disease, shall, by placing two pieces of straw on the surface, ascertain whether he will recover. If he is to get well, the straws will whirl round in opposite directions; if he is to die soon, they will remain motionless. The well referred to is generally thought to be the Craigie Well, dedicated to St Benedict and situated on the east shore of Munlochy Bay. It is a clootie or rag well, and is still visited on the first Sunday in May by local people who hang an offering of ribbon or lace as a gift to the fairy of the water. This custom dates back to the pre-Christian era when the Celts believed that every spring of pure water had its own spirit to be appeased. The first Christian evangelists blessed the wells and dedicated them to Christian saints, but the old rituals were and are still observed. Coinneach's test is still tried as a health prognosis, and there is at least one authenticated case of a woman requesting that the water be brought to her in hospital.

The Craigie Well is not to be confused with the other clootie well, which is on the side of the road between Munlochy and Tore and which is dedicated to St Boniface.

The name of the Lady Hill in Avoch has gone far and wide, but though thy owners were brave on the field of battle, they never decked thy brow. The day will come, however, when a white collar shall be put upon thee. The child that is unborn shall see it, but not I. The Lady Hill is sometimes called Ormond Hill, and the castle of that name was owned by the two Sir Andrew Murrays, father and son, who died in 1297 and 1338 respectively. The first raised the standard for William Wallace to defeat the English at the Battle of Stirling Bridge; the second was Guardian of Scotland in 1332, and ended his days at the castle on the Lady Hill with a reputation for being 'a lord of great beauty, sober and chaste-like, wise and stout, hardy and of great courage'. The castle was later destroyed by Cromwell's forces and the stones allegedly used to build the Citadel at Inverness.

The road that ran round the Lady Hill during the last century – the white collar of the prediction – was a favourite Sunday afternoon carriage drive for Victorians. It survives today as a forest track.

The Mackenzie Prophecies

The Mackenzies of Fairburn

The day will come when the Mackenzies of Fairburn shall lose their entire possessions and that branch of the clan shall disappear almost to a man from the face of the earth. Their castle shall become uninhabited, desolate and forsaken, and a cow shall give birth to a calf in the uppermost chamber of Fairburn Tower.

345

A Rowan tree will grow out of the walls of Fairburn Tower, and when it becomes large enough to form a cart axle, the Mackenzies will be so reduced in number that all could be taken in an open fishing-boat back to Ireland from whence they originally came.

A bird will plant a rowan tree on the top of Fairburn Tower and when it grows to the thickness of an axle, the glory of the Seaforths will rise again. The day' will come when the sow will litter in my lady's chamber at Fairburn Castle.

Fairburn Tower stands on a ridge between the Orrin and Conon valleys about five miles from Muir of Ord and dates from the sixteenth century. It rises four storeys high with a garret under the crow-stepped gables, and it is still just possible to climb the precarious spiral stair. During the mid-seventeenth century it belonged to Roderick Mackenzie, fifth laird of Fairburn, one of the richest and most respected chieftains in Ross-shire, who was a contemporary and friend of his clan chief, Kenneth, third Earl of Seaforth. The line ended with Major-General Sir Alexander Mackenzie who died unmarried in 1820, having sold the estate. The castle was left to ruin.

In 1827 Professor Sedgwick and Sir Roderick Murchison of Tarradale, President of the Geological and Geographical Societies, turned aside to visit his mother's old home. 'The professor and I', wrote Murchison, 'were groping our way up the broken staircase when we were almost knocked off our feet by a rush of two or three pigs that had been nestling upstairs in the very room in which my mother was born.' Alexander Geikie, biographer of Sir Roderick, states that he knew the prophecy.

Years later the ruin was used by the local farmer to dry grain. One of his cows, finding the door open, followed wisps of straw up the spiral stair all the way to the garret. Being in calf, she was unable to get down. The prophecy was so well known before its fulfilment that carriage-loads of sightseers arrived from Inverness to witness the event in the year 1851.

The rowan tree was growing on the north-west face of the tower at the turn of the century and achieved some girth by 1921. The 'glory of the Seaforths' may refer to James Alexander Stewart-Mackenzie, great-grandson of the 'Last Seaforth', who was created Baron Seaforth of Brahan as a reward for his war-time services, but who died without issue in 1923. The rowan tree died in the drought of 1957, but is still remembered and spoken about locally.

When the girls of Kilcoy House cry out,
'The cup of our murders is flowing over.'
A fox from Croy will come
Who shall be like a wolf among the people
During forty years and more,
And in his coat shall be many curses:
He shall then be thrown empty and sorrowful
Like an old broom behind the door.
And large farmers will be like merry birds
And the lairds as poor as sparrows –
There's a blessing in fine honesty
And curses in the shedding of blood.

When the stern Castle of Kilcoy
Shall stand cold and empty,
And the jackdaws and the rooks
Are artfully flying past it,
A loathsome man shall then dwell
Beside it, indecent and filthy,
Who will not keep his marriage vows,
Listen neither to cleric or friend,
But from Craigiehow to Ferintosh
The dirty fellow will be after every girl.
Ochan! Ochan! Woe is me,
The cunning dog will swallow up much land.

Kilcoy Castle was built in the early seventeenth century by Alexander Mackenzie, known as Alexander the Knife, who possessed a charter for the land in 1618. He is thought to have carved the handsome lintel over the fireplace in the hall, dated 1679. The Kilcoy Mackenzies owned the estate for about 300 years, though the last to live in the castle died in 1813.

According to Alexander Mackenzie the writer, part of the first verse may refer to a vicious deed alleged to have taken place during the lifetime of the third Earl of Seaforth, who was contemporaneous with the legendary Brahan Seer. A number of cattle belonging to the Kilcoy and Redcastle were dying of some disease, so the two lairds offered a reward for a cure. They were approached by a local wizard who promised to heal the beasts for the sum offered, provided he was supplied with a human sacrifice. Together the lairds selected a victim, and the barn at Parktown in the parish of Killearnan was set aside for the deed. A vagrant was persuaded to go to the barn where he was bound and disembowelled by the sorcerer, who dried and fed his organs to the cattle. As the victim was dying he uttered the following curse, which has often been ascribed to Coinneach Odhar: 'Let the day never come when the family of Redcastle shall be without a female idiot or the family of Kilcoy without a fool.'

There may however be another explanation of the prediction of murder, for a certain Kenneth, son of Donald, fifth of Kilcoy, was recorded as having been 'murdered in his own doorway' in or about 1760. Alexander Mackenzie writes: 'The history of the Kilcoy family has been an unfortunate one in late years, and the second and last lines of the first stanza clearly refer to a well-known tragic incident in the recent history of this once highly favoured and popular Highland family.' This cryptic remark may refer to the murder of Kenneth.

With reference to the curse, it is said that the last male heir was 'not wise', which is why the direct line came to an end. The ten and eleventh lines of the first stanza certainly came true for the family was impoverished at the end. Today Kilcoy Castle is restored and is now the fine property of Mr and Mrs E. I. Robinson.

Redcastle, a mile south of Kilcoy on the Beauly Firth, was originally the site of Eddydor, a stronghold built by David, the brother of William the Lyon, in 1179. In the thirteenth century it belonged to Sir John Bisset whose daughter brought Beauly to the Frasers as her dowry. After a period of violence it was annexed to the crown by James II. In 1492 it was seized by the Mackenzies and, in spite of continual rowing and raiding, it remained a Mackenzie stronghold until 1790, when it was sold to James Grant of Shewglie as a result of a debt incurred by Kenneth, the last but one laird of Redcastle. By raising a regiment he bankrupted an already impoverished estate. It was said that he was cursed by a witch for kidnapping a child for his force. He died in a duel – not the first he had fought – at Constantinople in 1789. His heir died unmarried in Jamaica ten years later. Redcastle is now a ruin, thought to be haunted by the ghost of a child – perhaps that of the boy said to have been kidnapped. With reference to the curse Alexander Mackenzie writes: 'It appears that this wild imprecation was to some extent realized.'

The Mackenzies of Rosehaugh

> *The heir of the Mackenzies will take*
> *A white rook out of the wood,*
> *And will take a wife from a music-hall,*
> *With his people against him.*
> *And the heir will be great*
> *In deeds and as an orator,*
> *When the Pope in Rome*
> *Will be thrown off his throne*
>
> *Over opposite Craigiehow*
> *Will dwell a diminutive lean tailor*
> *Also foolish James as the laird,*
> *And wise James as a measurer,*
> *Who will ride without a bridle*
> *The wild colt of his choice;*
> *But foolish pride without sense*
> *Will put in the place of the seed of the deer*
> *The seed of the goat;*
> *And the beautiful Black Isle will fall*
> *Under the management of the Fishermen of Avoch.*

The above stanzas taken from the Gaelic need some unravelling, and make better sense if the first four lines are placed in the second verse.

The heir who will be great in deeds and as an orator must refer to Sir George Mackenzie, Lord Advocate for Scotland during the reign of Charles II, who earned for himself the title of 'Bluidy Mackenzie' for his harsh dealings with the Covenanters. Sir George was the eldest son of Simon Mackenzie of Lochslin, progenitor of the Mackenzies of Allangrange and a contemporary of Kenneth, third Earl of Seaforth. He took for his title as law lord Mackenzie of Rosehaugh in the Black Isle, so called for the profusion of wild roses that grew there. He himself, as we have seen on page 36, experienced second sight. He was twice married, first to the daughter of a law lord and then to Margaret Halyburton of Pitcur, neither of them music-hall dancers. The reference to the Pope may refer obliquely to the troubled times that followed the Reformation.

Rosehaugh estate eventually came into the hands of the Mackenzies of Scatwell, but the second stanza refers not to that family but to the descendants of Sir Alexander Mackenzie, explorer, who gave his name to the Mackenzie River in Canada. Born in Stornoway, Sir Alexander Mackenzie emigrated to Canada at the age of sixteen and entered service of the North-West Company, whose work included exploration. He wrote an account of his voyages, was knighted in 1802, returned to Scotland, and bought the estate of Avoch, adjacent to that of Rosehaugh. At his death in 1820 he was succeeded by his son, 'foolish James' of the prediction. The 'diminutive lean tailor' was a certain worthy who lived at Bennetsfield, an estate that bordered Rosehaugh on one side and Munlochy Bay on the other. He constantly warned 'foolish James,' and by so doing 'cut his bounds for him'.

Wise James was a certain James Maclean who lived on the Rosehaugh estate. Like the tailor, he constantly corrected 'foolish James', thus earning the style of 'measurer' as he too set bounds to the laird's behaviour. The 'wild colt' is generally thought to be the music-hall lass, and it was 'foolish James's pride without sense' that was to bring about the most interesting part of the prophecy contained in the last four lines.

When Sir James Mackenzie of Scatwell – a distinguished man who was Lord Lieutenant of Ross-shire – died, Rosehaugh estate was sold to a certain James Fletcher in 1864. According to Walford's *County Families of the United Kingdom*, James Fletcher had been born in 1807, the son of William Jack and Isabel Fletcher. William Jack was a fisherman of Avoch who had left the village to set up as a small dealer in Elgin. His son James, a particularly bright boy, had been adopted by his maiden aunt Fletcher, who educated him and whose name he eventually took out of gratitude. Thereafter he had made his way to Liverpool to seek his fortune. He returned as a millionaire to buy not only the estate of Rosehaugh, but also a number of others including that of Avoch.

The 'deer' in the second stanza refers to the *cabarfeidh* or antlers which were the armorial bearings of the Mackenzies, while the 'goat' is that of the Fletchers. He and his son, James Douglas Fletcher, a financier and multi-millionaire, were responsible for many improvements in the fishing-village of Avoch. James Douglas built a magnificent Italianate chateau, which, on the death of his widow was demolished in 1959, when the Eagle Star Insurance Company owned the estate. In further fulfilment of the prediction, the fishermen of Avoch today now own their houses.

I see a chief, the last of his house, both deaf and dumb. He will be the father of four fair sons, all of whom he shall follow to the tomb. He shall live careworn, and die mourning, knowing that the honours of his house are to be extinguished for ever, and that no future chief of the Mackenzies shall rule in Kintail. After lamenting over the last and most promising of his sons, he himself shall sink into the grave, and the remnant of his possessions shall be inherited by a white-coifed widow from the East, and she shall kill her sister.

As a sign that these things are coming to pass, there shall be four great lairds in the days of the last Seaforth [Gairloch, Chisholm, Grant and Raasay], one of whom shall be buck-toothed, the second hare-lipped, the third half-witted, and the fourth a stammerer. Seaforth, when he looks round and sees them, may know that his sons are doomed to death, and that his broad lands shall pass away to the stranger, and that his line shall come to an end.

And of Brahan Castle itself, not a stone shall remain.

The fulfilment of the above prediction is given in detail on pages 213–15.

Briefly, the last chief was Francis Humberstone Mackenzie, created Baron Seaforth of Kintail in 1797, made Governor of Barbados in 1800, and a Lieutenant-General in 1808. He died in 1815. He caught scarlet fever at Eton which left him stone-deaf. In time he was virtually dumb as well. He had ten children, four of whom were sons, all of whom predeceased him. His estates, by now impoverished, were inherited by his eldest daughter, Mary, the widow of Admiral Hood, Commander of the Indian Seas. Owing to the entailment, she could not inherit the chieftainship of the clan. She and her sister were thrown from a pony carriage near Brahan when the ponies bolted. Her sister died of the injuries.

The four other lairds were said to have been disfigured as foreseen.

The estates were sold and the chieftainship was in dispute for nearly 150 years. The present Earl of Cromarty is now clan chief.

Brahan Castle was razed shortly after the Second World War.

BIBLIOGRAPHY

ADAMNAN, SAINT, *The Life of Saint Columba*, transl. by Wentworth Huyshe, Routledge & Kegan Paul, 1905

AUBREY, JOHN, *Three Prose Works*, Centaur Press, 1972

BAIN, GEORGE, *The Lordship of Petty*, Nairnshire Telegraph, 1925

BAIN, ROBERT, *History of the Ancient Province of Ross*, The Pefferside Press Ltd, Dingwall, 1899

BARKER, J. C., *Sacred to Death*, Frederick Muller, 1968

BISHOP, WASHINGTON IRVINE, *Second Sight Explained*, J. Menzies, 1880

BOSWELL, JAMES, *The Journal of a Tour to the Hebrides* (ed. Chapman), Oxford University Press, 1924

BRODIE, A., *Diaries of the Lairds of Brodie 1652–85*, Spalding Club, 1863

BYRD, ELIZABETH, *A Strange and Seeing Time*, Robert Hale, 1969

CAMERON, FLORENCE, *Told in the Furthest Hebrides*, Eneas Mackay, 1936

CAMPBELL, J. C. (ed.), *A Collection of Highland Rites and Customes*, D. S. Brewer and Rowman and Littlefield for the Folklore Society, 1975

CAMPBELL, J. C. and HALL, TREVOR H., *Strange Things*, Routledge & Kegan Paul, 1968

CAMPBELL, J. F., *Popular Tales of the West Highlands* (4 vols), A. Gardner, 1890/93

CAMPBELL, J. G., *Witchcraft and Second Sight in the Highlands and Islands of Scotland*, James Maclehose and Sons, 1902

CARMICHAEL, A., *Carmina Gadelica* (6 vols), Scottish Academic Press Ltd, 1928–71

CHADWICK, NORA, *The Celts*, Pelican, 1970

CHAMBERS, ROBERT, *Domestic Annals of Scotland* (Vol 1), W. and R. Chambers, 1858

CHAMBERS, WILLIAM, *Exploits and Anecdotes of the Scottish Gypsies*, W. and R. Chambers, 1886

CROMARTIE, EARL OF, *A Highland History*, Gavin Press, 1979

DALYELL, J. G., *Darker Superstitions of Scotland*, Richard Griffin and Co, 1835

DILLON, M. and CHADWICK, N., *The Celtic Realms*, Cardinal, 1977

DONALDSON, GORDON, and MORPETH, R. S., *A Dictionary of Scottish History*, John Donald, 1977

DUNNE, J. W., *An Experiment with Time*, Faber and Faber, 1929

DWELLY, E., *The Illustrated Gaelic Dictionary*, Gairm Publications, 1973

FINLAYSON, J. CLARENCE, *The Strath*, St Andrews Press, 1979

FORBES, ROBERT, *Bishop Forbes' Journal* (ed. J. B. Craven) Skefington and Sons, 1923

FRASER, JAMES, *Chronicles of the Frasers known as the Wardlaw Manuscript*, Scottish History Society, 1905

FRAZER, JOHN, *Deuteroscopia*, A. Sympson, Edinburgh, 1707

FRAZER, J. G., *The Golden Bough*, Macmillan, 1922

GALT, JOHN, *The Autobiography of John Galt* (2 vols), Fraser, 1833

GEIKIE, SIR ARCHIBALD, *The Life of Sir Roderick I. Murchison* (2 vols), Gregg International, 1973

GRANT, ANNE M., *Essays on the Superstitions of the Highlanders of Scotland*, Longman, Hurst, Rees, Orme, and Brown, 1811

GRANT, ELIZABETH, *Memoirs of a Highland Lady 1792–1827*, Murray, 1972

GREEN, CELIA, *The Decline and Fall of Science*, Hamish Hamilton, 1976

GRIMBLE, IAN, *Highland Men*, H.I.D.B., 1980

HENDERSON, ISABEL, *The Picts*, Thames & Hudson, 1967

HEYWOOD, ROSALIND, *The Sixth Sense*, Chatto & Windus, 1956

ISULANUS, THEOPHILUS, *A Treatise on Second Sight, Dreams and Apparitions*, Ruddiman, Auld and Co, 1763

JOHNSON, RAYNOR C., *The Imprisoned Splendour*, Hodder and Stoughton, 1953

JOHNSON, SAMUEL, *A Journey to the Western Islands of Scotland*, (ed. R. W. Chapman) Oxford University Press, 1924

JONES, G., *A History of the Vikings*, Oxford University Press, 1973

JUNG, C. G., *Memories, Dreams and Reflections*, Routledge & Kegan Paul, 1963

—— *Synchronicity*, Routledge & Kegan Paul, 1972

KENNEDY, JOHN, *The Days of the Fathers in Ross-shire*, Norman Macleod, 1897

KIRK, ROBERT, *The Secret Common-Wealth* (ed. Stewart Sanderson), D. S. Brewer for the Folklore Society, 1976

KIRK, WILLIAM, *Stories of Second-Sight in a Highland Regiment*, Eneas Mackay 1933

KOESTLER, ARTHUR, *The Roots of Coincidence*, Hutchinson, 1972

LANG, ANDREW, *Cock Lane and Common Sense*, Longmans, Green, and Co, 1894

Letter-Book of Bailie John Steuart, (ed. William Mackay), Scottish History Society, 1915

LOCKHART, JOHN, *Memoirs of the Life of Sir Walter Scott, Bart.*, (10 vols), Cadell, 1839

MACDONALD, DONALD, *Lewis*, Gordon Wright, 1978

MACECHERN, REVD DUGALD, *Highland Second Sight* (Vol 29), T.G.S.I.*, 1922

MACGREGOR, A., *Highland Superstitions*, Eneas Mackay, 1901

MACKENZIE, ALEXANDER, *The Celtic Magazine* (Vol 2), A. and W. Mackenzie, 1877

—— *Coinneach Odhar Fiosaiche* (Vols 3 and 4), T.G.S.I.,* 1875

—— *The Prophecies of the Brahan Seer* (ed. E. Sutherland) Constable, 1977

—— *History of Clan Mackenzie*, A. and W. Mackenzie, 1879

—— *History of Clan Munro*, A. and W. Mackenzie, 1898

MACKENZIE, ANDREW, *Hauntings and Apparitions*, Heinemann, 1982

MACKENZIE, DONALD A., *Article in Encyclopaedia of Occultism* (ed. Lewis Spence) 1920

MACKENZIE, OSGOOD, *A Hundred Years in the Highlands*, Geoffrey Bles, 1974

McKERRARCHER, A. C., 'The Lady of Lawers', *The Scots Magazine*, June 1982

MACLAGAN, R. C., *Evil Eye in the Western Highlands*, David Nutt, 1902

*Transactions of the Gaelic Society of Inverness

MACLEAN, JOHN, *Reminiscences of a Clachnacuddin Nonagenarian*, Donald Macdonald, 1886

MACLENNAN, A. B., *The Petty Seer*, The Highland News Printing and Publishing Coy, 1906

MACLEOD, DONALD, *Memoir of Dr Norman Macleod* (2 vols), Isbister, 1877

MACLEOD OF MACLEOD, REVD CANON R. C., *The Macleods of Dunvegan*, T. and A. Constable, 1927

MACPHERSON, A., *Glimpses of Church and Social Life in the Highlands of Olden Times*, Blackwood, 1893

MACRITCHIE, DAVID, *Scottish Gypsies under the Stewarts*, David Douglas, 1894

MARSHALL, ELIZABETH, *The Black Isle, a Portrait of the Past*, Protheroe, 1972

MARTIN, MARTIN, *A Description of the Western Islands of Scotland* (2nd edition, 1716), James Thin, 1981

MATHESON, REVD WILLIAM, *The Historical Coinneach Odhar and Some Prophecies Attributed to Him* (Vol 46), T.G.S.I.*, 1971

MILLER, HUGH, *Scenes and Legends of the North of Scotland*, Nimmo, 1834

—— *My Schools and Schoolmasters*, Nimmo, 1869

MOODY, R., *Life after Life*, Mockingbird Books, 1975

MORRISON, REVD W. and MACRAE, NORMAN, *Highland Second Sight*, George Soutar, 1908

MURRAY, W. H., *The Islands of Western Scotland*, Eyre Methuen, 1973

MYERS, F. W. H., *Human Personality and its Survival of Bodily Death* (2 vols), Longmans Green, 1903

PARSONS, COLEMAN O., *Witchcraft and Demonologie in Scott's Fiction*, Oliver & Boyd, 1964

PEDLER, KIT, *Mind over Matter*, Thames Methuen, 1981

PENNANT, THOMAS, *A Tour in Scotland*, Warrington, 1769

PEPYS, SAMUEL, *Letters and Second Diary of Samuel Pepys*, (ed. R. G. Haworth), Dent, 1933

PIGGOTT, STUART (ed.), *The Prehistoric Peoples of Scotland*, Routledge & Kegan Paul, 1962

—— *The Druids*, Thames & Hudson, 1975

*Transactions of the Gaelic Society of Inverness.

PITCAIRN, ROBERT, *Ancient Criminal Trials in Scotland* (Vol 2), The Maitland Club, 1833

PLAYFAIR, GUY, *The Infinite Boundary*, Souvenir Press, 1976

POWELL, T. E. G., *The Celts*, Thames & Hudson, 1958

RICHARD, JOHN, *But Deliver us from Evil*, Darton, Longman and Todd, 1974

RITCHIE, ANNA, *The Kingdom of the Picts*, Chambers, 1977

ROHWER, J. and HUMMELCHEN G., *Chronology of the War at Sea 1939–45* (Vol I), Ian Allen, 1974

ROSS, A., *Everyday Life of Pagan Celts*, Carousel, 1972

ROSS, ANNE, *The Folklore of the Scottish Highlands*, Batsford, 1976

ROSS, JOHN C., *The Great Clan Ross*, John Robert Ross, M.D., 1972

SALTMARSH, H. F., *Foreknowledge*, Bell & Sons Ltd, 1938

SANDERSON, STEWART, (ed.), *The Secret Common-Wealth*, D. S. Brewer for the Folklore Society, 1976

Scottish Record Society, containing the Calendar of Writs of Munro of Foulis, 1299–1823

SHARKEY, JOHN, *Celtic Mysteries*, Thames & Hudson, 1975

SINCLAR, GEORGE, *Satan's Invisible World Discovered*, Thomas G. Stevenson, 1871

SMOUT, T. C., *A History of the Scottish People*, Collins, 1969

SPENCE, LEWIS, *Second Sight: Its History And Origins*, Rider, 1951

SQUIRE, CHARLES, *Celtic Myths and Legends*, Newcastle Publishing Co. Inc., 1975

STEWART, REVD ALEXANDER, *Nether Lockaber*, Paterson, 1883

SULLOWAY, FRANK J., *Freud, Biologist of the Mind*, Fontana, 1980

SWIRE, OTTA F., *The Highlands and their Legends*, Oliver & Boyd, 1963

TAYLOR, JOHN, *Science and the Supernatural*, Temple Smith, 1980

THOMPSON, FRANCIS, *The Supernatural Highlands*, Robert Hale, 1976

TOMES, JOHN, *The Blue Guides Scotland*, Ernest Benn Ltd, 1975

TYRRELL, G. N. M., *Apparitions*, Duckworth, 1953

VYVYAN, JOHN, *A Case against Jones*, James Clarke, 1966

WAINWRIGHT, T. F., *The Problem of the Picts*, Nelson, 1955

WARRAND, DUNCAN, *More Culloden Papers* (Vol I), Robert Carruthers, 1923

WATSON, W. J., *Place-Names of Ross and Cromarty*, reprinted by Ross and Cromarty Heritage Society, 1976

ZOHAR, DANAH, *Through the Time Barrier*, Heinemann 1982

INDEX

357

A SELECTION OF NON FICTION
TITLES AVAILABLE FROM CORGI BOOKS

The prices shown below were correct at the time of going to press. However Transworld Publishers reserve the right to show new retail prices on covers which may differ from those previously advertised in the text or elsewhere.

☐ 12361 7	**UNFINISHED SYMPHONIES: VOICES FROM**		
	THE BEYOND	*Rosemary Brown*	£1.75
☐ 99160 0	**FIRE FROM WITHIN**	*Carlos Casteneda*	£3.95
☐ 12299 8	**THE FURTHER PROPHECIES OF NOSTRADAMUS**	*Erika Cheetham*	£2.50
☐ 09828 0	**THE PROPHECIES OF NOSTRADAMUS**	*Erika Cheetham*	£2.95
☐ 12501 6	**BEYOND THE HIGHLAND LINE**	*Richard Frere*	£1.95
☐ 07145 5	**THE THIRD EYE**	*T. Lobsang Rampa*	£2.50
☐ 08800 5	**CHARIOTS OF THE GODS?**	*Erich Von Daniken*	£1.95
☐ 12138 X	**THE HOLY BLOOD AND THE HOLY GRAIL**		
		Michael Baigent, Richard Leigh & Henry Lincoln	£3.50
☐ 12468 0	**THE ANATOMY OF POWER**	*John Kenneth Galbraith*	£2.95
☐ 11487 1	**LIFE AFTER DEATH**	*Neville Randall*	£2.50
☐ 12640 3	**IN GOD'S NAME**	*David Yallop*	£3.50

ORDER FORM

All these books are available at your book shop or newsagent, or can be ordered direct from the publisher. Just tick the titles you want and fill in the form below.

Transworld Publishers, Cash Sales Department,
61–63 Uxbridge Road, Ealing, London, W5 5SA

Please send cheque or postal order, not cash. All cheques and postal orders must be in £ sterling and made payable to Transworld Publishers Ltd.

Please allow cost of book(s) plus the following for postage and packing:

U.K./Republic of Ireland Customers:
Orders in excess of £5; no charge
Orders under £5; add 50p

Overseas Customers:
All orders; add £1.50

NAME (Block Letters) ....

ADDRESS .. ISOBEL McLOUGHLIN ....

....